# ACCA
## PRACTICE & REVISION KIT

Paper 3.6

## Advanced Corporate Reporting

BPP Publishing
*January 2002*

First edition 2001
Second edition January 2002

ISBN 0 7517 0524 1 (Previous edition 0 7517 0797 X)

**British Library Cataloguing-in-Publication Data**
A catalogue record for this book
is available from the British Library


Published by

BPP Publishing Limited
Aldine House, Aldine Place
London W12 8AW

www.bpp.com

Printed in Great Britain by Ashford Colour Press

We are grateful to the Association of Chartered Certified Accountants for permission to reproduce past examination questions. The answers to past examination questions have been prepared by BPP Publishing Limited.

# CONTENTS

BPP PUBLISHING

# Contents

**Order form**

**Review form & free prize draw**

The headings in this checklist/index indicate the main topics of questions, but questions often cover several different topics.

**Preparation questions**, listed in italics, provide you with a firm foundation for attempts at exam-standard questions.

Questions preceded by ★ are **key questions** which we think you must attempt in order to pass the exam. Tick them off on this list as you complete them.

Questions set under the old syllabus *Financial Reporting Environment* paper are included because their style and content are similar to those which will appear in the Paper 3.6 exam. The questions have generally been amended to reflect the current syllabus exam format.

BPP PUBLISHING

## Question and answer checklist/index

*Handwritten margin notes:* FRS 15; 11; 10; 4 (next to Capital and financial instruments); goodwill or Brand valuation (next to 38 MG); FRS 5. (next to 42 Timber Products); 17 (next to 45); 8 (next to 54 Maxpool)

# TOPIC INDEX

Listed below are the key Paper 3.6 syllabus topics and the numbers of the questions in this Kit covering those topics.

If you need to concentrate your practice and revision on certain topics, or if you want to attempt all available questions that refer to a particular subject (be they preparation or exam standard), you will find this index useful.

The New Syllabus *Advanced Corporate Reporting* paper differs from the Old Syllabus *Financial Reporting Environment* in a number of ways. Some of the questions in this kit are on topics which were not covered under the Old Syllabus, and these are marked with an asterisk (*).

> RETAKE STUDENTS SHOULD PAY PARTICULAR ATTENTION TO THE QUESTIONS ON THE TOPIC AREAS MARKED WITH A *. THESE ARE BEING EXAMINED FOR THE FIRST TIME UNDER THE NEW SYLLABUS.

*Handwritten annotations: "+ Porter." next to Cash flow statements – consolidated (with "consolidated" circled); "Timber Products" next to FRS 5; "MRA", "FV", "RP", "ASV", "GI", "I", "cA-cL", "FIXD", "EPS", "FA" in left margin beside FRS 6–15; "Q II(2)." beside FRS 7; "BADEN." beside FRS 9; "mock 2-(4b)." beside FRS 11; FRS 13 circled.*

### Topic index

# EFFECTIVE REVISION

This is a very important time as you approach the exam. You must remember three things.

> **Use time sensibly**
> **Set realistic goals**
> **Believe in yourself**

## Use time sensibly

1   **How much study time do you have?** Remember that you must EAT, SLEEP, and of course, RELAX.

2   **How will you split that available time between each subject?** What are your weaker subjects? They need more time.

3   **What is your learning style?** AM/PM? Little and often/long sessions? Evenings/ weekends?

4   **Are you taking regular breaks?** Most people absorb more if they do not attempt to study for long uninterrupted periods of time. A five minute break every hour (to make coffee, watch the news headlines) can make all the difference.

5   **Do you have quality study time?** Unplug the phone. Let everybody know that you're studying and shouldn't be disturbed.

## Set realistic goals

1   Have you set a **clearly defined objective** for each study period?

2   Is the objective **achievable**?

3   Will you **stick to your plan**? Will you make up for any **lost time**?

4   Are you **rewarding yourself** for your hard work?

5   Are you leading a **healthy lifestyle**?

## Believe in yourself

**Are you cultivating the right attitude of mind?** There is absolutely no reason why you should not pass this exam if you adopt the correct approach.

•   **Be confident** – you've passed exams before, you can pass them again

•   **Be calm** – plenty of adrenaline but no panicking

•   **Be focused** – commit yourself to passing the exam

## REVISING WITH THIS KIT

Here is some **general guidance** about how to get the most out of this Kit. In the following section we set out a detailed revision plan which you may find useful.

*A confidence boost*

To boost your morale and to give yourself a bit of confidence, **start** your practice and revision with a topic that you find **straightforward**.

*Diagnosis*

First look through the Paper 3.6 Passcards and do some revision. Then attempt any **preparation questions** included for the syllabus area. These provide you with a firm foundation from which to attempt exam-standard questions.

*Key questions*

Then try as many as possible of the **exam-standard questions**. Obviously the more questions you do, the more likely you are to pass the exam. But at the very least you should attempt the **key questions** that are highlighted in the following section. Even if you are short of time, you must prepare answers to these questions if you want to pass the exam - they incorporate the key techniques and concepts underpinning *Advanced Corporate Reporting* and they cover the principal areas of the syllabus.

*No cheating*

Produce **full answers** under **timed conditions**; practising exam technique is just as important as recalling knowledge. Don't cheat by looking at the answer. Look back at your notes or at your BPP Study Text instead. Produce answer plans if you are running short of time. In the guidance below we have distinguished between questions that should be answered in full and those for which you can prepare a plan.

*Imagine you're the marker*

It's a good idea to actually **mark your answers**. Don't be tempted to give yourself marks for what you meant to put down, or what you would have put down if you had time. And don't get despondent if you didn't do very well. Refer to the **topic index** and try another question that covers the same subject.

*Ignore them at your peril*

Always read the **Tutor's hints** in the answers. They are there to help you.

*Trial run for the big day*

Then, when you think you can successfully answer questions on the whole syllabus, attempt the **two mock exams** at the end of the Kit. You will get the most benefit by sitting them under strict exam conditions, so that you gain experience of the four vital exam processes.

- Selecting questions
- Deciding on the order in which to attempt them
- Managing your time
- Producing answers

# REVISION PROGRAMME

Below is a suggested **step-by-step revision programme**. Please note that this is not the only approach – you may prefer to do your revision in a different order, and your college may suggest a different approach. However, **as a minimum you must do the key questions if you want to pass the exam.**

The BPP programme requires you to devote a **minimum of 40 hours** to revision of Paper 3.6. Any time you can spend over and above this should only increase your chances of success.

## Suggested approach

1    For the topics covered in each revision period, **review** your notes and the relevant summaries in the **Paper 3.6 Passcards**.

2    Then do the **key questions** for that section. These are **shaded** in the table below, and, as we indicated earlier, are the questions you must attempt, even if you are short of time. Try to complete your answers without referring to our solutions.

3    For some questions we have suggested that you prepare **answer plans** rather than full solutions. This means that you should spend about 30% of the full time allowance for that question on brainstorming the question and drawing up a list of points to be included in an answer.

4    Once you have worked through all of the syllabus sections, **attempt at least one of the Mock Exams under strict exam conditions.** Mock Exam 1 is BPP's prediction of the topics likely to come up in June 2002. Mock Exam 2 is the Pilot Paper for this subject. If you don't have time to do both under exam conditions, have a look at the exam you didn't do to get an idea of the style of questions and the likely topics.

BPP PUBLISHING

## Revision programme

| Topic | 2001 Passcard Chapter | Questions in this Kit | Comments | Done √ |
|---|---|---|---|---|
| **Revision period 1**<br>*Regulatory framework* | | | | |
| | 1, 18 | 2 | Answer in full. This is a thorough test of your knowledge of FRS 8 | |
| **Revision period 2**<br>*Group accounts I* | | | | |
| Simple groups | 2 | 4 | Answer if you need to revise – a straightforward question | |
| Associates and joint ventures | 3 | 5 | Key question. Answer in full, addressing all parts of the requirements | |
| Multicompany structures | 4 | 6 | Answer in full under exam conditions, paying particular attention to layout and mark allocation | |
| | | 7 | A useful question – answer if you have time | |
| **Revision period 3**<br>*Group accounts II* | | | | |
| Changes in group composition | 5 | 8 | An unusual question. Do it if you have time | |
| | | 9 | Answer in full under exam conditions | |
| Merger accounting | 6 | 11 –10 –12· | Answer if you have time | |
| | | 12 | Answer in full under exam conditions | |
| **Revision period 4**<br>*Group accounts III* | | | | |
| Overseas transactions | 7 | 14 | Do only if you have time – this deals with a peripheral area | |
| | | 15 | Answer in full, using a methodical approach | |
| Cash flow statements | 8 | 17 | Answer in full under exam conditions to test your ability to work at speed | |
| **Revision period 5**<br>*Reports I* | | | | |
| Share valuation | 9 | 19 | An excellent question. Answer in full | |
| Ratio analysis | 10 | 22 | Answer in full | |
| *Reports II* | | | | |
| Measurement of performance | 11 | 23 | Answer in note form only | |
| Price changes | 12 | 25 | Answer plan only | |

| Topic | 2001 Passcard Chapter | Questions in this Kit | Comments | Done √ |
|---|---|---|---|---|
| **Revision period 6** *International, environmental and current issues* | | | | |
| International issues | 13 | 29 | A useful question. Do the written bits in note form | |
| Environment and culture | 14 | 31, 32 | Low priority questions | |
| **Revision period 7** *Accounting standards I* | | | | |
| Fixed assets | 16, 17 | 36 | Make notes from part (a) and attempt part (b) in full | |
| | | 37 | Make notes for parts (a) and (b) and work part (c) in full | |
| Capital and financial instruments | 18 | 40 | Answer in full under exam conditions | |
| **Revision period 8** *Accounting standards II* | | | | |
| Off balance sheet finance | 19 | 42 | Attempt parts (b) and (c) under exam conditions | |
| Leasing | 20 | 44 | Answer in full | |
| **Revision period 9** *Accounting standards III* | | | | |
| Retirement benefits | 21 | 45 | Answer in full | |
| Taxation | 22 | 47 | Answer in full | |
| **Revision period 10** *Accounting standards IV* | | | | |
| Reporting financial performance | 23, 24 | 49 | Answer in full. This is a topical issue | |
| | | 50 | Ignore part (a)(i), as it is unlikely to re-appear now FRS 14 is no longer 'new' | |
| | | 52 | A useful question to try if you have time | |
| **Revision period 11** *Accounting standards V* | | | | |
| PBSE, provisions and contingencies | 25 | 56 | Answer in full. This is a good indication of what may come up | |

## THE EXAM PAPER

The examination is a **three hour paper** divided into **two sections**.

Section A will normally comprise one compulsory question on group financial statements including group cash flows and foreign currency translation. This question will be technically demanding and could have a discursive element in it.

Section B will comprise four questions out of which candidates should select three questions. These questions will involve advising discussing and reporting on issues and topics in corporate financial reporting. The questions will view the subject matter from the perspective of the preparer of financial statements and from the perspective of the accountant as an advisor. Invariably a technical understanding of the subject matter will be required and candidates will have to apply their knowledge to given cases and scenarios.

Advice as to current and future reporting requirements and their impact on reported corporate performance will be an important element of these questions. Additionally current issues and developments in financial reporting will be examined on a discursive basis.

|  |  | *Number of Marks* |
|---|---|---|
| Section A: | One compulsory question | 25 |
| Section B: | Choice of 3 from 4 questions (25 marks each) | 75 |
|  |  | 100 |

### Additional information

Candidates need to be aware that questions involving knowledge of new examinable regulations will not be set until at least six months after the last day of the month in which the regulation was issued.

The Study Guide provides more detailed guidance on the syllabus. Examinable documents are listed in the 'Exam Notes' section of *Student Accountant*.

### Analysis of past papers

The analysis below shows the topics which were examined in the first sitting of the new syllabus and in the pilot paper.

*December 2001*

*Section A*

1    Consolidated financial statements and foreign currency

*Section B*

2    Effect of accounting treatments on EPS calculation
3    Closure of subsidiary: FRS 3, FRS 11, FRS 12 and FRS 17
4    IAS requirement; share based payment; impairment
5    Reporting business performance; analysis; corporate citizenship

*Pilot paper*

*Section A*

1   Group cash flow statement: preparation and commentary on usefulness of such statements

*Section B*

2   Leases - discussion of new approach
3   Changes in group structure
4   Related party transactions - discussion and applications
5   Environmental accounting

# CURRENT ISSUES

If you have been studying with the first edition of the BPP *Advanced Corporate Reporting* Study Text you will already be up to date for developments up to June 2001. Since then, however, there have been some developments of which you should be aware. The following notes also give guidance on the material which is examinable in this paper.

The contents of this section are as follows.

1    Current accounting standards and other documents

2    Discussion Paper *Revenue Recognition*

## 1    Current accounting standards and other documents

The following standards are extant at the date of writing. The SSAPs which were in force at the date the ASB was formed have been adopted by the Board. They are gradually being superseded by the new Financial Reporting Standards (FRSs).

*Accounting standards*

| No | Title | Issue date |
|----|-------|-----------|
|  | Foreword to accounting standards | Jun 93 |
| FRS 1 | Cash flow statements (revised) (see below) | Oct 96 |
| FRS 2 | Accounting for subsidiary undertakings | Jul 92 |
| FRS 3 | Reporting financial performance | Oct 92 |
| FRS 4 | Capital instruments | Dec 93 |
| FRS 5 | Reporting the substance of transactions (amended Sept 1998) | Apr 94 |
| FRS 6 | Acquisitions and mergers | Sep 94 |
| FRS 7 | Fair values in acquisition accounting | Sep 94 |
| FRS 8 | Related party disclosures | Oct 95 |
| FRS 9 | Associates and joint ventures | Nov 97 |
|  | Financial Reporting Standard for Smaller Entities (revised) | Dec 99 |
| FRS 10 | Goodwill and intangible assets | Dec 97 |
| FRS 11 | Impairment of fixed assets and goodwill | July 98 |
| FRS 12 | Provisions, contingent liabilities and contingent assets | Sept 98 |
| FRS 13 | Derivatives and other financial instruments: disclosures | Sept 98 |
| FRS 14 | Earnings per share | Oct 98 |
| FRS 15 | Tangible fixed assets | Feb 99 |
| FRS 16 | Current tax | Dec 99 |
| FRS 17 | Retirement benefits | Nov 00 |
| FRS 18 | Accounting policies | Dec 00 |
| FRS 19 | Deferred tax | Dec 00 |
| SSAP 4 | Accounting for government grants | Jul 90 |
| SSAP 5 | Accounting for value added tax | Apr 74 |
| SSAP 9 | Stocks and long-term contracts | Sep 88 |
| SSAP 13 | Accounting for research and development | Jan 89 |
| SSAP 17 | Accounting for post balance sheet events | Aug 80 |
| SSAP 19 | Accounting for investment properties (amended) | Nov 81 |
| SSAP 20 | Foreign currency translation | Apr 83 |
| SSAP 21 | Accounting for leases and hire purchase contracts | Aug 84 |
| SSAP 25 | Segmental reporting | Jun 90 |

*Accounting Standards Board (ASB): Statement*

| Title | Issue date |
| --- | --- |
| Statement of Principles for Financial Reporting | Dec 99 |
| FRED 22 *Revision of FRS 3 Reporting financial performance* | Dec 00 |

*ASB Drafts for Discussion (DDs)*

| Title | Issue date |
| --- | --- |
| Segmental reporting | May 96 |
| Discounting (working paper) | Apr 97 |
| Derivatives and other financial instruments | Jul 96 |
| Business combinations | Dec 98 |
| Leases: implementation of a new approach | Dec 99 |
| Year end financial reports: improving communication | Feb 00 |
| Share based payment | July 00 |
| Revenue recognition | July 01 |

## 2 Discussion paper: revenue recognition

There is no accounting standard in the UK and the Republic of Ireland that deals with the top line of the profit and loss account (usually called 'turnover' but referred to by the ASB as 'revenue'). Although not a problem in the past, the increasing complexity of business activities and the absence of a framework underlying existing practices have allowed inconsistencies to arise between industries and even between companies within a single industry.

These inconsistencies are not merely the result of practical difficulties in deciding how to proceed: they also reflect different views of what revenue should represent, and of how financial statements should portray a business's operating activities. There is a need for a coherent framework that can be used consistently to address revenue issues in different contexts. The Discussion Paper 'Revenue Recognition', published in July, was the first step in this process.

The ASB recognises that revenue recognition issues are not unique to the UK and the Republic of Ireland. It therefore sees its Discussion Paper as a contribution to the international debate. It hopes to develop, in conjunction with the IASB and other standard-setters, a framework that can be used as the basis for a standard dealing with general revenue principles.

## USEFUL WEBSITES

The websites below provide additional sources of information of relevance to your studies for *Advanced Corporate Reporting*.

- ACCA        www.accaglobal.com
- BPP        www.bpp.com
- Financial Times        www.ft.com
- Accounting Standards Board        www.asb.org.uk
- International Accounting Standards Board        www.iasb.org.uk

# SYLLABUS MINDMAP

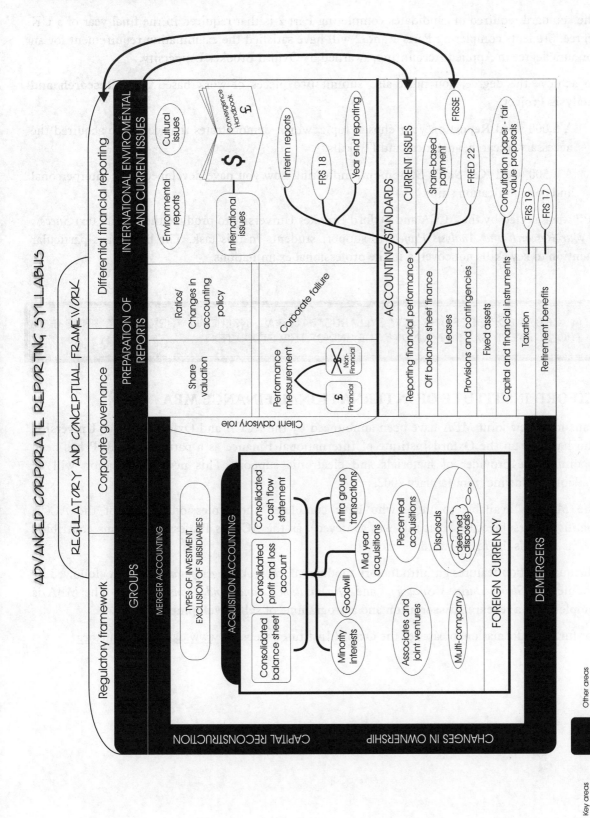

## OXFORD BROOKES BSc IN APPLIED ACCOUNTING

The standard required of candidates completing Part 2 is that required in the final year of a UK degree. Students completing Parts 1 and 2 will have satisfied the examination requirement for an honours degree in Applied Accounting, awarded by Oxford Brookes University.

To achieve the degree, you must also submit two pieces of work based on a **Research and Analysis Project.**

- A 5,000 word **Report** on your chosen topic, which demonstrates that you have acquired the necessary research, analytical and IT skills.

- A 1,500 word **Key Skills Statement**, indicating how you have developed your interpersonal and communication skills.

BPP was selected by the ACCA and Oxford Brookes University to produce the official text *Success in your Research and Analysis Project* to support students in this task. The book pays particular attention to key skills not covered in the professional examinations.

AN ORDER FORM FOR THE NEW SYLLABUS MATERIAL, INCLUDING THE OXFORD BROOKES PROJECT TEXT, CAN BE FOUND AT THE END OF THIS STUDY TEXT.

## OXFORD INSTITUTE OF INTERNATIONAL FINANCE MBA

Plans for a new joint MBA have been announced by the ACCA and Oxford Brookes University, who have set up the Oxford Institute of International Finance as a partnership. BPP has been appointed the provider of materials and electronic support. This new qualification will be available worldwide from January 2002.

The MBA is available to those who have completed the professional stage of the ACCA qualification (subject to when this was achieved), as the ACCA's Professional exams contribute credits towards the MBA award.

The qualification features an introductory module (*Markets, Management and Strategy*) followed by modules on *Global Business Strategy*, and *Organisation Change and Transformation*. The MBA is completed by a **research dissertation** and a programme of **self-development**.

For further information, please see the Oxford Institute's website: www.oxfordinstitute.org

# Questions

**REGULATORY FRAMEWORK**

Questions 1 and 2 cover the Regulatory Framework, the subject of Part A of the BPP Study Text for Paper 3.6.

# 1    PREPARATION QUESTION: PRESCRIPTIVE STANDARDS

Consider the following statement.

'Accounting standards permit such a wide variety of different accounting policies and practices that it would be wrong to assume any significant degree of comparability between companies' statutory accounts.'

*Required*

Discuss this statement, commenting on the extent to which comparability is achieved in practice and reaching a conclusion as to whether more prescriptive standards should be introduced.

# 2    ACCOUNTING POLICIES AND ESTIMATION TECHNIQUES    *45 mins*

FRS 18 *Accounting policies* distinguishes between accounting policies and estimation techniques and the accounting for changes in each is very different.

*Required*

(a) Distinguish between accounting policies and estimation techniques, as defined by FRS 18 and state the differences in accounting for a change in accounting policy and a change in an estimation technique.    (7 marks)

(b) For items (i) to (vii) below, state in each case whether the proposed changes represent changes in [accounting policies] or [estimation techniques] giving brief reasons.

> *P M R*

(i) **Capitalised finance costs.** An entity has previously charged to the profit and loss account interest incurred in connection with the construction of tangible fixed assets. It now proposes to capitalise such interest, as permitted by FRS 15 *Tangible fixed assets*, since it believes this better reflects the cost of constructing those assets.    (2 marks)

(ii) **Indirect overheads recorded in the value of stock.** A manufacturing entity has three cost centres (A, B and C). It has previously assessed that the indirect costs attributable to production are 30% of A and 40% of B. Having reassessed the nature of those cost centres' activities, it now assesses that the indirect costs attributable to production are 25% of A, 40% of B and 10% of C.    (2 marks)

(iii) **Classification of overheads.** An entity has previously shown certain overheads within cost of sales. It now proposes to show those overheads within administrative expenses.    (2 marks)

(iv) **Depreciation of vehicles**

(1) An entity has previously depreciated vehicles using the reducing balance method at 40% per year. It now proposes to depreciate vehicles using the straight-line method over five years, since it believes this better reflects the pattern of consumption of economic benefits.    (2 marks)

(2) As in (1), an entity has previously depreciated vehicles using the reducing balance method at 40% per year and now proposes to depreciate vehicles using the straight-line method over five years. In addition, it has previously

recorded the depreciation charge within cost of sales, but now proposes to include it within administrative expenses. (2 marks)

(v) **Accounting for fungible stocks.** An entity has fungible stocks and its accounting policy has previously been to consider those stocks in aggregate, measuring them at weighted average historical cost. However, it determines that the normal accounting policy in its industry is to measure such stocks at historical cost on a FIFO basis. It concludes, for reasons of comparability, that it should adopt the normal industry policy. (2 marks)

(vi) **Discounting**

(1) An entity has previously reported deferred tax on an undiscounted basis. However, the norm in its industry is to report deferred tax on a discounted basis. It concludes, for reasons of comparability, that it should adopt the normal industry approach. (2 marks)

(2) An entity has previously measured a particular provision on an undiscounted basis, in accordance with FRS 12 *Provisions, contingent liabilities and contingent assets*, as the effect of discounting was not material. However, this year it has revised upwards its estimates of future cash flows associated with the provision and, as a result, the effect of discounting is now material. FRS 12 therefore requires it to report the provision at the discounted amount. (2 marks)

(vii) **Translating the financial statements of a foreign subsidiary.** A group has previously translated the profit and loss account of its foreign subsidiary using the closing rate. However, it now proposes to use the average rate for the accounting period, on the basis that this reflects more fairly the group's profits and losses as they arise throughout the accounting period. (2 marks)

**(25 marks)**

---

**GROUP ACCOUNTS**

Questions 3 to 18 cover Group Accounts, the subject of Part B of the BPP Study Text for Paper 3.6.

---

## 3    PREPARATION QUESTION: SIMPLE CONSOLIDATION I

Aye plc purchased 1,450,000 ordinary shares in Bee plc in 20X0, when the general reserve of Bee plc stood at £400,000 and there was no balance of unappropriated profit.

The balance sheets of the two companies as at 31 December 20X4 are set out below.

| | *Aye plc* | | *Bee plc* | |
|---|---|---|---|---|
| | £'000 | £'000 | £'000 | £'000 |
| *Fixed assets* | | | | |
| Tangible assets | | | | |
| Buildings | 5,000 | | 1,000 | |
| Plant | 3,396 | | 543 | |
| Vehicles | 472 | | 244 | |
| | | 8,868 | | 1,787 |
| *Investment* | | | | |
| Shares in Bee plc at cost | | 1,450 | | - |
| | | 10,318 | | 1,787 |
| *Current assets* | | | | |
| Stock | 1,983 | | 1,425 | |
| Debtors | 1,462 | | 1,307 | |
| Cash | 25 | | 16 | |
| | 3,470 | | 2,748 | |
| *Creditors: amounts due within one year* | | | | |
| Overdraft | 1,176 | | 840 | |
| Trade creditors | 887 | | 1,077 | |
| Tax | 540 | | 218 | |
| Dividend | 280 | | - | |
| | 2,883 | | 2,135 | |
| *Net current assets* | | 587 | | 613 |
| *Total assets less current liabilities* | | 10,905 | | 2,400 |
| *Creditors: amounts due after one year* | | | | |
| 10% debentures | | 4,000 | | - |
| 15% debentures | | - | | 500 |
| | | 6,905 | | 1,900 |
| *Shareholders' funds* | | | | |
| Ordinary shares of 50p each | | 5,000 | | 1,000 |
| Share premium account | | 500 | | - |
| General reserve | | 1,200 | | 800 |
| Unappropriated profit | | 205 | | 100 |
| | | 6,905 | | 1,900 |

At the balance sheet date the current account of Aye plc with Bee plc was agreed at £23,000 owed by Bee plc. This account is included in the appropriate debtors and trade creditors balances shown above. Goodwill arising on consolidation is deemed to have an indefinite useful life and is to be retained in the balance sheet.

*Required*

(a)   Prepare a consolidated balance sheet for the Aye Bee Group.

(b)   Show the alterations necessary to the group balance sheet if the inter-company balance owed by Bee plc to Aye plc represented an invoice for goods sold by Aye to Bee at a mark-up of 15% on cost, and still unsold by Bee plc at 31 December 20X4.

**Guidance notes**

1   Lay out the pro-forma balance sheet, leaving plenty of space.

2   Lay out workings for: goodwill calculation; general reserve; unappropriated profit; and minority interest.

3   Fill in the easy numbers given in the question.

4   Work out the more complicated numbers using the workings and then add up the balance sheet.

5   Keep all your work very neat and tidy to make it easy to follow. Cross reference all your workings.

## 4   PREPARATION QUESTION: SIMPLE CONSOLIDATION II

Bath Ltd acquired 80% of the ordinary share capital of Jankin Ltd on 1 January 20X1 for the sum of £153,000 and 60% of the ordinary share capital of Arthur Ltd on 1 July 20X1 for the sum of £504,000.

From the information given below you are required to prepare the consolidated balance sheet of Bath Ltd at 31 December 20X1.

Comparative figures and notes to the accounts are not required.

Workings must be shown.

(a)   The balance sheets of the three companies at 31 December 20X1 are set out below.

|  | Bath Limited £ | Jankin Limited £ | Arthur Limited £ |
|---|---|---|---|
| Share capital |  |  |  |
|   Ordinary shares of £0.25 each | 750,000 | 100,000 | 400,000 |
| Share premium | 15,000 | - | - |
| Profit and loss account |  |  |  |
|   1 January 20X1 | 191,000 | 19,400 | 132,000 |
|   Retained profits for 20X1 | 37,000 | 3,000 | 54,000 |
| Taxation | 78,000 | 24,000 | 56,000 |
| Creditors | 162,000 | 74,400 | 149,000 |
| Bank overdraft: Bank A | 74,000 | - | - |
| Depreciation |  |  |  |
|   Freehold property | 9,000 | - | 40,000 |
|   Plant and machinery | 87,000 | 39,000 | 124,600 |
| Dividends proposed | 30,000 | 15,000 | 24,000 |
| Current account | - | 9,800 | - |
|  | 1,433,000 | 284,600 | 979,600 |
| Freehold property, at cost | 116,000 | - | 200,000 |
| Plant and machinery, at cost | 216,000 | 104,000 | 326,400 |
| Investments in subsidiaries |  |  |  |
|   Jankin Limited | 153,000 | - | - |
|   Arthur Limited | 504,000 | - | - |
| Trade investment | 52,000 | - | - |
| Stocks and work in progress | 206,000 | 99,000 | 294,200 |
| Debtors | 172,200 | 73,000 | 95,000 |
| Bank balance: Bank B | - | 7,900 | 62,800 |
| Cash | 1,100 | 700 | 1,200 |
| Current account | 12,700 | - | - |
|  | 1,433,000 | 284,600 | 979,600 |

(b)   No interim dividends were declared or paid in 20X1 out of 20X1 profits. Bath Ltd has not yet accounted for dividends receivable from its subsidiary companies.

(c) A remittance of £1,700 from Jankin Ltd in December 20X1 was not received by Bath Ltd until January 20X2.

(d) An invoice for £1,200 for stock material (including £240 profit) had been included in sales in 20X1 by Bath Ltd but it was not received by Jankin Ltd until 20X2.

(e) In Jankin Ltd's stock at 31 December 20X1, were goods to the value of £8,000 ex Bath Ltd on which the latter had taken profit of £1,600.

(f) Profits of Arthur Ltd are deemed to have accrued equally throughout the year.

(g) Any goodwill arising on consolidation is to be amortised over four years.

**Guidance notes**

1  Follow the guidance notes given in Question 3 above.

2  You may need workings for stocks and work in progress and creditors, as well as the other consolidation workings.

5    **BADEN (6/99)**                                                          *45 mins*

(a) FRS 9 *Associates and joint ventures* deals not only with the accounting treatment of associated companies and joint venture operations but covers certain types of joint business arrangements not carried on though a separate entity. The main changes made by FRS 9 are to restrict the circumstances in which equity accounting can be applied and to provide detailed rules for accounting for joint ventures.

*Required*

(i) Explain the criteria which distinguish an associate from ordinary fixed asset investment.                                                             (6 marks)

(ii) Explain the principal difference between a 'joint venture' and a 'joint arrangement' and the impact that this classification has upon the accounting for such relationships.                                                             (4 marks)

(b) The following financial statements relate to Baden, a public limited company.

PROFIT AND LOSS ACCOUNT
FOR THE YEAR ENDED 31 DECEMBER 20X8

|                                                | £m   | £m    |
|------------------------------------------------|------|-------|
| Turnover                                       |      | 212   |
| Cost of sales                                  |      | (170) |
| Gross profit                                   |      | 42    |
| Distribution costs                             | 17   |       |
| Administrative costs                           | 8    |       |
|                                                |      | (25)  |
|                                                |      | 17    |
| Other operating income                         |      | 12    |
| Operating profit                               |      | 29    |
| Exceptional item                               |      | (10)  |
| Interest payable                               |      | (4)   |
| Profit on ordinary activities before tax       |      | 15    |
| Taxation on profit on ordinary activities      |      | (3)   |
|                                                |      | 12    |
| Ordinary dividend – paid                       |      | (4)   |
| Retained profit for year                       |      | 8     |

BALANCE SHEET AT 31 DECEMBER 20X8

|  | £m | £m |
|---|---|---|
| Fixed assets:  tangible | 30 | |
| goodwill | 7 | |
| | | 37 |
| Current assets | 31 | |
| Creditors: amounts falling due within one year | (12) | |
| Net current assets | | 19 |
| Total assets less current liabilities | | 56 |
| Creditors: amounts due falling after more than one year | | (10) |
| | | 46 |
| Capital and reserves | | |
| Called up share capital | | |
| Ordinary shares of £1 | | 10 |
| Share premium account | | 4 |
| Profit and loss account | | 32 |
| | | 46 |

(i) Cable, a public limited company, acquired 30% of the ordinary share capital of Baden at a cost of £14 million on 1 January 20X7. The share capital of Baden has not changed since acquisition when the profit and loss reserve of Baden was £9 million.

(ii) At 1 January 20X7 the following fair values were attributed to the net assets of Baden but not incorporated in its accounting records.

|  | £m |  |
|---|---|---|
| Tangible fixed assets | 30 | (carrying value £20m) |
| Goodwill (estimate) | 10 | |
| Current assets | 31 | |
| Creditors: amount falling due within one year | 20 | |
| Creditors: amount falling after more than one year | 8 | |

(iii) Guy, an associate company of Cable, also holds a 25% interest in the ordinary share capital of Baden. This was acquired on 1 January 20X8.

(iv) During the year to 31 December 20X8, Baden sold goods to Cable to the value of £35 million. The inventory of Cable at 31 December 20X8 included goods purchased from Baden on which the company made a profit of £10 million.

(v) The policy of all companies in the Cable Group is to amortise goodwill over four years and to depreciate tangible fixed assets at 20% per annum on the straight line basis.

(vi) Baden does not represent a material part of the group and is significantly less than the 15% additional disclosure threshold required under FRS 9 *Associates and joint ventures*.

*Required*

(i) Show how the investment in Baden would be stated in the consolidated balance sheet and profit and loss account of the Cable group under FRS 9 *Associates and joint ventures*, for the year ended 31 December 20X8 on the assumption that Baden is an associate. (9 marks)

(ii) Show how the treatment of Baden would change if Baden was classified as an investment in a joint venture. (6 marks)

(25 marks)

## 6     EXOTIC (6/95, amended)                                                    *45 mins*

The Exotic Group carries on business as a distributor of warehouse equipment and importer of fruit into the United Kingdom. Exotic plc was incorporated in 20X1 to distribute warehouse equipment. It diversified its activities during 20X3 to include the import and distribution of fruit, and expanded its operations by the acquisition of shares in Madeira plc in 20X2, in Melon plc in 20X5 and in Kiwi plc in 20X7.

Accounts for all companies are made up to 31 December.

The draft profit and loss accounts for Exotic plc, Melon plc and Kiwi plc for the year ended 31 December 20X9 are as follows.

|                                         | Exotic plc | Melon plc | Kiwi plc |
|-----------------------------------------|-----------:|----------:|---------:|
|                                         | £'000      | £'000     | £'000    |
| Turnover                                | 45,600     | 24,700    | 22,800   |
| Cost of sales                           | 18,050     | 5,463     | 5,320    |
| Gross profit                            | 27,550     | 19,237    | 17,480   |
| Distribution costs                      | 3,325      | 2,137     | 1,900    |
| Administrative expenses                 | 3,475      | 950       | 1,900    |
| Operating profit                        | 20,750     | 16,150    | 13,680   |
| Interest paid                           | 325        |           | -        |
| Profit before tax                       | 20,425     | 16,150    | 13,680   |
| Tax on profit on ordinary activities    | 8,300      | 5,390     | 4,241    |
| Profit on ordinary activities after tax | 12,125     | 10,760    | 9,439    |
| Dividends: proposed                     | 9,500      | -         | -        |
| Retained profit for year                | 2,625      | 10,760    | 9,439    |
| Retained profit brought forward         | 20,013     | 13,315    | 10,459   |
| Retained profit carried forward         | 22,638     | 24,075    | 19,898   |

The draft balance sheets as at 31 December 20X9 are as follows.

|                             | Exotic plc | Melon plc | Kiwi plc |
|-----------------------------|-----------:|----------:|---------:|
|                             | £'000      | £'000     | £'000    |
| Fixed assets (NBV)          | 35,483     | 24,273    | 13,063   |
| Investments                 |            |           |          |
| Shares in Melon plc         | 6,650      |           |          |
| Shares in Kiwi plc          |            | 3,800     |          |
| Current assets              | 1,568      | 99,025    | 8,883    |
| Current liabilities         | (13,063)   | (10,023)  | (48)     |
|                             | 30,638     | 27,075    | 21,898   |
| *Share capital and reserves*|            |           |          |
| Ordinary £1 shares          | 8,000      | 3,000     | 2,000    |
| Profit and loss account     | 22,638     | 24,075    | 19,898   |
|                             | 30,638     | 27,075    | 21,898   |

The following information is available relating to Exotic plc, Melon plc and Kiwi plc.

(i)   On 1 January 20X5 Exotic plc acquired 2,700,000 £1 ordinary shares in Melon plc for £6,650,000 at which date there was a credit balance on the profit and loss account of Melon plc of £1,425,000. No shares have been issued by Melon plc since Exotic plc acquired its interest.

(ii)  On 1 January 20X7 Melon plc acquired 1,600,000 £1 ordinary shares in Kiwi plc for £3,800,000 at which date there was a credit balance on the profit and loss account of Kiwi plc of £950,000. No shares have been issued by Kiwi plc since Melon plc acquired its interest.

(iii) During 20X9, Kiwi plc had made inter-company sales to Melon plc of £480,000 making a profit of 25% on cost and £75,000 of these goods were in stock at 31 December 20X9.

(iv) During 20X9, Melon plc had made inter-company sales to Exotic plc of £260,000 making a profit of $33^{1}/_{3}\%$ on cost and £60,000 of these goods were in stock at 31 December 20X9.

(v) On 1 November 20X9 Exotic plc sold warehouse equipment to Melon plc for £240,000 from stock. Melon plc has included this equipment in its fixed assets. The equipment had been purchased on credit by Exotic plc for £200,000 in October 20X9 and this amount is included in its current liabilities as at 31 December 20X9.

(vi) Melon plc charges depreciation on its warehouse equipment at 20% on cost. It is company policy to charge a full year's depreciation in the year of acquisition to be included in the cost of sales.

(vii) Goodwill arising on consolidation was deemed to have an indefinite life and is to remain in the balance sheet.

The following information is available relating to Madeira plc.

(i) In 20X2 Madeira plc was incorporated as a wholly owned subsidiary of Exotic plc to carry on business importing bananas from Madeira to the United Kingdom. Increased competition from growers in other world markets has resulted in recurring trade losses.

(ii) In 20X7 the directors of the parent company arranged for all warehousing and distribution for Madeira plc to be physically handled by Melon plc. Madeira plc retained its office accommodation.

(iii) In the financial year ended 31 December 20X8 Exotic plc wrote off its investment in Madeira plc in its accounts.

(iv) In 20X8 Exotic plc decided to discontinue the trade carried on in Madeira plc's name as early as possible in 20X9. However, due to protracted negotiations with employees, the termination was not completed until November 20X9.

(v) The following data relates to Madeira plc in 20X9.

|  | £'000 |
| --- | --- |
| Turnover | 2,000 |
| Cost of sales | (2,682) |
| Distribution costs | (18) |
| Administrative expenses | (100) |
| Redundancy costs | (427) |
| Profit on sale of fixed assets | 115 |
| Loss on sale of net current assets | (36) |

*Required*

(a) Excluding Madeira plc:

 (i) Prepare a consolidated profit and loss account, including brought forward reserves, for the Exotic Group plc for the year ended 31 December 20X9

 (12 marks)

 (ii) Prepare a consolidated balance sheet as at that date (9 marks)

(b) Show the accounting treatment for Madeira plc in the consolidated profit and loss account of the Exotic Group for the year ended 31 December 20X9 in accordance with FRS 3 on the assumption that there has been a discontinuance and that a provision of £500,000 had been created in 20X8 in expectation of trading losses. (4 marks)

**(25 marks)**

7    **X AND Y (6/99, amended)**                                                          *45 mins*

X, a public limited company, acquired 100 million ordinary shares of £1 in Y, a public limited company on 1 April 20X6 when the accumulated reserves were £120 million. Y acquired 45 million ordinary shares of £1 in Z, a public limited company, on 1 April 20X4 when the accumulated reserves were £10 million. On 1 April 20X4 there were no material differences between the carrying values and the fair values of Z. On 1 April 20X6, the accumulated reserves of Z were £20 million.

Y acquired 30% of the ordinary shares of W, a limited company, on 1 April 20X6 for £50 million when the accumulated reserves of W were £7 million. Y exercises significant influence over W and there were no material differences between the carrying values and the fair values of W at that date.

There had been no share issues since 1 April 20X4 by any of the group companies. The following balance sheets relate to the group companies as at 31 March 20X9.

|  | X | Y | Z | W |
|---|---|---|---|---|
|  | £m | £m | £m | £m |
| Fixed assets:   tangible | 900 | 100 | 30 | 40 |
|              intangible |  | 30 |  |  |
| Investment in Y | 320 |  |  |  |
| Investment in Z |  | 90 |  |  |
| Investment in W |  | 50 |  |  |
| Net current assets | 640 | 360 | 75 | 73 |
| Creditors: amounts falling due after one year | (200) | (150) | (15) | (10) |
|  | 1,660 | 480 | 90 | 103 |
|  |  |  |  |  |
| Share capital | 360 | 150 | 50 | 80 |
| Share premium | 250 | 120 | 10 | 6 |
| Accumulated reserves | 1,050 | 210 | 30 | 17 |
|  | 1,660 | 480 | 90 | 103 |

(a)   The following fair value table sets out the carrying values and fair values of certain assets and liabilities of the group companies together with any accounting policy adjustments required to ensure consistent group policies at 1 April 20X6.

|  | Carrying value | | Accounting policy adj. | | Fair Value adj. | | New carrying value | |
|---|---|---|---|---|---|---|---|---|
|  | £m | £m | £m | £m | £m | £m | £m | £m |
|  | Y | Z | Y | Z | Y | Z | Y | Z |
| Tangible fixed assets | 90 | 20 |  |  | 30 | 10 | 120 | 30 |
| Intangible fixed assets | 30 |  | (30) |  |  |  | - |  |
| Stocks | 20 | 12 | 2 |  | (8) | (5) | 14 | 7 |
| Provision for bad debts | (15) |  |  |  | (9) |  | (24) |  |

These values had not been incorporated into the financial records. Group companies have consistent accounting policies as at 31 March 20X9.

(b)   During the year ended March 20X9 Z had sold goods to X and Y. At 31 March 20X9, there were £44 million of these goods in the stock of X and £16 million in the stock of Y. Z had made a profit of 25% on selling price on the goods.

(c)   On 1 June 20X6, an amount of £36 million was received by Y from an arbitration award against Q. This receipt was secured as a result of an action against Q prior to Y's acquisition by X but was not included in the assets of Y at 1 April 20X6.

(d)   The group charges depreciation on all tangible fixed assets on the straight line basis at 10% per annum. Goodwill is amortised over 11 years.

*Required*

Prepare a consolidated balance sheet as at 31 March 20X9 for the X group.     **(25 marks)**

**8   DEMERGER (6/97, amended)**                                    *45 mins*

The following financial statements relate to A plc, B plc, C Ltd and D Ltd for the year ended 31 May 20X7.

BALANCE SHEETS AT 31 MAY 20X7

|  | A plc £m | B plc £m | C Ltd £m | D Ltd £m |
|---|---|---|---|---|
| *Fixed assets* | | | | |
| Tangible assets | 3,500 | 550 | 60 | 90 |
| Investment in B | 900 | | | |
| Investment in C | | 90 | | |
| Investment in D | 50 | | | |
| | 4,450 | 640 | | |
| Net current assets | 1,830 | 400 | 70 | 60 |
| Creditors falling due after one year | 130 | 30 | 10 | 5 |
| | 6,150 | 1,010 | 120 | 145 |
| *Capital and reserves* | | | | |
| Called up share capital of £1 | 1,350 | 100 | 30 | 20 |
| Share premium account | 1,550 | 100 | 10 | 20 |
| Profit and loss account | 3,250 | 810 | 80 | 105 |
| | 6,150 | 1,010 | 120 | 145 |

PROFIT AND LOSS ACCOUNTS
FOR THE YEAR ENDED 31 MAY 20X7

|  | A plc £m | B plc £m | C Ltd £m | D Ltd £m |
|---|---|---|---|---|
| Turnover | 8,000 | 3,000 | 325 | 530 |
| Cost of sales | 5,000 | 2,000 | 195 | 320 |
| Gross profit | 3,000 | 1,000 | 130 | 210 |
| Administrative and distribution costs | 2,000 | 400 | 35 | 125 |
| Income from group companies | 13 | 4 | - | - |
| Operating profit before taxation | 1,013 | 604 | 95 | 85 |
| Taxation | 300 | 200 | 40 | 25 |
| Profit on ordinary activities after tax | 713 | 404 | 55 | 60 |
| Dividends paid | 30 | 10 | 5 | 5 |
| Retailed profit for year | 683 | 394 | 50 | 55 |

(a)  The directors of A plc decided to reconstruct the group at 31 May 20X7. Under the scheme the existing group of companies was split into two separate groups in order to separate their different trades. A plc has disposed of its shareholding in B plc to another company E plc. In return the shares in E plc were distributed to the shareholders in A plc. No profit or loss arose on the disposal of the shares in B plc as the 'demerger' simply involved a distribution to the shareholders of A plc of the shares of E plc.

(b)  After the 'demerger', there were two separate groups controlled by A plc and E plc. A plc and D Ltd formed one group. E plc and the B group plc formed another group. E plc issued 300 million ordinary shares of £1 in exchange for A plc's investment in B plc. The transaction took place on 31 May 20X7.

(c)  The following information relates to the dates of acquisition of the investments in group companies.

| Holding company | Company acquired | % acquired | Dates | Share premium account £m | Profit & loss account £m | NOA |
|---|---|---|---|---|---|---|
| A plc → B plc | → | 100 | 1.1.X4 | → 100 | → 250 | = 1350+ = 1700. |
| A plc → D Ltd | | 60 | 1.5.X5 | 20 | 90 = 20+ | = 130 |
| B plc → C Ltd | | 80 | 1.6.X5 | 10 | 60 = 30+ | = 100. |

(d) The group's policy is to amortise goodwill over ten years with a full year's amortisation in the year of acquisition and none in the year of disposal. No fair value adjustments are necessary.

(e) Dividends paid by group companies have been accounted for by the recipient companies. A Group plc has decided to show the effect of the distribution of the shares in E plc and the demerger of B Group plc in its profit and loss account and not as a movement on reserves.  *see (a).*

(f) The group is to take advantage of the provisions of the Companies Act 1985 regarding group reconstruction relief and the transaction qualifies as a merger.

*Required*

     *BxC*

(a) Prepare the consolidated balance sheet of the B Group plc for the year ended 31 May 20X7.     (7 marks)

(b) Prepare the consolidated profit and loss account and balance sheet of A Group plc for the year ended 31 May 20X7 after accounting for the demerger.     (15 marks)

    · P/L
    · B/S
    · STRSL
    - NOTES

     (Candidates should prepare the financial statements in accordance with FRS 3 *Reporting financial performance*.)

(c) Show the share capital and reserves of E Group plc at 31 May 20X7.     (3 marks)

         **(25 marks)**

## 9    WRIGHT (12/98)                 *45 mins*

Wright, a public limited company, acquired 80% of the issued equity capital of Berg, a public limited company, on 1 July 20X6 when the accumulated profits of Berg were £300 million. The cost of the shares was £600 million and the share capital and share premium account of Berg at that date were respectively £250 million and £50 million. The fair values of the net assets of Berg at the date of acquisition were equivalent to their book values. Wright sold half of its holding of the shares in Berg on 1 July 20X8 for £350 million.

On 1 April 20X8, Wright acquired 80% of the issued share capital of £500 million of Chang, a public limited company, at a cost of £700 million.

The draft profit and loss accounts for the year ended 31 December 20X8 are as follows.

13

|  | Wright £m | Berg £m | Chang £m |
|---|---|---|---|
| Turnover | 18,000 | 1,200 | 1,600 |
| Cost of sales | (12,000) | (840) | (1,020) |
| Gross profit | 6,000 | 360 | 580 |
| Distribution costs | (1,800) | (120) | (140) |
| Administrative expenses | (180) | (12) | (12) |
| Operating profit | 4,020 | 228 | 428 |
| Interest payable | (30) | (8) | (4) |
| Bank interest receivable | 15 | 10 | 20 |
| Dividends receivable (all inter company) | 112 | - | - |
| Profit on ordinary activities before taxation | 4,117 | 230 | 444 |
| Tax on profit on ordinary activities | (1,320) | (74) | (80) |
| Profit on ordinary activities after tax | 2,797 | 156 | 364 |
| Dividends – proposed | (200) | (80) | (100) |
| Retained profit for the year | 2,597 | 76 | 264 |
| Profit and loss reserve at 1.1.X8 | 8,500 | 324 | 249 |

The following information is relevant to the preparation of the group accounts:

(i)    During the period Wright plc closed down 15 of its 100 retail outlets because they were unprofitable and inefficient. These outlets contributed 5% of the turnover and operating costs of Wright plc. The costs of this downsizing included in cost of sales amounted to £14 million.

(ii)   The net assets of Chang acquired on 1 April 20X8 and their fair values were as follows.

|  | Carrying value £m | Fair value adjustment £m | Fair values £m |
|---|---|---|---|
| Tangible fixed assets | 500 | (30) | 470 |
| Stock and work-in-progress | 240 | (40) | 200 |
| Provision for re-organisation | (30) | (20) | (50) |
| Other net assets | 130 |  | 130 |
|  | 840 | (90) | 750 |

The provision for re-organisation of £30 million relates to the reorganisation of the retail outlets of Chang which had been committed and provided for on 31 December 20X7 and a further post acquisition provision of £20 million is required which relates to the re-organisation of the remaining retail outlets as a result of the acquisition. The reduction in the stock value relates to a change in the accounting policy for stocks in order to bring it into line with that of Wright. The required change in the closing stock value of Chang to ensure uniform group accounting policies is a decrease of £30 million. The stock of Chang at 1 January 20X8 was £150 million and at 31 December 20X8 was £350 million.

(iii)  Berg sold goods to Wright on 1 September 20X8 which had a selling value of £60 million. The profit made by Berg on these goods was £6 million and Wright had sold half of these goods by the year end.

(iv)   Goodwill arising on the acquisition of subsidiaries is amortised through the profit and loss account in cost of sales over four years with a full year's charge being made in the year of acquisition. Depreciation is charged on all group fixed assets at 20% per annum on the carrying value. The depreciation policy of Chang has been the same as the group's policy for several years. The fair value adjustments had not been incorporated into Chang's accounting records.

(v)    The sale of the shares in Berg has not been accounted for by Wright, although the dividends receivable reflect the change in Wright's shareholding. Assume that profits accrue evenly and that there are no other expenses or share capital in issue other than those stated in the question. Taxation on any capital gain is to be ignored.

*Required*

(a) Prepare a consolidated ~~profit and loss account~~ for the Wright Group plc for the year ended 31 December 20X8 in accordance with the Companies Acts and UK accounting standards. (The amount of the consolidated profit dealt with in the holding company's accounts is not required.)    *individual a/c*    (21 marks)

(b) Show the composition of the balance on the group profit and loss reserve at 31 December 20X8.    (4 marks)

**(25 marks)**

## 10    PREPARATION QUESTION: ACQUISITIONS VS MERGERS

'Accounting standards should narrow differences in reporting yet acquisition accounting and merger accounting result in significantly different results in the year of combination and thereafter.'

You are required to discuss the above statement stating, with reasons, whether there is a need for two different methods.

**Guidance notes**

1    Make sure you do not confuse the criteria for merger accounting with those for merger relief.

2    FRS 6 is mentioned a lot in the Study Guide for Paper 3.6, even though mergers are likely to be rarer in future.

## 11    GROWMOOR (12/96)    *45 mins*

Growmoor plc has carried on business as a food retailer since the last century. It had traded profitability until the late 20W0s when it suffered from fierce competition from larger retailers. Its turnover and margins were under severe pressure and its share price fell to an all time low. The directors formulated a strategic plan to grow by acquisition and merger. It has an agreement to be able to borrow funds to finance acquisition at an interest rate of 10% per annum. It is Growmoor plc's policy to amortise goodwill over ten years.

1    *Investment in Smelt plc*

*15.6.X4 as.*
*S*

*25    1500.*
*(240)*

On 15 June 20X4 Growmoor plc had an issued share capital of 1,625,000 ordinary shares of £1 each. On that date it acquired 240,000 of the 1,500,000 issued £1 ordinary shares of Smelt plc for a cash payment of £164,000.    *15.6.X4*

Growmoor plc makes up its accounts to 31 July. In early 20X6 the directors of Growmoor plc and Smelt plc were having discussions with a view to a combination of the two companies.    *JAN X6.*

The proposal was as follows.

*(1200)*

(i)    On 1 May 20X6 Growmoor plc should acquire 1,200,000 of the issued ordinary shares of Smelt plc which had a market price of £1.30 per share, in exchange for 1,500,000 newly issued ordinary shares in Growmoor plc which had a market price of £1.20p per share. There has been no change in Growmoor plc's share capital since 15 June 20X4. The market price of the Smelt plc shares had ranged from £1.20 to £1.50 during the year ended 30 April 20X6.

(ii)    It was agreed that the consideration would be increased by 200,000 shares if a contingent liability in Smelt plc in respect of a claim for wrongful dismissal by a former director did not crystallise.

(iii)   After the exchange the new board would consist of six directors from Growmoor plc and six directors from Smelt plc with the Managing Director of Growmoor plc becoming Managing Director of Smelt plc.

(iv)   The Growmoor plc head office should be closed and the staff made redundant and the Smelt plc head office should become the head office of the new combination.

(v)   Senior managers of <u>both</u> companies were to re-apply for their posts and be interviewed by an interview panel comprising a director and the personnel managers from each company. The age profile of the two companies differed with the average age of the Growmoor plc managers being 40 and that of Smelt plc being 54 and there was an expectation among the directors of both boards that most of the posts would be filled by Growmoor plc managers.

2   *Investment in Beaten Ltd*

Growmoor plc is planning to acquire all of the 800,000 £1 ordinary shares in Beaten Ltd on 30 June 20X6 for a deferred consideration of £500,000 and a contingent consideration payable on 30 June 2000 of 10% of the amount by which profits for the year ended 30 June 2000 exceeded £100,000. Beaten Ltd has suffered trading losses and its directors, who are the major shareholders, support a takeover by Growmoor plc. The fair value of net assets of Beaten Ltd was £685,000 and Growmoor plc <u>expected</u> that reorganisation costs <u>would</u> be £85,000 and future trading losses would be £100,000. Growmoor plc agreed to offer four year service contracts to the directors of Beaten Ltd.

The directors had expected to be able to create a provision for the reorganisation costs and future trading losses but were advised by the Financial Director that FRS 7 required these two items to be treated as post-acquisition items.

*Required*

(a)   (i)   Explain to the directors of Growmoor plc the extent to which the proposed terms of the combination with Smelt plc satisfied the requirements of the Companies Act 1985 and FRS 6 for the combination to be treated as a merger.

(ii)   If the proposed terms fail to satisfy any of the requirements, advise the directors on any changes that could be made so that the combination could be treated as a merger as at 31 July 20X6.   (10 marks)

(b)   Explain briefly the reasons for the application of the principles of recognition and measurement on an acquisition set out in FRS 7 to provisions for future operating losses and for re-organisation costs.   (5 marks)

(c)   (i)   Explain the treatment in the profit and loss account for the year ended 31 July 20X6 and the balance sheet as at that date of Growmoor plc on the assumption that the acquisition of Beaten Ltd took place on 30 June 20X6 and the consideration for the acquisition was deferred so that £100,000 was payable after one year, £150,000 after two years and the balance after three years. Show your calculations.

(ii)   Calculate the goodwill to be dealt with in the consolidated accounts for the year ending 31 July 20X6 and 20X7 explaining clearly the effect of deferred and contingent consideration.

(iii)   Explain and critically discuss the existing regulations for the treatment of negative goodwill.   (10 marks)

(25 marks)

## 12   MERGE AND ACQUIRE (12/97, amended)                         *45 mins*

A merger is 'a business combination that results in the creation of a new reporting entity formed from the combining parties, in which the combining entities come together in a partnership for the mutual sharing of the risks and benefits of the combined entity, and in which no party to the combination in substance obtains control over any other, or is otherwise seen to be dominant ...' FRS 6 *Acquisitions and mergers*. The continuity of ownership, control and the sharing of risks and benefits in the combined entity are seen as crucial to a combination being accounted for as a merger. There are certain criteria under FRS 6 which can be verified and substantiated in order to determine whether there is continuity of ownership. Similarly there are certain criteria in FRS 6 which could be said to be circumstantial or implied evidence of a merger and which cannot be exactly determined. This type of evidence is somewhat subjective. Finally FRS 6 has invoked certain criteria which attempt to prevent a company creating the superficial or cosmetic appearance of the occurrence of a merger.

*Required*

(a)   Analyse and describe the criteria that a business combination must meet under FRS 6 for it to be accounted for as a merger under the following classes.

  (i)     Verifiable and substantive signs of a merger

  (ii)    Implied or circumstantial evidence of a merger

  (iii)   Terms which prevent superficial mergers (anti-avoidance criteria)      (9 marks)

(b)   The following abridged financial statements relate to Merge plc and Acquire plc for the year ended 30 November 20X7.

PROFIT AND LOSS ACCOUNT FOR THE YEAR ENDED 30 NOVEMBER 20X7

|  | Merge plc £'000 | Acquire plc £'000 |
|---|---|---|
| Turnover | 21,285 | 18,000 |
| Cost of sales | (16,950) | (14,450) |
| Gross profit | 4,335 | 3,550 |
| Distribution and administrative expenses | (3,310) | (2,730) |
| Operating profit | 1,025 | 820 |
| Income from investments | 200 | 100 |
| Profit before taxation | 1,225 | 920 |
| Taxation | (365) | (274) |
| Dividends | (208) | (148) |
| Retained profit for year | 652 | 498 |

BALANCE SHEET AT 30 NOVEMBER 20X7

|  | £'000 | £'000 |
|---|---|---|
| Fixed assets (including cost of investment in Acquire plc) | 4,099 | 3,590 |
| Current assets | 5,530 | 4,350 |
| Creditors: amounts falling due within one year | (2,502) | (2,530) |
| Net current assets | 3,028 | 1,820 |
| Total assets less current liabilities | 7,127 | 5,410 |
| | | |
| Capital and reserves | | |
| Called up share capital - ordinary shares of £1 | 2,500 | 1,250 |
| Share premium account | 400 | 250 |
| Revaluation reserve | 75 | 185 |
| Other reserves | 100 | - |
| Profit and loss account | 4,052 | 3,725 |
| | 7,127 | 5,410 |

(i)   During the year the entire share capital of Acquire plc was acquired following a recommended offer by merchant bankers on 30 April 20X7. Ordinary shares were issued to those shareholders of Acquire plc who accepted the offer and, at the same time, £36,000 was paid in cash to those shareholders who took the cash alternative. The offer was made on the basis of six shares in Merge plc for every five shares in Acquire plc. A fully underwritten cash alternative of £2.25 per share was offered to the shareholders of Acquire plc. The offer became unconditional on 31 May 20X7 when the market value of shares in Merge plc was £2.50 per share. On 31 August 20X7 Merge plc compulsorily acquired 8,000 shares of Acquire plc for cash from shareholders who had not accepted the initial offer under the Companies Act 1985. The above transactions had been incorporated in the financial records of Merge plc at their nominal value.

(ii)   Merge plc incurred £156,000 of expenses in connection with the acquisition of Acquire plc. This figure included issue costs of shares of £58,000 and has been included in administrative expenses.   *Dr Share Premium £*

(iii)   Acquire plc paid dividends of £48,000 on 31 March 20X7 and has proposed a final dividend of £100,000. Merge plc's dividends are all proposed. The proposed dividend of Acquire plc has been taken into account in Merge plc's financial statements.

(iv)   The acquisition fulfils all of the criteria in the Companies Acts and FRS 6 for merger accounting except for the criteria relating to the purchase consideration which has not been tested.   *∴ needs to be tested*

(v)   There is no group election for tax purposes in force.

*∴ 100 ordinary*
*into co. s/n.*

*Required*

Prepare the group profit and loss account for the year ended 30 November 20X7 and the balance sheet as at 30 November 20X7 for the Merge Group plc.          (16 marks)

**(25 marks)**

## 13   PREPARATION QUESTION: FOREIGN CURRENCY

Groups of companies with overseas branches and subsidiaries have problems in determining the manner in which their results are included in the consolidated and parent company accounts.

*Required*

(a)   Explain the two alternative methods of foreign currency translation now in general use, and distinguish the circumstances in which each is appropriately used.

(b)   Give your views on the appropriateness of the two alternative methods of translating the 'foreign currency' annual accounts of an overseas branch or subsidiary.

**Guidance notes**

1   A plan is a good idea before you write your full answer.

2   You need a thorough knowledge of SSAP 20 to give an in-depth answer to this question. Make sure you can define major terms succinctly and accurately.

3   In part (b) you should consider a wider arena than just accounting treatment: look at the economic reality of the situation.

**14    GOLD (12/97)**                                           *45 mins*

SSAP 20 *Foreign currency translation* states that the method used to translate financial statements for consolidation purposes should reflect the financial and other operational relationships which exist between an investing company and its foreign enterprises. A key element in determining this relationship is the dependency of the trade of the foreign enterprise on the economic environment of the investing company's currency rather than that of its own reporting currency. Thus it is important to determine the dominant or functional currency in order to determine whether the temporal method should be utilised.

However, where the foreign enterprise operates in a country with a high rate of inflation, the translation process may not be sufficient to present fairly the financial position of the foreign enterprise. Some adjustment for inflation should be undertaken to the local currency financial statements before translation. UITF 9 *Accounting for operations in hyper-inflationary economies* deals with this issue.

*Required*

(a)    Explain the factors which should be taken into account in determining the dominant or functional currency and how these factors influence the choice of method to be used to translate the financial statements of a foreign enterprise.                     (10 marks)

(b)    Discuss the reasons why adjustments for hyper-inflation in the financial statements of foreign enterprises are felt necessary before their translation.                     (5 marks)

(c)    On 30 November 20X3, Gold plc, a UK company, set up a subsidiary in an overseas country where the local currency is effados. The principal assets of this subsidiary were a chain of hotels. The value of the hotels on this date was 20 million effados. The rate of inflation for the period 30 November 20X3 to 30 November 20X7 has been significantly high. The following inflation is relevant to the economy of the overseas country.

|  | *Effados in exchange for* | | *Consumer price index in overseas* | *Exchange rate* |
|  | *£UK* | *$US* | *country* | *UK£ to US$* |
|---|---|---|---|---|
| 30 November 20X3 | 1.34 | 0.93 | 100 | £0.69 to $1 |
| 30 November 20X7 | 17.87 | 11.91 | 3,254 | £0.66 to $1 |

There is no depreciation charged in the financial statements as the hotels are maintained to a high standard.

*Required*

(i)    Calculate the value at which the hotels would be included in the group financial statements of Gold plc on the following dates and using the methods outlined below.

(1)    At 30 November 20X3 and 30 November 20X7 using the closing rate/net investment method.

(2)    At 30 November 20X7 after adjusting for current price levels.

(3)    At 30 November 20X7 after remeasuring using the dollar as the stable currency.                     (5 marks)

(Methods (2) and (3) are those outlined in UITF 9 *Accounting for operations in hyper-inflationary economies*.)

(ii)    Discuss the results of the valuations of the hotels, commenting on the validity of the different bases outlined above.                     (5 marks)

                                                                **(25 marks)**

**15   FOREIGN (6/98)**                                                   *45 mins*

XY, a public limited company, owns 80% of AG, a public limited company which is situated in a foreign country. The currency of this country is the Kram (KR). XY acquired AG on 30 April 20X6 for £220 million when the retained profits of AG were KR 610 million. AG has not issued any share capital since acquisition. The following financial statements relate to XY and AG.

BALANCE SHEETS AT 31 DECEMBER 20X7

|  | XY £million | AG KRmillion |
|---|---|---|
| *Fixed assets* |  |  |
| Tangible assets | 945 | 1890 |
| Investment in AG | 270 | - |
| *Net current assets* | 735 | 645 |
| *Creditors: falling due after one year* | (375) | (1,115) |
|  | 1,575 | 1,420 |
| Share capital | 330 | 240 |
| Share premium | 350 | 80 |
| Profit and loss account | 895 | 1,100 |
|  | 1,575 | 1,420 |

PROFIT AND LOSS ACCOUNT
YEAR ENDED 31 DECEMBER 20X7

|  | XY £million | AG KRmillion |
|---|---|---|
| Turnover | 1,650 | 3,060 |
| Cost of sales | (945) | (2,550) |
| Gross profit | 705 | 510 |
| Administrative and distribution costs | (420) | (51) |
| Income from AG | 8 | - |
| Interest payable | (22) | (102) |
| Operating profit before taxation | 271 | 357 |
| Taxation | (79) | (153) |
| Profit on ordinary activities after tax | 192 | 204 |
| Dividends paid | (20) | (52) |
| Retained profit for year | 172 | 152 |

(i)   During the year AG sold goods to XY for KR 104 million. The subsidiary made a profit of KR 26 million on the transaction. The exchange rate ruling at the date of the transaction was £1 = KR5.2. All of the goods remained unsold at the year end of 31 December 20X7. XY had paid for the goods on receipt and there were no inter company current balances outstanding at 31 December 20X7. At 31 December 20X6 there were goods sold by AG to XY held in the stock of XY. These goods amounted to £6 million on which AG made a profit of £2 million.

(ii)  A loan of £50 million in sterling was raised by AG from XY on 31 May 20X7. The loan is interest free and is repayable in 20Y7. The loan to the subsidiary was translated at the temporal rate in the subsidiary's financial statements and had been included in the investment in AG figure in the balance sheet of XY. An amount of KR 65 million had been paid to XY by AG on 31 December 20X7 in part settlement of the loan. This amount had not been received by XY and was not included in its financial statements.

(iii) The fair value of the net assets of AG at the date of acquisition was KR 1,040 million. Goodwill on consolidation is to be amortised on a straight line basis over three years and is to be calculated using historical cost goodwill. Goodwill is treated as a sterling asset which does not fluctuate with changes in the exchange rate. The increase in the fair value of AG over carrying value is attributable to tangible fixed assets which are depreciated over five years on the straight line basis. Tangible and intangible assets are depreciated without time apportionment in the year of acquisition and the fair value adjustment was not incorporated into the books of AG.

(iv) AG paid the dividend for the year ended 31 December 20X7 on 30 June 20X7. No more dividends were paid or proposed by AG during the year. The tax effect of the dividend has been taken into account in the above figures and may be ignored.

(v) The following exchange rates are relevant to the financial statements.

|  | KRAMS to the £ |
| --- | --- |
| 30 April 20X6 | 4.0 |
| 31 December 20X6 | 4.6 |
| 1 January 20X7 | 4.7 |
| 31 May 20X7 | 5.3 |
| 30 June 20X7 | 5.2 |
| 31 December 20X7 | 5 |
| Weighted average 20X7 | 5.1 |

(vi) The group policy is to use the closing rate/net investment methods and translate the profit and loss account at the weighted average rate.

*Required*

(a) Prepare a consolidated profit and loss account for the year ended 31 December 20X7 and a balance sheet as at that date for the XY group.

(All calculations should be to one place of decimals.)                                  (18 marks)

(b) Prepare a statement of the movement in consolidated reserves for the financial year ended 31 December 20X7.                                                             (3 marks)

(c) Discuss why SSAP 20 *Foreign currency translation* fails to deal adequately with accounting for foreign currency translation.                                          (4 marks)

**(25 marks)**

## 16    PREPARATION QUESTION: CASH FLOW STATEMENTS

The draft results of Mansfield plc are as follows.

DRAFT BALANCE SHEETS
AS AT 31 DECEMBER

|  | 20X5 | | 20X6 | |
|---|---|---|---|---|
|  | £ | £ | £ | £ |
| *Fixed assets* | | | | |
| Freehold buildings | | | | |
| Cost | 440,000 | | 487,000 | |
| Depreciation | 100,000 | | 120,000 | |
|  | | 340,000 | | 367,000 |
| Machinery | | | | |
| Cost | 290,000 | | 500,000 | |
| Depreciation | 95,000 | | 105,000 | |
|  | | 195,000 | | 395,000 |
| Vehicles | | | | |
| Cost | 55,000 | | 116,000 | |
| Depreciation | 27,000 | | 30,000 | |
|  | | 28,000 | | 86,000 |
| Quoted investments at cost | | 18,000 | | 11,395 |
|  | | 581,000 | | 859,395 |
| *Current assets* | | | | |
| Stock | 77,667 | | 89,301 | |
| Debtors | 61,739 | | 75,630 | |
| Cash | 25,932 | | 4,000 | |
|  | 165,338 | | 168,931 | |
| *Current liabilities* | | | | |
| Trade creditors | 71,338 | | 69,872 | |
| Current tax | 15,000 | | 17,000 | |
| Proposed dividends | 10,000 | | 8,000 | |
| Bank overdraft | - | | 2,112 | |
|  | 96,338 | | 96,984 | |
| *Net current assets* | | 69,000 | | 71,947 |
|  | | 650,000 | | 931,342 |
| Ordinary shares, of £0.25 each | | 300,000 | | 522,500 |
| 15% convertible loan stock | | 50,000 | | 38,000 |
| Share premium | | 20,000 | | 22,300 |
| General premium | | 70,000 | | 97,000 |
| Retained profit | | 80,000 | | 131,542 |
| 10% debentures, redeemable 20X5/20X8 | | 130,000 | | 100,000 |
| Bank loan | | - | | 20,000 |
|  | | 650,000 | | 931,342 |

*Notes*

(a)   During February 20X6, the holders of £12,000 nominal value of 15% convertible loan stock opted to convert their holdings into ordinary shares. The terms of the conversion were two ordinary shares for every £1.50 nominal value of 15% convertible loan stock.

(b)   During June 20X6, there was a rights issue of one share for every four shares held at a price of £0.70 per share, all of which were subscribed.

(c)   In August 20X6, the directors of Mansfield plc authorised a bonus issue out of the share premium. The terms of the issue were three ordinary shares for every eight ordinary shares held.

(d) In November 20X6 the office buildings were revalued from £30,000 to £47,000 and the increase in valuation was transferred to the general reserve.

(e) The following disposals of fixed assets took place in the year ended 31 December 20X6.

   (i)   A building with a cost of £30,000 and a book value of £17,000 was sold at a profit of £500.

   (ii)  Two machines which had cost £5,000 each twenty years ago, and did not have any book values, were sold at a profit of £1,000 each.

   (iii) A vehicle with a cost of £1,000 and a book value of £300 was sold at a loss of £100.

(f) During August 20X6, some quoted trade investments which had cost £16,605 were sold at a profit of £10,395.

(g) Interest paid during the year was as follows.

|              | £      |
|--------------|--------|
| Loan Stock   | 6,600  |
| Debentures   | 11,500 |
| Overdraft    | 200    |

*Required*

From the above information prepare a cash flow statement for the year ended 31 December 20X6 suitable for inclusion in the financial statements of Mansfield plc as per FRS 1 (revised).

**Guidance notes**

1   First of all, draw up a proforma of the cashflow statement, leaving plenty of space.

2   Slot in the easy/given figures.

3   The reconciliation of operating profits to related cash flows will gain you plenty of marks.

4   Make sure you understand the reconciliation of net cash flow to movement in net debt and the analysis of changes in net debt.

17   **HEBDEN**                                                        *45 mins*

The following draft financial statements relate to the Hebden Group plc.

DRAFT PROFIT AND LOSS ACCOUNT FOR THE YEAR TO 31 JULY 20X6

|                                              | £m    | £m      |
|----------------------------------------------|-------|---------|
| Turnover                                     |       | 5,845   |
| Cost of sales                                |       | (2,160) |
| Gross profit                                 |       | 3,685   |
| Distribution costs                           | 510   |         |
| Administrative expenses                      | 210   |         |
|                                              |       | (720)   |
|                                              |       | 2,965   |
| Group share of associates' operating profit  |       | 990     |
| Group operating profit                       |       | 3,955   |
| Profit on disposal of tangible fixed assets  |       | 300     |
| Income from investments                      |       | 80      |
| Interest payable                             |       | (300)   |
| Profit on ordinary activities before taxation|       | 4,035   |
| Tax on profit on ordinary activities         |       | (1,345) |
| Profit on ordinary activities after tax      |       | 2,690   |
| Minority interest - equity                   |       | (200)   |
| Profit attributable to members of parent company |  | 2,490   |
| Dividends paid and proposed                  |       | (800)   |
|                                              |       | 1,690   |

DRAFT GROUP BALANCE SHEET AS AT 31 JULY 20X6

|  | 20X6 £m | 20X5 £m |
|---|---|---|
| *Fixed assets* | | |
| Intangible asset: goodwill | 200 | - |
| Tangible assets | 7,750 | 5,000 |
| Investment in associated undertaking | 2,200 | 2,000 |
| Other fixed asset investments | 820 | 820 |
|  | 10,970 | 7,820 |
| *Current assets* | | |
| Stocks | 3,950 | 2,000 |
| Debtors | 3,700 | 2,550 |
| Cash at bank and in hand | 9,030 | 3,640 |
|  | 16,680 | 8,190 |
| *Creditors: amounts falling due within one year* | (3,084) | (1,854) |
| Net current assets | 13,596 | 6,336 |
| Total assets less current liabilities | 24,566 | 14,156 |
| Creditors: amounts falling due after more than one year | (4,340) | (1,340) |
| *Provision for liabilities and charges* | | |
| Deferred taxation | (60) | (26) |
| Minority interests: equity | (230) | - |
|  | 19,936 | 12,790 |
| *Capital and reserves* | | |
| Called up share capital | 7,880 | 4,000 |
| Share premium account | 5,766 | 4,190 |
| Profit and loss account | 6,290 | 4,600 |
| Total shareholders' funds - equity | 19,936 | 12,790 |

The following information is relevant to Hebden Group plc.

(a) The Hebden Group plc has two wholly owned subsidiaries. In addition it acquired a 75% interest in Hendry Ltd on 1 August 20X5. It also holds a 40% interest in Sullivan Ltd which it acquired several years ago. Goodwill in Sullivan Ltd is fully amortised. However, goodwill on the acquisition of Hendry Ltd was deemed to have an indefinite useful life and is to remain in the balance sheet.

(b) The following balance sheet recorded at fair values refers to Hendry Ltd at the date of acquisition.

BALANCE SHEET AT 1 AUGUST 20X5

|  | £m | £m |
|---|---|---|
| Plant and machinery | | 330 |
| Current assets | | |
| Stocks | 64 | |
| Debtors | 56 | |
| Cash at bank and in hand | 224 | |
|  | 344 | |
| Creditors: amounts falling due within one year (including corporation tax £34m) | (170) | |
|  | | 174 |
|  | | 504 |
| Called up share capital | | 100 |
| Profit and loss account | | 404 |
|  | | 504 |

The consideration for the purchase of the shares in Hendry comprised 440 million ordinary shares of £1 of Hebden plc at a value of £550 million and a balance of £28 million was paid in cash.

24

(c)   The taxation charge in the profit and loss account is made up of the following items.

|  | £m |
|---|---|
| Corporation tax | 782 |
| Deferred taxation | 208 |
| Tax attributable to associated undertakings | 355 |
|  | 1,345 |

(d)   The tangible fixed assets of the Hebden Group plc comprise the following.

|  | Buildings £m | Plant and machinery £m | Total £m |
|---|---|---|---|
| 1 August 20X5 cost or valuation | 5,100 | 2,800 | 7,900 |
| Additions | - | 4,200 | 4,200 |
| Disposals | - | (1,000) | (1,000) |
| At 31 July 20X6 | 5,100 | 6,000 | 11,100 |
|  |  |  |  |
| Depreciation |  |  |  |
| At 1 August 20X5 | 700 | 2,200 | 2,900 |
| Provided during year | 250 | 400 | 650 |
| Disposals |  | (200) | (200) |
| At 31 July 20X6 | 950 | 2,400 | 3,350 |
|  |  |  |  |
| Net book value at 31 July 20X6 | 4,150 | 3,600 | 7,750 |
|  |  |  |  |
| Net book value at 1 August 20X5 | 4,400 | 600 | 5,000 |

Included in additions of plant and machinery, are items totalling £1,700m acquired under finance leases. The plant and machinery disposed of resulted in a profit of £300m. Because of the nature of the industry the finance leases are normally quite short term.

(e)   Creditors: amounts falling due within one year comprise the following items.

|  | 20X6 £m | 20X5 £m |
|---|---|---|
| Trade creditors | 1,000 | 560 |
| Obligations under finance leases | 480 | 400 ✓ |
| Corporation tax | 924 | 434 |
| Dividends | 600 | 400 |
| Accrued interest and finance charges | 80 | 60 |
|  | 3,084 | 1,854 |

The interest paid on the finance lease rental payments in the year was calculated by the accountant to be £100m.

(f)   Creditors: amounts falling due after more than one year included the following items.

|  | 20X6 £m | 20X5 £m |
|---|---|---|
| Obligations under finance leases | 1,434 | 1,340 |
| 6% debentures repayable 1.8.2005 | 2,906 | - |
|  | 4,340 | 1,340 |

There had been an issue of debentures on 1 August 20X5. The debentures of face value of £3,000 million had been issued at a discount of £100m effectively increasing the yield on the loan to 6.2% approximately.

*Required*

Prepare a group cash flow statement for the Hebden Group plc for the year ended 31 July 20X6 in accordance with the requirements of FRS 1 *Cash flow statements (revised)*. Your answer should only include the following notes.

(a)   A reconciliation of operating profit to net cash inflow from operating activities

(b)  An analysis of headings netted off in the cash flow statement
(c)  Analysis of net debt
(d)  Purchase of subsidiary undertaking                                              **(25 marks)**

## 18  CARVER (12/94, amended)                                              *45 mins*

Carver plc is a listed company incorporated in 20T8 to produce models carved from wood. In 20V5 it acquired a 100% interest in a wood importing company, Olio Ltd; in 20W9 it acquired a 40% interest in a competitor, Multi-products Ltd; and on 1 October 20X3 it acquired a 75% interest in Good Display Ltd. It is planning to make a number of additional acquisitions during the next three years.

The draft consolidated accounts for the Carver Group are as follows

DRAFT CONSOLIDATED PROFIT AND LOSS ACCOUNT
FOR THE YEAR ENDED 30 SEPTEMBER 20X4

|                                                          | £'000 | £'000 |
|----------------------------------------------------------|-------|-------|
| Operating profit                                         |       | 1,485 |
| Share of operating profit in associate                   |       | 495   |
| Income from fixed asset investment                       |       | 155   |
| Interest payable                                         |       | (150) |
| Profit on ordinary activities before taxation            |       | 1,985 |
| Tax on profit on ordinary activities                     |       |       |
| Corporation tax                                          | 391   |       |
| Deferred taxation                                        | 104   |       |
| Tax attributable to income of associated undertakings    | 145   |       |
|                                                          |       | (640) |
| Profit on ordinary activities after taxation             |       | 1,345 |
| Minority interests                                       |       | (100) |
| Profit for the financial year                            |       | 1,245 |
| Dividends paid and proposed                              |       | (400) |
| Retained profit for the year                             |       | 845   |

DRAFT CONSOLIDATED BALANCE SHEET
AS AT 30 SEPTEMBER

| | 20X3 | | 20X4 | |
|---|---|---|---|---|
| | £'000 | £'000 | £'000 | £'000 |
| *Fixed assets* | | | | |
| Intangible asset: goodwill | | - | | 100 |
| Tangible assets | | | | |
| Buildings at net book value | | 2,200 | | 2,075 |
| Machinery:    cost | 1,400 | | 3,000 | |
|         aggregate depreciation | (1,100) | | (1,200) | |
|         net book value | | 300 | | 1,800 |
| | | 2,500 | | 3,975 |
| Investments in associated undertaking | | 1,000 | | 1,100 |
| Fixed asset investments | | 410 | | 410 |
| *Current assets* | | | | |
| Stocks | | 1,000 | | 1,975 |
| Trade debtors | | 1,275 | | 1,850 |
| Cash | | 1,820 | | 4,515 |
| | | 4,095 | | 8,340 |
| *Creditors: amounts falling due within one year* | | | | |
| Trade creditors | | 280 | | 500 |
| Obligations under finance leases | | 200 | | 240 |
| Corporation tax | | 217 | | 462 |
| Dividends | | 200 | | 300 |
| Accrued interest and finance charges | | 30 | | 40 |
| | | 927 | | 1,542 |
| *Net current assets* | | 3,168 | | 6,798 |
| *Total assets less current liabilities* | | 7,078 | | 12,283 |
| *Creditors: amounts falling due after more than one year* | | | | |
| Obligations under finance leases | | 170 | | 710 |
| Loans | | 500 | | 1,460 |
| *Provisions for liabilities* | | | | |
| Deferred taxation | | 13 | | 30 |
| *Net assets* | | 6,395 | | 10,083 |
| *Capital and reserves* | | | | |
| Called up share capital in 25p shares | | 2,000 | | 3,940 |
| Share premium account | | 2,095 | | 2,883 |
| Profit and loss account | | 2,300 | | 3,145 |
| Total shareholders' equity | | 6,395 | | 9,968 |
| Minority interest | | - | | 115 |
| | | 6,395 | | 10,083 |

*Notes*

1    There had been no acquisitions or disposals of buildings during the year.

Machinery costing £500,000 was sold for £500,000 resulting in a profit of £100,000. New machinery was acquired in 20X4 including additions of £850,000 acquired under finance leases.

2    Information relating to the acquisition of Good Display Ltd.

|  | £'000 |
|---|---|
| Machinery | 165 |
| Stocks | 32 |
| Trade debtors | 28 |
| Cash | 112 |
| Trade creditors | ((68) |
| Corporation tax | (17) |
|  | 252 |
| Minority interest | (63) |
|  | 189 |
| Goodwill | 100 |
|  | 289 |
|  |  |
| 880,000 shares issued as part consideration | 275 |
| Balance of consideration paid in cash | 14 |
|  | 289 |

Goodwill in Olio Ltd and Multi-products Ltd is fully amortised. However, the goodwill arising on the acquisition of Good Display Ltd is considered to have an indefinite useful life and is to remain in the balance sheet.

3    Loans were issued at a discount in 20X4 and the carrying amount of the loans at 30 September 20X4 included £40,000 representing the finance cost attributable to the discount and allocated in respect of the current reporting period.

*Required*

(a)    Prepare a consolidated cash flow statement for the Carver Group for the year ended 30 September 20X4 as required by FRS 1 (revised) with supporting notes for the following.

     (i)     Reconciliation of operating profit to net cash flow from operating activities

     (ii)    Analysis of cash flows netted in the cash flow statement

     (iii)   Analysis of changes in net debt                      (20 marks)

(b)    Explain and illustrate any adjustments that you consider the company should make to the cash flow statement prepared in (a) above to take account of the following information.

     (i)     Carver plc had constructed a laser cutter which is included in the machinery cost figure at £73,000.

|  | £'000 |
|---|---|
| Materials | 50 |
| Labour | 12 |
| Overheads | 6 |
| Interest capitalised | 5 |
|  | 73 |

     (ii)    The cash figures comprised the following.

|  | 1.10.X3 | 30.9.X4 |
|---|---|---|
|  | £'000 | £'000 |
| Cash in hand | 10 | 15 |
| Bank overdrafts | (770) | (65) |
| Bank | 1,080 | 1,890 |
| 10% Treasury Stock 20X3 | 1,500 | - |
| Bank deposits | - | 1,125 |
| Gas 3% 20X0 - 20X5 | - | 1,550 |
|  | 1,820 | 4,515 |

     The 10% Treasury Stock 20X3 was acquired on 1 September 20X3 and redeemed on 31 October 20X3 at par.

The bank deposits were made on 1 September 20X4 for a 3 month term.

The Gas 3% was acquired on 1 June 20X4 and is traded on an active market.

(5 marks)

**(25 marks)**

**19    LANGUAGE-EASE (12/96, amended)**                                    *45 mins*

Language-ease Ltd is a company incorporated by Peter Wong and Daphne Hillier in 20V5 to provide English language teaching to foreign students. Peter and Daphne are the directors and each holds 50% of the issued shares. Since 20V5, 40 colleges have been opened in city centre locations in the UK and abroad. Each college is owned by a separate company of which Peter and Daphne are the directors and shareholders.

Each college has approximately 400 students for 30 weeks per year. Language-ease Ltd employs staff centrally to market the courses at all of the colleges. Peter and Daphne have appointed a different firm of auditors to audit each separate company and there are different dates for the financial year ends.

In 20X0 Student-Food Ltd was incorporated to sell food, mainly in long-life packs priced at approximately £5 per pack, to college students either to eat on the premises or to take away. The directors were Peter Wong's son and Daphne Hillier's sister who had previously taught at a college. Each held 30% of the issued share capital with the remaining share being held by private business investors.

In some of the colleges, Student-Food Ltd sold to the college and the college itself operated the sales outlet; in the other colleges, Student-Food Ltd operated the sales outlet under a licence granted by a college whereby it was permitted to rent space on the college premises for a period of eight years from 1 November 20X2 at a rental of £1 per square metre; the market rental was £6.50 per square metre. As at 31 October 20X4 the company had fixed assets with a gross cost of £650,000 and a book value of £400,000 consisting of motor vehicles £96,000, storage equipment £200,000 and fixtures and fittings £104,000. The company planned to sell 4 pre-packed units per week to at least 15% of the student population for the year ended 31 October 20X5.

In 20X5 the company incurred fixed asset expenditure to encourage students to remain on the premises for meals so that the company could achieve its planned sales: by installing a freezer unit costing £5,000 at each college to satisfy health and safety regulations; by installing fittings costing £7,500 per college and storage equipment costing £4,000 per college.

In 20X6 it incurred £12,500 per college for additional fittings. This fixed asset expenditure was considered to be necessary in order for the company to be able to compete with local city centre restaurants.

The directors considered that the fixed asset expenditure had been successful and they consequently revised their target for 20X6 to achieving sales of 4 packs per week to 30% of the student population. On the basis of this estimated increase in turnover, the company undertook further improvements to the college locations. It is company policy not to charge depreciation in the year of acquisition and to charge depreciation in the year of disposal. The bank overdraft and loan increased steadily during 20X5 and 20X6. Interest of 20% per annum was charged on the bank overdraft. The market rate of interest on loans was 12% per annum.

In 20X6 the shareholders decided to dispose of their shares in Student-Food Ltd. The audit of the accounts for the year ended 31 October 20X6 was to be completed by January 20X7. Extracts from the accounts of Student-Food Ltd for years ended 31 October were as follows.

PROFIT AND LOSS ACCOUNT FOR THE YEAR ENDED 31 OCTOBER

|  | 20X4 | | 20X5 | | 20X6 (draft) | |
|---|---|---|---|---|---|---|
|  | £'000 | £'000 | £'000 | £'000 | £'000 | £'000 |
| Sales |  | 900 |  | 1,200 |  | 1,240 |
| Gross profit |  | 252 |  | 272 |  | 320 |
| Less: expenses | 66 |  | 138 |  | 146 |  |
| rent | 6 |  | 6 |  | 6 |  |
| depreciation | 60 |  | 60 |  | 100 |  |
| interest | - |  | 28 |  | 84 |  |
|  |  | (132) |  | (232) |  | (336) |
| Profit/(loss) before tax |  | 120 |  | 40 |  | (16) |
| Tax |  | (28) |  | (7) |  |  |
|  |  | 92 |  | 33 |  | (16) |
| Dividends |  | (48) |  | (36) |  |  |
|  |  | 44 |  | (3) |  | (16) |

BALANCE SHEETS AS AT 31 OCTOBER

|  | 20X4 | | 20X5 | | 20X6 (draft) | |
|---|---|---|---|---|---|---|
|  | £'000 | £'000 | £'000 | £'000 | £'000 | £'000 |
| Ordinary shares of £1 each |  | 400 |  | 400 |  | 400 |
| Profit and loss account |  | 320 |  | 317 |  | 301 |
|  |  | 720 |  | 717 |  | 701 |
| Loan |  | - |  | 240 |  | 760 |
|  |  | 720 |  | 957 |  | 1,461 |
| Fixed assets |  | 400 |  | 1,000 |  | 1,400 |
| *Current assets* |  |  |  |  |  |  |
| Stock | 240 |  | 360 |  | 400 |  |
| Debtors | 160 |  | 360 |  | 480 |  |
| Bank | 80 |  | - |  | - |  |
|  | 480 |  | 720 |  | 880 |  |
| *Current liabilities* |  |  |  |  |  |  |
| Trade creditors | 112 |  | 431 |  | 518 |  |
| Expense creditors | 48 |  | 29 |  | 18 |  |
| Bank overdraft | - |  | 303 |  | 283 |  |
|  | 160 |  | 763 |  | 819 |  |
| Net current assets/(liabilities) |  | 320 |  | (43) |  | 61 |
|  |  | 720 |  | 957 |  | 1,461 |

Tan, Wether & Co, a firm of certified accountants, was informed by a client, Cold Pack Ltd, that the company was having preliminary discussions to acquire the issued share capital of Student-Food Ltd. Cold Pack Ltd has been following a strategy of growth by acquisition. It has been valuing its acquisitions using a price earnings multiple of between 10 and 15 applied to earnings after interest. It has been able to improve results by obtaining better terms from suppliers to the acquired companies through centralised purchasing and increasing the gross profit to 42.5% of sales.

On 25 November 20X6 Cold Pack Ltd instructed Tan, Wether & Co to prepare a report based on the accounts of Student-Food Ltd for the three years ended 31 October 20X6 and to prepare a valuation of the business. The valuation was to take into account Cold Pack Ltd's estimate that Student-Food Ltd could maintain its 20X6 level of sales and achieve a gross profit of 42.5% under new management.

BPP
PUBLISHING

Joseph Tan, the partner in Tan, Wether & Co responsible for the assignment, has requested Joyce Asprey, a trainee accountant with the firm, to draft a report and a share valuation.

*Required*

(a) Assuming that you are Joyce Asprey:

   (i)   Comment on the financial position of Student-Food Ltd as at 31 October 20X6 and on the changes that have occurred during the three years to that date for inclusion in a report to Cold Pack Ltd. Please include appropriate financial data

(15 marks)

   (ii)  Comment on the action that Cold Pack Ltd might need to take to improve the company's profitability

(5 marks)

(b) Assuming that you are Joseph Tan, prepare an initial valuation of the shares in Student-Food Ltd based on the information available at 25 November 20X6.

(5 marks)

**(25 marks)**

## 20 OLD PARCELS

*45 mins*

(a) The administrative and legislative burdens which have been imposed on small companies have been the subject of debate for several years. The application of accounting standards to small companies has been the subject of considerable research. It is the view of some accountants that accounting standards should apply to all financial statements whilst others feel that small companies should have a completely different set of accounting standards. In response to the continuing debate in this area, the Accounting Standards Board has issued a Financial Reporting Standard *Financial reporting standard for smaller entities*.

*Required*

Discuss the main issues in the development of an accounting framework for small companies with reference to the *Financial reporting standard for smaller entities*. (6 marks)

(b) The directors of the Old Parcels Ltd, an unlisted company, have drawn up their financial statements in accordance with the *Financial reporting standard for smaller entities* (FRSSE) for the year ended 31 May 20X8. All exemptions from compliance with accounting standards given to small companies by the FRSSE have been utilised by the company. They have been approached by a publicly quoted company, New Parcels plc, with a view to selling the whole of the share capital of Old Parcels Ltd to this company. New Parcels plc is in the same industry as Old Parcels Ltd and has a price earning ratio of 14. The shares in Old Parcels Ltd are held by one family who have agreed to sell all of the shares to New Parcels plc subject to an independently agreed valuation of the shares. Following the purchase of the shares, the two companies are to be joined together to form a single company.

FINANCIAL INFORMATION - OLD PARCELS LIMITED
BALANCE SHEET AT 31 MAY 20X8

|  | £'000 | £'000 |
|---|---|---|
| *Fixed assets* | | |
| Intangible asset | | 12 |
| Tangible assets | | 278 |
| | | 290 |
| | | |
| Current assets | 835 | |
| Creditors: amounts falling due within one year | (365) | |
| Net current assets | | 470 |
| Total assets less current liabilities | | 760 |
| Creditors: amounts falling due after more than one year | | (119) |
| Provisions for liabilities and charges | | (12) |
| | | 629 |
| | | |
| *Capital and reserves* | | |
| Share capital | | 204 |
| Profit and loss account | | 425 |
| | | 629 |

PROFITS AND DIVIDENDS 20X4 TO 20X9

| Year ended 31 May | Profit/(loss) on ordinary activities after tax £ | Dividends (including preference dividend) declared £ | Preference share redemption-additional finance cost £ |
|---|---|---|---|
| 20X4 | 60,000 | 6,000 | - |
| 20X5 | 66,000 | 6,500 | - |
| 20X6 | 75,000 | 8,000 | 510 |
| 20X7 | 45,000 | 2,100 | 554 |
| 20X8 | (30,000) | Nil | 603 |
| 20X9 (projected) | 35,000 | 6,200 | 654 |

The profit/loss amounts are before dividend payments.

(i) . The intangible asset is a licence to distribute a product and is estimated to generate net income before tax in the future of £10,000 per annum for the period of the licence which expires on 31 May 20Y0. The carrying value in the balance sheet represents the original cost of £20,000 less amortisation and it is estimated that the market value of the licence is £15,000.

(ii) . The tangible fixed assets were revalued on 31 May 20X7 by an independent valuer. The assets are depreciated at 10% per annum. The directors estimate that the market price of the fixed assets has increased by approximately 5% of their current carrying value during the year and that the net realisable value of the assets is £250,000.

(iii) The company has an employee share ownership scheme which is run by trustees with rules which prevent transfer of the schemes assets to the company. The assets of the scheme amount to £150,000 at 31 May 20X8 and have not been included in the balance sheet. The costs of the scheme have been charged to the profit and loss account for the year.

(iv) The current assets and liabilities are felt to be worth their balance sheet amounts. The creditors falling due after more than one year are 6% debentures which are repayable at a premium of 25% on 31 May 20X9. The original debenture loan was £100,000. Interest is payable on 31 May of each year and the finance cost has been allocated at a constant rate on the carrying amount.

33

(v) The provision for liabilities and charges in the accounts of Old Parcels Ltd represents the provision for deferred taxation calculated using the partial provision method. The basis of the calculation is the crystallisation of the accumulated net deferred timing differences of £52,000. There is no provision in the financial statements of New Parcels plc as their timing differences are anticipated to rise by £70,000 per annum from 31 May 20X8 until 31 May 20Y0.

(vi) The share capital comprises the following elements.

|  | £ |
|---|---|
| 30,000 7% cumulative redeemable preference shares of £1 | 33,767 |
| 170,000 ordinary shares of £1 | 170,000 |
|  | 203,767 |

There are one year's arrears of preference dividends at 31 May 20X8 included in the above figure for preference shares and the shares are redeemable at 31 May 20Y0 at a premium of 10%. There were no issue cost or premiums paid on the original issue of the preference shares on 1 June 20X5. The share capital is owned by the directors of Old Parcels Ltd. Share options have been granted to certain senior employees and these will be exercised in the event of a sale or stock market flotation of the company if it is financially beneficial. There are options outstanding at 31 May 20X8 to subscribe for 30,000 shares at £1 per share.

(vii) The company operates a computer system which will require adjustment for the effects of dealing with the Euro. The costs of a new system would be £100,000 and the cost of adjusting the existing system would be £30,000 as at 31 May 20X8.

(viii) During the current financial year, the company discontinued part of its business activities. The operating loss after tax of these activities was £6,000 and the loss on the disposal of the sale of the operation was £3,000. This part of the business normally contributed 20% of the annual post tax profit or loss of Old Parcels Ltd.

(ix) The appropriate discount rate to be used in any calculations is a rate of 8% per annum and corporation tax is 23%. Assume any future dividend payments are made at the year end.

*Required*

Calculate and discuss the range of share values which may be placed on the ordinary shares of Old Parcels Ltd utilising the following methods of valuation.

| (i) | Net assets valuation (going concern basis) | (11 marks) |
|---|---|---|
| (ii) | Earnings based valuation | (8 marks) |

**(25 marks)**

# 21    PREPARATION QUESTION: FINANCIAL ANALYSIS

The following five year summary relates to Wandafood Products plc, and is based on financial statements prepared under the historical cost convention.

|  |  |  | 20X5 | 20X4 | 20X3 | 20X2 | 20X1 |
|---|---|---|---|---|---|---|---|
| **Financial ratios** | | | | | | | |
| *Profitability* | | | | | | | |
| Margin | $\dfrac{\text{Trading profit}}{\text{Sales}}$ | % | 7.8 | 7.5 | 7.0 | 7.2 | 7.3 |
| Return on assets | $\dfrac{\text{Trading profit}}{\text{Net operating assets}}$ | % | 16.3 | 17.6 | 16.2 | 18.2 | 18.3 |
| *Interest and dividend cover* | | | | | | | |
| Interest cover | $\dfrac{\text{Trading profit}}{\text{Net finance charges}}$ | times | 2.9 | 4.8 | 5.1 | 6.5 | 3.6 |
| Dividend cover | $\dfrac{\text{Earnings per ord share}}{\text{Div per ord share}}$ | times | 2.7 | 2.6 | 2.1 | 2.5 | 3.1 |
| **Debt to equity ratios** | | | | | | | |
| | $\dfrac{\text{Net borrowings}}{\text{Shareholders funds}}$ | % | 65.9 | 61.3 | 48.3 | 10.8 | 36.5 |
| | $\dfrac{\text{Net borrowings}}{\text{Shareholders funds} + \text{minority interests}}$ | % | 59.3 | 55.5 | 44.0 | 10.1 | 33.9 |
| **Liquidity ratios** | | | | | | | |
| Quick ratio | $\dfrac{\text{Current assets less stock}}{\text{Current liabilities}}$ | % | 74.3 | 73.3 | 78.8 | 113.8 | 93.4 |
| Current ratio | $\dfrac{\text{Current assets}}{\text{Current liabilities}}$ | % | 133.6 | 130.3 | 142.2 | 178.9 | 174.7 |
| **Asset ratios** | | | | | | | |
| Operating asset turnover | $\dfrac{\text{Sales}}{\text{Net operating assets}}$ | times | 2.1 | 2.4 | 2.3 | 2.5 | 2.5 |
| Working capital turnover | $\dfrac{\text{Sales}}{\text{Working capital}}$ | times | 8.6 | 8.0 | 7.0 | 7.4 | 6.2 |
| **Per share** | | | | | | | |
| Earnings per share | - pre-tax basis | p | 23.62 | 21.25 | 17.96 | 17.72 | 15.06 |
| | - net basis | p | 15.65 | 13.60 | 10.98 | 11.32 | 12.18 |
| Dividends per share | | p | 5.90 | 5.40 | 4.90 | 4.60 | 4.10 |
| Net assets per share | | p | 102.10 | 89.22 | 85.95 | 85.79 | 78.11 |

Net opening assets include tangible fixed assets, stock, debtors and creditors. They exclude borrowings, taxation and dividends.

*Required*

Prepare a report on the company, clearly interpreting and evaluating the information given. Include comments on possible effects of price changes which may limit the quality of the report.

**Guidance notes**

1   You must get used to questions where a load of information is thrown at you.

2   You should read the information once carefully and then skim through it again, marking off the important points.

3   Produce an answer plan first, otherwise your answer will lack structure.

22   **THERMO (6/96, amended)**                                                                *45 mins*

Mike Ried and Jane Thurby were refrigeration engineers who were made redundant in 20X5. Whilst working together they had often discussed the idea of setting up on their own. They believed that there was a niche in the market for the manufacture of low temperature thermometers. Following their redundancy, they agreed to attempt to put their idea into practice.

They prepared a business plan which showed that after start up losses the business would be profitable. They estimated that they would need £350,000 to finance the business. They presented their plan to the bank which agreed to provide an overdraft facility of £175,000 for two years on condition that they raised share capital of £175,000.

A company, Thermo Ltd was formed and commenced trading on 1 July 20X6. It was financed by the issue of 100,000 shares at par value to Mike and Jane and 75,000 shares at par value to their relatives and friends.

The accounts for the period to 31 March are set out below.

PROFIT AND LOSS ACCOUNT FOR THE PERIOD ENDING 31 MARCH

|  | 20X7 | 20X8 |
|---|---|---|
|  | £ | £ |
| Sales | 304,500 | 549,500 |
| Cost of sales | 252,787 | 443,170 |
| Gross profit | 51,713 | 106,330 |
| Administrative expense | 15,100 | 18,050 |
| Selling expenses | 36,490 | 39,368 |
| Operating profit | 123 | 48,912 |
| Interest payable | 3,922 | 18,455 |
| (Loss)/profit before tax | (3,799) | 30,457 |
| Taxation | - | 6,637 |
| (Loss)/profit after tax | (3,799) | 23,820 |

BALANCE SHEETS AS AT 31 MARCH

| | | 20X7 | | | 20X8 | |
| | Cost | Dep'n | | Cost | Dep'n | |
| *Fixed assets* | £ | £ | £ | £ | £ | £ |
| Premises | 105,000 | 1,600 | 103,400 | 105,000 | 3,200 | 101,800 |
| Machinery | 87,500 | 8,750 | 78,750 | 122,500 | 21,000 | 101,500 |
| Office furniture | 3,500 | 700 | 2,800 | 5,250 | 1,750 | 3,500 |
| Motor vehicles | 21,000 | 3,937 | 17,063 | 21,000 | 9,187 | 11,813 |
| | | | 202,013 | | | 218,613 |
| *Current assets* | | | | | | |
| Stock | 47,775 | | | 138,375 | | |
| Debtors | 151,200 | | | 190,539 | | |
| Prepayments | - | | | 8,750 | | |
| Cash | - | | | 1,253 | | |
| | 198,975 | | | 338,917 | | |
| *Current liabilities* | | | | | | |
| Creditors | 93,445 | | | 125,675 | | |
| Accruals | 43,775 | | | 25,962 | | |
| Tax | | | | 5,851 | | |
| Overdraft | 74,567 | | | 188,235 | | |
| | 211,787 | | | 345,723 | | |
| *Net current liabilities* | | | (12,812) | | | (6,806) |
| *Total assets less current liabilities* | | | 189,201 | | | 211,807 |
| *Provisions for liabilities and charges* | | | | | | |
| Deferred income: grants | | | 18,000 | | 16,000 | |
| Deferred tax | | | | | 786 | |
| | | | | | | 16,786 |
| | | | 171,201 | | | 195,021 |
| *Capital and reserves* | | | | | | |
| Share capital | | | 175,000 | | | 175,000 |
| Profit and loss account | | | (3,799) | | | 20,021 |
| | | | 171,201 | | | 195,021 |

*Note.* Agreed credit terms were 90 days for collection and payment.

In April 20X7 Mike and Jane presented their first period's draft accounts to the bank. At the meeting the bank manager produced ratios which he used to analyse the year's results during their discussion.

The ratios prepared by the bank for 20X7 were as follows.

*Profitability*

| | |
|---|---|
| Gross profit % | 17.00% |
| Operating profit % | 0.04% |
| Profit before tax % | (1.25%) |
| Profit after tax % | (1.25%) |
| Return on share capital and reserves | (2.22%) |
| Net asset turnover | 1.78 |

*Liquidity*

| | |
|---|---|
| Current ratio | 0.94 |
| Liquid ratio | 0.71 |
| Collection period (days) | 136 |
| Stock period (days) based on cost of sales | 52 |
| Payment period (days) based on purchases | 85 |

*Leverage*

| | |
|---|---|
| Total liabilities/tangible net worth | 1.24 |
| Bank debt/tangible net worth | 0.43 |
| Profit cover for interest | 0.03 |

It was agreed that Mike and Jane would discuss the position with the bank in May 20X8. At that meeting they proposed to request a restructuring of the bank facility to take the form of a term loan of £200,000 repayable over three years. They were intending to suggest a repayment schedule of £100,000, £50,000 and £50,000 on 31 March 20X9, 31 March 20Y0 and 31 March 20Y1 respectively.

They produced projected profit and loss accounts and balance sheets for three years as follows.

|  | 20X9 | 20Y0 | 20Y1 |
|---|---|---|---|
|  | £'000 | £'000 | £'000 |
| Sales | 670 | 750 | 960 |
| Cost of sales | 545 | 600 | 760 |
| Gross profit | 125 | 150 | 200 |
| Administrative expenses | 18 | 20 | 21 |
| Selling expenses | 37 | 40 | 42 |
| Operating profit | 70 | 90 | 137 |
| Interest payable | 27 | 14 | 5 |
| Profit before tax | 43 | 76 | 132 |
| Taxation | 9 | 20 | 33 |
| Profit after tax | 34 | 56 | 99 |

|  | 20X9 | | 20Y0 | | 20Y1 | |
|---|---|---|---|---|---|---|
|  | £'000 | £'000 | £'000 | £'000 | £'000 | £'000 |
| *Fixed assets* | | 230 | | 230 | | 230 |
| *Current assets* | | | | | | |
| Stock | 120 | | 170 | | 190 | |
| Debtors | 145 | | 126 | | 200 | |
| Prepayments | 10 | | 10 | | 10 | |
|  | 275 | | 306 | | 400 | |
| *Current liabilities* | | | | | | |
| Creditors | 140 | | 150 | | 180 | |
| Accruals | 8 | | 9 | | 10 | |
| Tax | 4 | | 16 | | 27 | |
| Overdraft | 5 | | 5 | | 5 | |
|  | 157 | | 180 | | 222 | |
| *Net current assets* | | 118 | | 126 | | 178 |
| Total assets less current liabilities | | 348 | | 356 | | 408 |
| Less: | | | | | | |
| Term loan | 100 | | 50 | | - | |
| Deferred tax | 5 | | 9 | | 14 | |
| Deferred income | 14 | | 12 | | 10 | |
|  | | 119 | | 71 | | 24 |
|  | | 229 | | 285 | | 384 |
| Share capital | | 175 | | 175 | | 175 |
| Profit brought forward | | 20 | | 54 | | 110 |
| Profit for year | | 34 | | 56 | | 99 |
|  | | 229 | | 285 | | 384 |

Mike and Jane have asked you, as their accountant, to assist them in drafting a report to the bank, requesting the restructuring of the bank facility. The report to the bank is to be presented in two sections.

(i) A review of the company's performance in the two periods: from incorporation to 31 March 20X7 and from 1 April 20X7 to 31 March 20X8

(ii) The case for the request for restructuring of the bank's facility, supported by the projected accounts

*Required*

(a) Draft the first section of the report on the company's performance in the two periods from incorporation to 31 March 20X8 that Mike and Jane are to present to the bank.

(9 marks)

(b) Draft a report to Mike and Jane commenting on the projected accounts and their request for a restructuring of the bank facility.    (16 marks)

**(25 marks)**

## 23    ROI AND APPROPRIATE MEASURES
*45 mins*

You have just been appointed financial controller of an old-established family-controlled business which operates a large number of shops. These shops are located in most towns in the country. It also owns a number of factories which manufacture a variety of products, most of which are sold through the shops.

The new managing director, appointed at the same time as you, is very critical of the limited management information available for the various operations, which consists of:

(a) Quarterly internal financial accounts

(b) Daily and weekly sales

(c) Statements comparing ratios of gross profit and costs to sales

He wishes to introduce better ways of measuring performance, as a preliminary step towards assessing the quality of the management of the various operations, and towards starting some rationalisation. His initial view is that both management and the operations are very variable in quality.

His first thoughts on defining this requirement were that it could be useful to produce statements of the return on investment (ROI) for each operation.

*Required*

Write a report to the managing director which does the following.

(a) Explains the problems in measuring the 'investment' in the ROI and the practical problems this causes in developing and interpreting the ROI measure for the purposes envisaged    (15 marks)

(b) Explains the process of determining which performance measurements are appropriate in a particular business.    (10 marks)

**(25 marks)**

## 24    MUSIC SOCIETIES
*45 mins*

In a number of cities, music societies, which are charitable organisations, provide classical music concerts by operating concert halls and supporting orchestras employing full-time musicians. Earned income arises mainly from giving concerts, with additional earned income from catering activities, ancillary sales programmes, CDs and cassettes, and souvenirs, and hiring out the concert hall facilities. The earned income is much less than the cost of running the orchestras and concert halls, which are also supported by subsidies in the form of annual grants from local government authorities and the central government, and from business sponsorship, which is a form of corporate public relations expenditure.

The broad aims of the music societies are to provide the best possible standard of live performance of classical music in their home cities (supported by grants from their local government authority) and in other areas of the country (supported by grants from the central government), and to encourage new music and musicians.

As they are charities, music societies do not aim to make a profit. Any surpluses are invested in improvements to the concert halls and spent on additional musicians.

Costs are largely fixed and are broadly 75% orchestral and 25% concert hall and administration (mostly staff). Levels of remuneration, especially for musicians, are low, considering the skills and training required.

The scope for increases in income is very limited. Grants will not increase, and may decrease. The orchestras (allowing for rehearsal time) are fully occupied. Fees for engagements elsewhere in the country and abroad are falling due to the competition from orchestras from other countries.

The chairman of the manufacturing company for which you are a management accountant, has recently become a non-executive director of the local music society (X Music), which owns the concert hall and employs the orchestra. His first impressions are that the music is probably excellent, though he is no expert, but that the data available on operations is very limited.

Some comparisons are available with another music society (Y Music) in a smaller city: these are given below.

*Required*

(a)  On the basis of the available data, prepare a report for the Chairman, comparing the key features of the business and financial performance of X Music with that of Y Music.                                                                                  (18 marks)

(b)  Explain which cost management techniques should be most useful to X Music, where the accounting staff is very small and available data is limited.                         (7 marks)

**(25 marks)**

**Comparative data**

|  | 20X9 | | 20X4 | | 20X0 | |
|---|---|---|---|---|---|---|
| **Number of performances** | *X* | *Y* | *X* | *Y* | *X* | *Y* |
| Concerts in home city | 74 | 84 | 77 | 91 | 75 | 91 |
| Other concerts in home country | 63 | 26 | 88 | 38 | 81 | 52 |
| Overseas concerts | 8 | 8 | 15 | - | 11 | - |
| TV/radio/recording | 5 | 11 | 9 | 5 | 14 | 9 |
| Total | 150 | 129 | 189 | 134 | 181 | 152 |
| **Income** | £'000 | £'000 | £'000 | £'000 | £'000 | £'000 |
| Concerts in home city | 698 | 1,043 | 540 | 717 | 410 | 459 |
| Other concerts in home country | 916 | 762 | 697 | 361 | 518 | 371 |
| Overseas concerts | 282 | 333 | 154 | - | 100 | - |
| TV/radio/recording | 70 | 210 | 72 | 128 | 53 | 118 |
| Other earned income | 466 | 133 | 76 | 41 | 56 | 22 |
| Business sponsorship | 397 | 607 | 141 | 135 | 56 | 44 |
| Total earned income | 2,829 | 3,088 | 1,680 | 1,382 | 1,193 | 1,014 |
| Grant - central government | 1,300 | 1,500 | 900 | 1,000 | 500 | 900 |
| Grant - local government authority | 655 | 950 | 150 | 750 | 400 | 500 |
| Total income | 4,784 | 5,538 | 2,730 | 3,132 | 2,093 | 2,414 |
| Total costs | 4,872 | 5,356 | 2,703 | 3,147 | 2,059 | 2,402 |
| Surplus/(deficit) | (88) | 182 | 27 | (15) | 34 | 12 |
| Cumulative surplus/(deficit) | (686) | 311 | 80 | (26) | 141 | 62 |

## 25    LEWES (6/95, amended)                                    *45 mins*

Lewes Holdings plc is an international group whose principal activities are the manufacture of air-conditioning systems, the supply of packaging products and automated manufacturing systems.

The draft consolidated financial statements for the year ended 31 December 20X4 together with supporting extracts are set out below.

LEWES GROUP
CONSOLIDATED PROFIT AND LOSS ACCOUNT
FOR THE YEAR ENDED 31 DECEMBER

|  | £m | 20X4 £m | 20X3 £m |
|---|---|---|---|
| Turnover (Note 1) |  |  |  |
| Continuing operations |  | 2,928.6 | 1,966.3 |
| Acquisitions |  | 453.2 | - |
|  |  | 3,381.8 | 1,966.3 |
| Operating costs |  | (3,168.7) | (1,843.7) |
| Operating profit |  |  |  |
| Continuing operations | 183.2 |  |  |
| Acquisitions | 29.9 |  |  |
|  |  | 213.1 | 122.6 |
| Costs of restructuring UK subsidiaries |  | (18.9) | - |
| Profit on ordinary activities before interest |  | 194.2 | 122.6 |
| Income from associated undertakings |  | 6.0 | 4.6 |
| Interest |  | (23.9) | (5.6) |
| Profit on ordinary activities before tax |  | 176.3 | 121.6 |
| Tax on profit on ordinary activities |  | (42.4) | (25.4) |
| Profit on ordinary activities after tax |  | 133.9 | 96.2 |
| Dividends:  on preference shares |  | (4.2) | (4.2) |
|                  on ordinary shares |  | (61.1) | (35.0) |
| Retained profit transferred to reserves |  | 68.6 | 57.0 |
| EPS |  | 16p | 14p |

LEWES GROUP
CONSOLIDATED BALANCE SHEET OF THE AS AT 31 DECEMBER

|  | 20X4 £m | 20X3 £m |
|---|---|---|
| *Fixed assets* |  |  |
| Intangible assets | 0.7 | 0.5 |
| Tangible assets | 438.5 | 277.0 |
| Investments |  |  |
| Associate | 6.7 | 1.3 |
| Other listed investments | 7.4 | 0.5 |
|  | 453.3 | 279.3 |
| *Current assets* |  |  |
| Stocks | 259.8 | 129.5 |
| Debtors | 966.9 | 574.7 |
| Investments | 31.6 | 28.5 |
| Cash at bank | 165.1 | 108.7 |
|  | 1,423.4 | 841.4 |
| Creditors: amounts falling due within one year | (1,186.2) | (691.4) |
| Net current assets | 237.2 | 150.0 |
| Total assets less current liabilities | 690.5 | 429.3 |
| Creditors: amounts falling due after more than one year | (212.4) | (97.3) |
| Provision for liabilities and charges | (36.5) | (6.8) |
|  | 441.6 | 325.2 |

*Capital and reserves*
Called up share capital

| | | |
|---|---:|---:|
| Ordinary shares (20p each) | 172.7 | 148.0 |
| 9% preference shares (£1 each) | 47.0 | 47.0 |
| Share premium account | 9.9 | 9.2 |
| Revaluation reserve | 33.5 | 27.0 |
| Other reserves (distributable) | 39.5 | 43.9 |
| Capital redemption reserve | 00.6 | 0.6 |
| Profit and loss account (Note 2) | 138.4 | 49.5 |
| | 441.6 | 325.2 |

*Notes*

1   *Group turnover and profit on ordinary activities before tax*

    (a)  *Analysis by geographical area by destination*

| | 20X4 | | 20X3 | |
|---|---:|---:|---:|---:|
| | *Turnover* | *Profit* | *Turnover* | *Profit* |
| | *£m* | *£m* | *£m* | *£m* |
| United Kingdom | 1,892.3 | 133.3 | 1,191.5 | 137.5 |
| Continental Europe | 260.8 | 21.4 | 201.9 | 15.4 |
| North America: USA | 1,002.2 | 36.9 | 396.2 | (15.3) |
| Canada | 160.1 | 6.8 | 121.3 | (3.9) |
| Other areas | 66.4 | 3.5 | 55.4 | 3.1 |
| | 3,381.8 | 201.9 | 1,966.3 | 136.8 |
| Central items, including interest and investment income | | (25.6) | | (15.2) |
| | 3,381.8 | 176.3 | 1,966.3 | 121.6 |

    (b)  *Analysis by class of business*

| | 20X4 | | 20X3 | |
|---|---:|---:|---:|---:|
| | *Turnover* | *Profit* | *Turnover* | *Profit* |
| | *£m* | *£m* | *£m* | *£m* |
| Manufacturing | 1,041.4 | 65.5 | 533.4 | 60.1 |
| Distribution | 489.0 | 51.0 | 268.5 | 34.7 |
| Automated manufacturing systems | | | | |
| UK and Europe | 889.2 | 48.3 | 666.7 | 56.3 |
| North America | 962.2 | 37.1 | 497.7 | (14.3) |
| | 3,381.8 | 201.9 | 1,966.3 | 136.8 |
| Central items, including interest and investment income | | (25.6) | | (15.2) |
| | 3,381.8 | 176.3 | 1,966.3 | 121.6 |

2   *Profit and loss account*

| | £m |
|---|---:|
| Opening balance | 49.5 |
| Retained profit for year | 68.6 |
| Foreign exchange adjustments | 20.3 |
| Profit and loss account | 138.4 |

3   *Values of assets and liabilities of companies acquired on 1 January 20X4*

|                                      | £m       |
|--------------------------------------|----------|
| *Fixed assets*                       |          |
| Intangible assets                    | 0.3      |
| Tangible assets                      | 92.5     |
|                                      | 92.8     |
| *Current assets*                     |          |
| Stocks                               | 117.8    |
| Debtors                              | 197.0    |
| Cash at bank                         | 23.8     |
|                                      | 338.6    |
| *Creditors: amounts falling due within one year* |  |
| Bank overdrafts                      | (35.6)   |
| Other creditors                      | (245.7)  |
| *Net current assets*                 | 57.3     |
| Total assets less current liabilities | 150.1   |
| Creditors amounts falling due after more than one year | (11.4) |
| Provisions for liabilities and charges | (5.1)  |
|                                      | 133.6    |

Note that no acquisitions in 20X4 have been merger accounted. Fair goodwill arose on acquisition.

*Required*

(a)  (i)   Explain briefly the principal aim of the financial review section of an operating and financial review prepared in accordance with the ASB Statement *Operating and Financial Review*.

     (ii)  Explain briefly the matters that should be considered when discussing capital structure and treasury policy.   (5 marks)

(b)  (i)   Draft a brief report for an existing shareholder who was concerned that earnings per share in 20X4 had risen by only 14% although turnover had increased by more than 70% and who is considering whether to sell his shareholding in Lewes plc.

     (ii)  State any additional information arising from a review of the information given in the question that would assist the investor in making a hold or sell decision.

                                                                           (20 marks)
                                                                           **(25 marks)**

# 26   PREPARATION QUESTION: SUGGESTED ALTERNATIVES

Three suggested alternatives to historical cost accounting are:

(i)   Current purchasing power accounting
(ii)  Current cost accounting
(iii) 'Economic', or present value, accounting

*Required*

(a)  Indicate the basis on which each of the three methods values the shareholders' equity of a company as at the end of a financial year.

(b)  Evaluate critically the three methods of computation of annual profit, and retained earnings for the year as shown by each of the three methods mentioned in (a) above.

**Guidance notes**

1   Examination questions on this topic are as likely to be written ones as numerical ones. In any case, you should understand the topic sufficiently to give good definitions and descriptions of these three methods.

43

2    It would probably help to make an answer plan to part (b). Mark off the points in order of importance.

3    If you are still having problems with this topic, it is worth revising it in your BPP Study Text.

## 27   CORPORATE FAILURE (6/98)                                                    *45 mins*

There has been widespread debate for several years concerning the declining value of traditional methods of measuring corporate performance and the ability to predict corporate failure. Earnings per share, return on capital employed and other investment ratios are seemingly out of step with the needs of investors. The analysis of financial ratios is to a large extent concerned with the efficiency and effectiveness of management's use of resources and also with the financial stability of the company. Researchers have developed models which attempt to predict business failure. Altman's 'Z score', and Argenti's failure model are examples of such research.

However, many analysts feel that financial statements require several adjustments before any meaningful evaluation of corporate performance can be made. Analysts often make amendments to corporate profit and net assets before calculating even the most basic of ratios because of their disapproval of certain generally accepted accounting principles and in an attempt to obtain comparability.

*Required*

(a)   Evaluate the usefulness of traditional accounting ratios, calculated by reference to published financial statements, in providing adequate information for analysts and investors.                                                                       (8 marks)

(b)   Discuss the value and usefulness of the corporate failure prediction models such as those developed by Altman and Argenti.                                            (8 marks)

(c)   Describe, with reasons, an accounting adjustment which analysts might wish to make to financial statements before evaluating corporate performance in the case of each of the following elements.

(i)    Goodwill
(ii)   Depreciation                                                                   (9 marks)

                                                                                **(25 marks)**

---

**INTERNATIONAL, ENVIRONMENTAL AND CULTURAL ISSUES**

Questions 28 to 32 cover international, environmental and cultural issues, the subject of Part D of the BPP Study Text for Paper 3.6.

---

## 28    STATESIDE (6/95, amended)                                               *45 mins*

*Required*

(a)  Discuss the potential benefits of greater harmonisation of international accounting policies and disclosure requirements, and comment on the obstacles hindering its progress.                                                            **(9 marks)**

(b)  (i)   Explain why you think each of the adjustments has been made in the statement for Stateside plc reconciling UK to US GAAP as at 31 May 20X5.

| Income statement adjustments | £m |
|---|---|
| Net profit per UK GAAP | 45 |
| US GAAP adjustments (assumed net of tax) | |
| Capitalised interest amortised | (5) |
| Elimination of results prior to merger | (150) |
| Acquisition accounting: additional depreciation and | |
| amortisation of goodwill | (200) |
| Estimated reported loss as adjusted to accord with US GAAP | (310) |

(ii)   Explain whether the equity as reported per UK GAAP will be increased or decreased when reconciled to the equity as adjusted to accord with US GAAP for the items in (b)(i).

(iii)  Explain the effect on the equity of a proposed final dividend which under US GAAP has to be included in the year in which the directors propose to pay the dividends. *ie. to be included before B/sheet date* **(11 marks)**

(c)  Assume that the fixed assets were revalued from £20m to £30m on 1 June 20X3 at which date they had a remaining life of 10 years and disposed of for £40m on 31 May 20X5.

(i)   Show the accounting treatment in the accounts for 20X4 and 20X5 of the revaluation and disposal of fixed assets in accordance with FRS 3 (note that a full year's depreciation is charged in 20X4 and 20X5).

(ii)  Explain the reasons why the ASB required such accounting treatment.  **(5 marks)**

*sop.*

**(25 marks)**

## 29    MORGAN (6/97, amended)                                                  *45 mins*

Morgan plc is considering the acquisition of one of two companies. Their investment advisers have prepared a report on the acquisition of the companies, one of which is situated in the United Kingdom, UK Group plc. The other is situated overseas. The overseas company, Overseas Group Inc prepares its financial statements in accordance with local accounting standards. The following financial ratios had been prepared for discussion at a board meeting of Morgan plc based on the financial statements for the year ending 31 May 20X7.

**BPP**
PUBLISHING

| | | UK Group plc | Overseas Group Inc |
|---|---|---|---|
| Current ratio | $\dfrac{\text{Current assets}}{\text{Current liabilities}}$ | 1.75 to 1 | 1.2 to 1 |
| Stock turnover | $\dfrac{\text{Cost of goods sold}}{\text{Closing stock}}$ | 6.5 times | 2.6 times |
| Debtors collection period | $\dfrac{\text{Closing debtors}}{\text{Sales per day}}$ | 41.7 days | 85.5 days |
| Interest cover | $\dfrac{\text{Earnings before interest and tax}}{\text{Interest charges}}$ | 6 times | 1.8 times |

| | | UK Group plc | Overseas Group Inc |
|---|---|---|---|
| Profit margin | $\dfrac{\text{Net profit before sales}}{\text{Sales}}$ | 5.4% | 0.6% |
| Return on total assets | $\dfrac{\text{Earnings before interest and tax}}{\text{Total assets}}$ | 7.4% | 0.8% |
| Return on net worth | $\dfrac{\text{Net profit before tax}}{\text{Shareholders' funds (including minority interests)}}$ | 12.2% | 1.6% |
| Gearing ratio | $\dfrac{\text{Total long-term debt}}{\text{Total assets}}$ | 27.7% | 43.3% |
| Price earnings ratio | $\dfrac{\text{Market price per share}}{\text{Earnings per share}}$ | 15 | 81.6 |

The financial statements of Overseas Group Inc are as follows.

CONSOLIDATED PROFIT AND LOSS ACCOUNT
FOR YEAR ENDING 31 MAY 20X7

| | $'000 | $'000 |
|---|---|---|
| Sales | | 132,495 |
| Operating costs (see below) | | (130,655) |
| Operating profit | | 1,840 |
| Interest | | (1,020) |
| Profit before tax | | 820 |
| Income taxes | | (200) |
| Profit after tax | | 620 |
| Minority interests | | (80) |
| Net profit for the year before extraordinary item | | 540 |
| Extraordinary profit | 72 | |
| Taxation | (18) | |
| | | 54 |
| Net profit | | 594 |

*Note.* Operating costs comprise cost of goods sold of $110,100,000 and other expenses of $20,555,000.

CONSOLIDATED BALANCE SHEET AT 31 MAY 20X7

| | $'000 |
|---|---|
| *Assets* | |
| Current assets | |
|   Cash and deposits | 22,230 |
|   Debtors | 31,050 |
|   Stock | 42,020 |
| | 95,300 |
| Long term assets | 135,200 |
| *Total assets* | 230,500 |

|  | $'000 |
|---|---|
| *Liabilities and shareholders' equity* | |
| Current liabilities | 79,400 |
| Long-term liabilities | 99,700 |
| Minority interests in subsidiaries | 8,200 |
| Shareholders' equity | |
| Ordinary shares | 30,000 |
| Retained earnings | 13,200 |
| | 43,200 |
| Total liabilities and shareholders' equity | 230,500 |

At the board meeting the financial director questioned the validity of the financial ratios in view of the differences in the accounting practices of the UK and Overseas countries. She requested that the ratios be re-calculated on a common basis using UK generally accepted accounting practice. The following information is relevant to these calculations.

(a) Overseas Inc had purchased a 60% holding in a subsidiary on 1 June 20X6. For accounting purposes the purchase consideration was taken as $10 million to be satisfied by the issue of 8 million ordinary shares of $1 and $2 million in cash. Overseas Inc's shares were valued at $2 each on 1 June 20X6. If the subsidiary makes profits in excess of the profit for the year ended 31 May 20X7 in the financial year to 31 May 20X8, then a further cash sum of $200,000 is payable on 1 June 20X8. Preliminary indications suggest that the subsidiary will exceed this target profit.

(b) Overseas Inc had taken account of the above transaction by proportionately reducing the fixed assets of the subsidiary by the negative goodwill figure of $2 million which was calculated by using the book value of the net assets acquired of $20 million. The fair value of the net assets of the subsidiary at the date of acquisition was $25 million. The difference between the book value and fair value of the assets comprised the increase in the value of buildings which are depreciated at 2% per annum on cost. No adjustment to the depreciation charge is required for the treatment of negative goodwill. The current borrowing cost in the overseas country is 10%. UK plc assumes the goodwill to have an indefinite useful life and retains it in the balance sheet.

(c) Overseas Inc had capitalised the costs of developing computer software products totalling $1 million incurred in 20X7. The product's first revenues were received in the year to 31 May 20X7 and were expected to have an economic life of four years. Overseas Inc amortises such costs based on the economic life of the product. UK plc charges all such costs in the year in which they are incurred.

(d) Overseas Inc has a share option scheme under which options are granted to certain directors. On 1 December 20X6 100,000 ordinary shares were allotted for $175,000 upon the exercise of options. The company had accounted for the full market price of $250,000 of the shares with the discount on the share price being treated by Overseas Inc as directors' remuneration. Additionally the company had included an employee share ownership trust in its balance sheet at a cost of $7 million. The assets of the trust had been deducted from the reserves of Overseas Inc.

(e) The share capital of UK plc is 50 million ordinary shares of £1 and of Overseas Inc 30 million shares of $1 at 31 May 20X7. The earnings per share calculation used in the price earnings ratio calculations had utilised the above share capital figures. The market price of Overseas Inc's shares at 31 May 20X7 was $1.47.

(f) The extraordinary item in the profit and loss account of Overseas Inc is the profit on the repayment of long-term debt in the accounts of a subsidiary.

(g) Part of the stock in Overseas Inc has been valued at market value. Overseas Inc does not trade in commodities but purchases precious metals which it uses in the

47

production process. The stock of these precious metals and related values are as follows.

|  | Market value $'000 | Cost $'000 |
|---|---|---|
| Year end 31 May 20X6 | 30,000 | 21,000 |
| Year end 31 May 20X7 | 10,000 | 7,500 |

There is no tax impact of any change in policy regarding stock. Because of the poor quality of the initial report by the investment analyst, the financial director has asked the auditor to prepare another report on the potential acquisition taking into account the above factors.

*Required*

(a) Recalculate the financial ratios of Overseas Inc so that they can be compared to UK plc's ratios. (Candidates should describe the reasons for the adjustments to the financial statements of Overseas Inc.)                                                      (15 marks)

(b) Discuss the implications of the revision of the financial ratios on the decision to acquire UK plc or Overseas Inc.                                                         (5 marks)

(c) Explain what considerations other than differences in accounting practice should be taken into account when analysing the financial ratios of an overseas company, such as Overseas Inc.                                                                         (5 marks)

(All workings should be to the nearest thousand units of currency.)            **(25 marks)**

## 30   PREPARATION QUESTION: ENVIRONMENT

Identify the main factors in a business's general environment, and give an example of each.

**Guidance note**

Only a very brief answer is required.

## 31   STAKEHOLDERS                                                               *45 mins*

(a) Provide a classification of the key stakeholders in any public limited company and describe the relationship of each category to the company.                          (12 marks)

(b) Explain why stakeholders sometimes find themselves in conflict with each other yet for the most part find it in their interests to co-operate.                             (13 marks)

                                                                                **(25 marks)**

## 32   NEAR ENVIRONMENT                                                          *45 mins*

(a) What are the five forces in an organisation's competitive environment?       (13 marks)

(b) Who are the major stakeholders in an organisation and what will they each be looking for from the management of the organisation?                                       (12 marks)

                                                                                **(25 marks)**

> **ACCOUNTING STANDARDS**
>
> Questions 33 to 56 cover Accounting Standards, the subject of Part E of the BPP Study Text for Paper 3.6.

## 33   PREPARATION QUESTION: FRS 15

(a) (i)   FRS 15 *Tangible fixed assets* was published in February 1999. How does the standard define tangible fixed assets? Explain the significance of the definition.

(ii)   How should tangible fixed assets be measured initially?

(b)   Kabin Ltd, a retail company has previously not depreciated its land and buildings, including shop facias (which have all been treated as one asset) on the grounds that they were regularly maintained. Following FRS 15, the company has revised its policy and split its property into three separate components with different useful economic lives, which are to be depreciated as follows

| | |
|---|---|
| Land | No depreciation |
| Buildings | Depreciation over useful economic life of 40 years |
| Shop facias | Depreciation over useful economic life of 10 years |

*Required*

Comment on these proposals, stating how the change should be reflected in the accounts.

**Guidance notes**

1   Part (b) of this question is more difficult than part (a).

2   FRS 15 is fairly uncontroversial on the whole.

## 34   PREPARATION QUESTION: REVALUATIONS

You are the management accountant of Historic Ltd. Historic Ltd makes up its financial statements to 30 September each year. The financial statements for the year ended 30 September 20X1 are currently being prepared. The Directors have always included fixed assets under the historical cost convention. However, for the current year, they are considering revaluing some of the fixed assets. They obtained professional valuations as at 1 October 20X0 for the two properties owned by the company. Details of the valuations were as follows.

|  | *Historical cost NBV* | *Existing use value* | *Open market value* |
|---|---|---|---|
| | £'000 | £'000 | £'000 |
| Property One | 15,000 | 16,800 | 17,500 |
| Property Two | 14,000 | 12,000 | 12,500 |

No acquisitions or disposals of properties have taken place since 1 October 20X0 and none are expected in the near future. The buildings element of the two properties comprises 50% of both historical cost and the revalued amounts. Each property is reckoned to have a useful economic life to the company of 40 years from 1 October 20X0.

Given the results of the valuations, the Directors propose to include Property One at its open market value in the financial statements for the year to 30 September 20X1. They wish to leave Property Two at its historical cost. They have no plans to revalue the other fixed assets of the company which are plant and fixtures.

*Required*

(a) State briefly the key arguments for and against including fixed assets at revalued amounts.

(b) Evaluate the Directors' proposal to revalue Property One as at 1 October 20X0 but to leave all other fixed assets at historical cost. Your answer should include reference to appropriate accounting standards.

(c) The Directors have decided to revalue the fixed assets of the company in accordance with their original wishes, amended where necessary to comply with appropriate accounting standards. Compute the net book value of each property as at 30 September 20X1. You should clearly explain where any differences on revaluation will be shown in the financial statements.

## 35  PREPARATION QUESTION: INCOME-GENERATING UNITS

(a) FRS 11 *Impairment of fixed assets and goodwill* was published in July 1998. It introduced the term 'income generating units'.

Explain what an income generating unit is and why it is necessary.

(b) Identify the income generating unit in the following cases.

(i) A manufacturer can produce a product at a number of different sites. Not all the sites are used to full capacity and the manufacturer can choose how much to make at each site. However, there is not enough surplus capacity to enable any one site to be closed. The cash inflows generated by any one site therefore depend on the allocation of production across all sites.

(ii) A restaurant chain has a large number of restaurants across the country. The cash inflows of each restaurant can be individually monitored and sensible allocations of costs to each restaurant can be made.

**Guidance notes**

1   FRS 11 has been around for a while now and is a likely candidate for examination.

2   Identifying income generating units is a subjective exercise, so be prepared to argue your case.

## 36  IMPAIRMENT (12/98, amended)                                            *45 mins*

FRS 11 *Impairment of fixed assets and goodwill* was published in July 1998. Impairment is measured by comparing the value of a fixed asset with its recoverable amount. The issues of how one identifies an impaired asset, the measurement of an asset where impairment has occurred and the recognition of impairment losses are also dealt with in the standard.

*Required*

(a) (i) Describe the circumstances which indicate that an impairment loss relating to a fixed asset may have occurred.                                      (7 marks)

(ii) Explain how FRS 11 deals with the recognition and measurement of the impairment of fixed assets and the implications of this for future accounting periods.                                                          (7 marks)

(b) AB, a public limited company, complies with FRS 11 as regards the impairment of its fixed assets. The following information is relevant to the impairment review.

(i) Certain items of machinery appeared to have suffered a fall in value. The product produced by the machines was being sold below its cost and this occurrence had affected the value of the productive machinery. The carrying value at historical cost of these machines is £290,000 and their net realisable value was estimated at £120,000. The anticipated net cash inflows from the machines were £100,000 per annum for the next three years. A market discount rate of 10% per annum is to be used in any present value computations.                                         (4 marks)

(ii)    AB acquired a car taxi business on 1 January 20X8 for £230,000. The values of the assets of the business at that date based on net realisable values were as follows.

|                                   | £'000 |
|-----------------------------------|------:|
| Vehicles                          |   120 |
| Intangible assets (taxi licence)  |    30 |
| Debtors                           |    10 |
| Cash                              |    50 |
| Creditors                         |  (20) |
|                                   |   190 |

On 1 February 20X8, the taxi company had three of its vehicles stolen. The net realisable value of these vehicles was £30,000 and because of non-disclosure of certain risks to the insurance company, the vehicles were uninsured. As a result of this event, AB wishes to recognise an impairment loss of £45,000 (inclusive of the loss of the stolen vehicles) due to the decline in the value in use of the income generating unit, that is the taxi business. On 1 March 20X8 a rival taxi company commenced business in the same area. It is anticipated that the business revenue will be reduced by 25% and that a further impairment loss has occurred due to a decline in the present value in use of the business which is calculated at £150,000. The NRV of the taxi licence has fallen to £25,000 as a result of the rival taxi operator. The net realisable values of the other assets have remained the same as at 1 January 20X8 throughout the period.    (7 marks)

*Required*

Describe how AB should treat the above impairments of assets in its financial statements. (In part (b)(ii) candidates should show the treatment of the impairment loss at 1 February 20X8 and 1 March 20X8).

Please note that the mark allocation is shown after paragraph (b)(i) and (b)(ii) above.

**(25 marks)**

**37    YUKON (6/97, amended)**                                              *45 mins*

Accounting for goodwill has been a contentious issue in the UK for several years and FRS 10 *Goodwill and intangible assets* attempts to eliminate the problems associated with SSAP 22, *Accounting for goodwill.*

*Required*

(a)    Describe the requirements of FRS 10 regarding the initial recognition and measurement of goodwill and intangible assets.                               (8 marks)

(b)    Explain the approach set out in FRS 10 for the amortisation of positive goodwill and intangible assets.                                                       (6 marks)

(c)    Territory plc acquired 80% of the ordinary share capital of Yukon plc on 31 May 20X6. The balance sheet of Yukon plc at 31 May 20X6 was as follows.

YUKON PLC
BALANCE SHEET AT 31 MAY 20X6

| | £'000 |
|---|---|
| *Fixed assets* | |
| Intangible assets | 6,020 |
| Tangible assets | 38,300 |
| | 44,320 |
| *Current assets* | |
| Stocks | 21,600 |
| Debtors | 23,200 |
| Cash | 8,800 |
| | 53,600 |
| Creditors: amounts falling due within one year | 24,000 |
| *Net current assets* | 29,600 |
| *Total assets less current liabilities* | 73,920 |
| *Creditors: amounts falling due after more than one year* | 12,100 |
| *Provision for liabilities and charges* | 886 |
| *Accruals and deferred income* | |
| Deferred government grants | 2,700 |
| | 58,234 |
| *Capital and reserves* | |
| Called up share capital (ordinary shares of £1) | 10,000 |
| Share premium account | 5,570 |
| Profit and loss account | 42,664 |
| | 58,234 |

*Additional information relating to the above balance sheet*

(i) The intangible assets of Yukon plc were brand names currently utilised by the company. The directors felt that they were worth £7 million but there was no readily ascertainable market value at the balance sheet date, nor any information to verify the directors' estimated value.

(ii) The provisional market value of the land and buildings was £20 million at 31 May 20X6. This valuation had again been determined by the directors. A valuer's report received on 31 November 20X6 stated the market value of land and buildings to be £23 million as at 31 May 20X6. The depreciated replacement cost of the remainder of the tangible fixed assets was £18 million at 31 May 20X6, net of government grants.

(iii) The replacement cost of stocks was estimated at £25 million and its net realisable value was deemed to be £20 million. Debtors and creditors due within one year are stated at the amounts expected to be received and paid.

(iv) Creditors falling due after more than one year was a long-term loan with a bank. The initial loan on 1 June 20X5 was £11 million at a fixed interest rate of 10% per annum. The total amount of the interest is to be paid at the end of the loan period on 31 May 20X9. The current bank lending rate is 7% per annum.

(v) The provision for liabilities and charges relates to costs of reorganisation of Yukon plc. This provision had been set up by the directors of Yukon plc prior to the offer by Territory plc and the reorganisation would have taken place even if Territory plc had not purchased the shares of Yukon plc. Additionally Territory plc wishes to set up a provision for future losses of £10 million which it feels will be incurred by rationalising the group.

(vi) The offer made to all of the shareholders of Yukon plc was 2.5 £1 ordinary shares of Territory plc at the market price of £2.25 per share plus £1 cash, per Yukon plc ordinary share.

(vii) Goodwill is to be dealt with in accordance with FRS 10. The estimated useful economic life is deemed to be 10 years. The directors of Yukon plc informed Territory plc that as at 31 May 20X7, the brand names were worthless as the products to which they related had recently been withdrawn from sale because they were deemed to be a health hazard.

(viii) A full year's charge for amortisation of goodwill is included in the group profit and loss account of Territory plc in the year of purchase.

*Required*

Calculate the amortisation of goodwill in the Group profit and loss account of Territory plc for accounting periods ending on 31 May 20X6 and 31 May 20X7.

(11 marks)

**(25 marks)**

## 38   MG                                                                      *45 mins*

The following extract has been taken from the balance sheet of MG plc as at 30 September 20X6.

| Fixed assets | £m |
| --- | --- |
| Intangible assets: brands | 9,268 |
| Tangible assets | 15,024 |
| Investments | 856 |
| | 25,148 |

The accounting policy of MG plc was as follows.

Significant owned brands, acquired after 1 October 20X0, the value of which is not expected to diminish in the foreseeable future, are recorded in the balance sheet as fixed intangible assets. No amortisation is provided on these assets but their value is reviewed annually by the directors and the cost written down as an exceptional item where permanent diminution in value has occurred.

*Required*

(a) Explain why a company such as MG plc may have included purchased brands as fixed assets in their balance sheet.                                             (5 marks)

(b) Explain the criteria that should be met if a purchased brand is to be recognised as an asset in the balance sheet.                                           (5 marks)

(c) Explain the justification for including non-purchased brands in the balance sheet and how they should be valued.                                              (10 marks)

(d) Explain the steps taken by the profession to regulate this accounting treatment.

(5 marks)

**(25 marks)**

## 39   TALL                                                                    *45 mins*

You are the management accountant of Tall plc. The company is planning a number of acquisitions in 20Y0 and so you are aware that additional funding will be needed. Today's date is 30 November 20X9. The balance sheet of the company at 30 September 20X9 (the financial year-end of Tall plc) showed the following balances.

|                          | £m    |
|--------------------------|-------|
| Equity share capital     | 100.0 |
| Share premium account    | 35.8  |
| Profit and loss account  | 89.7  |
|                          | 225.5 |
| Net assets               | 225.5 |

On 1 October 20X9 Tall plc raised additional funding as follows.

(a) Tall plc issued 15 million £1 bonds at par. The bonds pay no interest but are redeemable on 1 October 20Y4 at £1.61 – the total payable on redemption being £24.15m. As an alternative to redemption, bondholders can elect to convert their holdings into £1 equity shares on the basis of one equity share for every bond held. The current price of a £1 share is £1.40 and it is reckoned that this will grow by at least 5 per cent per annum for the next five years.

(b) Tall plc issued 10 million £1 preference shares at £1.20 per share, incurring issue costs of £100,000. The preference shares carry no dividend and are redeemable on 1 October 20Y5 at £2.35 per share – the total payable on redemption being £23.5m.

Your assistant is unsure how to reflect the additional funding in the financial statements of Tall plc. He expresses the opinion that both of the new capital instruments should logically be reflected in the shareholders' funds section of the balance sheet. He justifies this as follows.

(a) The preference shares are legally shares and so shareholders' funds is the appropriate place to present them.

(b) The bonds and the preference shares seem to have very similar terms of issue and it is quite likely that the bonds will *become* shares in five years' time, given the projected growth in the equity share price.

He has no idea how to show the finance costs of the capital instruments in the profit and loss account. This is because he has never before encountered a capital instrument where no payments will be made to the holders of the instrument until the date of redemption.

*Required*

(a) Write a memorandum to your assistant which evaluates the comments he has made and explains the correct treatment where necessary. Your memorandum should refer to the provisions of relevant accounting standards.                     (10 marks)

(b) Prepare the relevant balances in the balance sheet of Tall plc immediately after the issue of the bonds and the preference shares.                     (5 marks)

(c) Calculate the finance cost that will be required to be shown in the profit and loss account of Tall plc for the year ended 30 September 20Y0 for the bonds and the preference shares. You should state where in the profit and loss account the costs should be shown.                     (10 marks)

**(25 marks)**

## 40   DERIVATIVES (12/99)                     *45 mins*

Standard setters have been struggling for several years with the practical issues of the disclosure, recognition and measurement of financial instruments. The ASB has issued a discussion paper on *Derivatives and Other Financial Instruments* and Financial Reporting Standard 13 on the disclosure of such instruments. The dynamic nature of international financial markets has resulted in the widespread use of a variety of financial instruments but present accounting rules in this area do not ensure that the financial statements portray effectively the impact and risks of the instruments currently being used.

*Required*

(a) (i) Discuss the concerns about the accounting practices used for financial instruments which led to demands for an accounting standard. (7 marks)

(ii) Explain why regulations dealing with disclosure alone cannot solve the problems of accounting for financial instruments.

(4 marks)

(b) (i) Discuss three ways in which gains and losses on financial instruments might be recorded in the financial statements, commenting on the relative merits of each method. (8 marks)

(ii) AX, a public limited company, issued a three year £30 million 5% debenture at par on 1 December 20X8 when the market rate of interest was 5%. Interest is paid annually on 30 November each year. Market rates of interest on debentures of equivalent term and risk are 6% and 4% at the end of the financial years to 30 November 20X9 and 30 November 20Y0. (Assume that the changes in interest rates took place on 30 November each year.)

Show the effect on 'profit' for the three years to 30 November 20Y1 if the debenture and the interest charge were valued on a fair value basis. (6 marks)

**(25 marks)**

## 41   FINALEYES (6/96)                                    *45 mins*

The following questions relate to Finaleyes plc, a car seat manufacturer. The company is pursuing a policy of growth by acquisition and it has targeted a number of specific companies for takeover during the next three years.

For the year ended 30 April 20X6 its turnover was £100m; post tax profits £13m applying a tax rate of 30%; net assets £80m and issued share capital £10m in 25p shares. At 30 April 20X6 its share price was £6 per share and at 31 May 20X6 its share price was £7 per share.

The financial director is reviewing the accounting treatment of various items prior to the signing of the 20X6 accounts which is planned for July 20X6.

The items are as follows.

(a) *A share issue*

On 31 January 20X6 it was announced that the company was raising £14m before expenses by the issue of shares for cash. The issue took place on 31 May 20X6 at market share price.

(b) *Acquisition of a plant*

On 1 May 20X5 the company acquired a factory in Norway for £4m. On 30 April 20X6 they obtained professional advice that the building had an expected life of 40 years with no residual value but that the heating systems would require replacing every 15 years at an expected cost of £450,000.

Depreciation on the buildings has been charged following the company's normal accounting policy of using the straight line method.

A charge of £30,000 has been made to the profit and loss account to create a provision for the replacement of the heating system assuming a 15 year life. The initial reasoning for making the charge for the heating system replacement was that it complied with the

ASB definition of a liability, ie 'liabilities are an entity's obligations to transfer economic benefits as a result of past transactions or events.'

(c) *Sale and lease back*

At 30 April 20X6 the balance sheet included the main offices of the company at a figure of £10m. On 15 May 20X6 the company exchanged contracts with the Helpful Friendly Society Ltd for the sale of the main offices for £12m with lease back for an initial period of 20 years at market rentals. The company intended to use the proceeds to invest in office property in Kuala Lumpur. The contract provided that the cash consideration would be paid to Finaleyes plc on 14 June 20X6.

(d) *Stock valuation errors*

The company's policy on stock valuation was to value stock in accordance with SSAP 9 at the lower of cost and net realisable value. The company discovered in May 20X6 that there had been an omission for three years to apply this policy to stock held in a warehouse in Cyprus; the provisions required to bring the stock down to net realisable value were £63,000 for 20X3, £70,000 for 20X4, £105,000 for 20X5 and £115,000 for 20X6.

The adjustment has been treated as a prior period adjustment and reduced the profit and loss account balance brought forward at 1 May 20X5 and the stock by £238,000 being the total of the provisions required for the years ended 30 April 20X3 to 20X5.

*Required*

For each of the items (a) to (d) above:

(i) State your view on the appropriate treatment in the financial statements as at 30 April 20X6 giving your reasons.

(ii) Draft an appropriate note to the accounts and/or state the adjustment that would be made to items in the accounts as required.

Each of the items (a) to (d) carries equal marks. **(25 marks)**

## 42 TIMBER PRODUCTS (12/95) *45 mins*

*Required*

(a) (i) Explain briefly the objective of FRS 5 *Reporting the substance of transactions.*

(ii) Explain the criteria for ceasing to recognise an asset and give an illustration of the application of each. (7 marks)

(b) Explain the appropriate accounting treatment for the following transactions and the entries that would appear in the balance sheet as at 31 October for transaction (i) and in the profit and loss account for the year ended 31 October 20X5 and balance sheet as at 31 October 20X5 for transactions (ii), (iii) and (iv).

(i) Timber Products plc supplied large industrial and commercial customers direct on three month credit terms. On 1 November 20X4 it entered into an agreement with Ready Support plc whereby it transferred title to the debtors to that company subject to a reduction for bad debts based on Timber Products plc's past experience and in return received an immediate payment of 90% of the net debtor total plus rights to a future sum the amount of which depended on whether and when the debtors paid. Ready Support plc had the right of recourse against Timber Products plc for any additional losses up to an agreed maximum amount.

The position at the year end, 31 October 20X5, was that title had been transferred to debtors with an invoice value of £15m less a bad debt provision of £600,000 and Timber Products plc was subject under the agreement to a maximum potential debit of £200,000 to cover losses.

(ii) Timber Products plc imports unseasoned hardwood and keeps it for five years under controlled conditions prior to manufacturing high quality furniture. In the year ended 31 October 20X5 it imported unseasoned timber at a cost of £40m. It contracted to sell the whole amount for £40m and to buy it back in five years time for £56.10m.

(iii) Timber Products plc manufactures and supplies retailers with furniture on a consignment basis such that either party can require the return of the furniture to the manufacturer within a period of six months from delivery. The retailers are required to pay a monthly charge for the facility to display the furniture. The manufacturer uses this monthly charge to pay for insurance cover and carriage costs. At the end of six months the retailer is required to pay Timber Products plc the trade price as at the date of delivery. No retailers have yet sent any goods back to Timber Products plc at the end of the six month period.

In the year ended 31 October 20X5, Timber Products plc had supplied furniture to retailers at the normal trade price of £10m being cost plus $33^{1}/_{3}\%$; received £50,000 in display charges; incurred insurance costs of £15,000 and carriage costs of £10,000; and received £6m from retailers.

(iv) On 1 December 20X4 Timber Products plc sold a factory that it owned in Scotland to Inter plc a wholly owned subsidiary of Offshore Banking plc for £10m. The factory had a book value of £8.5m. Inter plc was financed by a loan of £10m from Offshore Banking plc. Timber Products plc was paid a fee by Inter plc to continue to operate the factory, such fee representing the balance of profit remaining after Inter plc paid its parent company loan interest set at a level that represented current interest rates. If there was an operating loss, then Timber Products plc would be charged a fee that would cover the operating losses and interest payable.

For the year ended 31 October 20X5 the fee paid to Timber Products plc amounted to £3m and the loan interest paid by Inter plc amounted to £1.5m.

(14 marks)

(c) State what further information you would seek in order to determine the substance of the following transaction.

Timber Products plc has installed computer controlled equipment in its furniture making factory. This has created the need for large extractor fans to remove dust particles. The company has contracted with Extractor-Plus plc for that company to build and install extractor equipment. Timber Products plc will maintain and insure the equipment and make an annual payment to Extractor-Plus plc comprising a fixed quarterly rental and an hourly usage charge.

In the year ended 31 October 20X5 Timber Products plc has paid the fixed quarterly rentals totalling £80,000 and hourly charges totalling £120,000.          (4 marks)

(25 marks)

*Compound interest table*

| Number of years | 5% | 6% | 7% | 8% | 9% |
|---|---|---|---|---|---|
| | | | *Interest rate per year* | | |
| 1 | 1.050 | 1.060 | 1.070 | 1.080 | 1.090 |
| 2 | 1.102 | 1.124 | 1.143 | 1.166 | 1.188 |
| 3 | 1.158 | 1.191 | 1.225 | 1.260 | 1.295 |
| 4 | 1.216 | 1.262 | 1.311 | 1.360 | 1.412 |
| 5 | 1.276 | 1.338 | 1.403 | 1.469 | 1.539 |
| 6 | 1.340 | 1.419 | 1.501 | 1.587 | 1.677 |

## 43   LEASING (6/98)                                                    *45 mins*

(a)   The development of conceptual frameworks for financial reporting by accounting standard setters could fundamentally change the way in which financial contracts such as leases are accounted for. These frameworks identify the basic elements of financial statements as assets, liabilities, equity, gains and losses and set down their recognition rules. In analysing the definitions of assets an liabilities one could conclude that most leases, including non-cancellable operating leases, qualify for recognition as assets and liabilities because the lessee is likely to enjoy the future economic benefit embodied in the leased asset and will have an unavoidable obligation to transfer economic benefits to the lessor. Because of the problems of accounting for leases, there have been calls for the capitalisation of all non-cancellable operating leases so that the only problem would be the definition of the term 'non-cancellable'.

*Required*

(i)   Explain how leases are accounted for in the books of the lessee under SSAP 21 *Accounting for leases and hire-purchase contracts*.                    (7 marks)

(ii)   Discuss the current problems relating to the recognition and classification of leases in corporate financial statements. (Candidates should give examples where necessary.)                                                              (8 marks)

(b) (i)   During the financial year to 31 May 20X8, AB plc disposed of electrical distribution systems from its electrical power plants to CD plc for a consideration of £198m. At the same time AB plc entered into a long-term distribution agreement with CD plc whereby the assets were leased back under a 10-year operating lease. The fair value of the assets sold was £98m and the carrying value based on the depreciated historic cost of the assets was £33m. The lease rental payments were £24m per annum which represented twice the normal payment for leasing this type of asset.                             (5 marks)

(ii)   Additionally on 1 June 20X7, AB plc sold plant with a book value of £100m to EF plc when there was a balance on the revaluation reserve of £30m which related to the plant. The fair value and selling price of the plant at that date was £152m. The plant was immediately leased back over a lease term of four years which is the asset's remaining useful life. The residual value at the end of the lease period is estimated to be a negligible amount. AB plc can purchase the plant at the end of the lease for a nominal sum of £1. The lease is non-cancellable and requires equal rental payments of £43.5m at the commencement of each financial year. AB plc has to pay all of the costs of maintaining and insuring the plant. The implicit interest rate in the lease is 10% per annum. The plant is depreciated on a straight line basis. (The present value of an ordinary annuity of £1 per period for three years at 10% interest is £2.49.)      (5 marks)

*Required*

Show and explain how the above transactions should be dealt with in the financial statements of AB plc for the year ending 31 May 20X8 in accordance with SSAP 21 *Accounting for leases and hire purchase contracts* and FRS 5 *Reporting the substance of transactions.*

**(25 marks)**

## 44   HIRE

*45 mins*

Hire plc is a service sector company. Part of its usage of land and buildings and motor vehicles is currently financed by operating leases.

*Summarised financial statements as at 30 November 20X0*

HIRE PLC
PROFIT AND LOSS ACCOUNT (EXTRACT)
FOR THE YEAR ENDED 30 NOVEMBER 20X0

|  | £m |
|---|---|
| Turnover | 1,160 |
| Profit on ordinary activities before taxation | 176 |
| Taxation on profit on ordinary activities | (60) |
| Profit on ordinary activities after taxation | 116 |

HIRE PLC
BALANCE SHEET (EXTRACT)
AS AT 30 NOVEMBER 20X0

|  | £m |
|---|---|
| Fixed assets | 400 |
| Net current assets | 340 |
| Creditors: amounts falling due after more than one year | |
| (interest free loan from holding company) | (100) |
| | 640 |
| Share capital | 400 |
| Profit and loss account | 240 |
| | 640 |

*Notes*

Operating lease rentals for the year – paid 30 November 20X0:

|  | £m |
|---|---|
| Land and buildings | 60 |
| Motor vehicles | 20 |

Future minimum operating lease payments for leases payable on 30 November each year were as follows.

| | Land & buildings £m | Motor vehicles £m |
|---|---|---|
| 30 November 20X1 | 56 | 18 |
| 30 November 20X2 | 50 | 16 |
| 30 November 20X3 | 40 | 14 |
| Thereafter | 1,000 | - |
| Total future minimum operating lease payments (non-cancellable) | 1,146 | 48 |

The directors have heard that the Accounting Standards Board (ASB) is considering developing a standard which will bring operating leases onto the balance sheet and wish to seek advice on the implications for the company. The directors are concerned about the potential impact on profitability and key financial ratios.

In order to assess the impact of ASB's proposal, the directors have decided to value current year and future operating lease rentals at their present value.

The appropriate interest rate for discounting cash flows to present value is 5% and the current average remaining lease life for operating lease rentals after 30 November 20X3 is deemed to be 10 years.

Depreciation on land and buildings is 5% per annum and on motor vehicles it is 25% per annum with a full year's charge in the year of acquisition. Assume that the operating lease agreements commenced on 30 November 20X0. The rate of corporation tax is 30% and depreciation rates equate to those of capital allowances.

*Required*

(a) Explain why accounting standard setters are proposing to bring operating leases onto the balance sheets of companies. (7 marks)

(b) (i) Show the effect on the profit and loss account for the year ending 30 November 20X0 and the balance sheet as at 30 November 20X0 of Hire capitalising its operating leases. (10 marks)

       (ii) Discuss the specific impact on key performance ratios as well as the general business impact of Hire capitalising its operating leases. (8 marks)

                                                          **(25 marks)**

## 45   PREPARATION QUESTION: FRS 17

In November 2000, the ASB issued FRS 17 *Retirement benefits*. This covers the treatment of pensions and other retirement benefits in the employer's accounts, and replaces SSAP 24 *Accounting for pension costs*. The main changes are to defined benefit schemes.

(a) What are the main criticisms of SSAP 24 which gave rise to the need for change?
(b) What are the main provisions of FRS 17?
(c) What drawbacks can you foresee to the new approach?

**Guidance note**

This is a fairly straightforward discursive question on a recent standard.

## 46   PREPARATION QUESTION: DEFERRED TAX

(a) Grant Ltd had timing differences of £100,000 at 31 March 20X1. During the year ended 31 March 20X2, depreciation exceeded capital allowances by £10,000 and in the year ended 31 March 20X3, capital allowances exceeded depreciation by £25,000. Given a tax rate of 30%, calculate the deferred tax provision at 31 March 20X2 and 20X3. Show the deferred tax transfer to the P&L account.

(b) Haven Ltd had a balance on its deferred tax account of £60,000 at 31 December 20X1. During the year ended 31 December 20X2, depreciation was £100,000 and capital allowances were £125,000. Given a tax rate of 25%, calculate the deferred tax transfer to the profit and loss account and the balance carried forward at 31 December 20X2 on the deferred tax account.

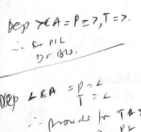

## 47   PLANGENT

*45 mins*

Until recently UK companies were required to provide for deferred tax using the partial provision method. However, this was recently changed to full provision by FRS 19 *Deferred tax*, issued in December 2000.

The different approaches are particularly significant when acquiring subsidiaries because of the fair value adjustments and also when dealing with revaluations of fixed assets as the IAS requires companies to provide for deferred tax on these amounts.

*Required*

(a)   Explain the main reasons why SSAP 15 was criticised.                              (6 marks)

(b)   Discuss the arguments in favour of and against providing for deferred tax on:

(i)    Fair value adjustments on the acquisition of a subsidiary
(ii)   Revaluations of fixed assets                                                        (5 marks)

(c)   Plangent plc, a company that operates solely in the UK, depreciates its plant and machinery on a straight line basis over 10 years. Residual value is estimated to be 1/11th of cost (at which point assume the asset will be sold). The company receives capital allowances at a rate of 25% per annum on a reducing balance basis. It is taxed on its profit at 30%.

The company has three assets that cost £1.1m each, purchased six years, three years and one year ago (in each case at the end of the financial year). The net book value of plant and machinery at 31 March 20X1 is:

|                          | £'000   |
|--------------------------|--------:|
| Original cost            | 3,300   |
| Cumulative depreciation  | (1,000) |
| Net book value           | 2,300   |

The tax written down values of the plant and machinery pool, and the consequential timing difference, at the balance sheet date are:

|                                | £'000   |
|--------------------------------|--------:|
| Net book value                 | 2,300   |
| Tax written-down value         | (1,114) |
| Timing difference at 31 March 20X1 | 1,186 |

*Required*

(i)    Produce a schedule of the future reversals of the deferred liability and calculate the undiscounted deferred tax liability of Plangent plc as at 31 March 20X1 as required by FRS 19 *Deferred tax*. (You should assume that the plant and machinery pool on which writing-down allowances are claimed will continue beyond year 20Y0.)                                                         (6 marks)

(ii)   Plangent plc has decided that it will adopt a policy of discounting its deferred tax liability, as permitted by FRS 19.

Discount rates for the years 20X2 to 20Y0 are as follows.

| Year | Rate |
|------|------|
| 20X2 | 4.7  |
| 20X3 | 4.4  |
| 20X4 | 4.2  |
| 20X5 | 4.0  |
| 20X6 | 3.9  |
| 20X7 | 3.9  |
| 20X8 | 3.8  |
| 20X9 | 3.8  |
| 20Y0 | 3.7  |

*Required*

Using the information in (i) above, calculate the discounted deferred tax liability of Plangent plc as at 31 March 20X1, as required by FRS 19.          (8 marks)

**(25 marks)**

## 48     RAPID RESPONSE (12/94, amended)                              *45 mins*

The accountant of Rapid Response plc has revised the accounts for the years ended 31 March 20X2 and 31 March 20X3 for the purposes of the 5 Year Summary that is being prepared in December 20X4 in order to comply with the provisions of FRS 3 *Reporting financial performance*.

The profit and loss accounts prepared prior to the implementation by the company of the provisions of FRS 3 are as follows.

|  | 20X2 £m | 20X3 £m |
|---|---|---|
| Turnover | 7,336.8 | 7,681.2 |
| Profit before interest | 505.7 | 509.0 |
| Net interest payable | (25.5) | (1.4) |
| Profit before exceptional items | 480.2 | 507.6 |
| Exceptional items |  |  |
| Development work in progress written down | - | (57.1) |
| Profit on disposal of group |  |  |
| occupied properties | 44.6 | 5.9 |
| Profit on ordinary activities before taxation | 524.8 | 456.4 |
| Tax on profit on ordinary activities | (136.1) | (118.7) |
| Profit on ordinary activities after taxation | 388.7 | 337.7 |
| Extraordinary item |  |  |
| Structural reorganisation costs |  |  |
| stated net of taxation of £13.2m | - | (31.8) |
| Net profit for financial year | 388.7 | 305.9 |
| Dividends | (137.3) | (162.6) |
| Retained profit for the year | 251.4 | s 143.3 |
| Earnings per share based on 500m shares | 77.7 pence | 67.5 pence |

The profit and loss accounts revised to comply with the provisions of FRS 3 are as follows.

|  | 20X2 £m | 20X3 £m |
|---|---|---|
| Turnover | 7,336.8 | 7,681.2 |
| Operating profit | 505.7 | 451.9 |
| Loss on disposal of properties | (24.7) | (6.9) |
| Structural reorganisation costs | - | (45.0) |
| Profit on ordinary activities before interest | 481.0 | 400.0 |
| Net interest payable | (25.5) | (1.4) |
| Profit on ordinary activities before taxation | 455.5 | 398.6 |
| Tax on ordinary activities | (136.1) | (105.5) |
| Profit on ordinary activities after taxation | 319.4 | 293.1 |
| Dividends | (137.3) | (162.6) |
| Retained profit for the year | 182.1 | 130.5 |
| Earnings per share | 63.9 pence | 58.6 pence |

*Required*

(a) Write a brief memo to the directors, explaining:

(i) Why the earnings per share figures are different under the two bases and reconciling the earnings per share figures for both years (5 marks)

(ii) How an analyst might appraise the company's performance under the two bases. (5 marks)

(b) Advise the company on the treatment of the following items in the accounts for the financial year ended 31 March 20X4.

(i) The company had regarded its region operations as four distinct geographical areas. These were served by staff located in London, Manchester, Glasgow and Newcastle.

In January 20X4 it made the staff in the London region redundant and transferred the work to Newcastle. The Newcastle staff absorbed the additional workload and provided the company's customers with the same level of support. The costs of closure were £20m. (5 marks)

(ii) In February 20X4 it made the staff in the Glasgow region redundant. Redundancy and other cost totalled £1m. The work was not transferred and the company ceased to service customers in Scotland and Ireland.

The company had not been able to dispose of its freehold premises in the Glasgow region by 31 March 20X4 and they were maintained at depreciated cost in the balance sheet. It is not expected that they will be sold until 20X5. (5 marks)

(c) Briefly discuss the statement that the application of financial reporting standards would be improved if they contained more detailed rules and explain the mechanism for giving companies guidance on reporting specific events where the standards are not explicit. (5 marks)

**(25 marks)**

**49   FRED 22**                                                    *45 mins*

The ASB has published FRED 22 *Revision of FRS 3 Reporting financial performance*. The FRED proposes that a single performance statement should replace the profit and loss account and the statement of total recognised gains and losses. In effect, they will be combined in one statement. FRED 22 also outlaws 'recycling'. In other words, it takes the view that gains and losses should be reported only once and in the period when they arise, and should not be reported again in another component of the financial statements at a later date.

*Required*

(a) (i) Discuss the views for and against recycling of gains and losses in the financial statements. (6 marks)

(ii) Explain the reasons for presenting financial performance in one statement rather than two or more statements. (8 marks)

(b) Describe how the following items are dealt with under current financial reporting standards, and how their treatment would change if FRED 22 were adopted.

(i) Revaluation gains and losses on fixed assets (4 marks)

(ii)   Foreign currency translation adjustments arising on the net investment in foreign operations                                                                                   (3 marks)

(iii)  Gains and losses on the disposal of fixed assets                          (4 marks)

**(25 marks)**

**50   JUNE (6/99)**                                                                                *45 mins*

Earnings per share is one of the most quoted statistics in financial analysis, coming into prominence because of the widespread use of the price earnings ratio as an investment decision making yardstick. In 1972 SSAP 3 *Earnings per share* was issued and revised in 1974, and the standard as amended was operating reasonably effectively. In fact the Accounting Standards Board (ASB) has stated that a review of earnings per share would not normally have been given priority at this stage of the Board programme. However, in October 1998 FRS 14 *Earnings per share* was published.

*Required*

(a)  (i)   Describe the main changes to SSAP 3 which have occurred as a result of FRS 14 and the main reasons for those changes.                                          (6 marks)

     (ii)  Explain why there is a need to disclose diluted earnings per share in financial statements.                                                                                      (5 marks)

(b)  The following financial statement extracts for the year ending 31 May 20X9 relates to Mayes, a public limited company.

|  | £'000 | £'000 |
|---|---:|---:|
| Operating profit | | |
| Continuing operations | 26,700 | |
| Discontinued operations | (1,120) | |
| | | 25,580 |
| Continuing operations | | |
| Profit on disposal of tangible assets | | 2,500 |
| Discontinued operations | | |
| (Loss) on sale of operations | | (5,080) |
| | | 23,000 |
| Interest payable | | (2,100) |
| Profit on ordinary activities before taxation | | 20,900 |
| Tax on profit on ordinary activities | | (7,500) |
| Profit on ordinary activities after tax | | 13,400 |
| Minority interest – equity | | (540) |
| Profit attributable to members of parent company | | 12,860 |
| Dividends | | |
| Preference dividend on non-equity shares | 210 | |
| Ordinary dividend on equity shares | 300 | |
| | | (510) |
| Other appropriations – non equity shares (note (iii)) | | (80) |
| Retained profit for year | | 12,270 |

| *Capital as at 31 May 20X9* | £'000 |
|---|---:|
| Allotted, called up and fully paid ordinary shares of £1 each | 12,500 |
| 7% convertible cumulative redeemable preference shares of £1 | 3,000 |
| | 15,500 |

*Additional Information*

(i)   On 1 January 20X9, 3·6 million ordinary shares were issued at £2·50 in consideration of the acquisition of June Ltd for £9 million. These shares do not rank for dividend in the current period. Additionally the company purchased and cancelled £2·4 million of its own £1 ordinary shares on 1 April 20X9. On 1

**64**

June 20X9, the company made a bonus issue of 1 for 5 ordinary shares before the financial statements were issued for the year ended 31 May 20X9.

(ii) The company has a share option scheme under which certain directors can subscribe for the company's shares. The following details relate to the scheme.

Options outstanding 31 May 20X8:

(1) 1·2 million ordinary shares at £2 each
(2) 2 million ordinary shares at £3 each

Both sets of options are exercisable before 31 May 20Y0.

Options granted during year 31 May 20X9

(1) One million ordinary shares at £4 each exercisable before 31 May 20X2, granted 1 June 20X8.

During the year to 31 May 20X9 the options relating to the 1.2 million ordinary shares (at a price of £2) were exercised on 1 March 20X9.

The average fair value of one ordinary share during the year was £5.

(iii) The 7% convertible cumulative redeemable preference shares are convertible at the option of the shareholder of the company on 1 July 20Y0, 20Y1, 20Y2 on the basis of two ordinary shares for every three preference shares. The preference share dividends are not in arrears. The shares are redeemable at the option of the shareholder on 1 July 200Y, 20Y1, 20Y2 at £1·50 per share. The 'other appropriations – non equity shares' item charged against the profits relates to the amortisation of the redemption premium and issue costs on the preference shares.

(iv) Mayes issued £6 million of 6% convertible bonds on 1 June 20X8 to finance the acquisition of Space Ltd. Each bond is convertible into 2 ordinary shares of £1. Assume a corporation tax rate of 35 %.

(v) The interest payable relates entirely to continuing operations and the taxation charge relating to discontinued operations is assessed at £100,000 despite the accounting losses. The loss on discontinued operations relating to the minority interest is £600,000.

*Required*

Calculate the basic and diluted earnings per share for the year ended 31 May 20X9 for Mayes plc utilising FRS 14 *Earning per share*.   (14 marks)

(Candidates should show a calculation of whether potential ordinary shares are dilutive or anti-dilutive.)

**(25 marks)**

## 51   PREPARATION QUESTION: SSAP 25

The Multitrade Group has three divisions (all based in the UK), A, B and C. Details of their turnover, results and net assets are given below.

| | £'000 |
|---|---|
| *Division A* | |
| Sales to B | 304,928 |
| Other UK sales | 57,223 |
| Middle East export sales | 406,082 |
| Pacific fringe export sales | 77,838 |
| | 846,071 |
| *Division B* | |
| Sales to C | 31,034 |
| Export sales to Europe | 195,915 |
| | 226,949 |
| *Division C* | |
| Export sales to North America | 127,003 |

| | Head office £'000 | Division A £'000 | Division B £'000 | Division C £'000 |
|---|---|---|---|---|
| Operational profit/(loss) before tax | | 162,367 | 18,754 | (8,303) |
| Re-allocated costs from | | | | |
| Head office | | 48,362 | 24,181 | 24,181 |
| Interest costs | | 3,459 | 6,042 | 527 |
| Fixed assets | 49,071 | 200,921 | 41,612 | 113,076 |
| Net current assets | 47,800 | 121,832 | 39,044 | 92,338 |
| Long-term liabilities | 28,636 | 16,959 | 6,295 | 120,841 |
| Deferred taxation | 1,024 | 24,671 | 9,013 | 4,028 |

*Required*

(a) Prepare a segmental report in accordance with SSAP 25 for publication in Multitrade's group.

(b) Comment on what the user of the accounts does and does not learn from this segmental report.

(c) Summarise the ASB's current proposals on segmental reporting.

**Guidance notes**

1   The calculations are very straightforward in this question, but be careful with your layout.

2   Make sure you show all the categories necessary for disclosure under SSAP 25.

3   As with all financial information, you have to be able to put it to good use for it to have a value, which is the point in part (b). Your answer should be in point form.

52   **AZ (6/99)**                                                                                     *45 mins*

(a) For enterprises that are engaged in different businesses with different risks and opportunities, the usefulness of financial information concerning these enterprises is greatly enhanced if it is supplemented by information on individual business segments. It is recognised that there are two main approaches to segmental reporting. The 'risk and returns' approach where segments are identified on the basis of different risks and returns arising from different lines of business and geographical areas, and the 'managerial' approach whereby segments are identified corresponding to the enterprises' internal organisational structure.

*Required*

(i) Explain why the information content of financial statements is improved by the inclusion of segmental data on individual business segments.                    (5 marks)

(ii) Discuss the advantages and disadvantages of analysing segmental data using:

   (1) The 'risk and return' approach                                                     (4 marks)
   (2) The 'managerial' approach                                                          (3 marks)

(b)  AZ, a public limited company, operates in the global marketplace.

(i)  The major revenue-earning asset is a fleet of aircraft which are now registered in the UK and its other main source of revenue comes from the sale of holidays. The directors are unsure as to how business segments are identified.    (3 marks)

(ii)  The company also owns a small aircraft manufacturing plant which supplies aircraft to its domestic airline and to third parties. The preferred method for determining transfer prices for these aircraft between the group companies is market price, but where the aircraft is of a specialised nature with no equivalent market price the companies fix the price by negotiation.    (2 marks)

(iii)  The company has incurred an exceptional loss on the sale of several aircraft to a foreign government. This loss occurred due to a fixed price contract signed several years ago for the sale of secondhand aircraft and resulted through the fluctuation of the exchange rates between the two countries.    (3 marks)

(iv)  During the year the company discontinued its holiday business due to competition in the sector.    (2 marks)

(v)  The company owns 40% of the ordinary shares of Eurocat Ltd, a specialist aircraft engine producer with operations in China and Russia. The investment is accounted for by the equity method and it is proposed to exclude the company's result from segment assets and revenue.    (3 marks)

*Required*

Discuss the implications of each of the above points for the determination of the segmental information required to be prepared and disclosed under SSAP 25 *Segmental reporting* and FRS 3 *Reporting financial performance*.

**(25 marks)**

Please note that the mark allocation is shown after each paragraph in part (b).

**53    RP GROUP (12/99)**                                                          *45 mins*

Related party relationships and transactions are a normal feature of business. Enterprises often carry on their business activities through subsidiaries and associates and its inevitable that transactions will occur between group companies. Until relatively recently the disclosure of related party relationships and transactions has been regarded as an area which has a relatively low priority. However, recent financial scandals have emphasised the importance of an accounting standard in this area.

*Required*

(a)  (i)  Explain why the disclosure of related party relationships and transactions is an important issue.    (6 marks)

(ii)  Discuss the view that small companies should be exempt from the disclosure of related party relationships and transactions on the grounds of their size.    (4 marks)

(b)  Discuss whether the following events would require disclosure in the financial statements of the RP Group plc under FRS 8 *Related party disclosures*.

RP Group plc, merchant bankers, has a number of subsidiaries, associates and joint ventures in its group structure. During the financial year to 31 October 20X9, the following events occurred.

(i)   The company agreed to finance a management buyout of a group company, AB, a limited company. In addition to providing loan finance, the company has retained a twenty-five per cent equity holding in the company and has a main board director on the board of AB, RP received management fees, interest payments and dividends from AB.                                    (6 marks)

(ii)  On 1 July 20X9, RP sold a wholly owned subsidiary, X, a limited company, to Z, a public limited company. During the year RP supplied X with second hand office equipment and X leased its factory from RP. The transactions were all contracted for at market rates.                                    (4 marks)

(iii) The pension scheme of the group is managed by another merchant bank. An investment manager of the group pension scheme is also a non-executive director of the RP Group and received an annual fee for his services of £25,000 which is not material in the group context. The company pays £16m per annum into the scheme and occasionally transfers assets into the scheme. In 20X9, fixed assets of £10m were transferred into the scheme and a recharge of administrative costs of £3m was made.                                    (5 marks)

                                                                          **(25 marks)**

## 54   MAXPOOL (6/97)        *See Q4-Mock2,*                    *45 mins*

The Companies Act 1985 and the Stock Exchange Listing rules contain requirements for disclosure of some related party transactions. The Accounting Standards Board has, however, published FRS 8 *Related party disclosures* in order to give users of financial information a more detailed insight into transactions. Without disclosure to the contrary, there is a general presumption that transactions reflected in financial statements have been conducted on an arm's length basis between independent parties. However, this presumption is not justified when related party transactions exist because the requisite conditions of competitive, free market dealings may not exist.

*Required*

(a)  (i)   Explain the reasons why the ASB felt that FRS 8 *Related party disclosures* was required when disclosure of such transactions was already deemed necessary under the Companies Act 1985 and the Stock Exchange Listing Rules.

                                                                          (8 marks)

     (ii)  Explain the reasons why the ASB feel that it is important to obtain comment on Financial Reporting Exposure Drafts prior to their acceptance as Financial Reporting Standards.                                    (4 marks)

(b)  Maxpool plc, a listed company, owned 60% of the shares in Ching Ltd. Bay plc, a listed company, owned the remaining 40% of the £1 ordinary shares in Ching Ltd. The holdings of shares were acquired on 1 January 20X6. Ching Ltd sold a factory outlet site to Bay at a price determined by an independent surveyor on 30 November 20X6. On 1 March 20X7 Maxpool plc purchased a further 30% of the £1 ordinary shares of Ching Ltd from Bay plc and purchased 25% of the ordinary shares of £1 of Bay plc. On 30 June 20X7 Ching Ltd sold the whole of its fleet of vehicles to Bay plc at a price determined by a vehicle auctioneer.

Explain the implications of the above transactions for the determination of related party relationships and disclosure of such transactions in the financial statements of Maxpool Group plc, Ching Ltd and Buy plc for the years ending 31 December 20X6 and 31 December 20X7.                                    (13 marks)

                                                                          **(25 marks)**

## 55   PREPARATION QUESTION: FRS 12

(a)   The release of FRS 12 *Provisions, contingent liabilities and contingent assets* means that prudence is no longer important in the balance sheet and that profits are highly volatile.

Discuss this statement.

(b)   Rita Ltd wishes to reduce its costs in order to remain competitive. It therefore intends to alter the terms and conditions of employment at its Wetherfield plant in such a way that overtime will be paid in future at 1.5 times the normal rate, rather than twice the normal rate as in the past. The company intends to compensate employees with a one-off payment and has put this offer to the union as one of a number of options. The employees are also aware of this impending change. No agreement has been reached with the union at the year-end. However, if the offer is not accepted, Rita Ltd is likely to switch overtime work to its Salford plant, and the union is aware that the company may do this.

*Required*

Discuss whether a provision should be made at the year end for the one-off compensation payment. Your answer should be based on FRS 12 Provisions, *contingent liabilities and contingent assets*.

**Guidance notes**

1   Part (a) sounds more difficult than it is – any sensible arguments would gain points.

2   In part (b), consider whether the expenditure can be avoided.

## 56   VACS

*45 mins*

(a)   Vacs Ltd is a manufacturing company which prepares financial statements to 30 September each year. The draft financial statements for the year ended 30 September 20X3 show a decrease in turnover and profit to £1,650,000 and £182,000 respectively with net assets of £232,000 at the year end. Before the financial statements can be finalised and approved by the directors, the following points need to be addressed.

(i)    Vacs Ltd has renewed the unlimited guarantee given in respect of the bank overdraft of an associated company.

(ii)   A former director, who was dismissed from the company's service for acting outside his authority, has given notice of his intention to claim substantial damages for loss of office. On 1 September 20X3 a claim was received for £150,000. The company's legal advisors do not think he will succeed in any claim and have been negotiating with the former director, who has reduced his claim to £100,000. A provision of £50,000 has been made in the accounts.

(iii)  Shortly after the year end the company's major competitor introduced its own version of Vacs' main product, the 'Dust Buster'. The rival version has received excellent reviews because of its technological superiority. In an attempt to maintain its market share, the directors have cut the price by 50%. At the moment stocks of the 'Dust Buster' are included in the draft accounts at £575,000, on which a normal mark-up of 30% would have been achieved.

(iv)   On 15 November 20X3 the company sold its former head office building, Whitley Wood, for £2.7 million. At the year end the building was unoccupied and carried at a value of £3.1 million.

(v)    Woodley Ltd, a subsidiary in Outer Sonning, was nationalised in December 20X3. The Outer Sonning authorities have refused to pay any compensation. The net assets of Woodley Ltd have been valued at £200,000 at the year end.

*Required*

Draft a memorandum to the directors of Vacs Ltd advising them of the implications of the above items for the financial statements for the year ended 30 September 20X3, giving reasons where necessary for the views taken.                                    (10 marks)

(b)    Vacs has a subsidiary, Scarey Ltd, a company manufacturing and selling bicycles. The directors of Scarey wish to provide for the following in its financial statements.

(i)     Costs of repairing bicycles under its two year warranty agreement.

(ii)    Costs of removing soil from its factory yard, which has been contaminated with toxic paint spillings. Under the terms of its lease it must make good any damage to its property in five years' time, when the lease expires.

(iii)   Costs of retraining staff in the manufacture of tandems.

(iv)    Future operating lease rentals for its factory in Wortley which is now disused.

*Required*

(i)     Explain the objectives of FRS 12 *Provisions, contingent liabilities and contingent assets* concerning the recognition of provisions, and explain in layman's terms the recognition criteria.                                                            (7 marks)

(ii)    Discus whether Scarey Ltd may provide for costs (i) to (iv) above and meet the recognition criteria of FRS 12.                                                        (8 marks)

                                                                                **(25 marks)**

# Answers

# 1    PREPARATION QUESTION: PRESCRIPTIVE STANDARDS

Accounting policies and practices have been increasingly regulated by the introduction of Companies Act requirements, SSAPs and FRSs. It has, however, always been recognised that financial reporting involves the exercise of judgement as the overriding requirements for each company is to present a true and fair view to its shareholders.

The statement attacks the wide variety of policies and practices, 25 years or so after the first SSAP was introduced. Is it fair to do so?

## Variety of acceptable policies and practices

The statement is correct to the extent that a wide variety does still exist. These varieties arise where there is still no accounting standard on an issue, eg accounting for intangible fixed assets. Companies are left to interpret imprecise CA 1985 requirements and a variety of solutions have emerged.

Even more seriously these differences exist in areas where standards have been introduced. For example, SSAPs 13 and 22 both permitted options on carrying intangibles. Both allowed the choice between carrying in the balance sheet or writing off to be based on which you believed to be true and fairer.

To be fair to the ASB, the indication from their FRSs to date is that, where they tackle an area, they are not going to let widely differing options still be allowed. FRS 6, which **requires** merger accounting to be used where the stringent criteria are met can be contrasted with SSAP 23. Under SSAP 23, even if the situation did qualify as a merger then merger accounting was an option but not compulsory.

Similarly, FRS 10 *Goodwill and intangible assets* has implemented a single rule for goodwill and all similar intangibles (capitalisation) rather than the choice given in SSAP 22.

On the whole though it is fair to say at the moment that there are too many grey areas and choices to be made.

## Wrong to assume any significant degree of comparability

This feeling flows logically out of the assertion in the first sentence. Clearly, it has some merit given the lack of standardisation of areas. On the other hand, it is perhaps too sweeping. Most of the more contentious accounting areas apply to more complicated groups of public companies. They are very aware of the impression their statutory accounts give and therefore are keen to find options that reflect their business well. Comparability is therefore diminished. Smaller, owner-managed companies, however, often have few contentious accounting policy areas to address and no real incentive to spend too long dressing things up. Consequently it is possible to see reasonable comparability between their accounts.

Overall though, for most public-interest companies only a skilled reader of accounts and accounting policies is able to make effective comparisons.

## Should more prescriptive standards be introduced?

This can be interpreted in two ways - should more standards be introduced and should they be more prescriptive.

Certainly it is uncontroversial to argue that more grey areas should be tackled in order to bring in standards where they are currently lacking. The ASB is moving into these areas with discussion papers and by continuing to work on the *Statement of Principles*. There are too many material areas where no real guidance exists, eg discounting.

Whether these new standards should be more prescriptive is more difficult. Two distinct views exist. There are those who lament the ever decreasing amount of judgement preparers and auditors are able to use. Others, however, welcome the moves towards standardisation taken by the ASB.

The key to resolving the debate is to clarify what users want. In many cases, the more prescriptive approach being taken by the ASB is being increasingly widely appreciated. There will always be a trade-off between comparability and flexibility. My feeling is that most users do not have the time or the expertise to worry about nuances of treatment and disclosure and prefer the increased confidence given by increasing comparability.

**Conclusion**

In conclusion, much has been done to cut down on some of the variety of options available. A lot still remains to be done, however, and the mood is that more prescriptive standards rather than less will best meet users' needs. In the meantime making effective comparisons between the accounts of large quoted companies remains a challenging task.

## 2   ACCOUNTING POLICIES AND ESTIMATION TECHNIQUES

> **Tutor's hint.** This question is a thorough test of your knowledge of FRS 18. In the exam you could be asked to explain the implications of the standard for the financial statements of a particular business, or to identify changes – such as those in part (b) – and explain their treatment in line with the new standard. When you review your answer make sure you understand the rationale behind all the answers in (b). The situations in (b) are taken directly from the standard, which was a short checklist to determine whether the change is to an accounting policy or just an estimation technique. To summarise the result of this for each part of (b):

| Does this involve a change to: | (i) | (ii) *ET* | (iii) | (iv) (1) | (iv) (2) | (v) | (vi) (1) | (vi) (2) *ET* | (vii) |
|---|---|---|---|---|---|---|---|---|---|
| Recognition? | ✓ | × | × | × | × | × | × | × | × |
| Presentation? | ✓ | × | ✓ | × | ✓ | × | × | × | × |
| Measurement basis? | × | × | × | × | × | ✓ | ✓ | × | ✓ |

(a) **Accounting policies** are defined by FRS 18 as those principles, bases, conventions, rules and practices, applied by an entity, that specify how the effects of transactions and other events are to be reflected in its financial statements through recognising, selecting measurement bases, and presenting assets, liabilities, gains, losses and changes to shareholders' funds. Accounting policies by definition do not include estimation techniques.

Accounting policies define the **process** whereby transactions and other events are reflected in financial statements. For example, an accounting policy for a particular type of expenditure may specify whether an asset or a loss is to be recognised; the basis on which it is to be measured; and where in the profit and loss account or balance sheet it is to be presented.

**Estimation techniques** are the methods adopted by an entity to arrive at estimated monetary amounts, corresponding to the **measurement bases** selected, for assets, liabilities, gains, losses and changes to shareholders' funds.

Estimation techniques implement the measurement aspects of accounting policies. An accounting policy will specify the basis on which an item is to be measured; where  there is uncertainty over the monetary amount corresponding to that basis, the amount will be arrived at by using an estimation technique.

The **distinction is important** because changes in accounting policy are accounted for as **prior period adjustments**, whereas the effects of changes in estimation techniques are taken through the current year profit and loss account.

(b) (i)    The transaction whose effects are being reflected is the incurring of directly attributable finance costs. That transaction is still being measured in the same way, but there is a change to recognition, in that it is now being recognised as (part of) an asset rather than as an expense. (FRS 18 states that where accounting standards allow a choice over what is to be recognised, that choice is a matter of accounting policy.) There is also, consequently, a change to the presentation of the transaction in the balance sheet and the profit and loss account. This is a **change of accounting policy**.

(ii)    This example has similarities with (i); cost centre C may be contrasted with interest in that example. The key difference is that, in (i), FRS 15 allows the entity a choice of how to treat directly attributable interest – as an asset or as an expense. There is no such choice here; directly attributable costs, once estimated, must be treated as part of an asset. Accordingly there is no change to recognition. In addition, both stocks and overheads continue to be presented in the same way and measured on the same basis (stocks are measured at the amount of directly attributable historical costs). This is a **change of estimation technique**.

(iii)    Although there is no change to the recognition and measurement of costs, they are being presented differently. This is therefore a **change of accounting policy**.

(iv)    (1)    Vehicles are being recognised and presented in the same way as before, and using the same, historical cost measurement basis. The only change is to the estimation technique used to measured the unexpired portion of each vehicle's economic benefits. This is **not a change of accounting policy**.

(2)    This accounting change involves both a change to presentation, as in (iii), and a change of estimation technique, as in (iv)(1) above. For the reasons set out in those examples, the former is a change of accounting policy but the latter is not. The two changes must therefore be **accounted for separately**. No change is made to the amount of depreciation charged in earlier periods, but the profit and loss account for the preceding period is restated to move the depreciation charge from cost of sales to administrative expenses.

(v)    There is explicitly a change of measurement basis. This is therefore a **change of accounting policy**, and it should be disclosed. However, a prior period adjustment will be required only if the difference between weighted average and FIFO is **material**.

(vi)    (1)    FRS 19 allows entities to report deferred tax on either a discounted or an undiscounted basis. These are two different measurement bases, and it is a matter of accounting policy which an entity chooses to adopt. This is therefore a **change of accounting policy**.

(2)    FRS 12 requires entities to report provisions at the best estimate of the expenditure required to settle the present obligation at the balance sheet date. Where that estimate is based on future cash flows, it is permissible to use undiscounted amounts only where the effect of the time value of money is not material. In such circumstances, the use of undiscounted future cash flows is, in effect, an estimation technique for arriving at the present value. Therefore this is **not a change of accounting policy**.

*= uncertainty PM.*

(vii) SSAP 20 *Foreign currency translation* allows a group translating the profit and loss account of a foreign subsidiary under the closing rate/net investment method to use either the closing rate or the average rate for the accounting period. These are two different measurement bases for the profit and loss account, and it is a matter of accounting policy which an entity chooses to adopt. This is thus a **change of accounting policy**.

## 3   PREPARATION QUESTION: SIMPLE CONSOLIDATION I

> **Tutor's hint**. This is a simpler question than any you will meet with in the examination. It is designed as a gentle introduction to the basic principles of consolidation, illustrating the calculation and accounting treatment of goodwill. Watch out, however, for the number of Bee shares in issue.

(a)   AYE PLC CONSOLIDATED BALANCE SHEET AS AT 31 DECEMBER 20X4

|  | £'000 | £'000 |
|---|---|---|
| *Intangible fixed asset: goodwill* |  | 435 |
| *Tangible fixed assets* |  |  |
| Buildings |  | 6,000 |
| Plant |  | 3,939 |
| Vehicles |  | 716 |
|  |  | 11,090 |
| *Current assets* |  |  |
| Stock | 3,408 |  |
| Debtors (less £23,000 inter-company) | 2,746 |  |
| Cash | 41 |  |
|  | 6,195 |  |
| *Creditors: amounts falling due within one year* |  |  |
| Overdraft | 2,016 |  |
| Trade creditors (less £23,000 inter-company) | 1,941 |  |
| Tax | 758 |  |
| Dividend | 280 |  |
|  | 4,995 |  |
| *Net current assets* |  | 1,200 |
| *Total assets less current liabilities* |  | 12,290 |
| *Creditors: amounts falling due after more than one year* |  |  |
| 10% debentures | 4,000 |  |
| 15% debentures | 500 |  |
|  |  | 4,500 |
|  |  | 7,790 |
| *Capital and reserves* |  |  |
| Called up share capital |  |  |
|   Ordinary shares of 50p each |  | 5,000.0 |
| Reserves |  |  |
|   Share premium account | 500.0 |  |
|   General reserve (W2) | 1,490.0 |  |
|   Unappropriated profit (W3) | 277.5 |  |
|  |  | 2,267.5 |
| Shareholders' funds |  | 7,267.5 |
| Minority interest (W4) |  | 522.5 |
|  |  | 7,790.0 |

(b)   Aye plc has made a profit of 15/115 × £23,000 = £3,000 on its sale of goods to Bee plc. Bee plc has <u>not yet sold goods</u> to an outside party and the profit is therefore <u>unrealised</u>

as far as the group is concerned. The adjustment is necessary to reduce the balance of unappropriated profit, and the value of stocks by £3,000.

*Workings*

1   *Goodwill*

|  | £'000 | £'000 |
|---|---|---|
| Cost of investment |  | 1,450 |
| Share of net assets acquired |  |  |
|   Share capital | 1,000 |  |
|   Reserves | 400 |  |
|  | 1,400 |  |
| Group share (72½%) |  | 1,015 |
|  |  | 435 |

2   *General reserve*

|  | Aye | Bee |
|---|---|---|
|  | £'000 | £'000 |
| Reserves per question | 1,200 | 800 |
| Bee at acquisition |  | (400) |
|  |  | 400 |
| Share of Bee: 72½ % × £400,000 | 290 |  |
|  | 1,490 |  |

3   *Unappropriated profit*

|  | Aye | Bee |
|---|---|---|
|  | £'000 | £'000 |
| Reserves per question | 205.0 | 100 |
| Bee at acquisition |  | 0 |
|  |  | 100 |
| Share of Bee: 72½ % × £100,000 | 72.5 |  |
|  | 277.5 |  |

4   *Minority interest*

|  | £'000 |
|---|---|
| Share capital (27½% × £1,000,000) | 275.0 |
| Reserves (27½% × £(800,000 + 100,000)) | 247.5 |
|  | 522.5 |

# 4   PREPARATION QUESTION: SIMPLE CONSOLIDATION II

**Tutor's hint**. This relatively straight forward question introduces the complication of dividends proposed by the subsidiaries but not yet accrued for by Bath Ltd. Notice that the profit and loss working must therefore include the proposed dividends.

*(handwritten notes)*

H sells to S = Dr con.P/L
                Cr stock

(pup)

S sells to H. = Dr m.I
               Dr con.P/L ] split
               Cr stocks in c/s

BATH LIMITED
CONSOLIDATED BALANCE SHEET AS AT 31 DECEMBER 20X1

| | £ | £ |
|---|---:|---:|
| *Fixed assets* | | |
| Intangible assets | | |
|    Goodwill arising on consolidation (W1) | | 164,160 |
| Tangible assets | | |
|    Freehold property at NBV | 267,000 | |
|    Plant and machinery at NBV | 395,800 | |
| | | 662,800 |
| Investment | | 52,000 |
| | | 878,960 |
| *Current assets* | | |
| Stocks and work in progress (W3) | 598,560 | |
| Debtors | 340,200 | |
| Cash at bank and in hand | 73,700 | |
| | 1,012,460 | |
| *Creditors: amounts falling due* | | |
| *within one year* | | |
| Bank overdraft | 72,300 | |
| Trade creditors | 385,400 | |
| Proposed dividend | 30,000 | |
| Other creditors (W4) | 170,600 | |
| | 658,300 | |
| *Net current assets* | | 354,160 |
| *Total assets less current liabilities* | | 1,233,120 |
| *Share capital and reserves* | | |
| Called up share capital | | 750,000 |
| Share premium account | | 15,000 |
| Profit and loss account (W6) | | 209,240 |
| Shareholders' funds | | 974,240 |
| Minority interest (W5) | | 258,880 |
| | | 1,233,120 |

*Workings*

1    *Goodwill*

| | | Jankin | | Arthur |
|---|---:|---:|---:|---:|
| | £ | £ | £ | £ |
| Cost of investment | | 153,000 | | 504,000 |
| Less dividend paid from | | | | |
|    pre-acquisition profits | | | | |
|    (24,000 × $^6/_{12}$ × 60%) | | - | | (7,200) |
| | | 153,000 | | 496,800 |
| Net assets acquired | | | | |
|    Share capital | 100,000 | | 400,000 | |
|    Reserves at acquisition (W2) | 19,400 | | 159,000 | |
| | 119,400 | | 559,000 | |
| Group share | @ 80% | 95,520 | @ 60% | 335,400 |
| | | 57,480 | | 161,400 |
| Amortisation at 25% | | (14,370) | | (40,350) |
| CBS | | 43,110 | | 121,050 |

Total goodwill = £164,160

2   *Reserves at acquisition*

|  | £ |
|---|---|
| **Arthur** | |
| Retained profits brought forward | 132,000 |
| To 30 June 20X1 (54,000 × $^6/_{12}$) | 27,000 |
|  | 159,000 |
| | |
| **Jankin** | |
| Retained profits brought forward | 19,400 |
| (no adjustment required as acquired at beginning of year) | |

3   *Stocks and work in progress*

|  | £ |
|---|---|
| Per question:  Bath | 206,000 |
| Jankin | 99,000 |
| Arthur | 294,200 |
|  | 599,200 |
| Add stock in transit (at cost to group) | 960 |
| Less profit in stock held by Jankin | (1,600) |
| Stocks in consolidated balance sheet | 598,560 |

4   *Other creditors*

|  | £ | £ |
|---|---|---|
| Taxation | | 158,000 |
| Dividends payable to minorities | | |
| Jankin (20% × £15,000) | 3,000 | |
| Arthur (40% × £24,000) | 9,600 | |
| | | 12,600 |
| | | 170,600 |

5   *Minority interests*

|  | *Jankin* | *Arthur* |
|---|---|---|
|  | £ | £ |
| Share capital | 100,000 | 400,000 |
| Reserves | 22,400 | 186,000 |
|  | 122,400 | 586,000 |
| | | |
| MI | 20% | 40% |
| | 24,480 | 234,400 |

CBS = £(234,400 + 24,480) = £258,880

6   *Profit and loss account*

|  | *Bath* | *Jankin* | *Arthur* |
|---|---|---|---|
|  | £ | £ | £ |
| Profit and loss account b/fwd | 191,000 | 19,400 | 132,000 |
| Dividends from: Jankin (W7) | 12,000 | | |
| Arthur (W7) | 7,200 | | |
| Unrealised profits (£240 + £1,600) | (1,840) | | |
| Retained profit 20X1 | 37,000 | 3,000 | 54,000 |
|  | 245,360 | 22,400 | 186,000 |
| | | | |
| Jankin/Arthur: pre-acquisition | | 19,400 | 159,000 |
| | | 3,000 | 27,000 |
| | | | |
| Share of Jankin: £3,000 × 80% | 2,400 | | |
| Share of Arthur: £27,000 × 60% | 16,200 | | |
| | | | |
| Less: amortisation of goodwill (£14,370 + £40,350) | (54,720) | | |
| | 209,240 | | |

7   *Dividends*

From Jankin (all post acquisition):  80% × £15,000 = £12,000

From Arthur (acquired 6 months through year so dividend must be split pre/post-acquisition):

Proposed dividend: £24,000

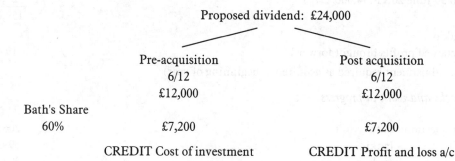

| | Pre-acquisition | Post acquisition |
|---|---|---|
| | 6/12 | 6/12 |
| | £12,000 | £12,000 |
| Bath's Share | | |
| 60% | £7,200 | £7,200 |
| | CREDIT Cost of investment | CREDIT Profit and loss a/c |

5   **BADEN**

> **Tutor's hint**. Part (a) of this question is quite straightforward, requiring you to distinguish between an associate and an ordinary investment. Part (b) required you to apply FRS 9. This question is a real test of your knowledge of FRS 9.
>
> Attempt the question under timed conditions making sure that you address all parts of the requirements.
>
> For part (b) you need to adopt a logical approach and should not get put off by any points where you are unsure but continue to deal with the rest of the question to get the marks where you are more confident.
>
> Review the solution carefully. Did you achieve a good presentation?
>
> * Understand the effect of the fair values on goodwill
>
> * Understand the effect of the transaction in note (iv)
>
> * Get the easy marks.
>
> **Examiner's comment.** Part (a) was well answered. Many candidates had learnt the various classifications in great detail and scored well. Part (b) was not well answered, however, with difficulties found in dealing with goodwill, post acquisition profits and elimination of inter-company profits.

(a)  (i)   An investor exercises **significant influence** over an associate, so the associate will often use **similar accounting policies**. In addition, the investor must retain a **participating interest** in the investee company. Under FRS 9, a holding of **20%** or more of voting rights **suggests but does not ensure**, significant influence. The investee's dividend policy is also a significant indicator of the status of the investment.

Where the investment is purely retained for the cash flow effect of dividend receipts and with no exercise of significant influence then an ordinary investment is suggested.

(ii)   A **joint venture** must be a **separate entity** (body corporate, partnership or unincorporated body carrying out a trade). All significant operational and financial decisions must be taken **jointly** by the participants. The **gross equity method** is used for accounting purposes.

A **joint arrangement** is in force where the participants derive benefits from products/services taken **in kind** rather than a share of financial results. Alternatively, a participant's share of output/results is determined by its supply of inputs to the arrangements.

Joint arrangements are accounted for by **participants** accounting for their **share of assets, liabilities and cash** flows. (*Note.* This will produce similar results to proportional consolidation.)

(b) (i) CALCULATION OF GOODWILL AT 1 JANUARY 20X7

| | £m | £m |
|---|---|---|
| Tangible fixed assets | 30 | |
| Current assets | 31 | |
| Creditors (short term) | (20) | |
| Creditors (long term) | (8) | |
| Fair value of net assets | 33 | |
| 30% thereof | | 9.9 |
| Cost | | 14.0 |
| Goodwill | | 4.1 ✓ |

*Note.* Goodwill in the balance sheet of investee is excluded by FRS 9.

CARRYING VALUE 31.20X8 IN THE BALANCE SHEET

| | £m |
|---|---|
| Investment cost | 14.0 ✓ |
| 30% post acquisition profit $(32 - 9 - 10)$ | 3.9 |
| Amortised goodwill $4.1 \times 2/4$ | (2.0) ✓ |
| Fair value adjustment for depreciation $2 \times 20\% \times (30 - 20) \times 30\%$ | (1.2) |
| | 14.7 |

*Alternative calculation*

| | £m | £m |
|---|---|---|
| Net assets | | |
| Per question | 46 | |
| Less PUP | (10) | |
| | 36 | |
| Group share: 30% | | 10.8 |
| Fair value increase | | |
| Net assets at 31.12.X8 | 46 | |
| Less profit for 20X7 and 20X8 $(32 - 9)$ | 23 | |
| Net assets at acquisition | 23 | |
| Fair value | 33 | |
| Increase in fair value | 10 | |
| Group share: 30% | | 3.0 |
| | | 13.8 |
| Goodwill | | 4.1 |
| | | 17.9 |
| Less goodwill amortisation | | (2.0) |
| Depreciation | | (1.2) |
| Investment in associate | | 14.7 |

CONSOLIDATED PROFIT AND LOSS ACCOUNT (EXTRACTS)
FOR THE YEAR ENDED 31 DECEMBER 20X8

| | £m | £m |
|---|---|---|
| Share of associate profit $(30\% \times 29)$ | 8.7 | |
| Less goodwill | (1.0) | |
| Intercompany profit | (3.0) | |
| Depreciation adjustment | (0.6) | |
| | | 4.1 |
| Exceptional item | | |
| Associate $(30\% \times 10)$ | | 3.0 |
| Interest payable $(30\% \times 4)$ | | 1.2 |
| Taxation on profit on ordinary activities $(30\% \times 3)$ | | 0.9 |

(ii) Under gross equity accounting for joint ventures, the above disclosures are expanded.

CONSOLIDATED PROFIT AND LOSS ACCOUNT

*inter co. sale,*

|  | £m |
|---|---|
| Turnover group and share of joint venture Y + | 53.1 |
| [(212 – 35) × 30% = 53.1] | |
| Less share of joint venture turnover | (53.1) |
| Group turnover | Y |

In the consolidated balance sheet the investment calculated above (£14.7m) is split between gross assets and liabilities.

CONSOLIDATED BALANCE SHEET (EXTRACT)

| | | £m |
|---|---|---|
| Share of gross assets | | |
| Fixed assets | 37 | |
| Current assets (31 – 10) | 21 | |
| | 58 × 30% | 17.4 |
| Fair value | | 3.0 |
| Goodwill | | 4.1 |
| Less written off | | (2.0) |
| Depreciation adjustment | | (1.2) |
| | | 21.3 |
| Share of gross liabilities: 30% × (12 + 10) | | (6.6) |
| | | 14.7 |

# 6 EXOTIC

**Tutor's hint**. The consolidation section of this question is quite straightforward as long as you remember how to calculate the MI of a sub-subsidiary. In part (b) you should be looking at the FRS 3 conditions for an operation to be discontinued. Points to watch in this question are the treatment of intercompany transactions, the calculation of minority interest, presentation and supporting workings and the correct treatment for part (b).

**Examiner's comment**. Some students could not deal with the sub-subsidiary and various errors were made in the consolidation, eg incorrect elimination of inter-company items. Most students know about FRS 3 but didn't apply it to the results given in the question.

(a) (i) EXOTIC GROUP
CONSOLIDATED PROFIT AND LOSS ACCOUNT
FOR THE YEAR ENDED 31 DECEMBER 20X9

| | £'000 |
|---|---|
| Turnover (W2) | 92,120 |
| Cost of sales (W3) | 27,915 |
| Gross profit | 64,205 |
| Distribution costs (3,325 + 2,137 + 1,900) | 7,362 |
| Administrative expenses (3,475 + 950 + 1,900) | 6,325 |
| Operating profit | 50,518 |
| Interest paid | 325 |
| Profit before tax | 50,193 |
| Taxation (8,300 + 5,390 + 4,241) | 17,931 |
| Profit after tax | 32,262 |
| Minority interest (W4) | 3,714 |
| | 28,548 |
| Dividends proposed | 9,500 |
| Retained profit for the year | 19,048 |
| Retained profit b/f (W5) | 37,560 |
| Retained profit c/f | 56,608 |

(ii)   EXOTIC GROUP
CONSOLIDATED BALANCE SHEET
AS AT 31 DECEMBER 20X9

|  | £'000 |
|---|---|
| Intangible fixed asset: goodwill (W6) | 4,107 |
| Tangible fixed assets (W7) | 72,787 |
| Current assets (W8) | 19,446 |
| Current liabilities (13,063 + 10,023 + 48) | (23,134) |
|  | 73,206 |
|  |  |
| Share capital | 8,000 |
| Profit and loss account (see note) | 56,608 |
| Shareholders' funds | 64,608 |
| Minority interest (W9) | 8,598 |
|  | 73,206 |

*Workings*

1   *Group structure*

Exotic
|   90%
Melon
|   80%
Kiwi

*Minority interest*
In Melon = 10%
In Kiwi = 100% – (90% × 80%) = 28%

2   *Turnover*

|  | £'000 | £'000 |
|---|---|---|
| Exotic |  | 45,600 |
| Melon |  | 24,700 |
| Kiwi |  | 22,800 |
|  |  | 93,100 |
| Less intercompany sales |  |  |
| Melon | 260 |  |
| Kiwi | 480 |  |
|  |  | (740) |
| Less intercompany sale of fixed assets |  | (240) |
|  |  | 92,120 |

3   *Cost of sales*

|  | £'000 |
|---|---|
| Exotic | 18,050 |
| Melon | 5,463 |
| Kiwi | 5,320 |
|  | 28,833 |
| Less intercompany sales (as above) | (740) |
| Less cost of intercompany fixed asset to Exotic | (200) |
| Less excess depreciation (240 – 200) × 20% | (8) |
| Add unrealised profit on stock |  |
| Melon ($60 \times 33^1/_3/133^1/_3$) | 15 |
| Kiwi ($75 \times 25/125$) | 15 |
|  | 27,915 |

4   *Minority interest*

|  | £'000 |
|---|---|
| Melon plc: 10% × (10,760 – 15 + 8) | 1,075 |
| Kiwi plc: 28% × (9,439 – 15) | 2,639 |
|  | 3,714 |

5     *Reserves b/f*

|  | £'000 |
|---|---|
| Exotic plc | 20,013 |
| Melon plc: 90% × (13,315 − 1,425) | 10,701 |
| Kiwi plc: 90% × 80% × (10,459 − 950) | 6,846 |
|  | 37,560 |

6     *Goodwill on acquisition*

|  | £'000 | £'000 |
|---|---|---|
| *Melon investment in Kiwi* | | |
| Investment cost | | 3,800 |
| Assets acquired | | |
|   Shares | 2,000 | |
|   Pre-acquisition reserves | 950 | |
| | 2,950 | |
| Group share (80%) | | 2,360 |
| | | 1,440 |
| *Exotic investment in Melon* | | |
| Investment cost | | 6,650 |
| Assets acquired | | |
|   Shares | 3,000 | |
|   Pre-acquisition reserves | 1,425 | |
| | 4,425 | |
| Group share (90%) | | 3,983 |
| Goodwill | | 2,667 |
| Total goodwill | | 4,107 |

7     *Tangible fixed assets*

|  | £'000 |
|---|---|
| Exotic | 35,483 |
| Melon | 24,273 |
| Kiwi | 13,063 |
|  | 72,819 |
| Less profit on sale of intercompany fixed asset: (240 − 200) | (40) |
| Add back excess depreciation: (240 − 200) × 20% | 8 |
|  | 72,787 |

8     *Current assets*

|  | £'000 |
|---|---|
| Exotic | 1,568 |
| Melon | 9,025 |
| Kiwi | 8,883 |
|  | 19,476 |
| Less unrealised profit on stock (W3) | |
|   Melon | (15) |
|   Kiwi | (15) |
|  | 19,446 |

9    Minority interest

|  | £'000 | £'000 |
|---|---|---|
| *In Kiwi* | | |
| Share capital | 2,000 | |
| Reserves (19,898 – 15) | 19,883 | |
|  | 21,883 | |
| MI (28%) | | 6,127 |
| Less cost of investment (10% × 3,800) | | (380) |
| Add goodwill (10% × 1,440) | | 144 |
| *In Melon* | | |
| Share capital | 3,000 | |
| Reserves (24,075 – 15 + 8) | 24,068 | |
|  | 27,068 | |
| MI (10%) | | 2,707 |
| Total MI | | 8,598 |

*Alternative working*

|  |  | £'000 | £'000 |
|---|---|---|---|
| Melon: | Net assets per question | 27,075 | |
|  | PUP | (15) | |
|  | Depreciation | 8 | |
|  | Investment in Kiwi | (3,800) | |
|  | Goodwill | 1,440 | |
|  |  | 24,708 | |
|  | × 10% | | 2,471 |
| Kiwi: | Per question | 21,898 | |
|  | PUP | (15) | |
|  |  | 21,883 | |
|  | × 28% | | 6,127 |
|  |  | | 8,598 |

*Note.* In this question you can insert the figure for consolidated reserves from the consolidated profit and loss account. However, for completeness, a reserve working may be shown as follows.

|  | Exotic £'000 | Melon £'000 | Kiwi £'000 |
|---|---|---|---|
| Reserves per question | 22,638 | 24,075 | 19,898 |
| Provision for unrealised profit | | (15) | (15) |
| Disposal of fixed assets: profit | (40) | | |
| depreciation | - | 8 | - |
|  | 22,598 | 24,068 | 19,883 |
| Melon: pre-acquisition | | (1,425) | |
| Kiwi: pre-acquisition | | - | (950) |
|  | | 22,643 | 18,933 |
| Share of Melon: 22,643 × 90% | 20,379 | | |
| Share of Kiwi: 18,933 × 72% | 13,631 | | |
|  | 56,608 | | |

(b)  *Effect of Madiera plc on consolidated P&L a/c*

|  | Discontinued operations | |
|---|---|---|
|  | £'000 | £'000 |
| Turnover |  | 2,000 |
| Cost of sales | (2,682) |  |
| Less provision at 31.12.X8 | 500 |  |
|  |  | (2,182) |
| Gross loss |  | (182) |
| Distribution costs |  | (18) |
| Administrative expenses |  | (100) |
| Operating loss |  | (300) |
| Loss on termination of discontinued operations (427 − 115 + 36) |  | (348) |
| Loss on ordinary activities before tax |  | (648) |

*FRS 3 (format 1)*

|  | £'000 |
|---|---|
| Turnover | 2,000 |
| Operating loss |  |
|   Discontinued operations | (800) |
|   Less provision at 31.12.X8 | 500 |
|  | (300) |
| Loss on termination of discontinued activities | (348) |
| Loss on ordinary activities before tax | (648) |

## 7    X AND Y

> **Tutor's hint.** This question covers various aspects of complex groups, including sub-subsidiaries, associates, intra-group profit elimination, contingencies, fair value adjustments and the write off of goodwill. It is important with this type of question to spend time clarifying the group structure and relationships before launching into it. Note that here we are dealing with two subsidiaries and an associate. The equity accounting of W uses 30% (this is what the group controls) and a minority interest is shown.
>
> **Examiner's comment.** Many candidates produced poor quality workings which were difficult to follow. Candidates had difficulty with the fair value and accounting policy adjustments quite difficult and often calculated the relative shareholdings of the group and minority interest incorrectly.

X GROUP
BALANCE SHEET AS AT 31 MARCH 20X9

|  | Workings | £m |
|---|---|---|
| Tangible fixed assets | 3 | 1,058 |
| Investment in associate | 4 | 47 |
| Goodwill (unamortised) | 2 | 40 |
| Net current assets | 5 | 1,060 |
| Long term creditors | 6 | (365) |
|  |  | 1,840 |
|  |  |  |
| Share capital |  | 360 |
| Share premium |  | 250 |
| Reserves |  | 1,071 |
|  |  | 1,681 |
| Minority interests | 7 | 159 |
|  |  | 1,840 |

*Workings*

1    *Group structure*

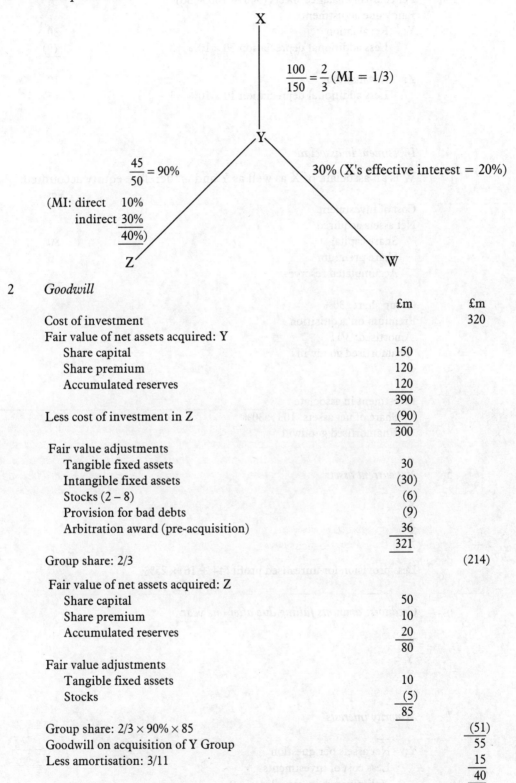

X

$$\frac{100}{150} = \frac{2}{3}(MI = 1/3)$$

Y

$$\frac{45}{50} = 90\%$$        30% (X's effective interest = 20%)

(MI: direct    10%
     indirect  30%
              40%)

Z                                    W

2    *Goodwill*

|  | £m | £m |
|---|---:|---:|
| Cost of investment | | 320 |
| Fair value of net assets acquired: Y | | |
| Share capital | 150 | |
| Share premium | 120 | |
| Accumulated reserves | 120 | |
|  | 390 | |
| Less cost of investment in Z | (90) | |
|  | 300 | |
| Fair value adjustments | | |
| Tangible fixed assets | 30 | |
| Intangible fixed assets | (30) | |
| Stocks (2 – 8) | (6) | |
| Provision for bad debts | (9) | |
| Arbitration award (pre-acquisition) | 36 | |
|  | 321 | |
| Group share: 2/3 | | (214) |
| Fair value of net assets acquired: Z | | |
| Share capital | 50 | |
| Share premium | 10 | |
| Accumulated reserves | 20 | |
|  | 80 | |
| Fair value adjustments | | |
| Tangible fixed assets | 10 | |
| Stocks | (5) | |
|  | 85 | |
| Group share: 2/3 × 90% × 85 | | (51) |
| Goodwill on acquisition of Y Group | | 55 |
| Less amortisation: 3/11 | | 15 |
|  | | 40 |

*Note.* Y had acquired Z *before* X acquired Y. You therefore compare the cost of X's investment in Y to Y's consolidated separable net assets, net of all goodwill.

3    *Tangible fixed assets*

|  |  | £m | £m |
|---|---|---|---|
| Per company balance sheets (900 + 100 + 30) |  |  | 1,030 |
| Fair value adjustments |  |  |  |
| Y: | Revaluation | 30 |  |
|  | Less additional depreciation $30 \times 10\% \times 3$ | (9) |  |
|  |  |  | 21 |
| Z: | Revaluation | 10 |  |
|  | Less additional depreciation $10 \times 10\% \times 3$ | (3) |  |
|  |  |  | 7 |
|  |  |  | 1,058 |

4    *Investment in associate*

W is an associate of X as well as Y and is therefore equity accounted.

|  | £m | £m |
|---|---|---|
| Cost of investment |  | 50 |
| Net assets acquired |  |  |
| Share capital | 80 |  |
| Share premium | 6 |  |
| Accumulated reserves | 7 |  |
|  | 93 |  |
| Group share: 30% |  | (28) |
| Premium on acquisition |  | 22 |
| Amortised: 3/11 |  | (6) |
| Unamortised goodwill |  | 16 |

|  | £m |
|---|---|
| Investment in associate |  |
| Share of net assets: $103 \times 30\%$ | 31 |
| Unamortised goodwill | 16 |
|  | 47 |

5    *Net current assets*

|  | £m |
|---|---|
| X | 640 |
| Y | 360 |
| Z | 75 |
|  | 1,075 |
| Less provision for unrealised profit $(44 + 16) \times 25\%$ | (15) |
|  | 1,060 |

6    *Creditors: amounts falling due after one year*

|  | £m |
|---|---|
| X | 200 |
| Y | 150 |
| Z | 15 |
|  | 365 |

7    *Minority interests*

|  |  | £m |
|---|---|---|
| Y: | Net assets per question | 480 |
|  | Less cost of investments (eliminated on consolidation) | (140) |
|  | Fair value adjustments: |  |
|  | Tangible (W3) | 21 |
|  | Intangible | (30) |
|  | Investment in associate (W4) | 47 |
|  |  | 378 |

∴Minority interest = $378 \times 1/3 = £126m$

£m

Z: Net assets per question
Fair value adjustments
    Tangible (W3)                     90
7
    Provision for unrealised profit      (15)

                                  82

Minority interests $82 \times 40\% = £33m$

∴ Total minority interest $(126 + 33) = £159m$

8   *Consolidated reserves*

|  | X £'m | Y £'m | Z £'m | W £'m |
|---|---|---|---|---|
| Reserves per question | 1050.0 | 210 | 30 | 17 |
| Depreciation (W3) |  | (9) | (3) |  |
| Goodwill amortisation (W4) |  | (6) |  |  |
| Intangible adjustment |  | (30) |  |  |
| Tangible assets adjustment |  | 30 | 10 |  |
| Provision for unrealised profit | - | - | (15) | - |
|  | 1,050.0 | 195 | 22 | 17 |
|  |  |  |  |  |
| Pre-acquisition profit |  |  |  |  |
|   Per question |  | 120 | 20 | 7 |
|   Arbitration |  | 36 |  |  |
|   Stock adjustment |  | (6) | (5) |  |
|   Bad debts adjustment |  | (9) |  |  |
|   Intangible adjustment |  | (30) |  |  |
|   Tangible assets adjustment |  | 30 | 10 | - |
|  |  | 141 | (25) | 7 |
| Post-acquisition |  | 54 | (3) | 10 |

Share of Y:   $2/3 \times 54$        36.0
Share of Z:   $60\% \times 3$        (1.8)
Share of W:   $20\% \times 10$      2.0
Amortisation of goodwill (W2)   (15.0)

                           1,071.2

## 8   DEMERGER

**Tutor's hint**. This is a challenging question in the time available. It is a good idea to sort out the group structures before and after the demerger.

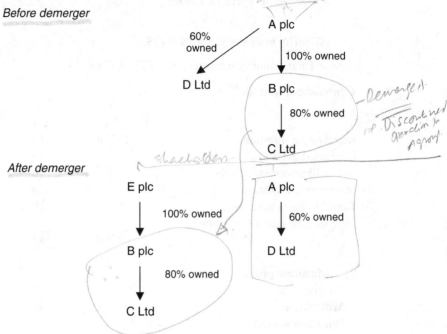

The demerger of the B group (B and C) from A plc to the newly formed company E plc means the shareholders in A plc will receive shares in E as compensation for the value of the assets demerged.

The demerger of the B group is really a disposal and the rules regarding the treatment of goodwill originally arising on the purchase of subsidiaries must be followed.

*Prizewinners' points.* The majority of marks were allocated to fundamental group accounting techniques. So if you did not get all aspects of the demerger right you could still get a pass.

**Examiner's comment**. As long as candidates did not panic and applied themselves, the marks they achieved were generally good.

(a)   B GROUP
CONSOLIDATED BALANCE SHEET FOR THE YEAR ENDED 31 MAY 20X7

|  | £m |
|---|---|
| Intangible assets: goodwill $(10 \times 8/10)$ | 8 |
| Tangible assets $(550 + 60)$ | 610 |
| Net current assets $(400 + 70)$ | 470 |
| Creditors due after one year $(30 + 10)$ | (40) |
| Minority interest (W1) | (24) |
|  | 1,024 |
|  |  |
| Called up share capital | 100 |
| Share premium a/c (*not 100+10*) | 100 |
| Profit and loss (W2) | 824 |
|  | 1,024 |

*Workings*

1    *Minority interest*

[handwritten: 20%(NA @ now)]

|  | £m |
|---|---|
| 20% ordinary shares in C | 6 |
| 20% share premium in C | 2 |
| 20% P&L in C | 16 |
| | 24 |

[handwritten: 20/ × 120.]

2 ✓  *Profit and loss*

|  | B plc | C Limited |
|---|---|---|
|  | £'m | £'m |
| Reserves per question | 810 | 80 |
| C Ltd pre-acquisition |  | (60) |
|  |  | 20 |
| Share of C Ltd: £20m × 80% | 16 |  |
|  | 826 |  |
| Less amortisation of goodwill: 10 × 2/10 | (2) |  |
|  | 824 |  |

[handwritten: ×2 = ×7]

3 ✓  *Goodwill* ✓

|  | £m | £m |
|---|---|---|
| Investment cost |  | 90 |
| Ordinary shares | 30 |  |
| Share premium | 10 |  |
| Pre acquisition profit | 60 |  |
|  | 100 |  |
| 80% thereof |  | (80) |
|  |  | 10 |

[handwritten: 9 =]

(b)  A GROUP
CONSOLIDATED BALANCE SHEET AT 31 MAY 20X7 (AFTER DEMERGER)

|  | £m |
|---|---|
| Tangible assets | 3,590 ✓ |
| Negative goodwill (W1) | (28) ✓ |
| Net current assets | 1,890 ✓ |
| Creditors due after one year | (135) |
| Minority interest (W2) | (58) |
|  | 5,259 |
| Called up share capital | 1,350 |
| Share premium account | 1,550 |
| Profit and loss account (W3) | 2,359 |
|  | 5,259 |

*Workings*

1    *Negative goodwill*

|  | £'000 |
|---|---|
| Investment in D |  | 50 |
| Ordinary shares | 20 |  |
| Share premium | 20 |  |
| Profit and loss | 90 |  |
|  | 130 ✓ |  |
| 60% thereof |  | 78 |
| Negative goodwill |  | (28) |

BPP PUBLISHING

2    *Minority interest*

|  | £m |
|---|---|
| 40% ordinary shares in D | 8 |
| 40% share premium in D | 8 |
| 40% P&L in D | 42 |
|  | 58 |

3    *Profit and loss account*

This can be calculated as a balancing figure but the detailed workings are as follows.

Consolidated P&L at 1 June 20X6

|  |  | £m |
|---|---|---|
| A | 3,250 – 683 | 2,567 |
| B | 810 – 394 – 250 | 166 |
| C | 80% × (80 – 50 – 60) | (24) |
| D | 60% × (105 – 55 – 90) | (24) |
| Less goodwill amortised |  | (182) |
|  |  | 2,503 |
| Retained loss for period (see workings to consolidated P&L account) |  | (144) |
|  |  | 2,359 |

|  |  | £m |
|---|---|---|
| Proof of reserves: |  |  |
| A: 3,250 – 900 |  | 2,350 |
| B: (105 – 90) × 60% |  | 9 |
|  |  | 2,359 |

A GROUP PLC
CONSOLIDATED PROFIT AND LOSS ACCOUNT
FOR THE YEAR ENDED 31 MAY 20X7

To comply with FRS 3, the demerged business will appear as 'discontinued operations'.

|  | £m | £m | £m |
|---|---|---|---|
|  | *Continuing operations* (A + D) | *Discontinued operations* (B + C) | *Total* |
| Turnover | 8,530 | 3,325 | 11,855 |
| Cost of sales | (5,320) | (2,195) | (7,515) |
| Gross profit | 3,210 | 1,130 | 4,340 |
| Net operating expenses | (2,125) | (435) | (2,560) |
| Operating profit | 1,085 | 695 | 1,780 |
| Goodwill on discontinued operations |  | (278) | (278) |
| Profit on ordinary activities before tax | 1,085 | 417 | 1,502 |
| Taxation |  |  | (565) |
| Profit on ordinary activities after tax |  |  | 937 |
| Minority interest |  |  | (35)[2] |
| Profit for financial year |  |  | 902 |
| Dividends |  |  | (1,046)[3] |
| Retained loss for financial year |  |  | (144) |

1 - see working 1
2 - see working 2
3 - see working 3

*Workings*

1  *Goodwill on discontinued operations (B + C)*

|  | £m | £m |
|---|---|---|
| Cost of investment in B |  | 900 |
| 100% ordinary shares in B | 100 |  |
| 100% P&L in B | 250 |  |
| 100% share premium in B | 100 |  |
|  |  | (450) |
|  |  | 450 |

*(handwritten left margin: 450 ; 450 × 4/10 = 180 ; 270.)*

*(handwritten: The Remaining)*

Of this, £450m, 4/10 ie 180 has been amortised. 6/10 ie 270 must be deducted in calculating the profit on disposal of B Ltd.

For the goodwill in C Ltd the figures are £2m and 8m respectively.

The split is therefore as follows.

|  | *Amortised in consolidated P&L* | *Brought into disposal calculation* |
|---|---|---|
| B Ltd | 180 | 270 *= 450.* |
| C Ltd | 2 | 8 *= 10.* |
|  | 182 | 278 |

2  *Minority interest share of profit for year*

|  | £m |
|---|---|
| In D: 40% of 60 | 24 |
| In C: 20% of 55 | 11 |
|  | 35 |

3  Dividends

|  | £m |
|---|---|
| Paid by A     *= Value of NA.* | 30 |
| Dividend *in specie* representing the consideration given to reflect the demerger of the net assets of B and C from the group = Net assets of the B group at 31 May 20X7 (see part (a) above) | 1,016 |
|  | 1,046 |

*(handwritten right: Se +R -9. ✓ ; 1024 -8 = 1016. ; T NA)*

Note that there is no profit or loss on demerger, the 'dividend *in specie*' simply compensates for the net assets demerged as shown in the consolidated balance sheet of the 'B' group in the answer to part (a) of this question.

(c)  E GROUP
SHARE CAPITAL AND RESERVES AT 31 MAY 20X7
(E + B + C)

*(handwritten: from A.it. ; See Diag. p90.)*

The share capital and reserves must equal the value of the demerged net assets of the B group, ie £1,016m.

|  | £m |
|---|---|
| This comprises 300m £1 ordinary shares (see question note ii) | 300 |
| Profit and loss account (balancing figure) | 716 |
|  | 1,016 |

*(handwritten: SC & Reserves of E group.)*

*(handwritten: E issued 300 0s in exchange for A's inv. in B)*

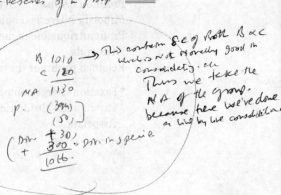

**9   WRIGHT**

> **Tutor's hint.** This question required consolidation of a subsidiary which became an associate during the year, consolidation of a subsidiary acquired during the year, dealing with a downsizing and provision and accounting for the sale of shares in a subsidiary. When you review your answer, check that you have produced clear workings which the examiner can follow and have calculated the gain on disposal correctly.
>
> **Examiner's comment.** Many candidates treated the downsizing as a discontinuance. They were not, however, penalised in the rest of their answer if they did this. Additionally, many candidates did not apply FRS 9 *Associates and joint ventures.* Many candidates forgot to accrue the profit for the half year to the date of sale of shares in the subsidiary. Very few candidates got part (b) completely right because of errors in part (a). However, credit was given where answers were consistent and logical.

(a)   WRIGHT GROUP PLC
CONSOLIDATED PROFIT AND LOSS ACCOUNT
FOR THE YEAR ENDED 31 DECEMBER 20X8

| | £m | £m | £m | *Working* |
|---|---:|---:|---:|---:|
| Turnover | | | | |
| Continuing operations | | 18,600 | | |
| Acquisition of Chang Plc | | 1,200 | | |
| | | | 19,800 | 1 |
| Cost of sales | | | (13,232) | 2 |
| Gross profit | | | 6,568 | |
| Distribution costs | | 1,965 | | 3 |
| Administrative expenses | | 195 | | |
| | | | (2,160) | 4 |
| Operating profit | | | | |
| Continuing operations | | 4,133 | | |
| Acquisition of Chang Plc | | 275 | | |
| | | | 4,408 | 6 |
| Share of operating profit in associate | | | 37 | 9 |
| Profit on disposal of shares | | | | |
| in the subsidiary | | 47 | | 7 |
| Cost of restructuring | | (34) | | |
| | | | 13 | 8 |
| | | | 4,458 | |
| Interest receivable:   group | 35 | | | 10 |
| associate | 2 | | | |
| | | 37 | | 9 |
| Interest payable:   group | 37 | | | 11 |
| associate | 2 | | | |
| | | (39) | | |
| | | | (2) | 9 |
| Profit on ordinary activities | | | 4,456 | |
| Tax on profit on ordinary activities* | | | (1,432) | |
| Profit on ordinary activities after taxation | | | 3,024 | |
| Minority interests (equity) | | | (61) | 12 |
| Profit attributable to members of the parent company | | | 2,963 | |
| Dividends | | | (200) | |
| Retained profit for the year | | | 2,763 | |
| | | | | |
| *Taxation charge comprises:* | | | | |
| Parent and subsidiaries | | | 1,417 | 13 |
| Associate | | | 15 | 9 |
| | | | 1,432 | |

*Workings*

1    *Turnover*

|  |  | £m |
|---|---|---|
| Wright |  | 18,000 |
| Berg | (6/12) | 600 |
| Chang | (9/12) | 1,200 |
|  |  | 19,800 |

Note that no adjustment for inter company sales is required because they occurred when Berg had become an associated company.

2    *Cost of sales*

|  | £m |  |
|---|---|---|
| Wright | 12,000 |  |
| Berg | 420 |  |
| Chang | 795 | (see below) |
| Depreciation (Chang) | (5) | (see below) |
| Restructuring costs (Wright) | (14) | (see below) |
| Goodwill (W5) | 36 |  |
|  | 13,232 |  |

*Chang: cost of sales*

|  | £m |
|---|---|
| Stock at acquisition less fair value adjustment | 200 |
| Purchases 9/12 × (1,020 − 150 + 350) | 915 |
| Stock at 31 December 20X8 after accounting policy change (350 − 30) | (320) |
|  | 795 |

Depreciation on Chang's assets is adjusted for fair value reduction.

£30m × 20% × 9/12 = £5m (rounded up)

The restructuring costs are not classified as discontinuing because they are considered immaterial. Instead they are included as a non-operating exceptional item.

3    *Distribution costs*

|  | £m |
|---|---|
| Wright | 1,800 |
| Berg (6/12) | 60 |
| Chang (9/12) | 105 |
|  | 1,965 |

4    *Administrative expenses*

|  | £m |
|---|---|
| Wright | 180 |
| Berg (6/12) | 6 |
| Chang (9/12) | 9 |
|  | 195 |

5    *Goodwill*

|  | £m | £m |
|---|---|---|
| Chang plc: purchase price |  | 700 |
| Net assets acquired at fair value per note (ii) to question | 750 |  |
| Add back *post acquisition* reorganisation provision |  |  |
| which is eliminated from the goodwill calculation | 20 |  |
|  | 770 |  |
| 80% thereof |  | 616 |
| Goodwill |  | 84 |
| Full year's charge for amortisation |  | 21 |

|  | £m | £m |
|---|---|---|
| Berg plc:  purchase price |  | 600 |
| share capital | 250 |  |
| share premium | 50 |  |
| pre-acquisition profits | 300 |  |
|  | 600 |  |
| 80% thereof |  | 480 |
|  |  | 120 |

|  | £m |
|---|---|
| Annual amortisation | 30 |
| *Total amortisation charge 20X8* |  |
| Chang | 21 |
| Berg (6/12 × 30) to date of sale | 15 |
|  | 36 |

6    *Operating profit: acquisition of Chang*

|  | £m |
|---|---|
| Turnover | 1,200 |
| Cost of sales (795 – 5) | (790) |
| Distribution | (105) |
| Administration | (9) |
| Goodwill | (21) |
|  | 275 |

7    *Share of profit in associated company*

Berg became an associate 1.7.X8, so the share of the associate's profit is calculated as follows.

|  | £m |
|---|---|
| Berg: operating profit for the year | 228 |

|  | £m |
|---|---|
| 6/12 as associate from 1.7.X8 | 114 |
| Less inter company profit in stock | (3) |
|  | 111 |

|  | £m |
|---|---|
| Group share as associate 40% | 44.4 |
| Less goodwill (15×50%) | (7.5) |
|  | 36.9 |
| Less interest payable (8 × 50% × 40%) | (1.6) |
| Plus interest receivable (10 × 50% × 40%) | 2.0 |
| Less taxation (74 × 50% × 40%) | (14.8) |
|  | 22.5 |

Share of pre-tax profit disclosed £22.5m+£14.8m= £37.3m

8    *Profit on disposal of shares in Berg*

|  | £m | £m |
|---|---|---|
| Sale proceeds |  | 350 |
| Share capital | 250 |  |
| Share premium | 50 |  |
| P+L Reserve 1.1.X8 | 324 |  |
| 50% profits 20X8 (156 × 6/12) | 78 |  |
|  | 702 |  |
| 40% disposed of (½ of holding) |  | (280.8) |
|  |  | 69.2 |
| Less goodwill not written off at 1.7.X8 (45 × 40/80*) |  | (22.5) |
|  |  | 46.7 |

* Portion relating to disposal.

9    *Restructuring costs*

|  | £m |
|---|---|
| Wright (from cost of sales) | 14 |
| Berg (treated as post acquisition) | 20 |
|  | 34 |

10    *Interest receivable*

|  | £m |
|---|---|
| Wright | 15 |
| Berg (6/12) | 5 |
| Chang (9/12) | 15 |
|  | 35 |

11    *Interest payable*

|  | £m |
|---|---|
| Wright | 30 |
| Berg (6/12) | 4 |
| Chang (9/12) | 3 |
|  | 37 |

12    *Minority interest*

*Chang:*

|  | £m | £m |
|---|---|---|
| Turnover (W1) | 1,200 |  |
| Cost of sales (W2) | (795) |  |
| Fixed assets depn (W3) | 5 |  |
| Distribution (W3) | (105) |  |
| Administrative expenses (W4) | (9) |  |
| Interest payable (W11) | (3) |  |
| Interest receivable (W10) | 15 |  |
| Exceptional item | (20) |  |
| Taxation 80 × 9/12 (W13) | (60) |  |
|  | 228×20% | 45.6 |
| Berg: 20% × 156 × 6/12 |  | 15.6 |
|  |  | 61.2 |

13    *Taxation*

|  | £m |
|---|---|
| Wright | 1,320 |
| Berg (6/12) | 37 |
| Chang (9/12) | 60 |
|  | 1,417 |

(b)    BALANCE ON WRIGHT GROUP RESERVES 31 DECEMBER 20X8

|  | £m |
|---|---|
| Reserves  1 January 20X8 | 8,500 |
| Berg (post acquisition at January 1 20X8) (324 – 300) × 80% | 19 |
| Retained profit 20X8 (see part (a) above) | 2,763 |
| Goodwill written off (Berg for two years) | (60) |
|  | 11,222 |

*Alternative calculation*

|  | Wright £m | Berg £m |
|---|---|---|
| Reserves per question |  |  |
| Brought forward | 8,500 | 324 |
| Profit for year | 2,597 | 76 |
|  | 11,097 | 400 |
|  |  |  |
| Profit on sale of shares in Berg | 50 |  |
| Provision for unrealised profit | - | (3) |
|  | 11,147 | 397 |
|  |  |  |
| Berg: pre-acquisition |  | (300) |
|  |  | 97 |
|  |  |  |
| Share of Berg: 40% × 97 | 39 |  |
| Chang: (228 (W12) – 100) × 80% | 102 |  |
|  |  |  |
| Less amortisation of goodwill |  |  |
| Berg:120(W5) × ½ × ¾ | ((45) |  |
| Chang: (W5) | (21) |  |
|  | 11,222 |  |

## 10   PREPARATION QUESTION: ACQUISITIONS VS MERGERS

In attempting to deal with accounting for business combinations both the ASC and ASB required that acquisition accounting be used in all cases except where merger accounting is appropriate. The standards issued have attempted to define those limited instances when merger accounting should be used.

### Results from mergers vs acquisitions

It is true that acquisition accounting and merger accounting result in significantly different results in the year of combination and thereafter. This comes about because, in acquisition accounting, the results of the acquired company are brought into the group accounts from the date of acquisition. In addition assets are included at fair value, ie at their cost to the acquirer. Conversely, in a merger the results of the two companies are combined as if both companies had always been one. Assets are included at original cost/value and reserves are not identified as pre- or post-acquisition.

### FRS 6

Whilst differences in reporting could be narrowed by only allowing acquisition accounting, there are some instances where merger accounting is the appropriate method as the combination is in fact a coming together of two enterprises where neither is the acquirer or acquiree. To use acquisition accounting under these circumstances would distort the true and fair view. Because merger accounting will usually enhance the financial statements, accounting standards have attempted to limit those instances when merger accounting is appropriate to those business combinations where a true merger has occurred, ie where there is no significant outflow of funds from the group.

FRS 6 removed areas of subjectivity. The five criteria which require merger accounting to be used are as follows.

(a)   No party to the combination is portrayed as either acquirer or acquired, either by its own board or management or by that of any other party to the combination.

(b) All parties to the combination, as represented by the boards of directors or their appointees, participate in establishing the management structure for the combined entity and in selecting the management personnel and such decisions are made on the basis of a consensus between parties to the combination rather than purely by exercise of voting rights.

(c) The relative sizes of the combining entities are not so disparate that one party effectively dominates the combined entity merely by virtue of its relative size.

(d) No more than an immaterial proportion of the fair value of the consideration received is represented by non-equity consideration or equity shares carrying substantially reduced voting or distribution rights.

(e) No equity shareholders of any of the combining entities retain any material interest in the future performance of part only of the combined entity.

FRS 6 states that, in applying these criteria, it is important to consider the **substance** and not just the form of the arrangement. It also requires extensive and onerous disclosures to enable users of the financial statements to understand the combination.

**Conclusion**

As can be seen, the accounting standards relating to business combinations have narrowed differences in reporting by ensuring that merger accounting is only used in exceptional circumstances when specific criteria apply. No choice is allowed in accounting for a business combination, which means that financial statements should reflect the reality of a business combination. Whilst removing the merger accounting option may seem to simplify the area of business combination accounting, to do so would result in those true mergers being accounted for as acquisition, so distorting the true and fair view of the group.

## 11 GROWMOOR

> **Tutor's hint**. Mergers are likely to be rarer in future because of the strict criteria of FRS 6 which look at the substance of the transaction, not at the legalistic rules. You must also be aware of the CA 1985 rules, however, because these can halt the use of merger accounting and they are included, in effect, in the FRS 6 provisions.
>
> **Examiner's comment**. Parts (a) and (b) were very well answered. Answers to parts (c)(i) were mixed. In part (c)(ii), marks were awarded for calculations consistent with parts (c)(i). In general candidates were well prepared and the question was well answered.

(a) (i) The FRS 6 and CA 1985 criteria can be considered separately.

*CA 1985*

CA 1985 lays out the following criteria for merger accounting to be used.

(1) At least 90% of the nominal value of the relevant shares in the undertaking acquired must be held by the group.

*· 90% E to be held by the group.*

(2) This must be achieved as a result of an arrangement providing for the issue of equity shares by the parent company (or one or more of its subsidiaries).

*· Issue of E*
*i.e. The consideration*

(3) The fair value of any consideration other than equity shares must not exceed 10% of the nominal value of the equity shares issues.

*· Fv of "NON E issue"*
*< 10% of E (N.v) issued*
*CASH paid*

(4) Adoption of the merger method must accord with generally accepted accounting principles or standards.

*GAAP / Stds.*

Point (1) is satisfied by the combination envisaged here as the group holds 240,000 + 1,200,000 = 96% shares, which is Smelt's share capital. Point (2) is

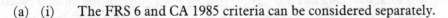

*[handwritten margin notes:*
*FV of the 'issued shares' ie. given*
*1 shares = 1.5m (x6).*
*2 cash.      (M).*
*Issue → consideration → paid cash £164000.*
*Receipt 240000s*
*? 10% > NV of shares (fixed) total 1.5m.]*

satisfied by Growmoor's issue of equity shares. The scheme fails on point (3), however, because the cash payment of £164,000 for the first 240,000 shares in Smelt is greater than 10% of the nominal value of the shares issued (£1,500,000 × 10% = £150,000). *[handwritten: £1/s]*

If the company forced the holders of the remaining 4% of Smelt's shares to sell under the same terms (as they can do under company law), the shares issued as consideration would increase by £75,000, but this is not sufficient to avoid the merger failing (10% × £1,500,000 + 75,000 = £157,500).

### FRS 6

Each of the five criteria under FRS 6 must be assessed in turn.

(1) **Neither party is portrayed as the acquirer or acquired**

*[handwritten margin: Acger/ee]*

FRS states that a premium on acquisition in the share for share exchange may indicate that an acquirer/acquiree situation exists. For the share exchange here, the following figures apply.

|  | £'000 |
|---|---|
| Value of shares given on consideration (1,500 × £1.20) | 1,800 |
| Value of shares acquired (1,200 × £1.30) | 1,560 |
| Premium on acquisition | 240 |

Although a premium would indicate that Growmoor was acting as the acquiring company, the exchange price is in the region of recent market prices for Smelt shares (£1.20 to £1.50), which explains why it was necessary to pay a premium, ie the premium was not paid merely as a cost of obtaining control over Smelt.

In addition, other circumstances indicate a merger, for example the fact the Growmoor is the company facing the closure of its head office and related redundancies, not Smelt.

(2) **All parties set up a management structure and select personnel based on consensus**

*[handwritten margin: All parties]*

The board is evenly divided between directors of the two companies. The managerial selection procedure is based on consensus.

(3) **Relative sizes are not disparate**

The nominal share values of Growmoor and Smelt are comparable, but it is necessary to consider the proportion of the equity of the combined entity held by each group of shareholders. If one is more then 50% larger than the other then an acquisition should be assumed, although this presumption is rebuttable.

|  | Shares held '000 |
|---|---|
| Shareholders of Growmoor | 1,625 |
| Shareholders of Smelt | 1,500 |

This criterion is therefore satisfied, even though the offer has only obtained 80% of Smelt shares. Note that although 80% has been acquired through the recent acquisition, the total is 96%. *[handwritten: 1200/1500.  240/1500]*

(4) **A substantial part of the consideration comprises equity shares**

FRS 6 required share purchases up to two years before the combination to be taken into account, which includes here the purchase of 240,000 shares on 15 June 20X4. FRS 6 uses the CA 1985 criteria, as discussed above, relating to non-equity consideration and so the combination would fail on this criterion to be treated as a merger.

(5) **No equity shareholders of the combination retains a material interest in the performance of only part of the combined entity**

The proposed combination satisfies this criterion because the contingent consideration is dependent on a specific liability crystallising, not upon the future performance of the combined entity.

(ii) The proposed merger fails under the CA 1985 rule of a 10% limit on non-equity consideration. In order to avoid this, the directors could authorise a small bonus issue, say one for every eight shares held, so that the number of shares offered as consideration is $1,500,000 \times 9/8 = 1,687,500$. The cash paid for the first share purchase (£164,600) is now less than 10% of the nominal value of the shares offered as consideration.

(b) **FRS 7** tackled the problem in acquisition accounting of the practice of attributing the **lowest values possible to the net assets** acquired so **that the goodwill figure** is correspondingly increased. Goodwill is generally deducted direct from reserves, the profit and loss account is bypassed, and profits are enhanced when the low asset values are subsequently charged against them in depreciation.

The commonest method of reducing the net assets acquired has been by establishing **provisions for reorganisation and restructuring costs,** reflecting the changes the acquirer intends to make to the business it has acquired. Since such provisions allow the subsequent expenditure to bypass the profit and loss account, the costs disappear into a 'black hole' as far as reported profits are concerned; and the profits of the acquirer benefit from the increased earnings resulting from the reorganisation, without bearing the costs involved.

In attributing fair values to assets and liabilities acquired, FRS 7 states that the basic principle is that fair values should reflect the circumstances at the time of the acquisition, and should not reflect either the acquirer's intentions or events subsequent to the acquisition. Thus, the assets and liabilities recognised are restricted to those of the acquired entity that existed at the date of acquisition, and **exclude** both provisions for reorganisation costs to be carried out by the acquirer and provisions for future losses. Such items are to be treated as part of the post-acquisition results of the enlarged group.

(c) (i) If Beaten Ltd is purchased, the treatment in Growmoor's accounts would be as follows.

*Balance sheet*

|  |  |  | £ |
|---|---|---|---|
| Cost of investment (W1) |  |  | 402,550 |
| Creditor: | due < 1 year |  | 90,900 |
|  | due > 1 year |  | 311,650 |
|  |  |  | 402,550 |

*Profit and loss account*

| Finance charge (W2) | 3,355 |
|---|---|

*Workings*

Cost of borrowing.

1   *Deferred consideration*

|  | Amount payable £ | Discount factor @10% | PV of cost. £ |
|---|---|---|---|
| Year 1 | 100,000 | 0.909 | 90,900 |
| Year 2 | 150,000 | 0.826 | 123,900 |
| Year 3 | 250,000 | 0.751 | 187,750 |
|  | 500,000 |  | 402,550 |

2   *Finance charge*

    PAID       cost

Total finance charge  = £(500,000 – 402,550)

                      = £97,450

For one month to 31 July 20X6 = 10% × £402,550 × $^1/_{12}$ = £3,355

*Cost of investment*

The deferred consideration is a type of debt instrument. FRS 7 states that the fair value of deferred consideration should be calculated by discounting the amounts payable using the rate at which the company could borrow similar amounts. The rate applicable here is therefore 10%.

Each component is discounted to give a total cost to the acquirer of £402,550, with the same amount shown in creditors, split between within one year and over one year.

*Finance charge*

The difference between the amount paid and the cost of investment calculated above is the finance charge, which should be charged as an interest expense in Growmoor's profit and loss account over the period of liability so that the annual cost gives a constant rate on the liability's carrying amount.

(ii)   Goodwill can be calculated as follows.

|  | £ |
|---|---|
| Cost of investment | 402,550 |
| Fair value of net assets acquired | 685,000 |
| Negative goodwill | (282,450) |

**Contingent consideration**

At the date of acquisition it is not possible to judge whether contingent consideration will be paid, or what amount it might be. It is therefore better to disclose details of the arrangement by a note to the accounts, rather than by making any provision.

**Deferred consideration**

*i.e D.C should be calculated to its PV.*

This has been calculated as shown in (i) above and no further adjustment will be made to goodwill as the payments are made. The cost of obtaining the benefit of deferred payment is charged to Growmoor's profit and loss account over the deferral period.   *= Interest*

**Service contracts**

It will be necessary to examine the service contracts given to Beaten's managers to determine whether they are in substance payment for services or part of the consideration for the shares in Beaten. If they are the latter, then a value must be assigned to them and which will be included in the goodwill calculation.

*of Cost of investment.*

*If contingency or deferred costs considered, then revision affect Reserve on acq.*

*cost ≠ 500000 but → 402,500 is given. Hence would affect gw if 500000 were used.*

(iii) **FRS 10** currently requires **negative goodwill** to be **recognised** and **separately disclosed** on the face of the balance sheet immediately below the goodwill heading.

There are other approaches. In particular in the **US**, negative goodwill is used to **reduce the separable net assets** to their cost to the acquiring company by proportionately writing down the value of the acquired company's fixed assets (other than any marketable securities). This is justified on the grounds that, although the separable net assets are worth more than the entity as a whole, the acquirer only had to pay the reduced amount. This may be criticised as arbitrary and it can seriously distort balance sheet values and thus mislead users.

An alternative is to assess the reasons negative goodwill arose and account for it accordingly, ie as an **expectation of future losses** or simply as a bargain. If the negative goodwill arose on an expectation of future losses as is (at least partly) the case with Beaten Ltd, it should be taken to a capital reserve and written off over the expected period of the losses.

## 12 MERGE AND ACQUIRE

> **Tutor's hint**. Part (a) of the question required you to analyse the current criteria for merger accounting under FRS 6 into various categories. Part (b) required the preparation of a group balance sheet and profit and loss account using merger accounting.
>
> _Prizewinners' points._ You may have classified the FRS 6 criteria in exactly the same way as the examiner, but if you didn't, you would still get credit provided you argued your case clearly.
>
> **Examiner's comment**. This question was well answered, although reserve movements were not well understood.

(a) **Verifiable signs of a merger**

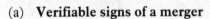

(i) No one party should have a dominant role or be the party which is 'acquired'. An example which would demonstrate that the party is seeking to control another party would be the issue of shares at a premium.

(ii) Only an immaterial proportion of the fair value of the consideration should be in the form of anything other than equity shares. (Under CA 1985 non-equity consideration is a maximum of 10% of the nominal value of the shares issued.)

(iii) Shares issued as consideration in a merger must not have reduced voting rights.

**Implied evidence of a merger**

(i) All parties must be involved in arriving at the management structure of the merged businesses. Where the senior management team is mostly drawn from personnel of only one of the combining parties then it is unlikely the combination is a merger in the terms of FRS 6.

(ii) The relative sizes of the combining parties must not be so disparate that it would dominate the other. There would be a presumption of dominance if one party is more than 50% larger than each of the parties to the combination.

(iii) Similarly there may be implied evidence that a true merger has occurred if the strategy for the combined business and its future corporate policies are determined by all parties to the combination.

**Anti avoidance terms** *Ll fyle to prevent creating a superficial merger.*

(i) All the arrangements made in conjunction with the business combination must be considered.

(ii) If equity shareholders are able to redeem or exchange the shares issued for other forms of non-equity consideration, then this will be taken into account in determining the maximum non-equity consideration.

(iii) Merger accounting cannot be used where an entity emerges as being sold off by a larger party. The entity sold off will not have established itself in its own right.

*Note.* The CA 1985 and FRS 6 merger accounting criteria are met (see (W6)).

(b) MERGE GROUP PLC
PROFIT AND LOSS ACCOUNT FOR THE YEAR ENDED 30 NOVEMBER 20X7

|  | £'000 |
|---|---:|
| Turnover | 39,285 |
| Cost of sales | (31,400) |
| Gross profit | 7,885 |
| Distribution and administration (W1) | (5,884) |
| Operating profit | 2,001 |
| Reorganisation expenses | (156) |
| Investment income (W2) | 200 |
| Profit before taxation | 2,045 |
| Taxation (W3) | (639) |
| Profit after taxation | 1,406 |
| Dividends (W4) | (256) |
| Retained profit of year | 1,150 |

MERGE GROUP PLC
BALANCE SHEET AT 30 NOVEMBER 20X7

|  | £'000 | £'000 |
|---|---:|---:|
| Fixed assets (W5) |  | 6,164 |
| Current assets (W10) | 9,780 |  |
| Creditors: amounts falling due within one year (W11) | (4,932) |  |
| Net current assets |  | 4,848 |
| Total assets less liabilities |  | 11,012 |
| Called up share capital |  | 2,500 |
| Share premium (W7) |  | 342 |
| Revaluation reserve |  | 260 |
| Other reserves (W9) |  | 75 |
| Profit and loss account (W8) |  | 7,835 |
|  |  | 11,012 |

*Workings*

1 *Distribution and administration expenses*

|  | £'000 |
|---|---:|
| Merge | 3,310 |
| Acquire | 2,730 |
|  | 6,040 |
| Less acquisition costs | (156) |
|  | 5,884 |

Acquisition costs are shown as an exceptional item in the combined P&L account.

*HB.*

**2**   *Investment income*

|  | £'000 |
|---|---|
| Merge | 200 |
| Acquire | 100 |
|  | 300 |
| Less inter company dividend | (100) ✓ |
|  | 200 |

**3**   *Taxation*

|  | £'000 |
|---|---|
| Merge | 365 |
| Acquire | 274 |
|  | 639 |

**4**   *Dividends*

|  | £'000 |
|---|---|
| Pre merger dividend — *by Acq.* | 48 |
| Merge plc proposed dividend | 208 |
|  | 256 |

**5**   *Fixed assets*

|  | £'000 |
|---|---|
| Merge | 4,099 |
| Acquire | 3,590 |
|  | 7,689 |
| Less cost of investment in Acquire (W6) | (1,525) |
|  | 6,164 |

**6**   *Merger accounting criteria*

Note (iv) in the question states that the FRS 6 and CA 1985 criteria regarding the non-equity element of the purchase consideration have not been tested.

The number of shares issued must be calculated.

|  |  | £'000 |
|---|---|---|
| Acquire share capital £1 shares |  | 1,250 *Shares* |
| Nominal value of shares represented by cash equivalent taken |  |  |
| Cash paid | 36,000 ✓ |  |
| Compulsory acquisition |  |  |
|     8,000 × 2.25 | 18,000 |  |
|     Cash paid | 54,000 |  |
|     divided by £2.25 |  | (24) |
|  |  | 1,226 |
| Shares issued 6/5 × 1,226 |  | 1,471 *Shares* |

*merger a/c.*

|  | £'000 |
|---|---|
| ∴ Purchase consideration: Shares 1,471 × £1 (at nominal value) | 1,471 ✓ |
| Cash | 54 |
|  | 1,525 ✓ |

|  | £'000 |
|---|---|
| Purchase consideration at fair value |  |
| Shares 1,471 × £2.50 | 3,678 |
| Cash | 54 |
|  | 3,732 |

Under CA 85 the non-equity consideration must not exceed 10% of the nominal value of the shares issued.

$$\frac{54}{1,525} \times 100 = 3.5\%$$ *∴ Passes test.*

Under FRS 6, all but an immaterial proportion of the fair value of the consideration is non-equity.

CASH $\dfrac{54}{3,732} \times 100 = 1.4\%$

Therefore the criteria under both FRS 6 and CA 85 are met and the transaction fully meets the merger accounting criteria.

7    *Share premium account*

|  | £'000 |
|---|---:|
| Balance per question | 400 |
| Less issue costs | (58) |
|  | 342 |

8    *Profit and loss account*

|  | £'000 |
|---|---:|
| Merge | 4,052 |
| Acquire | 3,725 |
|  | 7,777 |
| Add back issue costs charged to share premium account | 58 |
|  | 7,835 |

9    *Merger difference*

|  | £'000 |
|---|---:|
| Cost of investment | 1,525 |
| Share capital acquired (1,250 + 250) | 1,500 |
|  | 25 |

The merger difference is eliminated against other reserves of Merge: 100 – 25 = 75.

10    *Current assets*

|  | £'000 |
|---|---:|
| Merge | 5,530 |
| Acquire | 4,350 |
|  | 9,880 |
| Less intercompany dividend *proposed* | (100) |
|  | 9,780 |

11    *Creditors: amounts falling due within one year*

|  | £'000 |
|---|---:|
| Merge | 2,502 |
| Acquire | 2,530 |
|  | 5,032 |
| Less intercompany dividend *proposed* | (100) |
|  | 4,932 |

# 13    PREPARATION QUESTION: FOREIGN CURRENCY

(a)    The two alternative methods of foreign currency translation now in general use and which are featured in SSAP 20 are the temporal method and the closing rate method.

**Temporal method**

Under the temporal method, non-monetary items are translated at the exchange rates ruling at the time the relevant transactions occurred. Where non-monetary items, such as property, have been revalued they are translated at the exchange rates applicable at the time the revaluation occurred. Monetary items are translated at the closing rate; theoretically they should also be translated at the rate applicable at the time the transaction occurred but, for practical purposes, the transactions giving rise to monetary assets are assumed to have occurred at the end of the period. The theoretical exchange rate for monetary liabilities would be the future exchange rate when the liability would be settled. Since this is unknown, the year end rate is used as a reasonable surrogate. All translation gains and losses are taken to the consolidated profit and loss account.

### Temporal: justification

The theoretical justification for the use of the temporal method, which treats all foreign currency gains and losses as realised in the same way that transaction gains and losses are realised, is that the foreign currency operations of the subsidiary or branch are an extension of the activities of the parent or head office. The investment by the parent in the foreign currency denominated assets of the subsidiary or branch are considered to be historical events to be recorded at the historical cost to the shareholders of the parent. Thus the cost should be recorded at the cost to the parent in its own currency and this historical cost does not change as a result of subsequent changes in the exchange rate.

Monetary assets and liabilities, on the other hand, are seen as accruing directly to the parent and their value depends on changes in the exchange rate. Since changes in their value due to changes in the exchange rate affect the wealth of the parent it is considered appropriate that such changes should be reflected immediately in the parent's consolidated profit and loss account.

### Temporal: practical situations

The temporal method is considered to be an appropriate method of accounting for foreign currency translation where the trade of the foreign enterprise (branch or subsidiary) is more dependent on the economic environment of the investing company's currency than on that of its own reporting currency. This might occur, for example, when the foreign entity is essentially merely an extension of the business or the operations of the investing entity, such as operating as an agent for the investing entity.

### Closing rate method

The closing rate method, on the other hand, takes the view that the investing entity invests in the net worth of the foreign branch or subsidiary and that any gains or losses on translating non-monetary items are partially offset by corresponding losses or gains on the monetary assets and liabilities. Furthermore, the net resulting gain or loss on the net investment is regarded as a non-realised change in the value of the shareholders' investment in the foreign currency entity, due to the long term nature of the investment, from which it is implied that there is no intention to liquidate the investment in the foreseeable future. Consequently such translation gains and losses are recorded as changes in capital reserves and are transferred to realised reserves only when and to the extent that the related foreign currency denominated investment is disposed of.

### Closing rate method: practical situations

Thus the closing rate method is considered to be more appropriate to circumstances where the foreign currency denominated investment is regarded as being separate from the operations of the investor entity and not dependent on the economic environment of the investor entity's currency. This is the typical situation in which the branches and subsidiary companies of most major UK industrial and commercial companies operate and the closing rate method is the more usual in the UK.

(b) **Problems with temporal method**

Under the restricted conditions required by SSAP 20, the use of the temporal method is considered reasonable although it does give rise to some anomalies. For example, where a foreign currency denominated asset which produces income denominated in the same currency is financed 100% by loans denominated in the same currency, the temporal method produces gains and losses in the profit and loss account when the exchange rate changes.

This would not seem to correspond with economic reality since the foreign currency loan would fully hedge the foreign currency asset. It would seem more appropriate to limit the accounting exposure to the net investment if any.

**Problems with closing rate method**

On the other hand, the closing rate method produces charges or credits to reserves that can only properly be explained in bookkeeping terms unless they are considered to be a reflection of revaluations upwards or downwards. The subsequent transfer of these unrealised reserves to realised reserves makes more economic sense and is intuitively more understandable.

**Summary and conclusion**

On balance the closing rate method is considered more closely to reflect the underlying economic reality of an investment by a company in a foreign branch or subsidiary. Changes in the exchange rate do not in fact have the same economic effect as the temporal rate would imply; for example an investment in a subsidiary in a country whose currency devalues may become more valuable not less valuable depending on the effect of the devaluation on that country's relative competitive position. Thus the closing rate method correctly defers recognition of a profit or loss which is better reflected in subsequent cash flows whether from trading income or from disposal of the investment.

## 14 GOLD

> **Tutor's hint**. This question looks at the effect of inflation on accounting for foreign currency transactions. You would be advised to avoid a question like this in the exam as it is on a fairly peripheral subject.
>
> *Prizewinners' points.* If you were so familiar with the details of UITF 9 as to be able to attempt this question, you're probably on course for a prize.
>
> **Examiner's comment**. This question was well answered (perhaps because only the better candidates dared attempt it).

(a) The following factors will be taken into account if the *closing rate* is to be used:

(i) The foreign operation will be separate or independent.

(ii) The normal operations will be denominated in the local currency.

(iii) The normal operations are likely to be (at least partially) financed locally.

(iv) The foreign company will have a management team committed to maximisation of the local currency profits.

(v) The financial statements of the foreign company will be expressed in the local currency as the best indicator of the performance locally.

However, the *temporal method* will be appropriate when:

(i) The foreign company is merely an extension of the investing company operations overseas.

(ii) The foreign company is dependent upon the investing company for financing.

(iii) The foreign company cash flows have a material impact on those of the investing company.

(iv) The majority of the transactions are denominated in the investing company currency.

Factors which may be taken into account in determining the functional currency include the following.

(i) Pricing and market conditions. Are they determined locally or by the investing company?

(ii) Does the foreign operation buy goods and services locally or rely on imports?

(iii) How is the foreign operation financed? Locally or by the investing company?

(iv) What is the extent of inter company trading?

(v) The stability and marketability of the currency used in the country where the foreign operation is trading should be taken into account.

(b) If the effects of hyper inflation are not adjusted before translation, major distortions of the group accounts can occur.

The management of the parent will be better equipped to analyse the trading performance of the subsidiary if the hyper inflationary effects are stripped out.

Many of the emerging markets are subject to hyper inflation and in many large multinational groups it is essential that the effects are identified and adjusted for. SSAP 20 ignores the effect of hyper inflation in the translation process, hence the need for UITF 9.

(c) (i)

(1)

| | Value (E million) | Exchange rate | £m |
|---|---|---|---|
| 30 November 20X3 | 20 | 1.34 | 14.93 |
| 30 November 20X7 | 20 | 17.87 | 1.12 |

(A material reduction in value)

(2)

| | Value E million | Index | Exchange rate | £m |
|---|---|---|---|---|
| 30 November 20X7 | 20 × | 3254/100 | 17.87 | 36.42 |

(3)

| | Value E million | E/$ rate | Value $ m | £/$ rate | £m |
|---|---|---|---|---|---|
| 30 November 20X7 | 20 | 0.93* | 21.51 | 0.66 | 14.2 |

* The original cost is translated into a stable currency at the date when the subsidiary was set up.

(ii) In example (1) the tremendous reduction is due to severe exchange rate movements and has nothing at all to do with trading performance from the assets.

In example (2) a paper gain emerges simply as a result of revaluation locally, again this has little to do with trading performance and reflects an unrealised holding gain measured locally.

In example (3) the cost of the asset is effectively 'frozen' by using a stable currency as the original measurement base. The asset is then treated as if it were a dollar monetary amount not a fixed asset. The value of the hotel is then determined by the movement of the $/£ exchange rate and the effects of local price inflation and also the value of the property are then ignored.

As can be seen none of these methods are wholly satisfactory and UITF 9 allows 'other appropriate methods' to eliminate the distortions caused by hyper inflation.

## 15 FOREIGN

> **Tutor's hint.** You had to prepare a set of consolidated financial statements for a group with a foreign subsidiary. Adjustments had to be made for depreciation, cash in transit, fair value and inter-company items. The question is quite difficult and looks at the issues in a very practical way. Don't worry if you didn't get part (b) completely right. As long as it followed through your answer in part (a) you will get credit. In part (c) you had to discuss problems with SSAP 20. These are dealt with comprehensively in the BPP Study Text.
>
> **Examiner's comment.** Most candidates handled this tricky question quite well, although answers to part (c) were rather disappointing.

(a) XY

CONSOLIDATED BALANCE SHEET AS AT 31 DECEMBER 20X7

|  | £m |
|---|---|
| Intangible fixed asset (goodwill) (W3) | 4 |
| Tangible fixed assets (W5) | 1,340 |
| Net current assets (W6) | 872 |
| Long term creditors (W8) | (558) |
|  | 1,658 |
| | |
| Share capital | 330 |
| Share premium | 350 |
| Reserves (W10) | 918 |
|  | 1,598 |
| Minority interests (W4) | 60 |
|  | 1,658 |

XY GROUP
CONSOLIDATED PROFIT AND LOSS ACCOUNT
FOR THE YEAR ENDED 31 DECEMBER 20X7

|  | £m |
|---|---|
| Turnover (W11) | 2,230 |
| Cost of sales (W11) | (1,434) |
| Gross profit | 796 |
| Administrative and distribution expenses (W11) | (430) |
| Goodwill amortisation (W3) | (4) |
| Exchange gains (W9) | 3 |
| Interest payable | (42) |
| Profit before tax on ordinary activities | 323 |
| Taxation (W11) | (109) |
| Profit after tax on ordinary activities | 214 |
| Minority interest (W11) | (7) |
| Dividend | (20) |
|  | 187 |

*Workings*

**(1)** *Translation of subsidiary balance sheet* 31/12/X7.

|  | KRm | Rate | £m |
|---|---|---|---|
| Net assets | 1420 | 5 | 284 |
| Share capital | 240 | 4 | 60.0 |
| Share premium | 80 | 4 | 20.0 |
| Pre-acquisition profits | 610 | 4 | 152.5 |
| Post-acquisition profits | 490 | (bal fig) | 51.5 |
|  | 1,420 | | 284.0 |

*Note*. The closing rate method is stipulated in the question. The net assets are translated using the rate at 31 December 20X7 (5). Share capital and pre-acquisition profits are translated using the rate in force when XY acquired its interest in AG, 30 April 20X6 (4). Post-acquisition profits then become a balancing figure.

**(2)** *Translation of subsidiary profit and loss account*

|  | KRm | Rate | £m |
|---|---|---|---|
| Turnover | 3,060 | 5.1 | 600 |
| Cost of sales | (2,550) | 5.1 | 500 |
| Gross profit | 510 | | 100 |
| Administration and distribution expenses | (51) | 5.1 | (10) |
| Interest payable | (102) | 5.1 | (20) |
| Profit before tax | 357 | | 70 |
| Taxation | (153) | 5.1 | (30) |
| Profit after tax | 204 | | 40 |
| Dividends | (52) | 5.2 | (10) |
|  | 152 | | 30 |

*Note*. Dividends are translated using the rate in force when the dividend was paid, otherwise the average rate is used as stated in the question.

**(3)** *Calculation of goodwill arising on acquisition of AG*

|  | KR | £m | £m |
|---|---|---|---|
| Cost of investment 270 – 50 | | | |
| (loan see question note (ii)) | | | 220 |
| Share capital | | 60.0 | |
| Share premium | | 20.0 | |
| Pre-acquisition profits | | 152.5 | |
| | | 232.5 | |
| 80% thereof | | | (186) |
| Revaluation | | | |
| Fair value | 1,040 | | |
| Net assets at acquisition | | | |
| KR (240 + 80 + 610) | 930 | | |
| Increase | 110 | | |
| Translated at 4 KR/£1 = | | 27.5 | |
| 80% thereof | | | (22) |
| Goodwill | | | 12 |

Amortisation: £4m pa

Question note (iii) states that amortisation is over a three year period and that no time apportionment applies, therefore unamortised goodwill at 31 December 20X7 is £4m.

The fair value adjustment of £27.5m will lead to an additional depreciation charge of £5.5m pa which is incorporated in the consolidated balance sheet and profit and loss account workings (W5 and W6).

4    *Minority interests*

|  | £m |
|---|---|
| Share capital | 60.0 |
| Share premium | 20.0 |
| Reserves (152.5 + 51.5) | 204.0 |
| Revaluation | 27.5 |
| Depreciation (W5) | (11.0) |
| Intercompany (W7) | (5.0) |
| Translation gain (W9) | 3.0 |
|  | 298.5 |
|  |  |
| 20% thereof | 59.7 |

5    *Tangible fixed assets*

|  | £m |
|---|---|
| Per b/s |  |
| XY | 945.0 |
| AG per translated b/s | 378.0 |
| Revaluation (W3) | 27.5 |
| Less depreciation | (11.0) |
|  | 1,339.5 |

6    *Net current assets*

|  | £m |
|---|---|
| XY | 735 |
| AG | 129 |
| Intercompany (W7) | (5) |
| Cash in transit (W7) | 13 |
|  | 872 |

7    *Inter company stock transfers*

| Sale price: AG to XY | KR 104m | (all unsold 31 Dec 20X7) |
|---|---|---|
| Profit | KR 25m | |
| Transacted at 5.2 KR/ £1 | = £5m | |
| 80% thereof = | £4m | |

As the transaction is from subsidiary to parent an adjustment of the minority interest is required (£1m). Cash in transit of KR 65m is translated at KR 5.0/ £1 = £13m. Turnover and cost of sales in the consolidated profit and loss account will be reduced by 104 KR/ 5.2= £20m. The net adjustment to opening and closing stock will be:

|  |  | £m |
|---|---|---|
| Opening stock | (Note (i)) | 2 |
| Closing stock | (above) | 5 |
| Adjustment |  | 3 |

8    *Long-term creditors*

|  | £m |
|---|---|
| XY | 375 |
| AG | 223 |
| Intercompany (W9) | (40) |
|  | 558 |

9    *Inter company loan*

The loan from XY to AG is not a permanent loan (KR 65 repaid). The loan is retranslated at the closing rate and the exchange difference taken to the profit and loss account.

|  | KRm |
|---|---|
| Loan £50m × 5.3 | 265 |
| Repaid | 65 |
|  | 200 |

| | |
|---|---|
| At closing rate (KR5/£1) | £40m |
| Loan in the parent books: | £50m |

Repayment was £13m (KR 65/5.0) so an exchange gain of £3m (13 – 10) arises (group 80%, MI 20%).

## 10   Reserves

|  | XY £'m | AG £'m |
|---|---|---|
| XY – per question | 895.0 | 51.5 |
| AG – post-acquisition (W1) |  | ((11.0) |
| Fair value depreciation |  | 3.0 |
| Translation gain (W9) | - | (5.0) |
| Provision for unrealised profit (W7) | 895.0 | 38.5 |
| | | |
| Share of AG: 38.5 × 80% | 30.8 | |
| | | |
| Less amortisation of goodwill: 2 × £4m (W3) | (8.0) | |
| | 917.8 | |

## 11   Consolidated profit and loss account working schedule

|  | XY £m | AG £m | Inter Co £m | Minority £m | Goodwill £m | Total £m |
|---|---|---|---|---|---|---|
| Turnover | 1,650 | 600 | (20) (W7) |  |  | 2,230 |
| Cost of sales | (945) | (500) | 20 |  |  |  |
| Stock |  |  | (3) (W7) |  |  | (1,428) |
| Gross profit | 705 | 100 | (3) |  |  | 802 |
| Admin and dist | (420) | (10) |  |  |  | (430) |
| Exchange gain |  | 3 (W9) |  |  |  | 3 |
| Depreciation |  | (5.5) (W3) |  |  |  | (5.5) |
| Amortisation of goodwill |  |  |  |  | (4) (W3) | (4) |
| Interest | (22) | (20) |  |  |  | (42) |
| Taxation | (79) | (30) |  |  |  | (109) |
|  | 184 | 37.5 | (3) |  | (4) | 214.5 |
| Minority interest |  |  |  |  |  |  |
| (37.5 – 3) × 20% |  |  |  | (6.9) |  | (6.9) |
| Inter group div | 8 | (8) |  |  |  |  |
| Dividend | (20) |  |  |  |  | (20) |
|  | 172 | 29.5 | (3) | (6.9) | (4) | 187.6 |

Note that the elimination of the inter group dividend reflects the sterling receipt by XY, translated rate in force at the date of payment. If the weighted average rate was used an exchange difference would arise.

The cost of sales figure (1,428) is increased by the additional depreciation (5.5) for publication purposes.

## 12   Exchange differences on translation of subsidiary

|  | KRm | Rate | £m |
|---|---|---|---|
| Net assets at 31 Dec 20X6 | 1,268 | 4.6 | 275.7 |
| Share capital | 240 | 4 | 60.0 |
| Share premium | 80 | 4 | 20.0 |
| Pre-acquisition profits | 610 | 4 | 152.5 |
| Post-acquisition profits | 338 | Balance | 43.2 |
|  | 1,268 |  | 275.7 |

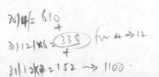

*XY Acd · Act on 30/4/X6.*

|  | £m |
|---|---|
| Post acquisition profits 31 December 20X6 | 43.2 |
| Post acquisition profits 31 December 20X7 (W1) | 51.5 |
| Increase  *X6→X7 ·* | 8.3 |
| Retained profit for year (W2) | 30.0 |
| Exchange loss | 21.7 |
| *Ex. Loss* Attributable to the group: 80% × 21.7 | 17.4 |

*Note.* The total exchange difference arises from retranslation of the opening equity interest at 5KR/£1 instead of 4.6KR/£1= £22.1m and the profit and loss account for the year translated using the weighted average rate compared with the closing rate (152/5 – 30)= £0.4m.

The difference is therefore:

(22.1 – 0.4) × 80%= £17.4m.

(b)  MOVEMENT ON CONSOLIDATED RESERVES

|  | £'m |
|---|---|
| Reserves as at 1 January 20X7 (W) | 747.6 |
| Retained profit for the year | 187.6 |
| Exchange loss (W12, part (a)) | (17.4) |
|  | 917.8 |

*Working: reserves as at 1 January 20X7*

|  | £'m | £'m |
|---|---|---|
| XY: 895 – 172 |  | 723.0 |
| AG: Opening net assets (W12, part (a)) | 275.7 |  |
| Net assets at acquisition: (240 + 80 + 610) ÷ 4 | 232.5 |  |
|  | 43.2 |  |
| Opening PUP | (2.0) |  |
| Fair value depreciation charged in 20X6 | (5.5) |  |
|  | 35.7 |  |
| Group share: 80% |  | 28.6 |
|  |  | 751.6 |
| Less amortisation of goodwill (W3) |  | 4.0 |
|  |  | 747.6 |

(c)  *A critical review of SSAP 20*  *FCT ·*

*· T· DATE*

(i)  SSAP 20 notes that transactions should be recorded at the rate in force at the date the transaction occurred. Should this be invoice date, delivery date or order date?

*Ave.Rate·*

(ii)  No guidance is given in SSAP 20 as to the calculation of an average rate. Why use an average when actual rates are known?

*NRA as  monma.*

(iii)  Some balance sheet items are not readily identifiable as monetary or non-monetary items for translation purposes. Certain types of securities held for investment purposes have this ambiguity.

*Hedge accounting &  fwd contracts*

(iv)  The treatment of hedge accounting and forward contracts is only dealt with by SSAP 20 to a limited extent. However, FRS 13 and the ASB work on derivatives has helped to clarify matters.

*FI*

114

(v) The treatment of cumulative exchange differences and the net investment in a foreign subsidiary when all or part of it is sold is not specifically covered by SSAP 20. Further questions arise.

   (1) Should the historic cost or current rate be used to calculate goodwill?

   (2) Should the rate to be used for elimination of intercompany profits be the closing or average rate?

(vi) The volume of overseas transactions and the proliferation of the use of derivatives and similar instruments makes a revision of SSAP 20 quite an urgent task for the ASB.

# 16   PREPARATION QUESTION: CASH FLOW STATEMENTS

CASH FLOW STATEMENT FOR THE YEAR ENDED 31 DECEMBER 20X6

|  | £ | £ |
|---|---|---|
| Net cash inflow from operating activities (Note 1) | | 121,756 |
| Returns on investments and servicing of finance | | |
| Interest paid | | (18,300) |
| Taxation | | |
| Corporation tax paid | | (15,000) |
| Capital expenditure | | |
| Purchase of fixed assets (W5) | (342,000) | |
| Purchase of investments (W5) | (10,000) | |
| Receipts from sale of fixed assets (W4) | 19,700 | |
| Receipts from sale of investments (W4) | 27,000 | |
| Net cash outflow from investing activities | | (305,300) |
| Equity dividends paid | | (10,000) |
| Financing | | |
| Issue of share capital | 212,800 | |
| Bank loan taken up | 20,000 | |
| Redemption of debentures | (30,000) | |
| Net cash inflow from financing | | 202,800 |
| Decrease in cash | | (24,044) |

NOTES TO THE CASH FLOW STATEMENT

1   *Reconciliation of operating profit to net cash inflow from operating activities*

|  | £ |
|---|---|
| Operating profit (W1) | 104,842 |
| Depreciation (W3) | 56,700 |
| Profit on disposal of assets (W3) | (2,400) |
| Profit on disposal of investments (W4) | (10,395) |
| Increase in stocks £(89,301 – 77,667) | (11,634) |
| Increase in debtors £(75,630 – 61,739) | (13,891) |
| Decrease in creditors £(69,872 – 71,338) | (1,466) |
| | 121,756 |

2   *Reconciliation of net cash flow to movement in net debt*

|  | £ |
|---|---|
| Decrease in cash in the period | (24,044) |
| Cash to repurchase debentures | 30,000 |
| Cash received from new bank loan | (20,000) |
| Conversion from debt to equity | 12,000 |
| Change in net debt | (2,044) |
| Net debt at 1 January 20X6 | (154,068) |
| Net debt at 31 December 20X6 | (156,112) |

3    *Analysis of changes in net debt*

| | At 1 January 20X6 £ | Cash flows £ | Other changes £ | At 31 December 20X6 £ |
|---|---|---|---|---|
| Cash at bank | 25,932 | (21,932) | | 4,000 |
| Overdraft | - | (2,112) | | (2,112) |
| | | (24,044) | | 1,888 |
| Debt due < 1 year | (42,000) | 30,000 | 12,000 | |
| Debt due > 1 year | (138,000) | (20,000) | | (158,000) |
| | (154,068) | (14,044) | 12,000 | (156,112) |

| | |
|---|---|
| Cash flows | (14,044) |
| Other changes | 12,000 |
| Change in debt | (2,044) |

*Workings*

1    *Profit before tax*

| | £ |
|---|---|
| Increased in retained profit £(131,542 – 80,000) | 51,542 |
| Dividends | 8,000 |
| Taxation | 17,000 |
| Transfer to general reserve (W2) | 10,000 |
| Interest | 18,300 |
| | 104,842 |

2    *Transfer to general reserve*

| | £ |
|---|---|
| Increase £(97,000 – 70,000) | 27,000 |
| Revaluation of office buildings | 17,000 |
| Transfer from profit and loss account | 10,000 |

3    *Depreciation*

| | Buildings £ | Machinery £ | Vehicles £ | Total £ |
|---|---|---|---|---|
| At 31.12.X6 | 120,000 | 105,000 | 30,000 | |
| At 31.12.X5 | 100,000 | 95,000 | 27,000 | |
| Increase in provision | 20,000 | 10,000 | 3,000 | 33,000 |
| On disposals | 13,000 | 10,000 | 700 | 23,700 |
| Provision for the year | 33,000 | 20,000 | 3,700 | 56,700 |

*Profit on disposal of fixed assets*

| | |
|---|---|
| On vehicle loss | (100) |
| Buildings | 500 |
| Machines | 2,000 |
| | 2,400 |

4    *Sale of fixed assets and investments*

| | Book value £ | Profit £ | Sale proceeds £ |
|---|---|---|---|
| Building | 17,000 | 500 | 17,500 |
| Machines | - | 2,000 | 2,000 |
| Vehicle | 300 | (100) | 200 |
| | | | 19,700 |
| Investments | 16,605 | 10,395 | 27,000 |

5   *Purchase of fixed assets*

| | *Buildings* | *Machinery* | *Vehicles* | *Total* |
|---|---|---|---|---|
| | £ | £ | £ | £ |
| Cost at 31.12.X6 | 487,000 | 500,000 | 116,000 | 1,103,000 |
| Cost at 31.12.X5 | 440,000 | 290,000 | 55,000 | 785,000 |
| Increase | 47,000 | 210,000 | 61,000 | 318,000 |
| Revaluation | 17,000 | | | 17,000 |
| | 30,000 | | | 301,000 |
| Disposals | 30,000 | 10,000 | 1,000 | 41,000 |
| Purchases | 60,000 | 220,000 | 62,000 | 342,000 |

*Purchase of investments*

| | £ |
|---|---|
| Cost at 31.12.X6 | 11,395 |
| Cost at 31.12.X5 | 18,000 |
| | (6,605) |
| Disposals | 16,605 |
| Purchases | 10,000 |

6   *Issue of shares*

| | *Number* | *Nominal value* £ | *Share premium* £ |
|---|---|---|---|
| At 31.12.X5 | 1,200,000 | 300,000 | 20,000 |
| Issued for loan stock converted | 16,000 | 4,000 | 8,000 |
| | 1,216,000 | 304,000 | 28,000 |
| 1 for 4 rights issues | 304,000 | 76,000 | 136,800 |
| | 1,520,000 | 380,000 | 164,800 |
| 3 for 8 bonus issue | 570,000 | 142,500 | (142,500) |
| | 2,090,000 | 522,500 | 22,300 |

Only movements involving flow of funds:

Rights issue for £(76,000 + 136,800) =                                £212,800

*Note*. This answer assumes that the only tax and dividends paid during the year were the current liabilities at 31.12.X5 also that the revaluation of buildings was added to 'cost'.

17   **HEBDEN**

**Tutor's hint**. At this level, a consolidated statement is certain to be required; make sure that you can deal with the complications that this involves, including associated undertakings and minority interests. Cash flow statements are a race against time, and marks will be awarded for the format as well as the calculations. Review your answer and look for presentation, easy marks and the trickier areas – work through these again.

HEBDEN GROUP
CONSOLIDATED CASH FLOW STATEMENT
FOR THE YEAR ENDED 31 JULY 20X6

|  | Note | £m |
|---|---|---|
| Cash flows from operating activities | 1 | 939 |
| Dividend received from associate (W1) |  | 435 |
| Returns on investment and servicing of finance | 2 | (290) |
| Taxation | 2 | (500) |
| Capital expenditure | 2 | (1,070) |
|  |  | (486) |
| Acquisitions and disposals | 2 | 196 |
| Dividends paid (400 + 800 – 600) |  | (600) |
|  |  | (890) |
| Financing | 2 |  |
|   Issue of shares |  | 4,906 |
|   Increase in debt |  | 1,374 |
| Increase in cash in the period |  | 5,390 |

*Reconciliation of net cash flow*
*to movement in net funds*     3

|  |  | £m |
|---|---|---|
| Increase in cash in the period   36u0 – 9070 |  | 5,390 |
| Cash inflow from increase in debt and lease financing |  | (1,374)✓ |
| New finance leases |  | (1,700)✓ |
| Other changes |  | (6)✓ |
| Movement in net funds in the period |  | 2,310 |
| Net funds at 1.8.X5 |  | 1,900 |
| Net funds at 31.7.X6 |  | 4,210 |

)sec(W3)

NOTES TO THE CASH FLOW STATEMENT

1    *Reconciliation of operating profit to operating cash flows*

|  | £m |
|---|---|
| Consolidated operating profit | 2,965 |
| Depreciation charges | 650 |
| Increase in stocks (3,950 – 2,000 – 64) | (1,886) |
| Increase in debtors (3,700 – 2,550 – 56) | (1,094) |
| Increase in creditors (1,000 – 560 – (170 – 34)) | 304 |
| Net cash inflow from operating activities | 939 |

2    *Analysis of cash flows for headings netted in the cash flow statements*

|  | £m | £m |
|---|---|---|
| *Returns on investment and servicing of finance* |  |  |
| Interest paid (W2) | (174) |  |
| Interest element of finance lease rental payments | (100) |  |
| Dividends from fixed asset investments | 80 |  |
| Minority interests (W3) | (96) |  |
|  |  | (290) |
| *Taxation* |  |  |
| UK corporation tax paid (W4) |  | (500) |
| *Capital expenditure* |  |  |
| Purchase of plant and machinery (4,200 – 1,700 – 330) | (2,170) |  |
| Sale of plant and machinery (W5) | 1,100 |  |
|  |  | (1,070) |
| *Acquisitions and disposals* |  |  |
| Purchase of subsidiary undertakings (note 4) | (28) |  |
| Net cash balances acquired with subsidiary (note 4) | 224 |  |
|  |  | 196 |

|  | £m | £m |
|---|---:|---:|
| *Financing* |  |  |
| Issues of ordinary share capital (W6) | 4,906 |  |
| Debt due in over one year |  |  |
| New loan repayable in 1.8.20Y5 (W7) | 2,900 |  |
| Capital element of finance lease rental payments (W8) | (1,526) |  |
|  |  | 6,280 |

## 3  Analysis of net funds

|  | At 1.8.X5 | Cash flow | Other non-cash changes | At 31.7.X6 |
|---|---:|---:|---:|---:|
|  | £m | £m | £m | £m |
| Cash in hand, at bank | 3,640 → | 5,390 ← | ← | → 9,030 |
| Debt due > 1 yr | - | (2,900) | (6) | (2,906) |
| Finance leases | (1,740) | 1,526 | (1,700) | (1,914)   480 + 1434. |
|  |  | (1,374) ✓ |  |  |
|  | 1,900 | 4,016 ← | → (1,706) | 4,210 |

## 4  Purchase of subsidiary undertaking

|  | £m | £m |
|---|---:|---:|
| *Net assets acquired* |  |  |
| Plant and machinery | 330 |  |
| Stocks | 64 |  |
| Debtors | 56 |  |
| Cash at bank and in hand | 224 |  |
| Creditors | (170) |  |
|  | 504 × 75% | 378 |
| Goodwill (balance) |  | 200 |
|  |  | 578 |
| *Satisfied by* |  |  |
| Shares allotted |  | 550 |
| Cash |  | 28 |
|  |  | 578 |

*Workings*

### 1  Dividend from associate

|  | £m | £m |
|---|---:|---:|
| Balance at 1.8.X5 |  | 2,000 |
| Profit and loss account income | 990 |  |
| Less taxation | (355) |  |
|  |  | 635 |
|  |  | 2,635 |
| Less balance at 31.7.X6 |  | (2,200) |
| Dividend received |  | 435 |

### 2  Interest paid

|  | £m |
|---|---:|
| Balance at 1.8.X5 | 60 |
| From profit and loss account | 300 |
| Discount on debt (W7) | (6) |
| Interest element: finance lease | (100) |
| Balance at 31.7.X6 | (80) |
| Interest paid | 174 |

3    *Minority interests*

|  | £m |
|---|---:|
| Balance at 1.8.X5 | - |
| Profit for the year | 200 |
| Acquisition of Hendry Ltd (504 × 25%) | 126 |
|  | 326 |
| Balance at 31.7.X6 | (230) |
| Paid to minority interests | 96 |

4    *UK corporation tax paid*

|  | £m | £m |
|---|---:|---:|
| Creditor b/f |  | 434 |
| Deferred tax balance b/f |  | 26 |
|  |  | 460 |
| Profit and loss account charge (782 + 208) |  | 990 |
| Tax on acquisition of Hendry plc |  | 34 |
|  |  | 1,484 |
| Creditor c/f | 924 |  |
| Deferred tax balance c/f | 60 |  |
| Tax paid |  | (984) |
|  |  | 500 |

5    *Sale of plant and machinery*

|  | £m |
|---|---:|
| Cost | 1,000 |
| Accumulated depreciation | 200 |
|  | 800 |
| Profit on sale | 300 |
| Proceeds | 1,100 |

6    *Issue of ordinary share capital*

|  | £m | £m |
|---|---:|---:|
| Balance b/f |  |  |
| Share capital |  | 4,000 |
| Share premium |  | 4,190 |
|  |  | 8,190 |
| Purchase of subsidiary |  |  |
| Ordinary shares |  | 440 |
| Premium |  | 110 |
|  |  | 8,740 |
| Balance c/f |  |  |
| Share capital | 7,880 |  |
| Share premium | 5,766 |  |
|  |  | 13,646 |
| Issue proceeds |  | 4,906 |

7    *Long-term loans*

|  | £m |
|---|---:|
| Balance at 31.7.X6 | 2,906 |
| Less finance cost discount (6.2% – 6.0%) × 3,000 | (6) |
| Cash inflow | 2,900 |

8     *Capital element of finance lease payments*

|  | £m | £m |
|---|---|---|
| Balance b/f |  |  |
| Due within one year |  | 400 |
| Due over one year |  | 1,340 |
|  |  | 1,740 ✓ |
| New leases undertaken |  | 1,700 ✓ |
|  |  | 3,440 |
| Balance c/f |  |  |
| Due within one year | 480 ✓ |  |
| Due over one year | 1,434 ✓ |  |
|  |  | 1,914 |
| Capital repaid — *see c flow* |  | 1,526 ✓ |

# 18    CARVER

> **Tutor's hint**. You must be able to deal with all the complications shown in the question, ie the discount, depreciation, profit on sale, assets and liabilities acquired from new subsidiary etc. Also don't forget premiums on share issues.
>
> **Examiner's comments**. Although workings to part (a) were often correct, candidates sometimes put figures in the wrong place in the statement. Answers to (b) were weak.

(a)   CARVER PLC
      CONSOLIDATED CASH FLOW STATEMENT
      FOR THE YEAR ENDED 30 SEPTEMBER 20X4

|  | Note | £'000 | £'000 |
|---|---|---|---|
| Cash flows from operating activities | 1 |  | 372 |
| Dividends from associates (W2) | 2 |  | 250 |
| Returns on investments and servicing of finance | 2 |  | 7 |
| Taxation (W9) |  |  | (250) |
| Capital expenditure and financial investment | 2 |  | (585) |
| Acquisitions and disposals | 2 |  | 98 |
| Equity dividends paid (200 + 400 − 300) |  |  | (300) |
| *Cash outflow before financing* |  |  | (408) |
| Financing | 2 |  |  |
| Issue of shares | 2 | 2,453 |  |
| Increase in debt | 2 | 650 |  |
|  |  |  | 3,103 |
| Increase in cash in the period |  |  | 2,695 |

|  | Note |  |  |
|---|---|---|---|
| *Reconciliation of net cash flow to movement in net funds* | 3 |  |  |
| Increase in cash in the period |  |  | 2,695 |
| Cash inflow from increase in debt and lease financing |  |  | (650) |
| Change in net debt resulting from cash flows |  |  | 2,045 |
| New finance leases |  |  | (850) |
| Other change |  |  | (40) |
| Movement in net debt in period |  |  | 1,155 |
| Net funds at 1 October 20X3 |  |  | 950 |
| Net funds at 30 September 20X4 |  |  | 2,105 |

NOTES TO THE CASH FLOW STATEMENT

1    *Reconciliation of operating profit to operating cash flows*

|  | £'000 |
|---|---|
| Operating profit | 1,485 |
| Depreciation charges (W1) | 325 |
| Profit on sale of machinery | (100) |
| Increase in stocks (1,975 – 1,000 – 32) | (943) |
| Increase in debtors (1,850 – 1,275 – 28) | (547) |
| Increase in creditors (500 – 280 – 68) | 152 |
| Net cash inflow from operating activities | 372 |

2    *Analysis of cash flows for headings netted in the cash flow statement*

|  | £'000 | £'000 |
|---|---|---|
| *Returns on investments and servicing of finance* | | |
| Interest paid (W3)* | (100) | |
| Dividends from fixed asset investment | 155 | |
| Dividends paid to minority interest (W4) | (48) | |
| | | 7 |
| *Capital expenditure and financial investment* | | |
| Purchase of tangible fixed assets (W5) | (1,085) | |
| Sale of tangible fixed assets | 500 | |
| | | (585) |
| *Acquisitions and disposals* | | |
| Purchase of subsidiary undertaking | (14) | |
| Cash balances acquired with subsidiary | 112 | |
| | | 98 |
| *Financing* | | |
| Issue of ordinary share capital (W6) | | 2,453 |
| Debt due beyond a year (W7) | 920 | |
| Capital element of finance lease rental payments (W8) | (270) | |
| | | 650 |
| | | 3,103 |

\* There is not sufficient information in the question to identify separately interest on finance leases.

3    *Analysis of changes in net debt*

|  | *At 1 Oct 20X3* | *Cash flow* | *Other changes* | *At 30 Sept 20X4* |
|---|---|---|---|---|
|  | £'000 | £'000 | £'000 | £'000 |
| Cash at bank | 1,820 | 2,695 | - | 4,515 |
| Debt due > 1yr | (500) | (920) | (40) | (1,460) |
| Finance leases | (370) | 270 | (850) | (950) |
|  | | (650) | | |
|  | 950 | 2,045 | (890) | 2,105 |

*Workings*

1    *Depreciation charges*

|  | £'000 | £'000 |
|---|---|---|
| Freehold buildings (2,200 – 2,075) | | 125 |
| Plant | | |
| Closing balance | 1,200 | |
| Opening balance | 1,100 | |
| | 100 | |
| Depreciation on disposal | 100 | |
| | | 200 |
| | | 325 |

2   *Dividends from associates*

|  | £'000 | £'000 |
|---|---|---|
| Opening balance | | 1,000 |
| Share of profit | 495 | |
| Taxation | (145) | |
| | | 350 |
| | | 1,350 |
| Closing balance | | 1,100 |
| | | 250 |

3   *Interest*

|  | £'000 |
|---|---|
| Accrued interest b/f | 30 |
| P & L account | 150 |
| Discount | (40) |
| Less accrued interest c/f | (40) |
| | 100 |

4   *Minority interests*

|  | £'000 |
|---|---|
| Opening balance | - |
| Profit for year | 100 |
| On acquisition | 63 |
| | 163 |
| Closing balance | (115) |
| Cash outflow | 48 |

5   *Purchase of tangible fixed assets: machinery*

|  | £'000 | £'000 |
|---|---|---|
| Cost at 30 September 20X4 | | 3,000 |
| Cost at 1 October 20X3 | | 1,400 |
| | | 1,600 |
| Disposal | | 500 |
| | | 2,100 |
| On acquisition | 165 | |
| Leased | 850 | |
| | | (1,015) |
| Cash outflow | | 1,085 |

6   *Issue of ordinary share capital*

|  | £'000 | £'000 |
|---|---|---|
| Closing balance | | |
| Shares | 3,940 | |
| Premium | 2,883 | |
| | | 6,823 |
| Non-cash consideration | | |
| Shares | 220 | |
| Premium | 55 | |
| | | (275) |
| Opening balance | | |
| Shares | 2,000 | |
| Premium | 2,095 | |
| | | (4,095) |
| Cash inflow | | 2,453 |

7    *Issue of loan stock*

|  | £'000 |
|---|---|
| Closing balance | 1,460 |
| Opening balance | 500 |
|  | 960 |
| Finance cost | 40 |
| Cash inflow | 920 |

8    *Capital payments under leases*

|  | £'000 | £'000 |
|---|---|---|
| Opening balances |  |  |
| Current |  | 200 |
| Long-term |  | 170 |
|  |  | 370 |
| New lease commitment |  | 850 |
| Closing balances |  |  |
| Current | 240 |  |
| Long-term | 710 |  |
|  |  | (950) |
| Cash outflow |  | 270 |

9    *Taxation*

|  | £'000 | £'000 |
|---|---|---|
| Opening balance |  |  |
| Corporation tax | 217 |  |
| Deferred tax | 13 |  |
|  |  | 230 |
| Profit and loss account transfer (391 + 104) |  | 495 |
| Closing balances |  |  |
| Corporation tax | 462 |  |
| Deferred tax | 30 |  |
|  |  | (492) |
|  |  | 233 |
| On acquisition |  | 17 |
| Cash outflow |  | 250 |

(b)  (i)    In relation to capitalised interest, FRS 1 states that cash outflows from returns on investments and servicing of finance includes interest paid, even if capitalised.

The capitalised interest should therefore be included in the 'Returns on investment and servicing of finance' section, increasing interest paid from £100,000 to £105,000. The purchase of fixed assets under 'Capital expenditure and financial investment' will be reduced from £1,085,000 to £1,080,000.

(ii)   FRS 1 gives the following definitions.

'*Cash*
Cash in hand and deposits repayable on demand …, less overdrafts … repayable on demand. Deposits are repayable on demand if they can be withdrawn at any time without notice and without penalty or if a maturity or period of notice of not more than 24 hours or one working day has been agreed.'

'*Liquid resources*
Current asset investments held as readily disposable stores of value. A readily disposable investment is one that:

(a)   is disposable by the reporting entity without curtailing or disrupting its business;
(b)   and is either:

(i)    readily convertible into known amounts of cash at or close to its carrying amount; or
(ii)   traded in an active market.'

Applying these definitions to the figures given in the question produces the following changes to the cash flow statement.

There will be a new note to the accounts

| | £'000 | £'000 |
|---|---|---|
| *Management of liquid resources* | | |
| Payments into short-term deposits | (1,125) | |
| Sale of government securities | 1,500 | |
| Purchase of corporate bonds | (1,550) | |
| *Net cash outflow from management of liquid resources* | | (1,175) |

The cash in hand, bank overdraft and bank figures are only included in cash. The increase in cash for the period is now (15 – 65 + 1,890) – (10 – 770 + 1,080) = 1,520. This represents a change from the original statement of 2,695 – 1,520 = 1,175, which represents the outflow from management of liquid resources.

Changes are also required in the analysis of change in net debt for the overdrafts, cash and current asset investments.

# 19   LANGUAGE-EASE

> **Tutor's hint.** This is a very long question. You must take some time to go through it, highlighting important points, because otherwise your solution will be meaningless. Your answers in part (a) should follow on from each other - do not look at each section in isolation. Make sure that you leave time for part (b) which should represent straightforward marks.
>
> This practical scenario is an excellent test of your report-writing skills. Before you write you report, make sure you have thought clearly through the requirements, identified the key issues and decided on a structure for your report. Remember, the examiner will be far more impressed by relevant comments than by dozens of calculations.
>
> In (b) notice that the question gives a clue as to the basis of valuation.
>
> When you review your answer, don't be over-awed by the suggested solution. It would be impossible to achieve in the time. Concentrate on assessing whether you made sufficient relevant points to achieve half marks. Also, in the exam it's better to keep calculations in a separate appendix to the report.
>
> *Prizewinners' points.* If you made all the points we make in our answer, well done. However, to get a pass you need only make the **main points**. The comparison of the cost of new fixed assets with internally generated funds is desirable, but not essential.
>
> **Examiner's comment.** Candidates need additional practice with attention given to establishing such matters as the overall picture, key balance sheet and performance aspects and the relationships between various ratios. This is an important part of the syllabus and requires continuing emphasis on the part of candidates. Performance is improving and this improvement needs to be maintained.

(a)
REPORT

To:     Joseph Tan
From:   Joyce Asprey
Date:   25 November 20X6
Re:     *Student Food Ltd*

This report examines the results of Student Food Ltd for the years 20X4 and 20X5 and the draft unaudited results for 20X6. The report falls into three parts.

(i)     General commentary/changes in the period
(ii)    Steps to improve profitability
(iii)   Initial valuation

### General commentary/changes in the period

The company has made some radical changes over the last few years and this has had a severe impact on the company's results.

*Fixed asset expenditure*

Student Food Ltd has invested heavily in fixed assets, as follows.

| | £ |
|---|---|
| 20X5 = £(5,000 + 7,500 + 4,000) × 40 | 660,000 |
| 20X6 = £12,500 × 40 | 500,000 |
| Total | 1,160,000 |

This represents an increase of 1,160/650 = 179% on 20X4 gross cost. This increase is partly due to expansion and partly due to health and safety problems. It has been almost entirely funded by loan finance as no new equity has been raised. The impact on turnover has been a rise of only (1,240 – 900)/900 = 38%.

The detailed financing picture can be produced by comparing the cost of new fixed assets with internally generated funds, increases in loan finance and movements in working capital, as follows.

| | 20X5 | | 20X6 | |
|---|---|---|---|---|
| | £'000 | £'000 | £'000 | £'000 |
| Cost of new fixed assets | | 660 | | 500 |
| *Financing* | | | | |
| Internally generated | | | | |
| Profit/(loss) | 33 | | (16) | |
| Deprecation | 60 | | 100 | |
| Dividends | (36) | | - | |
| | | (57) | | (84) |
| Loan capital | | (240) | | (520) |
| | | 363 | | (104) |
| *Working capital* | | | | |
| Increase in stocks | | 120 | | 40 |
| Increase in debtors | | 200 | | 120 |
| Increase in creditors | | (300) | | (76) |
| (Increase)/decrease in bank | | (383) | | 20 |
| | | (363) | | 104 |

It is clearer now how the purchase of fixed assets has been financed.

| | % |
|---|---|
| Loan finance: 760/1,160 | 66 |
| Internally generated funds: (57 + 84)/ 1,160 | 12 |
| Decrease in working capital: (363 – 104)/1,160 | 22 |
| | 100 |

No funds have been raised through the issue of share capital.

*Depreciation*

The depreciation charge is very low and requires further attention. A large part of the fixed asset expenditure has been on fixtures and fittings during 20X5 and 20X6 ((£7,500 + £12,500) × 40 = £800,000) and yet the rental agreements on the shops have only four years left to run from the end of 20X6. This would indicate that the depreciation charge is too low and that fixtures and fittings (and perhaps other assets) are being depreciated over lives which are too long).

*Working capital*

The company could not fund working capital requirements out of internally generated funds (as well as being unable to fund the purchase of fixed assets). Student Food Ltd has become totally reliant on loans for its capital requirements. In addition, the level of creditors has increased rapidly. The individual components of working capital are as follows.

*Stock turnover*

| 20X4 | 20X5 | 20X6 |
|---|---|---|
| $\dfrac{900-252}{240}=2.7$ | $\dfrac{1,200-272}{360}=2.58$ | $\dfrac{1,240-320}{400}=2.3$ times |

Stock turnover has decreased, perhaps reflecting falling demand (and therefore higher stocks). Shelf life should be investigated in case stock is out of date or about to be so. The level of stock write-offs for 20X4 and 20X5 and projected for 20X6 should be checked.

*Debtors/sales*

The level of debtors to sales has risen from 160/900 = 17.8% in 20X4 to 480/1,240 = 38.7% and this must also be checked. Are the outlets switching from cash to credit sales (in which case this rise is acceptable), or is Student Food Ltd granting extended credit to the outlets because of the related party situation? The credit offered may not be on normal commercial terms.

*Liquidity*

The current and acid test ratios are as follows.

| | | *Current* | *Acid test* |
|---|---|---|---|
| *20X4* | $\dfrac{480}{160}\,/\,\dfrac{480-240}{160}$ | 3 | 1.5 |
| *20X5* | $\dfrac{720}{763}\,/\,\dfrac{720-360}{763}$ | 0.94 | 0.47 |
| *20X6* | $\dfrac{880}{819}\,/\,\dfrac{880-400}{819}$ | 1.07 | 0.58 |

However, the acid test ratio in 20X6 would have been much worse if the level of debtors had remained at 20X4 levels: $(1,240 \times 17.8\%)/819 = 0.27$.

*Creditors turnover*

| 20X4 | 20X5 | 20X6 |
|---|---|---|
| $\dfrac{900-252}{112}=5.79$ | $\dfrac{1,200-272}{431}=2.15$ | $\dfrac{1,240-320}{518}=1.78$ |

Based on cost of sales, creditors turnover has also declined significantly over the last three years as the company's reliance on creditors for funding has grown.

*Turnover*

The rise in turnover has not matched the increases in fixed assets as noted above. We can compare actual turnover achieved to the budgeted plans for each year. Expected sales:

| 20X5 | £5 × 4 × 15% (40 × 400 × 30) | = | £1,440,000 |
| 20X6 | £5 × 4 × 30% (40 × 400 × 30) | = | £2,880,000 |

In 20X5 the budgeted rise in turnover was (1,440 – 900)/900 = 60%. The actual turnover for 20X5 was (1,440 – 1,200)/1,440 = 16.7% below budget. The 20X6 forecast was for another 140% ((2,880 – 1,200) rise on the 20X5 actual turnover. This was extremely optimistic, and in fact the rise achieved was only 3.33% ((1,240 – 1,200)/1,200).

*Profitability*

The gross profit margin has fallen from 28% in 20X4 (252/900) to 22.7% in 20X5 (272/1,200) and 25.8% in 20X6 (320/1,240). This fall may be due to competition from local city centre restaurants, but it may also indicate that customers of the outlets are not keen on the product offered and improvements are required.

Profit before tax has fallen to a loss and expenses have increased as a percentage of turnover from 7.3% in 20X4 to 11.8% in 20X6. A breakdown of these expenses is required before they can be analysed properly.

The company is currently paying below-market rents. Rents at market levels would have been:

$$\frac{£6,000}{£1} \times £6.50 = £39,000$$

This would have a further adverse impact on profitability, creating greater losses in 20X5 and 20X6.

*Interest*

Examining interest charged for 20X6 only, it may be assumed that the interest accrued evenly on the bank overdraft for the year. Interest charged would be:

$$20\% \times \frac{(303 + 283)}{2} = £58,600$$

The rate of interest charged on the loan is therefore

$$\frac{84 - 58.6}{(240 + 760) \div 2} = 5.08\%$$

This is well below the market rate of 12% and this discrepancy must be investigated. It is possible that the loans have been obtained from related parties at favourable rates, or even that the loans have low initial interest rates and have not been treated correctly under FRS 4. The average loan charged at the market rate in 20X6 would increase the interest charge to 12% × (240 + 760)/2 = £60,000, giving a total interest charge of £99,000 and increasing the company loss dramatically.

*Conclusion*

Student Food Ltd has increased its sales over the period, but not in line with the rise in investments in fixed assets. Profitability has deteriorated and there are suspect figures in the account which must be investigated, ie low depreciation and low interest, plus the impact of market rents must be considered. The directors have been almost naively optimistic in their forecasts for the rise in turnover in 20X6.

The company's financing is based entirely on creditors, overdraft and debt; loans on their own exceeded shareholders' funds in 20X6. The company is facing a liquidity crisis as it is unlikely that the bank will continue to fund such a high overdraft. The interest rate charged on loans is also suspect and may be due to related parties.

**Steps to improve profitability**

There are many steps which could be taken.

*Cost of sales/expenses*

A breakdown is required of both these figures in order to identify potential savings. Each component can be compared to turnover on an outlet by outlet basis and large variations can be investigated. Purchasing procedures should be reviewed and there may be scope for switching to centralised buying by Language-ease Ltd to cut costs.

*Turnover/profitability*

The poor turnover figures (compared to budget) may reflect reduced prices which would affect the gross margin. Alternatively the fall is accounted for by cost rises (see above). If the sales prices are under pressure then marketing and selling strategies should be assessed, as well as product pricing.

Underperformance on an individual outlet basis may require staff changes or the introduction of staff incentive schemes. Competition from local city centre restaurants may be addressed using local advertising or offering enhanced product features.

*Asset management*

Investment in assets is very high and should be reduced. The management of both cash/debt and working capital should be improved.

The debt situation may be improved by injecting new investor funds, which would be contributed by Language-ease Ltd and thereby reducing the level of debt, particularly overdrafts.

Stock turnover should be improved by either reducing stock or increasing sales. One method would be to agree with each shop how many days stock should be held, taking into account the shelf life of the products. For example, by holding four weeks stock in the shops, the stock level will be reduced to:

$$\frac{4}{30} \times (1,240 - 320) = £122,667$$

A question arises here about how constant the number of meals per student is. If the 4 per week is an average of very variable figures, then the year end figures may be distorted.

This timing problem also applies to debtors. The level of debtors should also be reduced, but the figures require further investigation first, as noted above.

The creditors turnover figures could also be improved and creditors should be reduced as part of the overall improvement in the liquidity of the company. Credit terms may be renegotiated.

Fixed asset disposals could be considered, although fixtures and fittings are unlikely to have any sales value.

Budgets and forecasts should be recalculated, and a detailed cash forecast prepared.

(b) **Initial valuation**

An initial valuation should take account of the expected savings by Student Food Ltd.

|  | £'000 |
|---|---|
| Turnover (as 20X6) | 1,240 |
| Gross profit (at 42.5%) | 527 |
| Projected interest as currently stated | (84) |
| Depreciation at, say, 15% × 1,400 | (210) |
| Expenses, assumed as for 20X6 | (146) |
| Rental, as currently stated | (6) |
|  | 81 |
| Adjustments for: |  |
| Market interest (99 – 84) | (15) |
| Market rent (39 – 6) | (33) |
|  | 33 |

As Cold Pack Ltd aims for control of Student Food Ltd, it would be normal to use an earnings basis to value the company.

Using a P/E multiple of, say, 12, the price calculated on profit after interest without accounting for market rent or interest, is 12 × £81,000 = £972,000, or £2.43 per share. However, if the rent and interest figures are adjusted, the price falls to 12 × £33,000 = £396,000 or .99 per share.

An alternative method would be to use the net assets basis. Based on book values this would produce a price of (1,461 – 760)/400 = £1.75, but adjustments may be required to the book value of the assets (depending on recoverability of debtors etc).

## 20 OLD PARCELS

> **Tutor's hint.** Part (a) required a knowledge of the thinking behind the FRSSE and associated problems. Part (b), on share valuation, required a knowledge of current accounting standards and an application of common sense. The question was unusual in combining current accounting standards with share valuation. The solution depended on various assumptions and alternative solutions were possible.
>
> **Examiner's comment.** Part (a) was generally well answered. In part (b), however, candidates often failed to discuss and explain their calculations – if the calculations are wrong, credit cannot easily be given in the absence of supporting reasoning.

(a) The issues are as follows.

(i) The overriding objective is to provide users with reliable, relevant and useful information. There is **little difference** between a small and a large company **simply as a function of relative sizes**. A better definition of 'small' would be by reference to the **ownership and management** characteristics of the small companies.

(ii) The principles of recognition, measurement and disclosure used as a basis for developing an accounting framework, **apply as much** to small companies as to large companies. Should **alternative accounting standards**, aimed at small companies, deal with different methods of recognition, measurement and disclosure specific to small companies?

(iii) The **nature of accountability is different** for large companies and owner managed concerns. The nature of the accounts and the objectives of financial reporting should satisfy those differing needs. The accounting framework should follow the objectives.

(iv) The approach of the ASB has been to develop the FRSSE which uses size criteria to determine the nature of the company as **'small' or 'large'**. This seems an **illogical approach**.

(v) In reality, **cost savings** accruing from the introduction of the FRSSE are **minimal**. Most small companies use external accountants to produce financial statements. Such small companies face precisely the same problems in recognising, measuring and disclosing transactions as their larger cousins.

(vi) Many small companies do undertake **complex transactions** and the full standards will continue to be appropriate.

(vii) The FRSSE may **increase the work** involved in the production of the financial statements in the short term until the companies concerned fully appreciate the application of the FRSSE.

(viii) Despite the problems, the principle that accounting standards are not equally applicable to all companies remains valid. Perhaps the criteria need to be re-defined.

(b)  (i)    *Net assets basis*

A **dividend yield** basis is **inappropriate** because all of the family capital is being sold and the companies are to merge.

|  |  |  | *Valuation* £000 |
|---|---|---|---|
| (i) (1) | Intangible asset (licence) | | |
| | Estimated market value: £15,000. If valued on an income basis it is £10,000 discounted for two years at 8%: £17,832 – a prudent valuation uses market value. | | 15 |
| (ii) (2) | Tangible assets valued at going concern, so NRV is not used. Tax is ignored as the assets are not sold: 278 × 1.05 | | 292 |
| (3) | Current assets | | 835 |
| (4) | Creditors due within one year | | (365) |
| (iv) (5) | Creditors due after one year: | | |

The debenture could be calculated as the NPV of the future interest payments and redemption costs.

| | | £ |
|---|---|---|
| ie | Loan interest due 31.5.X9 6% × 100 | 6,000 |
| | Loan and premium due 31.5.X9 1·25 | 125,000 |
| | | 131,000 |

Discounted at 8% pa                                                (121)

(6)    Preference shareholders interests valued at NPV:

| | £ |
|---|---|
| Dividend 31.5.X9 £4,200; PV at 8% = | 3,889 |
| Dividend/redemption 31.5.Y0 | |
| (2,100 + 33,000) at 8% | 30,093 |
| | 33,982 |

(34)

(v) (7)    Deferred tax is ignored as it is subjective and the timing differences of New Parcels are in excess of the fall in net cumulative timing differences of Old Parcels.

(vi) (8)    Euro costs: these could be ignored or taken into account, depending upon the use to which New Parcels put the existing systems. Prudently they are included. The shareholders of Old Parcels would not include the costs of a replacement system.                          (30)

(9)    Share issue proceeds: we have assumed the options would be exercised, as the option price is less that the offer price.

30
622

$$\text{Value} = \frac{£622,000}{£170,000 + £30,000} = £3.11$$

(issued + options)

(ii)    *Earnings yield basis*

The **market value** is arrived at by multiplying the P/E ratio by the earnings per share. The results from **discontinued operations** should be **ignored**, although the FRSSE does not require them to be disclosed.

| | £'000 |
|---|---|
| Profits 20X4 - 20X8 | 216.0 |
| Less discontinued operations (20% × 216) | (43.0) |
| Less preference dividends (3 years × 7% × 30,000) | (6.3) |
| Less preference share redemption (510 + 554 + 603) | (1.7) |
| Net profit attributable to ordinary shareholders | 165.0 |
| | |
| Average (÷5) | 33 |

The projected profit is:

|  | £'000 |
|---|---|
| As forecast | 35.0 |
| Less preference dividend | (2.1) |
| Less redemption cost | (0.7) |
|  | 32.2 |

Therefore the average profit of £33,000 seems reasonable.

New parcels has a P/E of 14 but this should be marked down because:

- Profit growth is uncertain.
- Old Parcels is unquoted and the shares are less marketable.

However, the mark-down may be reduced because of the additional capital to flow in from the share options.

An appropriate P/E would be (say) 10.

Therefore market value is $\dfrac{10 \times £33,000}{200,000} = £1.65$

*Note.* If a P/E ratio of 14 was applied the value would be £2.31.

*Summary*

| Asset value basis | £3.11 |
|---|---|
| Earnings basis | £2.31- £1.65 |

## 21 PREPARATION QUESTION: FINANCIAL ANALYSIS

> **Tutor's hint**. This is a straightforward question on interpretation of accounts, of a manageable size and providing you with all the ratios you need. You should, as with all interpretation questions, spend some time *thinking* about the ratios before you start writing. Mark what you think are the significant trends shown in the question and make brief notes which will serve as an answer plan. Then proceed to discuss each area, using sensible headings to break your report up, and including a brief introduction and conclusion.

WANDAFOOD PRODUCTS
FIVE YEAR SUMMARY: 20X1 TO 20X5

| Prepared by: | An Accountant |
|---|---|
| Date: | 28 February 20X6 |

**Introduction**

This report discusses the trends shown in the five year summary prepared from the published accounts for the five years ended 31 December 20X5. It also considers how price changes over that period may have limited the usefulness of the historical cost data provided.

**Profitability**

The net profit margin has remained fairly constant, although it dropped in 20X3. Asset turnover has decreased over the five years, pulling back a little in 20X4. Return on capital (or return on assets), the primary ratio produced by combining these two secondary ratios, has therefore decreased over the period but was at its lowest in 20X3.

These findings seem to indicate that assets are not being used more efficiently and that this has caused the decrease in return on assets. Inflation may be responsible for increases in turnover which would mask even worse decreases in efficiency.

### Interest and dividend cover

Interest cover improved markedly between 20X1 and 20X2, falling back a little in 20X3 and 20X4 but now below the 20X1 level, indicating increases in debt and/or interest rates. Dividend cover, however, after dropping below 20X1 levels for three years, has now recovered some lost ground. In both cases cover was adequate, even at the lowest points; however, since there has been a substantial increase in gearing, interest cover ought to be watched carefully. Profits may be available to cover interest and dividends but this must be matched by good cash flow.

### Debt to equity

Debt: equity fell in 20X2 but has steadily increased until in 20X5 it was almost double its 20X1 level. Minority interests appear to have remained a relatively insignificant element in the group's funding. It is more likely that debt has increased than that equity has decreased (for example, because of a purchase or redemption of own shares). Interest cover has fallen in line with this increase in borrowing as a proportion of long-term capital.

### Liquidity

Both the current and the quick ratios have declined over the period, although in 20X2 they both improved. However, they have been fairly constant between 20X3 and 20X5 and are quite high, although comments on the adequacy of these ratios are of very limited utility in the absence of information about the company's activities and industry averages.

The reduction may have been planned to reduce the costs involved in maintaining high levels of stock and allowing generous credit to customers. From the differential between the quick and current ratios it would seem that stock is a significant asset here. However, current liabilities must not be allowed to increase to the extent that current assets (and especially liquid assets) are insufficient to cover them, as this can lead to a liquidity crisis. Worsening liquidity ratios can be an indicator of overtrading but this most often arises when expansion is funded from short-term borrowings, whereas here new long-term capital in the form of debt appears to have been found.

Because working capital has fallen in size, it is now being used more efficiently, generating more sales from a reduced base. It would seem likely, given the slight fall in asset turnover, that fixed asset turnover has worsened considerably and that the improvement in working capital turnover has compensated for this in calculating total asset turnover. It may be that long-term borrowings have financed capital expenditure which has not yet affected operations. (An increase in the amount of fixed assets would decrease fixed asset turnover if turnover did not increase correspondingly.)

### Investors' ratios

Earnings, dividends and net assets per share have all increased over the period. There has therefore been no need to increase dividends regardless of fluctuations in earnings.

The increase in net assets per share seems to indicate either that retained profits and borrowings have been used to increase fixed asset expenditure or (less likely) that assets have been revalued each year.

### Inflation

Historical cost accounts do not show the effect on the group's operating capacity of rising prices over a period. The modest increases in EPS and dividend do not suggest that profit has increased sufficiently to compensate for more than a very low level of inflation. It is also possible that the value of assets is understated, so that ROCE and asset turnover measures are all understated. The underlying trends in real terms may be very much worse than those shown in historical cost terms.

### Conclusion

The group would appear, from this superficial analysis, to be a steady performer but not expanding fast. This may be an advantage in times of recession: debt is probably not so high as to cause liquidity problems nor have shareholders come to expect a high payout ratio. However, inflation may be eroding its profits. The possible recent expansion of fixed assets may help it to grow in future, as will its improved working capital management.

## 22 THERMO

> **Tutor's hint.** Do not be alarmed by the length of our answer. Marks are awarded for all valid points made, and you will be expected to have made some but not all of the points we make. You *must* be clear as to the purpose of the report, to whom it is addressed and the key issues. Ratio analysis at this level requires an in-depth understanding of such issues. The key to success is ensuring your answer is targeted to the question set and is concise and to the point.
>
> Review the information and consider anything which is significant and useful to your report. Plan your headings. Produce a report which highlights in a logical order the most salient points. Do not go through the information on a line by line basis and comment on everything – you will run out of time.
>
> **Examiner's comment.** Candidates failed to achieve marks by not taking time to form a clear picture of the question requirement and rushing into calculations. Also too much time was spent on part (a), for only 9

(a)

**REPORT**

To:    ABC Bank
From:    An Accountant on behalf of Mike Reid and Jane Thurby
Date:    14 June 20X8
Subject:    Thermo Ltd trading performance for 20X7 and 20X8

This report looks at the trading performance of Thermo Ltd over the two full periods trading from incorporation on 1 July 20X6: 9 months to 31 March 20X7 and the year to 31 March 20X8. A detailed breakdown of ratios is given in an appendix to this report and these are generally based on the standard ratio table. Your ratios calculated for the period to 31 March 20X7 are included for comparison.

### Liquidity

The current ratio has risen slightly from 0.94 to 0.98, but the quick ratio has fallen from 0.71 to 0.58 as a result of the substantial lengthening of the stock turnover period. In addition, the overdraft has increased sharply, more than doubling between 20X7 and 20X8. In fact the company has now exceeded its overdraft limit of £175,000.

The creditor payment period and debtor collection period have remained almost static. However although the creditor payment period is within the 90 day normal credit period, the debtor collection period is much longer at 127 days in 20X8. This may indicate that debts are not being collected efficiently and that the company is having difficulty obtaining payment. A reduction in the collection period to match that relating to creditor payments would have improved cash flow by £190,539 – (£549,500 × $^{86}/_{365}$) = £61,068. This would reduce the overdraft to well within its limit.

### Profitability

As would be expected now that trading has become established, 20X8 profitability is far better than 20X7.

Return on share capital and reserves and asset turnover have reached respectable levels. The gross profit % has risen by over two points and this has partly contributed to the rise in operating profit % from almost zero to 9%. It can also be assumed that parts of the administrative and selling costs are fixed, and as these have been spread over 12 rather than 9 months, they are lower pro-rata which has boosted the operating margin.

The rise in the profit before tax % and profit after tax % has been diluted by the increase in interest payable and the fact that the company has incurred a tax charge for the year (at an effective rate of 21.7% (£6,637/£30,457).

### Gearing

In spite of the increase in the interest charge, the increase in operating profits has produced a much better interest cover figure for 20X8.

The steep rise in the bank overdraft has, however, had a significantly adverse impact on the bank/total liabilities vs net assets ratios. The improved interest cover should reassure the bank that, although its investment in the business is now almost the same as that of the owners, profits appear sufficient to pay the current level of interest charges.

### Cash generation

In 20X8, adding back depreciation of £20,150 to profit of £30,457, the company generated cash of £50,607 from trading activities. Increases in sales meant additional working capital was required and this rose by £125,525. This meant that there was a net cash outflow from operations of £74,918 (£125,525 – £50,607) which together with the capital investment of £36,750 was financed by the increase in the bank overdraft.

### Conclusion

The company seems to have established itself quite well in its market. Profitability figures are all reasonably healthy, particularly the 15.6% return on net assets and 19.35% gross profit %. It is, however, still rather early to say that the company has settled into a steady trading pattern.

The increase in sales has put pressure on liquidity due to increased working capital requirements and particularly because of the longer stockholding period. Although this has increased the bank's risk from a gearing perspective, it has comfort of a relatively high interest cover, showing that the company is currently able to service the overdraft.

### APPENDIX

| | | 12 months to 31.3.X8 | *(For comparison)* 9 months to 31 3.X7 |
|---|---|---|---|
| Current ratio | $\dfrac{338,917}{345,723}$ | 0.98 | 0.94 |
| | $(\dfrac{198,975}{211,787}$ | | 0.94) |
| Quick ratio | $\dfrac{(338,917-138,375)}{345,723}$ | 0.58 | 0.71 |
| | $\dfrac{(198,975-47,775)}{211,787}$ | | 0.71) |
| Creditor payment | $\dfrac{125,675}{(443,170+138,375-47,775)}\times365$ | 86 days | 85 days |
| | $(\dfrac{93,445}{(252,787+47,775-0)}\times365\div12\times9$ | | 85 days) |

*BPP* PUBLISHING

| | | 12 months to 31.3.X8 | (For comparison) 9 months to 31 3.X7 |
|---|---|---|---|
| Debtor collection | $\dfrac{190{,}539}{549{,}500} \times 365$ | 127 days | 136 days |
| | $(\dfrac{151{,}200}{304{,}500} \times 365 \div 12 \times 9$ | | 136 days) |
| Stock turnover period | $\dfrac{138{,}375}{443{,}170} \times 365$ | 114 days | 52 days |
| | $(\dfrac{47{,}779}{252{,}787} \times 365 \div 12 \times 9$ | | 52 days) |
| *Profitability* | | | |
| Return on share capital and reserves | $\dfrac{30{,}457}{195{,}021}$ | 15.6% | (2.22%) |
| | $(\dfrac{(3{,}799)}{171{,}201}$ | | (2.22%)) |
| Net asset turnover | $\dfrac{549{,}500}{195{,}021}$ | 2.82 | 1.78 |
| | $(\dfrac{304{,}500}{171{,}201}$ | | 1.78) |
| Gross profit % | $\dfrac{106{,}330}{549{,}500}$ | 19.3% | 17% |
| | $(\dfrac{51{,}713}{304{,}500}$ | | 17%) |
| Operating profit % | $\dfrac{48{,}912}{549{,}500}$ | 9% | 0.04% |
| | $(\dfrac{123}{304{,}500}$ | | −0.04%) |
| Profit before tax % | $\dfrac{30{,}457}{549{,}500}$ | 5.5% | − 1.25% |
| | $(\dfrac{(3{,}799)}{304{,}500}$ | | − 1.25%) |
| Profit after tax % | $\dfrac{23{,}820}{549{,}500}$ | 4.3% | − 1.25% |
| | $(\dfrac{(3{,}799)}{304{,}500}$ | | − 1.25%) |
| *Gearing* | | | |
| Interest cover | $\dfrac{48{,}912}{18{,}455}$ | 2.65 | 0.03 |
| | $(\dfrac{123}{3{,}922}$ | | 0.03) |

|  |  | *12 months to 31.3.X8* | *(For comparison) 9 months to 31 3.X7* |
|---|---|---|---|
| Total liabilities/tangible net worth | $\dfrac{345,723}{(195,021+786)}$ | 1.77 | 1.24 |
|  | $(\dfrac{211,787}{171,201}$ |  | 1.24) |
| Book debt/tangible net worth | $\dfrac{188,235}{(195,021+786)}$ | 0.96 | 0.43 |
|  | $(\dfrac{74,567}{171,201}$ |  | 0.43) |

(b)

## REPORT

To:       Mike and Jane
From:     An Accountant
Date:     12 May 20X8
Subject:  *Forecasts and loan application*

As instructed by you we have examined the forecasts prepared by you for the three years to 31 March 20X9, 20Y0 and 20Y1 on the basis that these will be used to apply for a restructuring of bank finance, namely a term loan.

The main areas which will concern the bank are projected growth and overall profitability, working capital management, interest cover and gearing. The bank will then determine that risk attached to lending to Thermo and then decide whether to agree to further funding and what rate of interest to charge.

### Growth

The company is forecasting sales growth of 21.8%, 11.9% and 28% in 20X9, 20Y0 and 20Y1 respectively. Given the youth of the company, the bank may accept this variability in growth, but the company should present valid reasons for forecasting them. In particular, the large rise in 2001 should be explained, eg an expected new large contract, as the later figures in the forecast, while being less accurate, are more likely to indicate future performance.

Overall, the growth figures must be shown to be realistic, based on assumptions which can be verified at the current time. The bank wants to see a quality earnings stream from which interest and loan capital will be paid.

### Profitability

The forecast gross profit % is 18.7%, 20.0% and 20.8%, for 20X9, 20Y0 and 20Y1, showing very modest improvement. However, the relevant operating profit % figures are 10.4%, 12.0% and 14.2%, showing much greater improvements than the gross margin. This is mainly due to projected steady administration and selling expenses over the three years. It may be unrealistic to assume that these expenses will rise less than or on a par with inflation, particularly when the company is so new and increases in such expenditure might be expected.

### Interest cover

As the company is forecasting a fall in debt to zero over the next three years, interest cover is predicted to rise substantially. This does depend, however, on the company's ability to repay the loan as envisaged.

### Working capital management

This was the cause of most of the increase in the overdraft in 20X8 and the bank is likely to examine your figures in detail. These is scope for improvement in most areas, but any forecast improvement must be realistic and must involve practical proposals for action.

### Stock

The stock turnover lengthened dramatically in 20X8 to 114 days. In 20X9, however, it is forecast to fall to $120/545 \times 365 = 80$ days, rising to $170/600 \times 365 = 103$ days in 20Y0 and back down to $190/760 \times 365 = 91$ days in 20Y1. The company will have to provide evidence to the bank that the fall in 20X9 is realistic.

Perhaps a better approach would be to forecast (and put procedures in place to achieve) a regular fall in the stock turnover period each year. A fall of 12 days per year will still have a significant impact on cash flow and will produce the following variations to the projected working capital.

|  | 20X9 | | 20Y0 | | 20Y1 | |
|---|---|---|---|---|---|---|
| Turnover period (days) | 102 | (114 – 12) | 90 | (102 – 12) | 78 | (90 – 12) |
|  | £'000 | | £'000 | | £'000 | |
| Cost of sales | 545 | | 600 | | 760 | |
| Revised stock figure | 152 | | 148 | | 162 | |
| Forecast stock figure | 120 | | 170 | | 190 | |
| Increase/(decrease) in working capital | 32 | | (22) | | (28) | |

### Debtors

The debtors collection period fell a little in 20X8 to 127 days, but again the company is projecting a substantial fall in 20X9 to $145/670 \times 365 = 79$ days in 20X9, a further fall to $126/750 \times 365 = 61$ days in 20Y0 and a rise again to $200/960 \times 365 = 76$ days in 20Y1. Again, the large fall predicted in 20X9 appears unrealistic and the company should aim for an achievable steady fall, say to around the 90 day credit limit over three years. The bank is likely to prefer steadily improving figures rather than volatility.

Assuming a fall of 12 days per year in the collection period, the effects on the forecast working capital will be as follows.

|  | 20X9 | 20Y0 | 20Y1 |
|---|---|---|---|
| Debtors' collection period (days) | 115 | 103 | 91 |
|  | £'000 | £'000 | £'000 |
| Sales | 670 | 750 | 960 |
| Revised debtors figure | 211 | 212 | 239 |
| Projected debtors figure | 145 | 126 | 200 |
| Increase in working capital | 66 | 86 | 39 |

### Creditors' payment period

The creditors' payment period was at a reasonable level in 20X7 and 20X8, commensurate with suppliers' trading terms. This is forecast to continue in 20X9 which is acceptable and realistic.

### Fixed assets/security

Fixed assets are not projected to change; however, depreciation should have been charged (unless expected additions are exactly equal to the depreciation charged) and the profit projection should be adjusted accordingly.

The level of fixed assets is not high and you should consider what type of security you can offer the bank. The bank may accept a floating charge over the assets of the company, or may require personal guarantees from the directors.

**Overall revised forecasts**

The changes in working capital calculated above will have a direct impact on the projected overdraft and the overall effect will be as follows.

|  | *20X9* | *20Y0* | *20Y1* |
|---|---|---|---|
| Forecast overdraft | 5 | 5 | 5 |
| Stock increase/(decrease) | 32 | (22) | (28) |
| Debtors increase | 66 | 86 | 39 |
| Revised overdraft | 103 | 69 | 16 |

It appears therefore (even with minor adjustments to the above) that the projected loan repayments are not achievable, or at least the first repayments in 20X9, and that an overdraft will still be required by the end of 20Y1.

**Summary and conclusion**

It would certainly be in the company's best interests to revise the projected figures along the lines suggested above. All assumptions and reasoning should be given in full, concentrating on those aspects addressed in this report as being most important from the bank's point of view. You should also consider submitting a detailed cash flow forecast.

Please contact me if you have any queries regarding this report or if you require any further information.

## 23  ROI AND APPROPRIATE MEASURES

> **Tutor's hint**. In part (a) you are given a reasonable amount of information about the context in which the question is being asked, so do try to use this rather than just producing an answer learnt by rote.
>
> Part (b) is quite hard: it is about the *process* of selecting measures, not about the measures themselves. We have answered by borrowing ideas you will have encountered in your Financial Management studies. Another valid approach would be to talk about critical success factors.

REPORT

To:        The Managing Director
From:      The Management Accountant                    Date: XX.XX.XX
Subject:   Return on investment and other performance measurements

(a)  **The problems of measuring investment**

Return on investment (ROI) is a simple measure to compute in theory: it is the percentage given by dividing the profit made by a business by the amount of capital invested in order to make that profit. However, both elements of the ROI fraction present problems in practice. In this report the **focus is on the 'investment' element.**

'Investment' is likely to comprise the fixed assets of a business plus its net current assets. For the business as a whole these figures may be easy to identify, but when judging the **performance of the separate operations** that make up the business it will be **hard to decide what element of assets shared by several different operations should be taken into account.** For example debtors and creditors may be managed centrally by head office, or motor vehicles used by individual shops for deliveries might be part of a pool covering several shops in a region.

Even if the assets used by separate operations can be identified there is the further **problem of ascribing a value to them.**

(i)     If assets are valued at historic cost then an older asset will have a lower value than an identical one acquired more recently.

(ii)    If the value is restated at current cost, this may disguise the impact of the relative inefficiency of older assets compared with newer ones (for example repair costs and lack of technological improvements).

(iii)   If depreciation is taken into account, are all similar assets being depreciated according to the same accounting policy?

The ROI measure may, in any case, **not be a reliable guide to the quality of the management of the various operations.**

(i)     There is a considerable difference between the return likely to be achievable by a factory on its assets compared with a shop and its, quite different, assets. **Like should be compared with like,** or allowances should be made for differences, otherwise the exercise has no validity.

(ii)    If **investment decisions are made centrally** it may not be fair to measure a manager's ability to earn a return on assets that he or she might not have chosen to invest in, in the first place.

(iii)   If **managers have control over the assets** in use in their operation, they may be **inclined to under-invest in new assets** in order to keep the investment figure low and their ROI high. This is **unlikely to be in the interests of the company as a whole.**

(b)  **Determining which performance measurements are appropriate for particular businesses**

Overriding factors that will determine what performance measures are used in any business are the **costs of setting up information systems to provide them and the benefits of having them.**

The process is a matter of looking at **what the business is aiming to achieve (its mission) and what it actually does.** For example, one company may be aiming to be the biggest player in its market while another aims to corner the niche, luxury end of a market. Speed of delivery may be crucial to the success of one business, whereas quality of the finished product, no matter how long this takes, may be crucial to another.

The **mission of an organisation can be split into four elements and performance measures can be devised to reflect each of these.**

(i)     **Purpose,** for example maximising shareholder wealth, or satisfying the needs of all stakeholders.

(ii)    **Strategy,** defining the business the company is in (eg luxury cars), and the special competences it intends to use to prosper (eg hand built by craftsmen).

(iii)   **Policies and standards of behaviour,** for example speed of answering telephones, courtesy in redressing complaints.

(iv)    **Values,** related to the organisation's culture. For example in a role culture, or bureaucracy, measurements might be attached to the effectiveness of administrative systems and procedures.

**Measures are more likely to compare performance against that of competitors.**

It is less easy to generalise about **measures of what the business does**. It is necessary to have a **detailed understanding of how the business operates**, how its production systems or service delivery systems work, what channels it uses for sales, and so on. Measures such as output per machine, number of trains running on time, sales per region, or room occupancy rate can then be devised as appropriate.

Signed: Management Accountant

# 24    MUSIC SOCIETIES

> **Tutor's hint**. It is vital in part (b) that you take account of the fact that X Music is just a small organisation, with few staff and limited resources. There is little point in recommending modern cost management techniques.

(a)

## REPORT

To:        The Chairman
From:      Management Accountant                              Date: XX.XX.XX
Subject:   Comparison of the performances of X Music and Y Music

This report provides a comparison of the key features of the business and financial performance of X Music and Y Music.

### Overview

**X Music's** results for **20X9** show a **marked deterioration** in financial performance. The society reported a **deficit** of £88,000 in 20X9 (compared with surpluses of £27,000 and £34,000 in 20X4 and 20X0 respectively) and a worrying **cumulative deficit** of £686,000 (compared with surpluses of £80,000 in 20X4 and £141,000 in 20X9).

**Y Music**, on the other hand, was **more successful** and reported a **surplus** of £182,000 and a cumulative surplus of £311,000 in 20X9. A deficit of £15,000 in 20X4 and a surplus of £12,000 in 20X0, and a cumulative deficit in 20X4 (£26,000) and a cumulative surplus in 20X0 (£62,000) point to the possibility that the society's **results have been fluctuating widely** over the last decade, however.

An analysis of business and financial data for the two societies highlights a number of factors which may well have played their part in these results.

### Number of performances

Since 20X0, the **number of performance** given by **X Music** has **dropped** by 17% (from 181 to 150), while the number given by **Y Music** has **dropped** by 15% (from 152 to 129). The similarity in these figures tends to suggest that both societies have been **affected to a similar degree by competition from foreign orchestras**. Despite this fall, however, Y Music has reported both a surplus and a cumulative surplus in 20X9.

The **number of performances of all types of concert** given by **X Music** in **20X9** have **dropped** from those in 20X0 and 20X9. The number of concerts in other areas of the country (not the home city) in particular has dropped by over 28% to 63 from the 88 reported in 20X4. The number of performances in the home city has remained fairly constant (75 in 20X0 and 74 in 20X9).

**Y Music** has seen a significant **fall in the number of concerts played elsewhere in the home country** (a drop of 50% from 52 in 20X0 to 26 in 20X9). From playing no concerts abroad in 20X4, Y Music played 8 in 20X9 (as did X Music), and made 11 TV/radio/recording appearances in 20X9, compared with only five in 20X4.

141

In 20X9, **Y Music** gave 84 **concerts in its home city**, 10 **more than** the number of performances by **X Music** in its home city. This is **surprising** given that Y Music is based in a smaller city with, one assumes, a smaller concert-going population. **Overall**, however, **X Music** gave 150 performances in 20X9, 21 **more than Y Music**, principally because it made 63 performances in other areas of the country. X Music's disappointing results cannot therefore be attributed to the number of concerts it performed.

### Income

**Both societies** have reported a **significant increase** in total earned income over the ten-year period. X Music's earned income was 137% higher in 20X9 (£2,829,000) compared with that in 20X0 (£1,193,000). Y Music's was 205% higher (£3,088,000) compared with £1,014,000. It is, however, the **income per concert** that has **led to X Music's poor financial performance,** as illustrated by the following figures for 20X9.

|  | *20X9* | |
| --- | --- | --- |
|  | *X Music* | *Y Music* |
| Income per concert in home city | £9,432 | £12,417 |
| Income per concert in home country | £14,540 | £29,308 |
| Income per overseas concert | £35,250 | £41,625 |
| Income per TV/radio/recording event | £14,000 | £19,091 |

X Music achieves a significantly lower income per performance for all types of performance than that achieved by Y Music. The difference is most marked when comparing **concerts in the home country**, with **Y Music's income per performance is over double that of X Music's.** This could be because audience sizes are smaller at X Music's performances or ticket prices may be lower, but on the basis of the data provided it is not possible to state definite causes. If you were able to provide me with attendance figures and information about ticket prices I could provide you with a more detailed analysis.

**X Music's other earned income** of £466,000 in 20X9 (16% of total earned income) is significantly **higher than that of Y Music** (£133,000, representing 4% of total earned income) and hence its catering and merchandising activities are probably considerably more effective than those of Y Music. X Music's figure also compares well with the £56,000 earned ten years previously.

On the other hand, **business sponsorship** appears to have been extremely **lucrative for Y Music** in 20X9, bringing in £607,000, almost the same income as that earned for concerts in other parts of the country. X Music's business sponsorship at £397,000 was only 65% of Y Music's, although both societies have shown significant increases from the levels in 20X0 (X Music £56,000; Y Music £44,000) and 20X4 (X Music £141,000; Y Music £135,000).

The **grants** from both central government and the local authority **awarded to Y Music** in 20X0, 20X4 and 20X9 were **higher than those awarded to X Music**. In 20X9, grants represented 44% of Y Music's total income, compared with 41% of X Music's, with Y Music receiving £2,450,000 in grants compared with £1,955,000 by X Music. **Y Music's committee** appear to be **far more effective** in **applying for grants** and X Music's committee should be encouraged to actively pursue this source of income.

### Costs

Despite the fact that X Music put on more performances than Y Music in 20X0, 20X4 and 20X9, **X Music's costs have always been lower**. In 20X9, X Music's costs per performance were £32,480 (£4,872,000/150) whereas Y Music's were £41,519 (£5,356,000/129). Given that one would expect overseas concerts to be the most expensive to put on, and both societies gave eight overseas concerts, this cost difference

**may highlight particular cost control skills at X Music** (or alternatively, of course, particularly poor cost control at Y Music). On the other hand, because 75% of the costs are related to the orchestra, it **could point to lower quality performances by X Music** (which might explain X Music's lower income per performance) **or to different forms of performance** by the two societies, the two forms requiring different numbers of musicians.

Given that **X Music's total costs were not covered by total income** in 20X9, and that there is no guaranteed level of grant income, **X Music should carry out a detailed review of expenditure**.

I hope this information has proved useful. If I can be of any further assistance, please do not hesitate to contact me.

Signed: Management Accountant

(b) It is clear from the analysis in (a) above that X Music should pay close attention to the level of costs being incurred. **Seventy five percent of costs are orchestra related** and given the low levels of remuneration, especially for musicians, cost cutting will be difficult. The society therefore needs to consider ways of managing its costs more effectively. There are a number of cost management techniques which might prove particularly useful to an organisation such as X Music, with a small number of accounting staff and limited available data.

All of these techniques would involve setting up a more **detailed cost recording system** than exists at the moment. Until costs can be traced to and identified with performances, they cannot be managed.

**Budgeting**

Even the smallest of organisations needs to operate some form of **budgeting system**. It is vital that X Music undertakes a simple **planning exercise** to ensure that it is able to **finance its activities** during the next accounting period. The planning exercise needs to start with an **estimate of the number of performances** that are likely to be given in the home city, the home country and overseas and the TV/radio/recording work likely to be available. On the basis of these estimates, monthly **budgets for the various costs** (musicians, administration, concert hall and so on) can be set. Although these costs are largely fixed, they may behave in a step fashion and so could vary to a certain extent with the number of performances given. Each month, **costs can be compared against budgeted costs** and **control action** initiated if budgeted cost levels are being exceeded.

Using the estimates of the number of performances, budgets for the various forms of **income** can be drawn up. If grant income is not known with certainty, estimates will need to be made. **Contingency plans** (such as other sources of income or cost reduction measures) will need to be made, however, to ensure that the society is able to continue operating should the grant income be significantly less than anticipated. Once budgets for monthly income have been set, **cash budgets** can be drawn up to ensure that the society has sufficient funds to finance its activities during the coming accounting period.

**Cost benefit analysis**

On the basis of the information available, it does not appear that X Music is aware of whether particular activities make a profit or a loss. It is possible to determine average income per concert in home city, concert in home country and so on, but it does not appear that the **actual income per performance** is available from the current recording system. Such data needs to be available. What's more, there is currently no analysis of costs into those associated with, for example, concerts in the home city. A basic cost recording system therefore needs to be established so that **costs** can be **traced to specific types of concert**.

Although the majority of costs are fixed, it is still possible to **apportion** staff costs, for example, on the basis of how many members were in the orchestra during a particular performance. **Profitability** per home city concert, overseas concert and so on could be ascertained and it will then be possible to ascertain which are the profitable forms of performance, which type of performance result in a loss and the committee will be able to determine the **range of concerts that should be provided**.

### Contribution analysis

Rather than look at the profitability of each type of concert, the society could look at the **contribution** earned by each type of performance or each individual performance. If a revised cost recording system were set up, fixed costs associated with each type of performance could be ascertained, the contribution compared with the fixed costs, and the **breakeven** number of concerts and breakeven revenue determined. The society would then have more of an idea of the type of performance it should be putting on.

### Activity based costing

Given that the majority of costs are fixed, some sort of activity based costing analysis might be appropriate. The identification of the **drivers of the various costs** would enable the society's committee to control those drivers and hence manage the costs. For example, concert hall costs might be driven by the length of the concert and so the committee might try to avoid putting on particularly long concerts.

### Summary

Whatever cost management technique is adopted it should be simple and enable the society to control finances more effectively.

## 25   LEWES

> **Tutor's hint**. In questions of this nature, particularly those involving a report to a client, you must devise an answer plan. You will then be assured of addressing all the important issues in a structured and coherent manner. You must focus on the core issues and keep your answer brief and succinct. Most importantly, you must use the data given in the question as much as possible.
>
> **Examiner's comment**. Report writing is a core competence and students must develop their skills in this area. Few candidates had knowledge of the OFR. Good answers to (b) pinpointed the principle causes of the lack of correlation for 20X3 and 20X4 as far as possible.

(a)   (i)   The principal aim of the financial review section of the **OFR** is to **explain** to the user of the annual report the capital structure of the business, its treasury policy and the dynamics of its financial position - its sources of liquidity and their application, including the implications of the financing requirements arising from its capital expenditure plans.

The review will usually be in a **narrative** style, with figures used to support the points made where necessary. The review should highlight important issues for the business as a whole.

(ii)   The capital structure and treasury policy section should include information on the maturity profile of dept, type of capital instruments used, currency and interest rate structure. Capital funding and treasury policies should be discussed and the implementation of these policies, in terms of:

(1) The way in which treasury policy is controlled

(2) How financial instruments are used for hedging purposes

(3) Whether foreign currency investments are hedged by foreign currency borrowings or other hedging instrument

(4) The currencies in which borrowings are made and cash (equivalents) held

(5) The extent to which borrowings are at fixed/variable rates

The purpose and effect of major financing decisions taken should also be examined, as should the effect of interest costs on profits and the potential impact of interest rate changes.

(b)                                     REPORT

To:         A Shareholder
From:       An Accountant
Re:         *Performance of Lewes Holdings plc*                    Date: 5/5/X5

In compliance with your instructions I have examined the draft consolidated accounts for Lewes Holdings plc for the year ended 31 December 20X4 and the audited comparatives.

Your primary concern is that the earnings per share figure does not reflect the rise in turnover for the period. As well as looking at this specific concern, my report goes on to look at other information which may aid your decision on the sale of your holding.

**Rise in turnover/EPS**

There are several reasons why EPS has not risen as fast as turnover, which are discussed in turn here. First of all, it is worth making a general point, that turnover and EPS do not necessarily correlate to any great extent. The main causes of the lack of correlation in this case relate to the overall upheaval in the group in terms of acquisitions and restructurings.

(i)    **Share issue**

The group has made a major share issue during the year of 123.5m shares which has raised additional finance towards restructuring costs, acquisitions of other companies, purchases of fixed assets and expansion of working capital. (The increase in stock, debtors, fixed assets etc is only explained in part by the acquisitions - see note (iv).) The share issue has a direct impact on the EPS calculation, sharing the available earnings between more shares in 20X4 than in 20X3. If EPS were calculated on the basis of last year's share capital, the EPS for 20X4 would be:

$$133.9 \div \frac{148.0}{0.2} = 18.1 \text{ pence.}$$

The EPS would then have risen over 29% compared to 20X3. It might be expected that the EPS would reflect the increased earnings produced by new capital investment, but it may be early days yet and the benefit of restructuring and acquisitions has yet to filter through to earnings.

(ii)   **Profitability**

The operating profit margin of the group as a whole has risen only slightly from approximately 6.2% (122.6/1,966.3 × 100%) to 6.3% (213.1/3,381.8 × 100%). It would appear that no economies of scale have been produced by the increase in turnover as operating costs have risen in the same proportion. However, the restructuring operation may be recent and reductions in operating costs may be expected in the near future. The question arises of whether the group is becoming less profitable, but this is difficult to gauge as the group is (or was during 20X4) in a state of flux. Looking at items below the operating profit line, interest costs have risen sharply (by 327%) and restructuring costs have occurred. These two items, along with the changes in capital structure, have produced the greatest impact on EPS.

(iii) **Acquisitions**

The group's acquisitions are slightly more profitable at 6.6% (29.9/453.2 × 100%) than the rest of the group at 6.3% (183.2/2,928.6 × 100%) indicating sound decisions on acquisitions perhaps, but having no great impact as yet on group profitability.

(iv) **Restructuring costs**

The restructuring costs incurred by the group are shown here as an exceptional item. In previous years such an item might have been shown as extraordinary and thereby excluded from the EPS calculation, but an accounting standard (FRS 3) outlaws this treatment. As a cost with no related turnover the £18.9m has a direct impact on EPS. Without it, EPS for 20X4 would have been stated at (133.9 + 18.9)/(172.7 ÷ 0.20) = 17.7 pence, a 26.4% increase on 20X3. The question here is whether this cost in 20X4 will be reflected in savings in the next few years.

(v) **Gearing/interest costs**

Interest has risen sharply and this may reflect a significant increase in both short-term and long-term creditors. In particular the group will be paying interest to long-term creditors.

(vi) **Geographical analysis**

The geographical analysis given in the question gives an indication of which markets and product sectors are becoming more important to the group. It also shows the relative profitability of the markets. Turnover has risen by nearly 60% in the UK, but profitability has fallen dramatically from 11.5% to 7.0%. This may indicate where the increased turnover originates: the company may have pursued a deliberate strategy of increasing market share in the UK, allowing prices to fall and creating a significant impact on profitability.

This situation is not reflected in the rest of the world. In Europe, profitability has remained steady and in North America, loss-making operations have been turned around (perhaps causing the restructuring costs?). The profitability is still low in North America, as it is in the rest of the world, where markets seem to be very small.

The drop in profitability is most noticeable in the manufacturing sector, whereas the situation with distribution has declined only slightly and has actually improved in the case of automated manufacturing systems, in spite of significant expansion in all three classes of business.

**Further information**

The decision whether to sell or hold a share will be based on a variety of factors but the most direct concern is value, in both the dividend stream from the share and its market value (the two are connected, but perhaps only to a certain extent). This requires a shareholder to estimate what will happen in the future, whereas the historical accounts show only past data. I would be concerned with the following issues, some of which may be covered by the directors' report, operating and financial review etc.

### Profitability

Is profitability in certain areas likely to improve in the near future, ie in the UK and in the manufacturing side of the business? These aspects both represent significant parts of the group's turnover and only recovery in these areas is likely to improve profitability in a noticeable way. It is therefore necessary to ask whether the restructuring has come to an end or whether any further costs are likely. Also, what improvement in profitability is the restructuring expected to produce?

### Liquidity

Although cash balances are improved, creditors have increased greatly and questions may arise as to the group's ability to pay cash in distributions when it becomes harder to pay creditors. A breakdown of both short-term and long-term creditors would therefore be helpful to judge whether the rise in creditors will be permanent or not.

Similarly, the maturity dates of all loans and preference shares would be required to determine whether proper planning was in process for future funding requirements. It would then be possible to assess how such funding would affect ordinary shareholders.

### Conclusion

Lewes Holdings is expanding, particularly in the UK and North American markets. The main operations of the business which are expanding are manufacturing and (in a smaller way) distribution, although the North American market in automated manufacturing systems also seems to be expanding. The expansion has taken place partly through acquisition and partly through development of existing businesses. This expansion programme makes the group a riskier investment, but the rewards might thereby be greater.

## 26   PREPARATION QUESTION: SUGGESTED ALTERNATIVES

### (a)   CPP accounting

Shareholders' equity (= net assets) is valued as the purchasing power, stated in year-end pounds, invested by the shareholders in the net assets of the company. Non-monetary items therefore have their cost, less depreciation, indexed up from the date of acquisition to the balance sheet date. Monetary assets and liabilities are automatically already stated in year-end pounds, so no adjustment is required for them.

### CCA

Shareholders' equity is valued as the aggregate of the deprival values of the net assets of the business. Non-monetary items are therefore quoted at the lower of net replacement cost and recoverable amount (recoverable amount being defined as the higher of net realisable value and economic value). Monetary assets and liabilities are automatically already stated at their balance sheet date deprival value, so no adjustment is required for them.

### Present value accounting

Shareholders' equity is valued as the aggregate of the economic values of the net assets of the business. 'Economic value' is defined in the ASC *Handbook* as 'a measure of the value of an asset (or liability) based on the present value of the net cash flows likely to be generated by it (or, if a liability, incurred in discharging it) in future. The discount rate on which the DCF calculations should be based is the company's weighted average cost of capital.

(b) **CPP accounting**

The reported profit is the amount available for distribution to the shareholders after maintaining the purchasing power of shareholders' equity. This profit can be determined either via the CPP profit and loss account or via a determination of net asset values. In the profit and loss account both sales and cost of sales must be revalued to year-end pounds from pounds at the date of each transaction. If sales and purchases occur evenly through a year, it is convenient to restate each to year-end pounds from average pounds for the year. Depreciation charged will be the amount of the year-end balance sheet value of the fixed assets consumed in the period, and there will also be a gain/loss recognised in holding net monetary liabilities/assets in the period.

Via the balance sheet the CPP net profit can be determined by the following.

$$P = D + (E_1 - E_0)$$

Where    $P$    is the CPP accounting profit;

         $D$    is the distributions made to shareholders, restated in terms of year-end pounds;

         $E_0$    is the shareholders' equity at the start of the year, restated in terms of pounds at the end of the year;

         $E_1$    is the shareholders' equity at the end of the year, expressed in terms of pounds at the end of the year.

The retained earnings for the year will be the excess of $P$ over $D$ above. CPP is generally regarded as being more useful than straight historical cost accounting, but suffers from the weakness that the balance sheet amounts are difficult to interpret.

**Current cost accounting**

CCA profits are obtained by applying current cost adjustments to historical cost figures. The appendix to SSAP 16 gives an illustrative format for the presentation of a CCA profit and loss account as summarised below.

|  | £ | £ |
|---|---|---|
| Historical cost PBIT |  | X |
| Less current cost operating adjustments |  |  |
|   COSA | X |  |
|   ADA | X |  |
|   MWCA | X |  |
|   Others | X |  |
|  |  | (X) |
| Current cost operating profit |  | X |
|   Gearing adjustment | X |  |
|   Net interest payable | (X) |  |
|  |  | X |
| Current cost PBT |  | X |
| Tax (HC charge) |  | (X) |
| Current cost profit attributable |  |  |
|  to shareholders |  | X |
| Dividends (HC amount) |  | (X) |
| Current cost retained profit |  | X |

The current cost operating profit is therefore the amount of profits that the company has generated, after sufficient retentions have been made to maintain the operating capability of the business (maintain the fixed assets, stocks and level of monetary working capital).

The main problems with CCA have been a general lack of understanding of what the method is trying to achieve, coupled with a lack of enthusiasm for any seemingly complicated set of adjustments, at a period of time when inflation levels are generally low. None of the proposals in SSAP 16, ED 35 or the ASC *Handbook* have gained general acceptance, and further consultation is probably advisable before the ASB attempts another mandatory CCA accounting standard. This consultation may also help to iron out the technical flaws that some commentators identified in SSAP 16, for example that the crediting of the gearing adjustment to the profit and loss account appears to be contravening the stated aim of maintaining operating capability.

### Present value accounting

Economic value accounting has been proposed by economists such as Sir John Hicks (in *Value and capital* 1946) as the purest theoretical form of assessing the profits of an individual. Hicks wrote that income is the maximum amount that an individual could spend and still expect to be as well off at the end of a period as he was at the beginning. These ideas have been carried forward into the business world by suggesting that the profits of a business are the maximum dividends that could be paid, such that the business is as well off at the end of the period as at the beginning. The concept of well-offness is equated with economic values, in other words the present value of future cash flows arising from the asset. The present value accounting retained earnings will be the net profits less dividends paid (measured in cash terms).

The major drawback to the theory is the large element of subjective judgement involved, even in an ex post model, in determining the size and timing of the cash flows and the discount rate to choose. Although theoretically sound, in practice the use of present value accounting to a user of a set of accounts will be very small indeed.

## 27   CORPORATE FAILURE

> **Tutor's hint.** It is no good simply listing ratios and discussing them – you need to take a step back and consider the usefulness of ratios in general.
>
> **Examiner's comment.** Most candidates did reasonably well on this question.

(a)   Ratio analysis is a useful tool, but it suffers from certain limitations.

   (i)   Ratios calculated using historical cost accounts **do not reflect current values** or current costs and are of less use for predictive purposes.

   (ii)   **Differences in accounting policies** can make comparisons difficult between companies even where adequate disclosures are made in accounts.

   (iii)   Return on capital employed is a key ratio but the **capital employed** figure traditionally uses the **historical value** of capital employed. The real cost of shareholders' investments is their **opportunity cost** (the amount lost by *not* selling shares at market price). The return to shareholders used is based upon dividends received *not* future dividends expected.

   (iv)   Recent accounting standards have improved the balance sheet presentation but some assets and liabilities may still be held **off balance sheet**, for example operating leases. (The proposals in the recent Discussion Paper on leasing would remedy this.)

   (v)   There is still a trend for **creative accounting**, especially where management remuneration is linked to profits. However, new accounting standards have reduced the scope for this.

   (vi)   The **business environment changes rapidly**. Traditional ratio analysis may not reflect this.

**149**

(b) The essence of such corporate failure prediction models is that **a company may exhibit similar characteristics to companies** which have failed. Altman's model determined multiple predictors of business failure using multiple discriminant analysis for the development of a linear function, used to predict corporate failure. The 'Z' score selected five financial ratios as a basis for the final discriminant function. The basis of the ratios was data extracted from US companies. The effectiveness of the 'Z' score in predicting failure fell when used on data other than that used in the empirical study.

Argenti's model was derived using both financial and non-financial data such as accounting systems, mistakes and management styles.

The main problem with failure prediction models is that the financial statements used **cannot be directly compared** and may be influenced by creative accounting practices when a company is experiencing failure symptoms.

As outlined in part (a) above the accounting ratios used are subject to serious problems, and ideally failure prediction should use **prospective financial information** which is rarely available. Many financial statements contain information in a mixed form, ie replacement cost, historic cost or current values.

The underlying theory behind these models has been considered suspect and the logic hard to follow, so confidence in the models has fallen away.

The models were developed many years ago when business systems and the business environment was totally different from the current position.

Another possible shortcoming is that the models make **no allowance for inflation**.

To conclude, whilst the models are still used, for example by banks, it is dangerous to use them in isolation without other information.

(c) (i) FRS 10 *Goodwill and intangible assets* allows **capitalisation and amortisation** of goodwill over a period of 20 years. Goodwill may be assessed as having an indefinite life subject to impairment rules. Analysts will need to examine the accountancy policy for goodwill carefully where a company employs an 'unusual' treatment, albeit one which is permitted by FRS 10. Further adjustments may also be necessary in respect of 'old goodwill' which has been written off against reserves and not been reinstated.

(ii) Differences in depreciation methods and asset revaluations tend to cause **distortions in ratios**. Analysts may wish to see the effect of incorporating a common basis for depreciation accounting for companies within a particular industry or sector.

The additional disclosures and rules contained in recent changes to accounting standards may assists analysts.

## 28   STATESIDE

> **Tutor's hint**. This question combines two distinct topics: international considerations (in this case the reconciliation of UK/US GAAP often given in accounts by multinational companies) and the rules governing profit on disposal after a revaluation under FRS 3.
>
> **Examiners' comment**. Candidates were well-prepared for part (a), which was well answered. Answers to part (b) were confused and, although part (c) was generally well answered, candidates did not seem to know about FRS 3 and the statement of recognised gains and losses.

(a)   **Advantages of harmonisation**   *I - M_NC - G - T -*

These will be based on the benefits to users and preparers of accounts, as follows.

**Investors**

Individual and corporate investors would like to be able to compare the financial results of different companies internationally as well as nationally in making investment decisions. There is a "growing amount of investment across borders" and there are few financial analysts able to follow shares in international markets. For example, it is not easy for an analyst familiar with UK accounting principles to analyse the financial statements of a Dutch or German company.

**Multinational companies**

Multinationals benefit from harmonisation for many reasons.

(i)   Better access is gained to foreign investor funds.

(ii)   Management control is improved, because harmonisation aids internal communication of financial information.

(iii)   Appraisal of 'foreign enterprises' for take-overs and mergers is more straightforward.

(iv)   It is easier to comply with the reporting requirements of overseas stock exchanges.

(v)   Consolidation of foreign subsidiaries and associated companies is easier.

(vi)   A reduction in audit costs can be achieved.

(vii)   Transfer of accounting staff across national borders is easier.

**Governments**

Governments of developing countries would save time and money if they could adopt international standards and, if these were used internally, governments of developing countries could attempt to control the activities of foreign multinational companies in their own country. These companies could not 'hide' behind foreign accounting practices which are difficult to understand.

**Other interested parties**

For *tax authorities* it is easier to calculate the tax liability of investors, including multinationals who receive income from overseas sources.

**Regional economic groups** usually promote trade within a specific geographical region. This is aided by common accounting practices within the region.

**Large international accounting firms** can benefit as accounting and auditing is much easier if similar accounting practices existed throughout the world.

**Barriers to international harmonisation** - *L-u-p.*

*PESTL*
*COST.*

The main barriers are as follows.

(i)   **Different purposes of financial reporting.** In some countries the purpose is solely for tax assessment, while in others it is for investor decision-making.

(ii) *L*   **Different legal systems.** These prevent the development of certain accounting practices and restrict the options available.

(iii) *S*   **Different user groups.** Countries have different ideas about who the relevant user groups are and their respective importance. In the USA investor and creditor groups are given prominence, while in Europe employees enjoy a higher profile.

(iv)   **Needs of developing countries.** Developing countries are obviously behind in the standard setting process and they need to develop the basic standards and principles already in place in most developed countries.

(v)   **Nationalism** is demonstrated in an unwillingness to accept another country's standard.

(vi)   **Cultural differences** result in objectives for accounting systems differing from country to country.

(vii)   **Unique circumstances.** Some countries may be experiencing unusual circumstances which affect all aspects of everyday life and impinge on the ability of companies to produce proper reports, for example hyperinflation, civil war, currency restriction and so on.

(viii)   **The lack of strong accountancy bodies.** Many countries do not have strong independent accountancy or business bodies which would press for better standards and greater harmonisation.

(b)   (i)   The adjustments have been made to the income statement reconciliation between UK and US GAAP for the following reasons.

**Capitalised interest amortised**

Under UK GAAP companies have the choice of expensing or capitalising interest as there is no accounting standard governing this area. Under US GAAP the group has capitalised the interest (whereas in the UK it appears to have been written off) and the amortisation charge relating to this interest is £5m.

**Merger accounting adjustments**

It appears that a merger has taken place during the year which satisfies UK criteria for the use of merger accounting (per FRS 6). This is not allowed under US GAAP so adjustments have been made to adopt acquisition accounting, including the removal of £150m of pre-acquisition profits and the additional depreciation and amortisation of £200m.

(ii)   The effect of the above items on the UK/US GAAP equity reconciliation is as follows.

**Capitalised interest amortised**

US GAAP equity will be increased by the unamortised balance outstanding.

**Merger accounting adjustment**

The adjustments required to switch UK GAAP merger accounting to US GAAP acquisition accounting will *probably* cause an increase in equity because of the uplift to net assets given by a fair value exercise (a fall is possible, but unlikely).

(iii)   If such a dividend was proposed, the effect on equity would be to increase it because under UK GAAP the dividend must be accounted for in the fiscal year to which it relates. Under US GAAP the reduction in equity caused by the dividend is delayed until the period it is paid, ie the following period.

(c)   (i)   **Year ended 31 May 20X4**

(1)   **Profit and loss account**

Depreciation charge = £3m

(2)   **Statement of recognised gains and losses**

Gain = £10m

(3) **Note of historical cost profits and losses**

Difference between the historical cost depreciation charge and the actual depreciation charge based on the revalued amount = £1m.

(4) **Balance sheet**

| | £m |
|---|---|
| Fixed asset at revalued amount | 30.0 |
| Accumulated depreciation | (3.0) |
| | 27.0 |
| Revaluation reserve | |
| Revaluation during year | 10.0 |
| Transfer to realised reserves | (1.0) |
| | 9.0 |

## Year ended 31 May 20X5

(1) **Profit and loss account**

Depreciation charge = £3m

Gain on disposal = £40m – (£30m – £6m) = £16m

(2) **Note of historical cost profits and losses**

Realisation of property gains = £8m (W)

Difference between the historical cost depreciation charge and the actual depreciation charge based on the revalued amount = £1m.

(3) **Balance sheet**

Revaluation reserve: transfer £9m to realised profits (£8m shown above plus £1m excess depreciation, also shown above).

**Working: profit on disposal vs historical NBV**

| | £m | £m |
|---|---|---|
| Proceeds | | 40.0 |
| NBV at historical cost | | |
| Cost | 20.0 | |
| Accumulated depreciation | (4.0) | |
| | | 16.0 |
| (£16m + £8m) | | 24.0 |

(ii) **Statement of Principles**

The accounting treatment required by the ASB is based on the recognition of assets, liabilities, gains and losses in the accounts. According to the *Statement of Principles*:

'At any stage in the recognition process, where a change in total assets is not offset by an equal change in total liabilities or a transaction with owners, a gain or a loss will arise. Gains and losses should be recognised in one of the two performance statements, ie the profit and loss account and the statement of total recognised gains and losses.'

It is necessary to consider all gains and losses recognised in a period when assessing financial performance and so FRS 3 requires a statement of recognised gains and losses in addition to the profit and loss account.

**Statement of recognised gains and losses**

The statement of recognised gains and losses shows the profit or loss for the period along with all other movements on reserves which reflect recognised gains and losses attributable to shareholders. It does not deal with the *realisation* of gains in previous periods, nor with transfers between reserves. This means that the excess of the revalued amount over historical cost will never be recognised in the profit and loss account; profit or loss on disposal will be calculated as the difference between the net proceeds and the net carrying amount. This is a very important FRS 3 rule; previously, on disposal of a revalued asset, companies could transfer the surplus in the revaluation reserve which related to the asset to the profit and loss account.

The difference between historical cost depreciation and depreciation on a revaluation will appear in the note of historical cost profits and losses.

### Recognition of holding gains

The basic principle here is that the same gains should not be *recognised* twice, for example, a holding gain *recognised* when a fixed asset is revalued should not be *recognised* again when the asset is sold. This approach reflects the effect of allowing figures not related to current values to distort the measurement of performance in the profit and loss account because profit measured by return on assets is distorted.

## 29    MORGAN

> **Tutor's hint.** This question tests your knowledge of accounting standards by requiring you to adjust a set of overseas accounts and bring them into compliance with local accounting standards. You should have started by reconstructing the profit and loss account and balance sheet of the overseas company to bring it into line with local standards. This question is set in the context of a business decision and puts different accounting frameworks into a very practical context. It also tests your ability to link the effect of specific accounting treatments to key ratios. In part (a) you should
>
> - Avoid getting bogged down in any single bit of information; it's better to deal with the adjustments you can do than to waste time on those you can't.
>
> - Notice that 'reasons' for the adjustments are required, not just numbers.
>
> Make sure you allocate enough time to parts (b) and (c) as these probably contain the easier marks.
>
> *Prizewinners' points.* You will have done very well to calculate the ratios accurately, but if you made a few mistakes you will still have been given credit for valid interpretations of them.
>
> **Examiner's comment.** Few candidates approached the question in a systematic way.

(a)    *Working* (all $'000)

Firstly it is necessary to restate the financial accounts of the Overseas group using UK plc GAAP. (Negative figures are credits.)

| | Balance sheet | Subsid-iary | Software | Share option | ESOT | Stock and extraordi-nary item | Revised total |
|---|---|---|---|---|---|---|---|
| **Fixed assets:** | | | | | | | |
| tangible | 135,200 | 6,900 | 750 | | 7,000 | | 148,350 |
| Intangible | | 3,165 | | | | | 3,165 |
| **Current assets** | | | | | | | |
| Stock | 42,020 | | | | | (2,500) | 39,520 |
| Debtors | 31,050 | | | | | | 31,050 |
| Cash | 22,230 | | | | | | 22,230 |
| | 95,300 | | | | | | 92,800 |
| **Current** | | | | | | | |
| liabilities | (79,400) | | | | | | (79,400) |
| Debt | (99,700) | (181) | | | | | (99,881) |
| **Shareholders'** | | | | | | | |
| funds | 51,400 | | | | | | 65,034 |
| | | | | | | | |
| Share capital | 30,000 | | | | | | 30,000 |
| Other reserves | | (40) | | | | | |
| (inc minority) | 20,806 | 10,000 | | (75) | 7,000 | (9,000) | 28,691 |
| Profit for year | 594 | (60)/ (16) | (750) | 75 | | 6,500 | 6,343 |
| | 51,400 | | | | | | 65,034 |
| | | W1 | W2 | W3 | W4 | W5 | |

*Profit and loss*

| | Balance sheet | Subsid-iary | Software | Share option | ESOT | Stock and extraordi-nary item | Revised total |
|---|---|---|---|---|---|---|---|
| Profit before tax/interest | 1,840 | (100) | (750) | 75 | | 120 | 7,685 |
| | | | | | | 6,500 | |
| Interest | (1,020) | (16) | | | | | (1,036) |
| Pre tax profit | 820 | | | | | | 6,649 |
| Tax | (200) | | | | | (30) | (230) |
| | 620 | | | | | | 6,419 |
| Minority interest | (80) | 40 | | | | (36) | (76) |
| Group earnings | 540 | | | | | | |
| Extraordinary item | 54 | | | | | (54) | - |
| | 594 | | | | | | 6,343 |
| EPS | 1.8c | W1 | W2 | W3 | W4 | W5 | 21.2c |

## Workings

1    *Purchase of subsidiary*

Consideration:

| | | |
|---|---|---|
| 8m ordinary shares at market value | | 16,000 |
| Cash | | 2,000 |
| Deferred consideration | | |
| 200,000 at present value (10% discount) $\frac{200,000}{1.21}$ (say) | | 165 |
| | | 18,165 |
| Fair value of assets acquired 60% × $25m | | 15,000 |
| Goodwill | | 3,165 |

The negative goodwill created under the overseas GAAP is to be added back to fixed assets.

| | |
|---|---|
| Negative goodwill add back | 2,000 |
| In addition fixed assets are revalued by | 5,000 |
| Less increase in depreciation (50 year life) | (100) |
| Increase in fixed assets | 6,900 |

Note that the negative goodwill will be shown separately as a deduction from positive goodwill.

P&L account will be reduced by 100 (depreciation) and minority interest will also reduce by 40% × 100 = 40.

There will be an interest charge on the deferred purchase consideration of 165,000 × 10%, say 16.

The notional interest and deferred purchase consideration will increase balance sheet 'debt' by 165 + 16 = 181.

Other reserves will change by:

| | |
|---|---:|
| The premium accounted for by issue of shares at fair value 8,000 × ($2 – $1) | 8,000 |
| Minority interest share of revaluation 40% × 5,000 | 2,000 |
| | 10,000 |

2   Computer software would be written off to comply with normal UK GAAP reducing fixed assets and profits by 750.

3/4   *Share options and employee share ownership trusts*

Applying FRS 4, the options should be recorded at the discounted price.

| | | |
|---|---:|---|
| ie Market price | 250 | |
| Proceeds | 175 | |
| Directors' remuneration | 75 | eliminated |

Hence other reserves (share premium) will reduce by 75 and profits increase by 75.

ESOTs are to be recorded as fixed asset investments in the UK *not* deducted from shareholders funds, therefore assets will increase by 7,000 and reserves will increase by 7,000.

5   Extraordinary profits are not expected to arise under FRS 3, therefore pre-tax profits and also the minority interest calculations will be affected. The amount included in the profit and loss account is 60% therefore the gross extraordinary item is:

| | |
|---|---:|
| 72 × 100/60 | 120 |
| Tax = 18 × 100/60 | 30 |
| | 90 |

(Minority interest @ 40% = 36)

The adjustments required are:

| | |
|---|---:|
| Increase profit by | 120 |
| Increase tax by | 30 |
| Increase minority interest by | 36 |

The adjustments to stock involve a reduction to the lower of cost or market value.

| | |
|---|---:|
| Closing stock reduce by | 2,500 |
| Opening stock reduce by | 9,000 |
| Profit increase by | 6,500 |
| B/S stock reduce by | 2,500 |
| Opening reserves reduce by | 9,000 |

*Calculation of amended ratios*

|  |  | *Overseas Inc* | *UK Group* |
|---|---|---|---|
| Current ratio | $\dfrac{92,800}{79,400}$ | 1.17:1 | 1.75:1 |
| Stock turnover | $\dfrac{110,100 - 6,500\,*}{39,520}$ | 2.62 times | 6.5 times |

*Stock reduction to cost of sales

|  |  | | |
|---|---|---|---|
| Debtors collection | | 85.5 days (unchanged) | 41.7 days |
| Interest cover | $\dfrac{7,685}{1,036}$ | 7.4 times | 6 times |
| Profit margin | $\dfrac{6,649}{132,495} \times 100$ | 5% | 5.4% |
| Return on total assets | $\dfrac{7,685}{148,350 + 3,165 + 92,800} \times 100$ | 3.1% | 7.4% |
| Return on net worth | $\dfrac{6,649}{65,034} \times 100$ | 10.2% | 12.2% |
| Gearing ratio | $\dfrac{99,881}{148,350 + 3,165 + 92,800} \times 100$ | 40.9% | 27.7% |
| P/E ratio | $\dfrac{147}{21.2c}$ | 6.9 | 15 |

*EPS*

| | | |
|---|---|---|
| Shares issued 1.6.X6 | | 8,000 |
| Options | $100 \times 6/12$ (mid year) | 50 |
| Balance | | 21,900 |
| | | 29,950 |

$$\text{EPS} = \frac{6,343}{29,950} = 21.2 \text{ cents}$$

(b)  (i)   The incorporation of UK GAAP has **increased pre tax** profits and improved all ratios using profitability.

    (ii)   **Liquidity** is almost **unchanged.**

    (iii)   **Interest** cover is **much improved** as a result of profitability increases.

    (iv)   **Return** on assets, margins and return on net worth have also **improved** considerably.

The **decision to purchase may be affected by the use of UK GAAP.**

    (i)   Overseas Inc is much more highly geared than UK although the impact on interest as a result of the changes is minimal.

    (ii)   P/E ratios are significantly different as a composite result of all the changes.

    (iii)   UK appears more profitable, less highly geared and more liquid.

(c)   Other factors could include the following.

    (i)   Trading conditions may be completely different, eg gearing levels may be acceptable at much higher levels than the UK norm.

    (ii)   Relationships between banks, creditors and companies may be much closer. For example, bank officials may be on the board of directors.

  (iii) Capital structures may be quite different with long-term debt being a permanent feature of capital structure, possibly with a conversion option.

  (iv) UK plc would not normally finance-long term assets by short term borrowings but this could be normal practice abroad.

## 30 PREPARATION QUESTION: ENVIRONMENT

A widely-used framework for describing a business's general environment is PEST (political/legal, economic, social/cultural, technological factors).

(a) **Political and legal factors.** Examples include war, a change of government and new legislation.

(b) **Economic factors.** Examples include inflation, economic growth and exchange rates.

(c) **Social/cultural factors** include changes in the population as a whole (eg more elderly people) and people's attitudes and lifestyles (eg fashion trends, the trend towards single-person households).

(d) **Technological factors** include new products and production processes leading to increased productivity.

## 31 STAKEHOLDERS

> **Tutor's hint.** Part (a) consisted of identifying, classifying and working out the relationship between the various stakeholder groups.
>
> *Prizewinner's points.* Assuming that each stakeholder you mention will earn you approximately 2 marks, there is no need to be as comprehensive in your coverage as we are here. In part (b), mentioning the recent anger over 'fat cat' pay rises demonstrates the application of theory to real life and will identify a strong student.
>
> *Other points.* In part (b) you could have picked out any combination, although the easiest would be management v employees, shareholders v directors, pressure groups v company and management v unions.

(a) A stakeholder is an individual or an organisation that has a financial interest or a stake in a company.

  Stakeholders can be sub-divided into **three categories**.

  (i)  **Internal stakeholders** such as employees and managers.
  (ii)  **External stakeholders** such as government and pressure groups.
  (iii) **Connected stakeholders** such as customers and suppliers.

  The owners of the organisation are the **shareholders**. They are seeking a return on their investment in terms of an annual return or dividend and they are also looking to see a capital gain on their investment over a period of time.

  **Customers** are also stakeholders. They are seeking high quality products at competitive prices and may also be concerned with side issues such as environmental awareness.

  **Suppliers** want regular orders and to be paid on time.

  **Managers** tend to be concerned with their own status and with issues such as salary, company car, share options, responsibility and promotion. **Employees** are interested in pay, conditions and security of employment.

**Trade unions** look after their members and will seek to negotiate pay, holiday, sickness benefit and other employee related issues.

**The bank** will usually be a stakeholder since the company is likely to have an overdraft or loan. The bank will look for prudent financial management and will share similar concerns to the shareholder.

**The government** is a stakeholder since the company will be paying tax (if profitable). On the other hand, the government may have given the company financial assistance.

Finally, in recent years **pressure groups**, especially those concerned with environmental issues, have become integrated in firms' environmental policies.

(b) In theory, stakeholders should be working together since the company's long term survival is in everyone's interest. However, there are **numerous potential conflicts between the various stakeholders**.

In recent years there has been a conflict **between shareholders and senior management** over the large salary increases awarded to directors. This was especially the case in some of the privatised utilities where directors awarded themselves large salary increases which did not reflect the performance of the company. However, this was not confined to shareholders. Customers were angry at having to pay higher charges and trade unions were unhappy because many of their members had lost their jobs.

On a day to day level, there is often conflict **between management and employees** over pay and working conditions, although threat of job loss and redundancy has minimised this during the 1990's.

**Conflict with pressure groups** can be extremely damaging for a company. In recent times there was a well-publicised confrontation between Greenpeace and Shell over the dumping of an oilrig in the North Sea. In the end Greenpeace was successful in forcing the Oil Company to dismantle the rig.

There is also a potential conflict **between companies and government**. An increase in corporation tax may see firms try to reduce their profits. A trade embargo on a certain country might have a devastating effect on export orders.

Despite these potential conflicts, companies are working in a more harmonious way than they were twenty years ago. The publication of **the Cadbury report has raised** firm's **awareness of issues such as corporate governance and social responsibility**. Moreover, in the light of criticism of excessive pay awards the Greenbury committee was set up to take a look at directors salaries.

## 32   NEAR ENVIRONMENT

(a) **Competitive forces**

**Five forces in** the competitive environment.

(i)    **The threat of new entrants**. A new entrant will bring **extra capacity** into an industry and poses a threat to established firms because they may lose market share with a consequent potential loss of economies of scale. The strength of the threat from new entrants depends on the strength of the **barriers to entry** and on the likely **response of existing competitors** to the new entrant.

(ii)   **The threat of substitute products or services**. Substitute products are produced by a different industry but satisfy the same customer need. For example, railway travel is a substitute for private motor travel. Substitutes pose a threat because they limit the ability of a firm to charge high prices for its products and the firm is likely to find the demand for its products is relatively sensitive to price.

(iii) **The bargaining power of customers.** Customers require better quality products and services at lower prices. The strength of the threat from the bargaining power of customers will depend on how important the product is to the customer, the cost to the customer of switching from one supplier to another and whether a customer's purchases from the industry represent a large or small proportion of the customer's total purchases.

(iv) **The bargaining power of suppliers.** Suppliers can influence the profitability of a firm by exerting pressure for higher prices or by reducing the quality of the goods and services which they supply. The bargaining power of the supplier depends on the number of suppliers in the industry, the importance of the supplier's product to the firm, the cost to the firm of switching from one supplier to another.

(v) **The rivalry amongst current competitors.** Although rivalry can be beneficial in helping the industry to expand, it might leave demand unchanged. In this case the individual firms will be incurring costs on sales promotion campaigns, advertising battles and new product development and they will be charging lower prices and so making lower profits without gaining any benefits except maintaining market share.

(b) A **stakeholder** is any person or organisation with an interest in the organisation.

(i) **Internal stakeholders. Management and employees** are key stakeholders and are interested in the following.

(1) The **organisation's continuation and growth.** The organisation is a place where management and employees spend a great deal of their time and energy. It pays them.

(2) Satisfaction of **personal goals** such as pay, security, social needs, self actualisation etc.

(ii) **Shareholders.** Their main interest is a **return on their investment,** whether in the short or long term. As shareholders own the business, this is a commercial organisation's prime objective (at least in the UK).

(iii) **Bankers** are interested in cash flow, so that interest is paid, overdrafts do not get out of hand, loans are repaid and any security is adequate.

(iv) **Customers** want products and services, their prime interest. But customer may also be concerned with after-sales service (eg complaints-handling).

(v) **Suppliers** will expect to be paid and will be interested in future business.

(vi) The government has an interest in:

(1) Tax revenue (corporation tax, VAT) or other revenue (in the case of the public sector)

(2) Compliance with legislation (eg on health and safety)

(3) Statistics

(4) Regional development (as companies, all employers and wealth creators)

(vii) **Local authorities** are also interested, because companies can:

(1) Bring local employment

(2) Affect the local environment (eg by increasing road traffic).

(viii) **Professional bodies** are interested to ensure that members who work for companies comply with professional ethics and standards.

(ix) **Pressure groups** are interested in the organisation in so far as its activities affects their areas of concern (eg the environment).

## 33    PREPARATION QUESTION: FRS 15

(a) (i)    FRS 15 defines tangible assets as follows.

'Assets that have physical substance and are held for use in the production or supply of goods or services, for rental to others, or for administrative purposes on a continuing basis in the reporting entity's activities.'

The two important aspects of this definition to consider are the fact that the assets **have physical substance**, and are thus distinguished from intangible fixed assets, and that the assets are **held for use on a continuing basis**, differentiating fixed assets from current assets.

(ii)    FRS 15 requires that tangible fixed assets should initially be measured at **cost**. This applies whether the asset is purchased or whether it is constructed. 'Cost', broadly speaking, is purchase cost less any trade discounts plus any costs **directly attributable** to bringing it into working condition for its intended use. Examples of directly attributable costs include the following

- The incremental costs to the entity that would have been avoided only if the tangible fixed asset had not been constructed or acquired    *unavoidable*

- The labour costs of own employees arising directly from the construction or acquisition of the tangible fixed asset

Administration and other general overhead costs would, logically, be excluded form the cost of a tangible fixed asset.

*decommissioning costs.*

Directly attributable costs include costs of site preparation and clearance. Also included is the estimated cost of dismantling and removing the asset and restoring the site but only to the extent that it is recognised as a provision under FRS 12 *Provisions, contingent liabilities and contingent assets*. The amount to be ✓ capitalised in accordance with the principles of FRS 12 would be the amount of **foreseeable expenditure**, discounted where appropriate.

(b)    In this situation, Kabin Ltd is **changing from not providing depreciation to providing depreciation on its properties**. The company is correct in separating the property into **different components** with significantly different useful economic lives, as this is required by FRS 15. However, the question arises as to whether the carrying amount of the components are to be depreciated prospectively over their remaining useful economic lives or whether the change should be reflected as a prior year adjustment.

Generally FRS 15 states that revisions to useful economic lives, including those where assets are now being depreciated for the first time, should be treated as a change in estimate and recognised *etc* prospectively. However, a specific exception is made in circumstances where assets are being split into different components with significantly different useful economic lives for depreciation purposes for the first time. Such changes should be treated as a **change in accounting policy**, in other words as a prior year adjustment.

In the case of the split of the property between land and buildings, a case **cannot** be made for **providing backlog depreciation** as a **prior year adjustment**. Both the

Companies Act 1985 and SSAP 12, the forerunner of FRS 15 required that land and buildings should be treated separately for the purposes of depreciation on the grounds that buildings have a limited useful life while land does not. Therefore splitting the property between land and buildings is not identifying separate components for the first time, and consequently the **carrying amount of the building should be depreciated prospectively** over its remaining (revised) useful economic life.

However, the **shop facias** of the retail stores are different. In the past they have been treated as an integral part of the building of which they formed a part. However, under FRS 15 they are separate components because they have **substantially different useful economic lives**. Accordingly, where this asset is separated out for the first time and depreciated over its (shorter) useful life, there should be an **adjustment** for the accumulated depreciation that would have been charged if the new policy had always been in force. FRS 15 therefore allows a prior year adjustment in this case.

## 34 PREPARATION QUESTION: REVLAUATIONS

(a) **Arguments for revaluing tangible fixed assets**

   (i)   **Consistency and comparability** are important qualities of financial information. If all the assets in a particular class are revalued at the same time, there is consistency and comparability in the financial statements.

   (ii)   Subsequent **depreciation charges** are a **better reflection of the economic benefits consumed** by such assets.

   (iii)   Higher carrying values for tangible fixed assets have a **favourable effect** on the reporting entity's **capital gearing**.

   (iv)   **Relevance and reliability** also commonly seen a desirable characteristics of financial information. Gross amounts for revalued assets are up-to-date, relevant and fairly reliable.

**Arguments against revaluing tangible fixed assets**

   (i)   Carrying out fixed asset revaluations is a **costly and time-consuming** exercise.

   (ii)   It may not be practical to carry out all revaluations at the same time. This can lead to **inconsistencies in reported carrying** values, particularly if the market for the assets is highly volatile.

   (iii)   The revaluation process is **very subjective** and there is a danger that users will believe the balance sheet it a statement of the worth of the reporting entity.

   (iv)   Upward revaluations lead to **higher depreciation charges** and therefore **lower reported profits,** with subsequent effects on financial performance measures such as ROCE.

   (v)   The above may mean that only some fixed assets are revalued (even if this includes all of one class of fixed asset such as freehold properties). The resulting **financial statements may then be a hybrid of replacement** of market values and historical cost.

(b) **Proposal to revalue Property One only**

The required treatment is governed by FRS 15 *Tangible fixed assets*. If the directors agree to a **policy of revaluing** tangible fixed assets, **all the assets in a particular class must be revalued**. These valuations must be **kept up-to-date**. Both properties should be revalued at the same date (1 October 20X0) and then every five years with a full professional valuation. An interim valuation should take place at the end of the third year, which may be undertaken internally. Alternatively, the class of fixed assets may be revalued under a **rolling programme** over five years. This would allow the properties to be revalued individually at different times. There would still need to be an interim valuation.

Both properties are intended for **continuing use**. It is therefore **appropriate** for their **current use value** (rather than market value) to form the basis of their valuation in the financial statements. It will also be the basis for subsequent depreciation of the buildings element.

The directors cannot 'cherry pick' which properties they chose to revalue; the process must be consistent. They will need to report all revaluation gains and losses if they adopt a policy of revaluing properties. The **fall in value of Property Two will need to be recognised** as part of this policy.

Following FRS 15, it will be quite acceptable to retain the carrying values of other classes of tangible fixed assets (namely plant and fixtures) at their historical cost, less depreciation.

(c) NET BOOK VALUES OF REVALUED PROPERTIES AT 30 SEPTEMBER 20X1

|  | Property One | Property Two | Totals |
|---|---|---|---|
|  | £'000 | £'000 | £'000 |
| Historical cost net book value at 1.1.X0 | 15,000 | 14,000 | 29,000 |
| Revaluation gain | 1,800 |  | 1,800 |
| Revaluation loss/deficit |  | (2,000) | (2,000) |
| Gross value at 30.9.X1 | 16,800 | 12,000 | 28,800 |
| Depreciation to 30.9.X1 |  |  |  |
| (16,800 × 50% × 1/40) | 210 |  |  |
| (12,000 × 50% × 1.40) |  | 150 | 360 |
| Net book value at 30.9.X1 | 16,5090 | 11,850 | 28,440 |

The £1.8m **revaluation gain** on Property One should be credited to the non-distributable revaluation reserve. It should also be reported/recognised in the statement of **total recognised gains and losses** (STRGL) for the year ended 30 September 20X1.

As Property Two has not been previously revalued, the **£2m deficit** should be reported/recognised in the **profit and loss account** for the year ended 30 September 20X1. This is **effectively an impairment charge** or a reflection of the fact that depreciation over the property's previous years of use was understated.

# 35 PREPARATION QUESTION: INCOME-GENERATING UNITS

(a) To determine whether impairment of a fixed asset has incurred, it is necessary to compare the **carrying amount** of the asset with its **recoverable amount**. The recoverable amount is the **higher of net realisable value and value in use**. It is not always easy to estimate value in use. In particular, it is not always practicable to identify cash flows arising from an individual fixed asset. If this is the case, value in use should be calculated as the level of **income-generating units**.

An **income-generating unit** is defined as a group of assets, liabilities and associated goodwill that generates income that is **largely independent of the reporting entity's other income streams.** The assets and liabilities include those already involved in generating the income and an appropriate portion of those used to generate more than one income stream.

(b) (i) The income-generating unit comprises **all the sites** at which the product can be made.

(ii) **Each restaurant** is an **income-generating unit** by itself. However, any impairment of individual restaurants is unlikely to be material. A material impairment is likely to occur only when a number of restaurants are affected together by the same economic factors. It may therefore be acceptable to consider **groupings of restaurants** affected by the same economic factors rather than each individual restaurant.

## 36   IMPAIRMENT

> **Tutor's hint**. This question required you to discuss the impairment of assets in terms of the indicators of the impairment loss under FRS 11. The final part of the question required candidates to apply the principles of part (a) to two small cases. Part (b) is a good illustration of how the examiner could test your ability to apply an accounting standard by asking you to explain how certain events will be reflected in the financial statements. Notice that the requirement in part (b) asks you to 'describe' – number-crunching alone is not sufficient.
>
> Review your answer carefully
>
> **Examiner's comment**. Candidates performed very well on this question, particularly parts (a) and (b)(i). In part (b)(ii) some candidates did not realise that the carrying amount of the asset should not be reduced below net realisable value.

(a) (i) **Indications** of an impairment loss include the following.

(1) A significant **decrease in the market value** of an asset in excess of normal depreciation

(2) Adverse, significant **changes in the value of the business** or market in which the asset is used

(3) **Technological, economic, legal** or **environmental changes** affecting the business in which the asset is used

(4) **Financial factors** such as interest rate changes, market profitability, current period operating losses and net cash outflows adversely affecting the entity which uses the asset

(5) A major loss of **key employees**

(6) Damage, obsolescence or other **physical changes** to the asset

(7) An indication that construction or purchase **costs have increased** so that expected profits from new assets will not arise as originally expected

(8) **Management commitment** to **reorganisation or redundancy programmes**

(9) **Adverse changes in the fair value indicators** used to establish the fair value of an asset, eg multiples of turnover

(ii) Under FRS 11 possible impairment losses are **treated** as follows.

(1) If any of the above indicators suggest an impairment has occurred then an **impairment review** must be carried out.

(2) The **carrying value** of an asset is **compared to its recoverable amount** (the higher of NRV and value in use).

(3) For assets held at cost less depreciation if the **carrying amount exceeds** the **recoverable amount**, the asset is impaired and must be **written down** through the profit and loss account.

(4) Where assets are held at **valuation impairment losses** are recognised in the **statement of total recognised gains and losses** until the carrying value falls below depreciated historical cost. Impairments below depreciated historical cost are recognised in profit and loss account.

(5) It may be more convenient to test impairment for **groups of assets** known as **income generating units** (IGU). Impairment should be tested for the smallest IGU which produces an independent income stream. Impairment **losses** in an IGU should be **allocated firstly to goodwill, then capitalised intangibles and finally to tangible assets.**

(6) **Past impairment losses may be reversed** if the recoverable amount increases because of changed economic conditions. The losses should only be reversed to the original carrying amount, i.e. the amount it would have been if the original impairment had not occurred.

(7) When impairment losses arise on fixed assets, the **remaining useful economic life should be reviewed** and revised if necessary.

(b) (i) Impaired assets need to be written down to their recoverable amount, which is the higher of NRV and value in use.

For the productive assets:

| | |
|---|---|
| Carrying value | £290,000 |
| Value in use | £248,000 |
| NRV | £120,000 |

*Note.* Value in use is calculated as the discounted present value of cash flows from use of the asset. The cash flows are three years of £100,000, therefore use a discount factor (from tables) of 2.487.

The impairment loss is therefore £(290,000 – 248,700) = £41,300.

This will be written off to the profit and loss account.

(ii) Impairment losses should be recognised if the recoverable amount of the income generating unit is less than the carrying value of the unit (the taxi business).

At February 1 20X8

| | 1.1.X8 £'000 | Impairment loss £'000 | 1.2.X8 £'000 |
|---|---|---|---|
| Goodwill (230 – 190) | 40 | (15) | 25 |
| Intangibles | 30 | - | 30 |
| Vehicles | 120 | (30) | 90 |
| Sundry net assets | 40 | - | 40 |
| | 230 | (45) | 185 |

An impairment loss of £30,000 is recognised for the stolen vehicle the balance of £15,000 attributable to the IGU is applied initially to goodwill.

At 1 March 20X8

|  | 1.2.X8 | Impairment loss | 1.3.X8 |
|---|---|---|---|
|  | £'000 | £'000 | £'000 |
| Goodwill (230 – 190 – 15) | 25 | (25) | - |
| Intangibles | 30 | (5) | 25 |
| Vehicles | 90 | - | 90 |
| Sundry net assets | 40 | - | 40 |
|  | 185 | | 155 |

In this case, there is an indication that the value of the intangible asset, the licence, has fallen to £25,000 so an impairment loss of £5000 is recognised. There is no indication that the other tangible assets are impaired but value in use has fallen to £150,000.

NRV is therefore assumed to be £185,000 – £25,000 (goodwill) – £5,000 (licence)= £155,000.

The carrying amount is reduced to the higher of NRV or value in use as the recoverable amount.

## 37 YUKON

> **Tutor's hint**. You should by now be familiar with FRS 10. When reviewing your answer you must consider how easy marks could have been generated. There are some conceptually very difficult points in this question where you could have become bogged down. However, there are many basic elements to the goodwill calculation which easily represent more than 50% of the marks.

(a) **Goodwill** is the **difference** between the **cost** of an acquired entity and the aggregate of the **fair value of the entity's identifiable assets and liabilities**. FRS 10 deals with goodwill and intangible assets.

**Positive purchased goodwill** is **capitalised and amortised** in the P&L account over its useful economic life.

**Purchased intangible assets** may be **capitalised** provided they can be **reliably measured** (at fair value assessed by reference to replacement cost or market value). It would be expected that there is an active market for the items concerned in order that fair values may be determined. Non-purchased goodwill is not to be recogniscd. Non-purchased intangible assets may be recognised provided that there is a readily ascertainable market value. FRS 10 gives items such as franchises as examples. Brand names are unlikely to have a readily ascertainable market value and are thus not items that would be capitalised.

FRS 10 deals with the recognition and treatment of both positive and negative goodwill.

(b) The amortisation treatments required by FRS 10 are as follows.

(i) **Amortisation** is carried out on a **systematic basis** over the useful economic life which is presumed to be **20 years**

(ii) If the life is deemed to be less than 20 years, the shorter period will be used

(iii) If the life is considered **indefinite**, goodwill is **not amortised**, subject to **annual impairment reviews** as now required by FRS 11 *Impairment of fixed assets and goodwill*. Note that where goodwill is not amortised, a 'true and fair override' disclosure will be needed since CA 1985 requires depreciation to be applied.

(iv)   Where negative goodwill exists, it may be credited on a prudent basis to the P&L account in the periods in which the items leading to the creation of negative goodwill (mainly stock and fixed assets) are realised by sale or depreciation.

(c)   Fair values of net assets acquired at 31 May 20X6 by Territory plc:

|  | £'000 |
|---|---|
| Intangible assets (expected to be included in goodwill) | nil |
| Land and buildings (market value) | 20,000 |
| Other tangible assets | 18,000 |
| Stocks (at NRV) | 20,000 |
| Debtors | 23,200 |
| Cash | 8,800 |
| Creditors due within 1 year | (24,000) |
| Creditors after more than 1 year (W) | (13,147) |
| Provisions for liabilities and charges | (886) |
| Fair value | 51,967 |
| Purchase consideration (fair value) | |
| 25m shares at market price £2.25 | 56,250 |
| Cash | 10,000 |
| | 66,250 |
| Goodwill arising on acceptance by 80% of shareholders | |
| $(66,250 - 51,967) \times 80\%$ | 11,426 |

*Working: Amount due 31 May 20X9*

Initial loan                                                £11m

Amount repayable £11m $\times (1.1)^4$ =                     £16.1051m

(present value £11m of an amount of £16.1051m repayable after 4 years at 10%)

The market rates of interest are taken into account in determining fair values of this liability. Therefore the fair value of the loan at 31 May 20X6 is:

$$\frac{£16,105,100}{(1.07)^3} = £13,146,599$$

*Amortisation*

Year ended 31 May 20X6 = £11,426,000 $\times$ 1/10 = £1,143,000

|  | £'000 |
|---|---|
| Year ended 31 May 20X7 | |
| Carrying value at 1 June 20X6 = 11,426,000 − 1,143,000 | 10,283 |
| Adjustment to fair value of land and buildings per valuer's report | |
| £23,000,000 − 20,000,000 = £3,000,000 | |
| 80% thereof £2,400,000; £2,400,000 $\times$ 0.9 (Note 1) | (2,160) |
| Intangible assets: adjustment (Note 2) | (4,334) |
| Revised goodwill figure | 3,789 |
| Amortisation (1/9) | 421 |
| Write off of tangible assets | 4,334 |
| P&L account charge | 4,755 |

*Notes*

1   The goodwill figure would be £2.4m less at 1 June 20X6 had the new valuation been incorporated, therefore as 1 year's amortisation of goodwill has occurred the adjustment to goodwill is 9/10 of the revaluation increase.

2   The intangible assets were deemed worthless but included in the original goodwill calculation. Therefore the deduction is

$$£6,020,000 \times 80\% \times 9/10 = £4,344,400$$

**38   MG**

> **Tutor's hint**. This is still quite a controversial topic. You should construct sound logical arguments in each part.

(a)   In the past (before FRS 10 was published), the main reasons for capitalising purchased brands were as follows.

(i)   **Goodwill reduction**

In the acquisition of another business, by attributing some of the excess of consideration over the fair value of net assets acquired to purchased brands, the value of goodwill was reduced. This meant that there was less goodwill to write off immediately to reserves (the preferred treatment under SSAP 22), or to amortise over its useful life. Brands capitalised in such a way were rarely amortised as they were claimed to hold their value through promotional costs in the profit and loss account.

(ii)   **Gearing improvement**

When brands were recognised as an asset rather than a reduction in net worth, the structure of the balance sheet was improved and gearing was reduced.

(iii)   **Share price/earnings effect**

If brands are recognised as non-depreciating assets, there is no adverse effect on earnings in the future, as there would be if goodwill was being amortised. These improved earnings improve the share price, although the market may discount the effect of such brands. This practice is no longer permitted, because FRS 10 requires separately identifiable brands to be treated in the same way as goodwill.

(b)   The main requirements which should be met when such brands are capitalised are as follows.

(i)   The asset should only be recognised if a **distinguishable cash flow stream** can be identified which relates to the brand in question.

(ii)   The value of the brands should be **reviewed yearly**. Any diminution in value should be written off immediately to reserves. This diminution could relate to a reduction in expected cash flows or a new strong competitor in the market.

(iii)   All brands should be **treated in the same way**, using the same criteria for recognition and valuation.

(iv)   Brands can only be **revalued downwards**, not upwards.

(c)   **Arguments for capitalisation**

The main argument used in favour of capitalising non-purchased (and purchased) brands is that it reflects commercial reality by making the balance sheet an indicator of the true financial strength of an enterprise. Obviously, the arguments concerning goodwill do not apply to non-purchased brands. However, the gearing position of the company will be improved.

If non-purchased brands are capitalised, it is argued that predators would not be able to acquire companies with valuable brands at less than their true value. An example of this was Nestle's takeover of Rowntree.

Many companies might argue that the inclusion of non-purchased brands will provide valuable information to the users of accounts.

**Brand valuation**

The value of purchased brands are probably quite easy to determine because the acquiring company may have decided on their 'fair value' when deciding how much to offer for the company.

There are various methods of valuation for non-purchased brands. Some years ago Ranks Hovis McDougall (RHM) used an earnings multiple approach rather similar to valuing a share on a P/E basis. Confusingly, this valuation was not intended to produce a market value for its brands but to help in ensuring that the consolidated balance sheet showed 'the underlying financial strength of the business'. It was also intended to increase management awareness of the importance of brand management.

Methods of accounting for brands include the use of SSAP 13 rules and capitalisation at directors' valuation, as well as the prudent approach of ignoring their value.

The scope for creative accounting for brands using SSAP 13 is strictly limited and revaluation of development expenditure is not possible (except downwards). If directors' valuation is used, the directors usually refer the detailed valuation work to a specialist firm like Interbrand UK Ltd (which valued RHM's brands). The methods adopted include use of discounted cash flow techniques, earnings multiple approaches, return on investment approaches and reference to market transactions. A mixture of techniques may be used and all must take into account a multiplicity of factors such as:

(i)     Market share and strength of competition
(ii)    Stability and nature of market
(iii)   Market conditions
(iv)   Marketing and technical back-up invested by the owner
(v)    Internationality
(vi)   Legal protection for the brand name and concept

(d) **Regulation of brand accounting**

FRS 10 tackles the subject of non-purchased brands by stating unequivocally that:

> 'An internally developed intangible asset may be recognised only if it has a readily ascertainable market value.'

Readily ascertainable market value is defined as:

> 'The value of an intangible asset that is established by reference to a market where:
>
> (a)   the asset belongs to a homogeneous population of asset that are equivalent in all material respects; and
>
> (b)   an active market, evidenced by frequent transactions, exists for that population of assets.'

Where this is not the case, such brands must be subsumed in internally-generated goodwill, which 'should not be recognised'.

## 39  TALL

(a)

MEMORANDUM

To:     Assistant Accountant
From:   Management Accountant
Date:   10 October 20X9

**Treatment of Capital Instruments**

Although there may be some similarities between the bonds and the preference shares, they should not be treated in the same way. The accounting standard governing their treatment is FRS 4 *Capital instruments.*

The **bonds** are not legally shares and they carry an **obligation to transfer economic events** on redemption. Under FRS 4 they would therefore be regarded as **debt instruments** and shown as **a long-term liability** in the creditors section of the balance sheet. The **finance cost** should be allocated to individual accounting periods so that a **uniform percentage** of the amount outstanding is charged in the period. This is unaffected by the fact that no payments are made until redemption.

The **preference shares**, by contrast, would be shown in as part of **shareholders' funds** in the balance sheet under FRS 4. They are **non-equity** shares – although legally shares they are redeemable at a fixed future date and are therefore less 'permanent' than equity shares. FRS 4 requires that they be **disclosed separately from equity shares,** but the disclosure can be given in a note to the financial statements.

The **finance cost** should be **allocated uniformly** to individual accounting periods, despite the fact that no payments are to be made until redemption.

(b)

| | £'000 |
|---|---:|
| Equity shares capital | 100,000 |
| Non equity share capital | |
| Preference shares | 10,000 |
| Share premium account (W1) | 37,700 |
| Profit and loss account | 89,700 |
| | 237,400 |
| | |
| Net assets (W2) | 237,400 |

*Workings*

1   *Share premium account*

| | £'000 | £'000 |
|---|---:|---:|
| Existing balance | | 35,800 |
| Premium on issue of preference shares | 2,000 | |
| Less issues costs | 100 | |
| | | 1,900 |
| New balance | | 37,700 |

2   *Net assets*

| | £'000 |
|---|---:|
| Existing balance | 225,500 |
| Net proceeds of preference | |
| Share issue (10,000 + 1,900) | 11,900 |
| Net proceeds from issue of bonds | 15,000 |
| Creditor for bonds | (15,000) |
| New balance | 237,400 |

(c) *Finance cost of bonds*

$$\frac{\text{Carrying value}}{\text{Value on redemption}} = \frac{15}{24.15} = 0.621$$

From present value tables, implicit interest rate (5 years) is 10%.

∴Interest for the year is 10% × £15m = £1.5m. this should be shown under 'interest payable and similar charges'.

*Finance cost of preference shares*

$$\frac{\text{Carrying value}}{\text{Value on redemption}} = \frac{11.9}{23.5} = 0.506$$

From present value tables, implicit interest rate (6 years) is 12%.

∴Interest for the year is £11.9m × 12% = £1,428,000. This should be shown as an appropriation of profit.

# 40 DERIVATIVES

> **Tutor's hint.** This was an introductory question to the subject of derivatives, and perhaps therefore not typical of the sort of question that is likely to be set. The examples given in part (b) were fairly simple. There are basic marks available in the main written elements.
>
> **Examiner's comment.** Most people answered the written parts of this question well but fell down on the numerical bits.

(a) (i) **Concerns**

(1) The **growth and complexity** of financial instruments has increased dramatically in recent years.

(2) Companies tend to use a **range of instruments** to transform and manage **risk**.

(3) **Accounting standards did not deal adequately** with the growth of these complex capital instruments.

(4) Many derivatives are **not recognised in the balance sheet** because they have **no cost** and the financial statements use the historic cost concept.

(5) Derivatives may expose an entity to **significant risks.**

(6) Financial assets are often recognised at depreciated historic cost even where **market values differ** considerably.

(7) **Unrealised gains and losses** arising from changes in value of financial instruments are **often ignored**. Unrealised losses often arise where an instrument is regarded as a hedge.

(8) Companies have tended to vary the timing of profit recognition on instruments in order to engage in profit smoothing.

(9) Circumstances can change rapidly because of volatile capital markets and undisclosed risks can increase dramatically.

(ii) Accounting standards in recent years have generally dealt with issues of recognition, measurement and disclosure. However, FRS 13 deals only with disclosure. Disclosure is very important, but **recognition and measurement** issues also need addressing.

(1) At present many derivatives are **kept off the balance sheets** and unrealised gains and losses are ignored.

(2) Narrative disclosures are not sufficient to deal with **hedge accounting issues.**

(3) The possible **measurement bases** need to be considered and agreed upon, specifically whether current values should be used.

(4) The question of **impairment** of financial instruments also needs to be addressed.

(b) (i) The alternatives are (only three required)

(1) **All gains and losses to the profit and loss account**

This would ensure that management decisions are reflected in reported results and it would restrict the ability to be creative through the way in which gains and losses are reported.

(2) **Some gains/losses to the profit and loss account, others to the statement of total recognised gains and losses.**

Gains and losses on long term items could go into the STRGL, with short term items in the profit and loss account. The main issue would be enforcing rules concerning the distinction between the types of gains and losses to avoid creative accounting and to ensure consistency.

(3) **Some gains and losses recorded within assets and liabilities or as a part of shareholders funds and then transferred to the profit and loss account in future periods as they become realised.**

Gains and losses are effectively deferred until realised over the life of the instrument.

This reflects present practice on many capital instruments required by FRS 4. However, the opportunity to defer from the year in which gains and losses occur could give rise to creative accounting. Showing deferred debits or credits as a component of shareholders' funds is 'reserve accounting' which is difficult to justify.

(4) **Some gains and losses could be held in the STRGL and then transferred to the profit and loss account as they become realised.**

This has the advantage that all gains and losses would be recorded as they occur. However, there is a danger that the STRGL would become a temporary holding account, and would therefore be devalued as a financial statement.

Future plans to combine the STRGL and the profit and loss account into an all embracing statement of performance may rationalise the options discussed. This is the subject of a discussion paper.

(ii)

|  | 20X9 £'000 | 20Y0 £'000 | 20Y1 £'000 |
|---|---|---|---|
| Interest at 5% | 1,500 | 1,500 | 1,500 |
| Adjustment to fair value | - | 267 (W3) | (288) (W4) |
| Effective interest | 1,500 | 1,767 | 1,212 |
| Gains/loss due to change in fair value | (550) (W1) | 571 (W2) | - |
| Net charge to P&L | 950 | 2,338 | 1,212 |

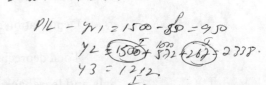

*Workings*

1   *Loss due to change in fair value*

Fair value of debt at 30 November 20X9:

|  | £m | *Discounted at 6%* £ |
|---|---|---|
| Interest payable 30.11.Y0 | 1.5 | 1,415,094 |
| Interest on capital due 30.11.Y1 | 31.5 | 28,034,887 |
|  |  | 29,449,981 |

Gain on fair value = £(30m – 29.45m) = £550,000 ✓

2   *Loss due to change in fair value*

|  | £m | *Discounted at 4%* £ |
|---|---|---|
| Fair value of debt at 30.11.20Y0 |  |  |
| Interest and capital due | 31.5 | 30,288,461 |

Loss due to change in fair value = £30,288m – (0.267m + 29.45m) = £571,000

3   *Interest adjustment*

6% × £29.45m (W1) = £1.767

∴ Adjustment is £1.767 – £1.5m = £0.267m

4   *Interest adjustment*

4% × £30.288m (W2) = £1.212m

∴ Adjustment is £1.212m – £1.5m = £(0.288m)

---

## 41   FINALEYES

> **Tutor's hint**. This question covers a variety of post balance sheet events, but standards other than SSAP 17 are involved and you should identify these where relevant. Make sure you identify the correct standard, for example in (c) SSAP 21 is not an issue, nor is FRS 4 in (a). Make sure you state the correct accounting treatment (with reasons) and then give the correct adjustments or disclosure. The examiner may not identify the relevant standard in the exam.
>
> **Examiner's comment**. Candidates fared badly if they applied the inappropriate FRS or where the accounting entries were incorrect. However, there were some excellent answers with some candidates displaying a good range of knowledge and skills.

(a)   **Share issue**

(i)   *Accounting treatment*

This is a **non-adjusting post balance sheet event** because, although the announcement was made before the year end, the conditions for receipt of the funds did not exist at the balance sheet date. Nor did the entitlement to receive the funds exist at the year end as the intention to issue the shares might not eventually have been carried out.

(ii)   *Required adjustment/disclosure*

Disclosure should be by note, because of the **materiality** of the issue, giving the date of issue, the number of shares issued (£14m/£7.00 = 2m shares), the price at which they were issued (£7.00) and the total funds raised (£14m). The percentage increase in the company's share capital should be noted (2m/40m = 5%) and the use for which the funds were raised.

(b) **Acquisition of a plant**

(i) *Accounting treatment*

Considering the definition of liabilities given by the ASB, the first part is satisfied in that it seems clear that in 15 years' time the company must replace the heating system, ie **transfer economic benefits**. The question of whether a liability arises out of past transactions or events is more vexed. Arguments could range from the extremes of full provision of £30,000 per year (anticipating all losses but no profits, ie prudence) to no provision at all because the 'past event' will be the actual replacement in 15 years' time.

When the system is replaced, the **assets** of the company will be **increased, not** its **liabilities**. Thus, the most sensible approach seems to be to make a provision for depreciation of £30,000 per year, thereby matching the cost of the heating system to the benefit received from it. The useful life should be 15 years, not the 40 year life of the buildings.

(ii) *Required adjustment/disclosure*

The company should not have depreciated the entire £4m over the 40 years and then made an additional provision of £30,000 for the heating system. Instead, depreciation should be calculated separately on buildings and plant and machinery.

$$\text{Depreciation on buildings} = \frac{\text{£4m} - \text{£0.45m}}{40} = \text{£88,750}$$

Total depreciation = £88,750 + £30,000 = £118,750

(c) **Sale and leaseback of factory**

(i) *Accounting treatment*

This is a **post balance sheet event which is non-adjusting** because it concerns conditions which did not exist at the balance sheet date. It must be disclosed by way of a note, however, because its materiality (£10m/£80m = 12.5% of net assets) is such that its non-disclosure would prevent users obtaining a true and fair view of the financial statements.

(ii) *Required adjustment/disclosure*

A note is required, as in (a) above, laying out the particulars of the transaction, namely: the sale price and book value of the factory (at 30 April 20X6), the intention to lease back over 20 years at market rents, and the date the contracts were signed.

(d) **Stock valuation errors**

(i) *Accounting treatment*

**Prior year adjustments** are defined by FRS 3 *Reporting financial performance* as material adjustments applicable to prior periods arising from changes in accounting policies or from the correction of fundamental errors.

The problem here is that the item is **not material** enough in relation to the company's overall results to be considered fundamental. In addition, because stock entries reverse each year, it is not the cumulative figure which should be adjusted, even if the item qualified as a prior year adjustment.

There has also been no change in accounting policy, only a failure to apply an existing one.

(ii)    *Required adjustment/disclosure*

The prior year adjustment should be **reversed** and so should the stock valuation adjustment.

The stock valuation at 30 April 20X6 should be reduced by £115,000. For the profit and loss account the same amount should be debited to cost of sales.

## 42    TIMBER PRODUCTS

> **Tutor's hint**. This question covers all the major types of off balance sheet finance which appear in the application notes of FRS 5. You should therefore be familiar with the way each should be treated. Part (a) should earn you some easy marks.
>
> Review solution to check that for each part of the question you have:
>
> Met the specific requirements for each part (eg. explain, entries in balance sheet and profit and loss accounts, giving reasons etc)
>
> Demonstrated your technical knowledge of FRS 5
>
> Clearly identified the issues in each of the transactions.
>
> **Examiner's comment**. Part (a) was often well answered, as long as candidates didn't just write down all they knew on FRS 5. In part (b), candidates knew more about transactions (i) to (iii) than about transaction (iv), where they failed to identify the quasi subsidiary. Candidates approached part (b) as a finance vs operating lease decision and credit was given for this approach.

(a)    (i)    **FRS 5's objective** is:

> 'to ensure that the substance of an entity's transactions is reported in its financial statements. The commercial effect of the entity's transactions and any resulting assets, liabilities, gains or losses, should be faithfully represented in its financial statements.'

FRS 5's **fundamental principle** is that the substance of an entity's transactions should be reflected in its accounts, ie the substance of a transaction should be shown, not just its legal form. The key considerations are whether a transaction has given rise to new assets and liabilities, and whether it has changed any existing assets and liabilities. Sometimes there will be a series of connected transactions to be evaluated, not just a single transaction. It is necessary to identify and account for the substance of the series of transactions as a whole, rather than addressing each transaction individually.

The standard defines assets and liabilities and these definitions tie in to the *Statement of Principles*.

(ii)    There are two main types of transaction where the FRS states that derecognition would be appropriate.

Firstly, where a transaction results in the transfer to another party of all **significant benefits and risks** relating to an asset, the entire asset should cease to be recognised. An example here is the sale of photocopy paper and toner at list price to a customer in a shop.

Secondly, the standard deals with **partial derecognition** where, although not all significant benefits and risks have been transferred, the transaction is more than a mere financing and has transferred enough of the benefits and risks to warrant at least some derecognition of the asset. An example is the sale of a photocopier by a manufacturer under a residual value guarantee.

(b) (i) **Factored debts**

Linked presentation would seem to be appropriate in this situation according to FRS 5 because:

(1)  some non-returnable proceeds have been received, but Timber Products has the right to further sums from Ready Support, the amounts of which depend on whether/when debtors will pay;

(2)  recourse for losses has a fixed monetary ceiling; and

(3)  Ready Support is paid only out of amounts collected from the factored debts and Timber Products has no right/obligation to repurchase the debts.

The accounting treatment in the balance sheet will be as follows.

|  | £m | £m |
|---|---|---|
| *Current assets: receivables subject to financing arrangements* | | |
| Gross receivables (15.0 – 0.6) | | 14.40 |
| Non-returnable proceeds | | |
| 90% × net debtors | 12.96 | |
| Potential recourse | (0.20) | |
| | | 12.76 |
| | | 1.64 |
| Cash | | 12.96 |
| *Creditors* | | |
| Recourse under factored debts | | 0.20 |

(ii) **Sale and repurchase agreement**

The characteristics of this transaction indicate that it is a secured loan, not a true sale of an asset, because Timber Products has not transferred the risks and benefits of ownership of the unseasoned hard wood to the buyer. FRS 5 therefore requires that the unseasoned hardwood should still be recognised as an asset (ie stock), that interest should be accrued, the carrying amount of the asset should be reviewed and that full disclosure should be made.

The accounting treatment is as follows.

|  | £m |
|---|---|
| *Year ended 31 October 20X5* | |
| *Profit and loss account* | |
| Interest payable (W) | 2.8 |

|  | £m |
|---|---|
| *Balance sheet* | |
| Stock | 40.0 |
| Loan payable after more than one year (W) | 42.8 |

*Working: interest payable*

You can work the interest rate on the loan from first principles without using the tables.

$$40(1 + r)^5 = 56.10$$

$$(1 + r)^5 = \frac{56.1}{40} = 1.4025 \text{ (see tables), } or$$

$$1 + r = \sqrt[5]{1.4025} = 1.07$$

$$r = 7\%$$

∴ Interest for first year = 7% × £40m = £2.8m ✓

∴ Balance outstanding = £42.8m

(iii)   **Consignment stock**

The characteristics of the consignment stock transaction indicate that the furniture is *not* an asset of the retailer on delivery, ie it remains an asset of Timber Products (mainly because the retailer has the right to return it). An indication that the stock *is* an asset of the retailer on delivery is the fact that the retailer is charged the price prevailing on the delivery date (rather than the date the stock is used by the retailer or the date the six month period expires).

On balance, the transaction should be treated as a genuine sale or return, with the price held for six months by the manufacturer. This is the more prudent view, indicating that the risks and benefits remain with Timber Products and this view is supported by the fact that retailers can return the stock just before the expiry of the six month period. The stock which has not been paid for should therefore be recognised by Timber Products at cost. The accounting treatment would therefore be as follows.

*Year ended 31 October 20X5*

| *Profit and loss account* | £'000 |
|---|---|
| Sales | 6,000 |
| Cost of sales (6,000 × 100/133$^1/_3$) | 4,500 |
| Gross profit | 1,500 |
| | |
| Other income | 50 |
| Other costs | |
| Insurance | 15 |
| Carriage | 10 |
| | 25 |

| *Balance sheet* | £'000 |
|---|---|
| Stock at cost (4,000 × 100/133$^1/_3$) | 3,000 |

*Note.* There is no absolute answer here. You could have argued that derecognition of the stock and recognition of the sale was more appropriate, in which case the figures would have been as follows.

| *Profit and loss account* | £'000 |
|---|---|
| Sales | 10,000 |
| Cost of sales | 7,500 |
| | 2,500 |

Other income and cost figures as above.

| *Balance sheet* | £'000 |
|---|---|
| Debtors | 4,000 |

A provision for returns would also be made based on past experience. A further point is that prudence might dictate that the stock should be recognised by both the retailer and Timber Products in their balance sheets.

(iv)   **Quasi subsidiary**

The circumstances of this transaction are such that, in effect, Inter plc is acting as a subsidiary to Timber Products, ie it is a quasi subsidiary under FRS 5. The transaction has been set up this way in order to avoid the definition of a subsidiary in FRS 2.

The accounting treatment will show the results of Inter plc relating to the factory consolidated into Timber Products results. The factory will appear in the balance sheet at £8.5m (cost to the group) and the loan to Offshore Banking plc will be shown at £10m under creditors. The profit on the sale of the factory will be cancelled out, as will the fee, as intra-group transactions. The consolidated profit and loss account will include the profit or loss made by the plant and the interest of £1.5m paid to Offshore Banking plc.

(c) There are two aspects to examine in relation to this transaction.

(i) Is this transaction a **secured loan**? Timber Products is bearing risks in terms of insurance and maintenance payments. If it was also shown that Timber Products was paying a financing cost for the construction of the asset, then the equipment should be recognised as an asset in the Timber Product balance sheet with a loan for the same amount secured on the asset. More information is required in order to determine whether the amounts paid to Extractor-Plus represent a lender's return or whether they are market-rate rental amounts.

(ii) Is this a **leasing transaction**? The company may be attempting to circumvent the SSAP 21 definition of a finance lease. Information required would include the cost of the equipment, any minimum lease payments (if the hourly use falls below a certain level) and the length of the contract.

## 43 LEASING

> **Tutor's hint.** Part (a) of this question allows you to get easy marks for knowledge of the distinction between operating leases and finance leases. It also asks for some of the shortcomings in the way leases are currently accounted for. This area is being debated at the moment by the standard-setting bodies, and a Discussion Paper has recently been published. Part (b) of the question required an explanation of how certain sale and leaseback transactions should be dealt with.
>
> **Examiner's comment.** Answers to part (a) showed that many candidates were not aware of current issues. In part (b) many candidates did not discuss the various elements of the question in sufficient detail, relying on a numerical answer.

(a) (i) A distinction must be made between finance and operating leases.

A finance lease is one which substantially transfers all of the risks and rewards of ownership of an asset to a lessee. An operating lease is any other type of lease.

Finance leases are capitalised in the accounts at the present value of the minimum lease payments using the lease term and the interest rate implicit in the lease. Any residual payments guaranteed by the lessee should also be taken into account. Assets are depreciated over the shorter of the lease term or useful economic life. The interest and principal elements of the lease repayments must be identified and the interest element allocated to appropriate periods. The lease liability is then appropriately reduced for the capital element. Finance charges should produce a constant periodic rate of charge.

Operating lease rentals are simply charged to the profit and loss account on a straight line basis over the lease term regardless of when the payments are due. The charges reflect the pattern of benefits from the leased asset.

(ii) Deficiencies in lease accounting are as follows.

(1) The distinction between treatment as a finance or operating lease is determined by the **substantial transfer** of risks and rewards of ownership to a lessee. If this occurs, a recognisable asset and liability are created in the lessee accounts. (This is normally taken as being the case if the lessee is non cancellable and the present value of the minimum lease payment is equal to

or greater than 90% of the fair value of the leased asset.) In other words, 'substantial' is normally judged against **quantitative not qualitative** criteria.

(2) Many operating leasing transactions have been **designed to fit** the **quantitative criteria**, while **in substance they are finance leases**. Typical areas of concern are responsibility for maintenance, insurance and so on.

(3) The 90% present value criterion may be satisfied by using a **contingent rental clause**. Contingent rentals would not come into the present value calculation.

(4) The **interest rate** implicit in the lease may not be available in which case an alternative **estimated** rate can be used. This again can lead to the present value criterion being circumvented.

(5) **Leases of land and buildings can be distorted** because land normally has an indefinite life and its title will not pass to a lessee, so that the lessee does not receive the risks and rewards of ownership. Companies can therefore distort the accounting treatment by allocating as large a value as possible to the land element so the lease is classified as an operating lease rather than a finance lease.

(6) The relative **ease of classifying a lease as operating** rather than finance by avoiding the criteria to determine the substantial transfer of risks and rewards of ownership is a **major deficiency of SSAP 21** leading to assets and liabilities not being recognised in the lessee's financial statements.

(b) (i) Where a lessee enters a **sale and leaseback transaction** resulting in an **operating lease** then the original asset should be **treated as sold**. If the transaction is at **fair value** then **immediate recognition** of the profit or loss should occur. If the transaction is **above fair value**, the **profit based on fair value** (98 – 33) ie £65m may be recognised immediately. The balance of profit in **excess of fair value** (198 – 98) ie £100m should be **deferred and amortised** over the shorter of the lease term and the period to the next lease rental review. In this case this would be amortised over 10 years, ie £10m pa.

However, as the sales value is not the fair value, the operating lease rentals (£24m) are likely to have been adjusted for the excess price paid for the assets. For AB plc the sales value is more than twice the fair value, and according to FRS 5 the substance of the transaction is one of sale of asset and a loan equalling the deferred income element, ie £100m. Therefore at least half of the commitments under the agreement, £24m/2 ie £12m pa could be viewed as repayment of the loan plus interest. The company could show the excess over fair value as a loan and part of the operating lease cost as a repayment of capital and interest on this amount.

(ii) The sale and leaseback appears to create a **finance lease** as the present value of the minimum lease payments is greater than 90% of the fair value of the plant (£43.5m + £43.5m × 2.49 = £151.82m compared with £152m). AB has to pay all the costs of maintenance and insurance and the lease covers the remaining life of the plant after which it can be purchased at a nominal amount.

Under FRS 5 the asset should **remain in the lessee's balance sheet at carrying value** and the sale proceeds (£152m) are shown as a creditor representing the finance lease liability. As payments are made they are treated partly as a repayment of the creditor and partly as a finance charge against income.

The revaluation reserve will continue to be treated as before, and if it is transferred to the profit and loss reserve, this will done over the lease term/asset life of four years.

## 44  HIRE

(a)  Many companies use operating leases to finance their use of assets, particularly land and buildings. Current accounting standards treat operating leases as if they were rental agreements, rather than financing arrangements. Neither the leased asset nor the liability for future payments appears in the lessee's balance sheet.

Companies wish to keep leased assets off the balance sheet. Problems have arisen because of the way in which SSAP 21 *Accounting for leases and hire purchase contracts* defines the two types of lease: finance lease and operating lease. A lease is presumed to be a finance lease if the present value of the minimum lease payments amounts to 90% or more of the fair value of the leased asset. SSAP 21 makes it clear that a finance lease is a lease which transfers the risks and rewards of ownership of the leased asset to the lessee and that it is possible for a lease to be a finance lease even if it fails the '90% test'. Factors such as the length of the lease and the arrangements for insuring and maintaining the asset should also be taken into account in determining the substance of an agreement.

In practice, the **'90% test' has been treated as an absolute threshold**. Lease agreements which are essentially finance leases are **deliberately structured** so that the present value of the lease payments is **just below 90%** of the fair value of the asset. These leases are then classified as operating leases. As a result, lessees may have **material assets and liabilities** that are **not recognised** in the financial statements. This means that key performance measures are distorted and the financial statements may be misleading to users. Further problems arise because under current standards it is possible for a lease to be classified as an operating lease by the lessee and as a finance lease by the lessor (so that neither party recognises the leased asset). If all leases were treated as finance leases these problems would be overcome.

Even where a lease is genuinely an operating lease, lessees may have **significant obligations** under lease agreements. A recent survey reported that in one sample of companies the average operating lease liability was £51 million compared with the average reported finance lease liability of £4 million. It is argued that keeping these amounts 'off balance sheet' **reduces the comparability** and usefulness of the financial statements.

Companies are required to **disclose** future operating lease commitments. This means that users can gain some idea of the materiality of the amounts involved. It is known that analysts use this information to adjust financial statements to show the effect of capitalising operating leases. Standard setters argue that the **market already takes account of operating leases,** so that in practice companies would have **little to lose** by bringing them onto the balance sheet.

(b) (i) **Effect of capitalising operating leases on the profit and loss account**

PROFIT AND LOSS ACCOUNT (EXTRACT)
FOR THE YEAR ENDED 30 NOVEMBER 20X0

|  | £m |
|---|---|
| Profit on ordinary activities before taxation | 176.0 |
| Add: operating lease rentals | 80.0 |
| Less: depreciation | (56.0) |
| Adjusted profit on ordinary activities before taxation | 200.0 |
| Tax on profit on ordinary activities: 60 + ((80 – 56) × 30%) | (67.2) |
| Profit on ordinary activities after taxation | 132.8 |

**Effect of capitalising operating leases on the balance sheet**

BALANCE SHEET (EXTRACT)
AS AT 30 NOVEMBER 20X0

|  | £m |
|---|---|
| Fixed assets (400 + 871 – 56) (W1) | 1,215.0 |
| Net current assets (W2) | 262.8 |
| Creditors: Amounts falling due after more than one year (W3) | (821.0) |
|  | 656.8 |
|  |  |
| Share capital | 400.0 |
| Profit and loss account (240 + 132.8 – 116) | 256.8 |
|  | 656.8 |

*Workings*

1  *Net present value of operating lease commitments (discount rate 5%)*

| Rental payable | Land and buildings £m | Motor vehicles £m | Total £m |
|---|---|---|---|
| 30 November 20X0 | 60.00 | 20.00 | 80.00 |
| 30 November 20X1 | 53.31 | 17.14 | 70.45 |
| 30 November 20X2 | 45.35 | 14.51 | 59.86 |
| 30 November 20X3 | 34.56 | 12.10 | 46.66 |
| Thereafter | 614.00 |  | 614.00 |
|  | 807.22 | 63.75 | 870.97 |
|  |  |  |  |
| Depreciation (5% × 807.22/ 25% × 63.75) | 40.36 | 15.94 | 56.30 |

2  *Net current assets*

|  | £m |
|---|---|
| Per balance sheet | 340.0 |
| Less current liability for operating lease (W1) | (70.0) |
| Less increase in taxation: 30% × (80 – 56) | (7.2) |
|  | 262.8 |

3  *Creditors: amounts falling due after more than one year*

|  | £m |
|---|---|
| Per balance sheet | 100 |
| Add net present value of operating lease rentals (W1) | 871 |
| Less rental paid 30 November 20X0 | (80) |
| Less current liabilities (payable 30 November 20X1) | (70) |
|  | 821 |

(ii)    **Key performance ratios**

|  | *Before capitalisation* | *After capitalisation* |
|---|---|---|

Return on capital employed:

$$\frac{\text{Profit before tax}}{\text{Capital employed}} \qquad \frac{176}{740} \times 100 = 23.8\% \qquad \frac{200}{1,477.8} \times 100 = 13.5\%$$

Net profit margin:

$$\frac{\text{Profit before tax}}{\text{Sales}} \qquad \frac{176}{1,160} \times 100 = 15.2\% \qquad \frac{200}{1,160} \times 100 = 17.2\%$$

Gearing:

$$\frac{\text{Long term liabilities}}{\text{Share capital} + \text{reserves}} \qquad \frac{100}{640} \times 100 = 16\% \qquad \frac{821}{656.8} \times 100 = 125\%$$

**Impact on key performance ratios**

**All the key performance ratios** are **affected**. **Return on capital employed** (ROCE) **falls significantly** from 23.8% to 13.5% as a result of the increase in net assets. The net profit margin increases from 15.2% to 17.2% as depreciation on the leased assets is less than the operating lease rental for the year. However, the **most dramatic change** is to the **gearing ratio**. This **increases** from 16% to 125%.

There are several implications of the changes. The fall in ROCE may be of particular concern to the holding company, especially if it is considering selling its investment. Users of the financial statements normally assess the performance of a company in relation to that of **similar companies** or industry averages. Most companies would probably be affected by the new standard to some extent. However, other companies are unlikely to have such **significant operating lease commitments** extending over a long period and therefore Hire's performance and gearing would **probably deteriorate** significantly **in relation** to that of **other companies** in the same sector.

In practice, the company's market value may not be significantly affected. Analysts can estimate the present value of operating lease commitments from the disclosures in the financial statements. Therefore this **information is already reflected in the market price** of the shares. Less sophisticated users of the financial statements would probably regard Hire as a relatively poor performer and a potentially risky investment.

The company may consider changing the way in which it finances its use of assets. A sale and leaseback that results in an operating lease would also have to be recognised in the balance sheet. However, some commentators believe that the leasing industry will **design forms of agreement** that will still enable lessees to **keep** some **leased assets off the balance sheet**.

Operating leases and finance leases are treated **differently for tax purposes**. Operating lease rentals are an allowable expense, while finance leases attract capital allowances. Although finance costs are also an allowable expense, the finance cost in this case is nil. Therefore the **new standard** may result in an **increase in the tax charge** for the period.

## 45   PREPARATION QUESTION: FRS 17

> **Tutor's hint**. Review our solution carefully, it gives a fairly comprehensive outline of the new rules.

(a)  Under **SSAP 24** the assets and liabilities in a defined benefit pension scheme were valued on an **actuarial basis**. The objective was to arrive at a regular pension cost each year that was a substantially level percentage of the pensionable payroll. Any **variations from regular cost** were spread forward and **recognised** gradually **over the average remaining service lives** of the employees. SSAP 24 was criticised for several reasons.

   (i)   There were **too many options** available to the preparers of accounts, leading to inconsistency in accounting practice and allowing a great deal of flexibility to adjust results on a short-term basis.

   (ii)  The **disclosure requirements** did **not** necessarily ensure that the pension cost and related amounts in the balance sheet were **adequately explained**.

   (iii) It is **inconsistent** with **international accounting standards**.

(b)  **FRS 17** abandons the use of actuarial values for assets in a pension scheme in favour of a **market value approach**. They are to be measured at **fair value**. Likewise, pension **liabilities** must be measured on a **market basis**, using the **projected unit basis**. Liabilities will be discounted at the current rate of return on a high quality corporate bond of equivalent term and currency to the liability.

An asset will be recognised to the extent that an employer can recover a surplus through reduced contributions and refunds. A liability will be recognised to the extent that the deficit reflects the employer's legal or constructive obligation. The resulting asset or liability is presented separately on the face of the balance sheet after other net assets.

The use of market values at the balance sheet date introduces **volatility** into the measurement of the surplus or deficit in the pension scheme. Such volatility was largely absent from the actuarial values used under SSAP 24. Internationally the volatility stemming from market values is dealt with by averaging the market values over a number of years and/or spreading the gains and losses forward in the accounts over the service lives of the employees. There are problems with this approach.

   (i)   It gives rise to figures in the balance sheet that do not represent the current surplus or deficit in the scheme.

   (ii)  It creates charges in the profit and loss account that are contaminated by gains and losses that occurred up to fifteen years previously.

The ASB has developed an alternative approach to cope with the volatility. The **profit and loss account** shows the relatively stable ongoing **service cost, interest cost** and **expected return** on assets measured on a basis consistent with international standards. The effects of the **fluctuations in market values**, on the other hand, are not part of the operating results of the business and are treated in the same way as revaluations of fixed assets, ie are recognised immediately in the second performance statement, the **statement of total recognised gains and losses**. This has two advantages over the international approach.

   (i)   The balance sheet shows the deficit or recoverable surplus in the scheme.

   (ii)  The total profit and loss charge is more stable than it would be if the market value fluctuations were spread forward.

(c) There are possible disadvantages to the new approach.

(i) The new standard is very **complicated**. ✓

(ii) It could be argued that the disclosure requirements are so extensive that preparers and users of accounts will get **lost in the detail**.

(iii) Concerns about the new accounting standard may cause more **employers to move to defined contribution schemes**, thereby putting the risk on the employee. ✓

(iv) The standard aims to aid consistency by the use of market values. However, much depends on the 'expected return on assets' which the actuary will be free to choose. Using a high expected return will increase profits, but since variations in future years go through the STRGL and not the profit and loss account, profits will not suffer in future years if the expected return is not realised. In other words **there will still be room for manoeuvre**.

## 46 PREPARATION QUESTION: DEFERRED TAX

(a) **Grant Ltd**

| | £'000 |
|---|---|
| Timing differences at 31 March 20X1 | 100 |
| Depreciation exceeds capital allowances | (10) |
| Timing differences at 31 March 20X2 | 90 |
| Capital allowances exceed depreciation | 25 |
| | 115 |

*Deferred tax provision :-*

| | £'000 |
|---|---|
| Balance b/f at 1 April 20X1 (£100,000 @ 30%) | 30 |
| To P&L account (£10,000 @ 30%) | (3) |
| Balance c/f at 31 March 20X2 | 27 |
| | |
| Balance b/f at 1 April 20X2 | 27 |
| To P&L account (£25,000 @ 30%) | 7 |
| Balance c/f at 31 March 20X3 | 34 |

*Profit and loss account*

31.3.20X2: Reduction in deferred tax charge – credit: £3,000

31.3.20X3: Increase in deferred tax charge – debit: £7,000

(b) **Haven Ltd**

| | £'000 |
|---|---|
| *Deferred tax account* | |
| Balance b/f at 1 January 20X2 | 60 |
| Increase in charge (W) | 6 |
| Balance c/f at 31 December 20X2 | 66 |

*Working: Deferred tax charge*

| | £'000 |
|---|---|
| Capital allowances | 125 |
| Depreciation | (100) |
| Increase in timing differences | 25 |
| | |
| Transfer to P&L account (25 @ 25%) | 6 |

## 47   PLANGENT

> **Tutor's hint**. Parts (a) and (b) are a good illustration of how in this paper it is just as important to understand the reasons for the rules as it is to be able to apply the rules to numerical examples. Review your answer carefully, noting particularly the method of scheduling reversals when discounting deferred tax provisions.

(a)   SSAP 15 was criticised on the following grounds.

(i)   The *Statement of Principles* published by the ASB defines assets and liabilities in relation to **past events,** whereas, the liabilities which emerge under **SSAP 15** for deferred tax depended upon **future events.**

(ii)   Under SSAP 15 deferred tax was only provided when the management of an entity believed a liability would **crystallise. Managerial intentions/beliefs** do not (by themselves) give rise to liabilities (and assets) under the *Statement of Principles*.

(iii)   The position of deferred taxation provisions in relation to **revaluation** and **fair value adjustments** under SSAP 15 was **unclear**. Some companies provided for deferred taxation on such items, some did not.

(iv)   The partial provision method under SSAP 15 was **inconsistent with international practice**. The ASB is increasingly seeking international harmonisation.

(b)   (i)   **Deferred tax arising on fair value adjustments**

*Against*

(1)   Under SSAP 15 fair value adjustments were seen as **permanent not timing differences**. Therefore no provision was made.

(2)   Fair value adjustments are **only made** for the purpose of **consolidation** and do not affect the tax position of the entities concerned.

(3)   Differences emerging as a result of fair value adjustments **affect goodwill** and no deferred tax is required.

*For*

(1)   Fair value adjustments **may affect post-acquisition profits and tax charges,** eg adjustments to stock values, therefore the tax effect of such changes should be included in the pre-acquisition period by providing deferred tax at acquisition on revaluation adjustments.

(2)   Deferred tax should be provided on assets purchased at acquisition which are revalued since if the asset had been purchased at market value its cost would have been tax deductible. Therefore deferred tax should be provided **as a valuation adjustment**.

FRS 19 *Deferred tax* requires that deferred tax should be provided as if the adjustment had been gains and losses recognised in the acquirer's own accounts. Thus this provision would not normally be made on adjusting assets to their market values. No provision is to be recognised in respect of acquired goodwill.

(ii)   **Revaluations of fixed assets**

*For*

(1)   Revaluations of fixed assets **create further timing differences** as a result of adjustments to depreciation.

(2) If the revaluation produces a surplus, a **chargeable gain could arise** which should be provided for.

(3) **Rollover relief** on chargeable gains **merely postpones tax liabilities** and does not eliminate the liability, so tax should be provided for.

*Against*

(1) Taxation on revaluation surpluses can be seen as a **permanent difference** since there is no equivalent in a tax computation.

(2) The **additional depreciation** charge arising from revaluation has no **tax equivalent** and it is incorrect to make tax adjustments.

FRS 19 states that deferred tax should not be provided on revaluation gains and losses unless, by the balance sheet date, the reporting entity has entered into a binding agreement to sell the revalued assets and recognised the gain or loss on sale. Similarly, deferred tax would not be recognised where rollover relief is available.

(c) (i) The future depreciation of the existing pool of fixed assets is compared with the future writing-down allowances available on the pool to determine the years of reversal of the capital allowances.

When forecasting capital allowances for future periods, it is assumed that allowance will be claimed as early as possible and that the residual values of the assets will equal those forecast for depreciation purposes.

| Year ended 31 March | Depreciation (a) £'000 | Capital allowances (b) £'000 | Reversal of timing difference ((a) – (b)) £'000 | Deferred tax liability @ 30% (undiscounted) ((a) – (b)) × 30% £'000 |
|---|---|---|---|---|
| 20X2 | 300 > | 278 | 22 | 7 |
| 20X3 | 300 | 209 | 91 | 27 |
| 20X4 | 300 | 157 | 143 | 43 |
| 20X5 | 300 | 93 | 207 | 62 |
| 20X6 | 200 | 69 | 131 | 39 |
| 20X7 | 200 | 52 | 148 | 44 |
| 20X8 | 200 | 14 | 186 | 56 |
| 20X9 | 100 | 11 | 89 | 27 |
| 20Y0 | 100 | (69) | 169 | 51 |
| Total | 2,000* (W1) | 814 (W2) | 1,186 | 356 |

(ii)

| Years ending 31 March | Deferred liability (undiscounted) £'000 | Discount rate | Deferred tax liability (discounted) £'000 |
|---|---|---|---|
| 20X2 | 7 | 4.7% | 7 |
| 20X3 | 27 | 4.4 | 25 |
| 20X4 | 43 | 4.2 | 38 |
| 20X5 | 62 | 4.0 | 53 |
| 20X6 | 39 | 3.9 | 33 |
| 20X7 | 44 | 3.8 | 35 |
| 20X8 | 56 | 3.8 | 43 |
| 20X9 | 27 | 3.8 | 20 |
| 20Y0 | 51 | 3.7 | 36 |
| Total | 356 | | 290 |

*Workings*

1 *Depreciation*

For each asset, annual depreciation is £(1,100,000 – 100,000)/10 = £100,000 pa. The residual value of £100,000 is £1,100,000/11. Each asset has a life of 10 years and is then assumed to be sold for residual value.

For the years ended 20X2, 20X3, 20X4, 20X5, depreciation $= £100,000 \times 3$
$= £300,000$

At the end of 20X5, asset 1 has been depreciated to residual value and is assumed to be sold for that value.

For the years ended 20X6, 20X7, 20X8, depreciation $= £100,000 \times 2$
$= £200,000$

At the end of 20X8, asset 2 is assumed to be sold for residual value.

For the years ended 20X9, 20Y0, depreciation $= £100,000 \times 1$
$= £100,000$

At the end of 20Y0, asset 3 is assumed to be sold for residual value.

2 *Capital allowances*

|  |  | £'000 |  |
|---|---|---|---|
| Tax written down value at 31.3.X1 |  | 1,114 |  |
| 20X2: | Capital allowances at 25% | (278) | 278 |
|  |  | 836 |  |
| 20X3: | Capital allowances at 25% | (209) | 209 |
|  |  | 627 |  |
| 20X4: | Capital allowances at 25% | (157) | 157 |
|  |  | 470 |  |
| 20X5: | Sales proceeds for asset 1 | (100) |  |
|  |  | 370 |  |
|  | Capital allowances at 25% | (93) | 93 |
|  |  | 277 |  |
| 20X6: | Capital allowances at 25% | (69) | 69 |
|  |  | 208 |  |
| 20X7: | Capital allowances at 25% | (52) | 52 |
|  |  | 156 |  |
| 20X8: | Sales proceeds for asset 2 | (100) |  |
|  |  | 56 |  |
|  | Capital allowances at 25% | (14) | 14 |
|  |  | 42 |  |
| 20X9: | Capital allowances at 25% | (11) | 11 |
|  |  | 31 |  |
| 20Y0 | Sale proceeds for asset 3 | (100) |  |
|  | Balancing charge | (69) | (69) |

## 48   RAPID RESPONSE

(a)                                             MEMO

To:      The Directors, Rapid Response plc
From:    An Accountant
Re:      *EPS and company performance*

As you have requested, I have analysed below the main differences between the pre- and post-FRS 3 accounts, in particular the changes in EPS and how an analyst might judge the company performance.

(i)   **Differences in EPS**

A summary of the reconciliation of the EPS figures is as follows.

|  | Note | 20X2 pence | 20X3 pence |
|---|---|---|---|
| As stated originally |  | 77.7 | 67.5 |
| Classification of restructuring costs | 1 |  | (6.3) |
| Sale of property adjustments | 2 | (13.8) | (2.6) |
| EPS as revised by FRS 3 |  | 63.9 | 58.6 |

*Notes*

1   **Reclassification of restructuring costs**

The company had originally classified these restructuring costs as an extraordinary item shown after the profit after tax figure, net of the tax attributable to those costs. In the EPS calculation, the earnings figure has been taken as the profit after tax but *before* extraordinary items.

FRS 3 does not allow such costs to be treated as extraordinary as they are not considered to be unusual enough - they are part of normal business operations. In any case, had they still been treated as extraordinary, the EPS figure would still require adjustment because under FRS 3 the earnings figure should be *after* extraordinary items. The restructuring costs have been grossed up, to take out the taxation credit, which had been included in the tax on profit on ordinary activities.

The effect on the EPS calculation is to decrease the earnings figure by £31.8m. On 500m shares, this reduces the EPS figure by 6.3 pence.

2   **Sale of property**

The treatment of the sale of properties has obviously changed, creating losses where previously a profit was reported. The proceeds received on the sales cannot have changed, so the figures which have been changed by the requirements of FRS 3 are those attached to the asset, which were compared with the proceeds to calculate the profit or loss.

It appears that, in the original profit and loss accounts, the gain was calculated by comparing the proceeds to historical cost less depreciation. Under FRS 3, it is necessary to compare the proceeds to the net carrying amount, which here seems to have been affected by upward revaluations. The net change is as follows.

|  | 20X2 | 20X3 |
|---|---|---|
| Earnings decrease (44.6 + 24.7/5.9 + 6.9) | £69.3m | £12.8m |
| Effect on EPS on 500m shares | 13.8p | 2.6p |

(ii) **Attitude of analysts**

The effects of FRS 3 on the calculation of EPS have caused much concern to analysts and other users of accounts. By including the effect of almost all events in the operating activities (as extraordinary items are now all but non-existent), many analysts feel that it will be difficult to judge the real trends in operating results of any company.

There is, however, increased disclosure under FRS 3. Most material items, which might not be expected to occur too often or which are not necessarily seen as a direct effect of normal trading, will be disclosed as exceptional items. There are more notes to the accounts, and an extra primary statement (the statement of total recognised gains and losses). Companies will need to explain their results more carefully to all users and analysts. In the case of Rapid Response plc, a rise in profits from 20X2 to 20X3 pre-FRS 3 has become a *fall* in profits under FRS 3.

The fall in EPS, however, is slightly less under FRS 3 (a fall of 8.3%) compared to the fall in EPS before FRS 3 (13.1%), indicating a stronger overall performance.

Analysts have produced their own version of EPS which may be used frequently in the financial press and even by companies themselves, but companies will still have to show the FRS 3 EPS figure with equal prominence *and* with a reconciliation between the two figures.

*Signed: An Accountant*

(b) (i) **Closure of London operation**

The criteria of a discontinued operation under FRS 3 are that the operation's assets, liabilities and operating results can be distinguished clearly from the rest of the business and 'it represents to the business a material reduction in its operating facilities resulting ... from its withdrawal from a particular market (whether class of business or geographical)' (FRS 3). It does not appear that there has been either a material reduction in operations, nor withdrawal from any geographical or business market. This is therefore *not* a discontinued operation.

The costs associated with the closure need not be disclosed as exceptional on the face of the profit and loss account under FRS 3 (paragraph 20). However, an assessment of the materiality of the amount may require disclosure in the notes to the accounts.

(ii) **Closure of Glasgow operation**

This situation would appear to meet the criteria for a discontinued operation quoted from FRS 3 above. The geographical market is clearly defined here.

The only problem is the freehold building which remains unsold, and will not be sold within three months of the year end. However, the building is for general use (rather than a specific purpose) and it seems fairly clear that the operations in Glasgow have ceased permanently. The closure costs should therefore be shown on the face of the profit and loss account as an exceptional item, described as 'loss on closure of discontinued operations'. Note that this is one of the types of exceptional item which FRS 3 *requires* to be disclosed on the face of the profit and loss account.

(c) **Current regulatory regime**

The present regulatory regime was set up with the intention of approaching the regulation of financial reporting on a more conceptual basis. It has been seen in the past that, as soon as a new set of detailed rules was formulated, then companies found some way of circumventing them through sophisticated accounting and legal procedures. This led to a circle of attempts to 'plug the gaps' by the standard setters followed by 'finding the loopholes' by companies.

**Criticism of ASB**

The ASB's approach has been criticised for not providing rules for specific situations which are seen as ambiguous and borderline. The attitude of the ASB is that the spirit of accounting standards must be followed in each specific situation as it arises. Every situation will be different and so attempting to produce detailed rules is bound to fail. Ambiguous situations are unlikely if standards are applied in the correct spirit.

Where this does not take place, there are two mechanisms in place to allow the regulatory authorities to correct the defects.

**UITF**

Where a practice arises which is widespread but is considered undesirable, and where a full standard is considered unnecessary or would take too long to produce, then the Urgent Issues Task Force can issue a judgement (called an Abstract) outlawing or changing the practice. For example, UITF Abstract 5 *Transfers from current assets to fixed assets* was produced to halt the practice of transferring current assets to fixed assets at revalued amounts, rather than the lower of cost and net realisable value.

**Financial Reporting Review Panel**

In more isolated cases of bad practice, particularly non-compliance with accounting standards or CA 1985 provisions, the Financial Reporting Review Panel has the power to force companies to revise their accounts, through the courts if necessary.

Underpinning the standard-setting process (and the UITF Abstracts and Review Panel decisions) will be the *Statement of Principles*. This outlines the conceptual framework on which all accounting procedure will be based.

**49 FRED 22**

> **Tutor's hint**. A good illustration of how you can be asked to explain the reasons for proposed changes to accounting standards. In part (b), note that the requirement asks for the treatment under current FRS as well as under the proposed new rules.

(a) (i) **Views for and against recycling**

There are **conflicting views** as to whether recycling of gains and losses should be permitted. In the UK FRS 3 prohibits recycling and states that gains and losses should only be reported once in the period when they arise. In contrast, IAS 21 *The effects of changes in foreign exchange rates* allows the recycling of gains and losses on overseas net investments on disposal.

### Arguments for recycling

(1) Traditionally, only realised profits have been recognised in the income statement. Unrealised profits have been reported in a second performance statement or as part of movements in equity. **When unrealised items become realised they should be recycled to the income statement.**

(2) The precise amount of a gain or loss may be uncertain. **Uncertain items may be recognised immediately** in the **second performance statement**. When the estimated amount of the gain or loss is subsequently **confirmed** or changed the item is **recycled** into the income statement.

(3) It can be argued that all items should appear in operating activities or financing activities at some point because **all items are ultimately part of operations**. There is a **critical** event, which **triggers** the introduction or **recycling** of a gain or loss.

### Arguments against recycling

(1) Realisation is no longer viewed as a critical concept in reporting financial performance. In many cases the realisation of an item provides information that is of limited value. For example, a gain on the revaluation of a fixed asset is always a holding gain. **Realisation simply represents confirmation of the gain** and the realisation of the gain does not change its characteristics. It does not justify further inclusion in the performance statements. The effect of realisation is better explained in the cash flow statement.

(2) If measurement of a gain or loss is sufficiently certain for recognition of the gain or loss to be possible, then the **nature of the item** itself **should determine how it is classified** in the statement(s) of financial performance. Recycling is not required.

(3) There is **no conceptual basis** for **delaying recognition** of items in the financial statements. The desire to recycle an item on the occurrence of a 'critical event' may reflect concerns about its volatility and size, rather than its nature. A **volatile item** of performance **should not be disguised**, even if the item is material.

(ii) **Reasons for presenting financial performance in one statement**

FRS 3 *Reporting financial performance* represented an important step towards providing users of the financial statements with useful information. Its objective was to enable users to analyse and understand the different components of an entity's financial performance. Since the issue of FRS 3 there have been a number of **developments in UK and international financial reporting practice**. These have led to the **review of the standard**.

Law and accounting standards require certain items to be taken directly to reserves, rather than included in the profit and loss account. These items include gains on revaluation of fixed assets and some gains and losses on foreign currency translation. Although the resulting changes in net assets are recognised in the financial statements, the **gains and losses are often hidden in reserves**. FRS 3 introduced the statement of total recognised gains and losses (**STRGL**) which **highlighted these items** and made users aware that although they were not included in the profit and loss account they were part of an entity's financial performance.

However, it is still possible for preparers of financial statements to display items in the performance statements in such a way as to draw users' attention to favourable aspects of performance and to **divert attention** from the entity's performance as a whole. A single performance statement would make this practice more difficult.

A further disadvantage of reporting financial performance in two statements is that **users may downgrade the importance of one statement** and attach undue significance to the other. There is some evidence that in the UK some users concentrate on the profit and loss account and largely **ignore the STRGL**. In addition, it is easier to compare the financial statements of different entities if only one statement is prepared.

Only realised items are included in the profit and loss account. Standard setters increasingly believe that the **concept of realisation is out of date** and that it should no longer be used to determine the way in which components of financial performance should be reported. Where performance is based on the realisation of assets, preparers of financial statements are able to **manipulate reported profits**. A single performance statement would largely overcome this problem.

One of the main objectives of financial reporting is to provide information that helps users of the financial statements to make and confirm predictions of the amount, probability and timing of **future cash flows**. This means that **all gains and losses**, whether **realised or unrealised**, are **relevant** in understanding an entity's financial performance and position. If all components of financial performance are reported in a single statement users will be able to judge the significance of each aspect and focus on the information that is of particular importance to them. This will enable them to gain insight into past performance and to estimate likely future trends.

(b) **How the treatment of items would change**

(i) Under **FRS 15 revaluation gains** are normally **recognised in the STRGL**. They are recognised in the profit and loss account to the extent (after adjusting for depreciation) that they reverse revaluation losses on the same asset which were previously recognised in the profit and loss account. All revaluation losses caused by **consumption of economic benefits** are reported in the **profit and loss account**. Other **revaluation losses** should be recognised in the **STRGL** until the carrying value falls below depreciated historical cost after which the losses should be recognised in the profit and loss account. Where it can be demonstrated that the recoverable amount is greater than the revalued amount, the loss should be recognised in the STRGL to the extent that the recoverable amount of the asset is greater than its revalued amount.

Under **FRED 22 revaluation gains and losses** would be reported in the 'other gains and losses' section of the statement of financial performance. However, where revaluation losses are **due to impairment**, they would be reported in the **operating section** of the performance statement.

(ii) Under **FRS 3 and SSAP 20** *Foreign currency translation*, **foreign currency translation adjustments** arising on the net investment in foreign operations are not included in the profit and loss account. Instead they are taken directly to **reserves** and reported in the **STRGL**.

Under **FRED 22**, these translation adjustments would be reported in the 'other gains and losses' section of the statement of financial performance. As at present, they would not be included in operating profit.

(iii)  **FRS 3 and FRS 15** *Tangible fixed assets* both require gains and losses on disposal to be calculated as the difference between the carrying amount and the net sale proceeds. Gains and losses on disposal are reported in the profit and loss account as part of profit on ordinary activities before taxation. If an asset has been revalued the balance on the revaluation reserve is transferred to the profit and loss account reserve by means of a **transfer between the reserves**. It is not included in the profit and loss account for the period. The reserve transfer is disclosed in the reconciliation of the opening and closing shareholders' funds and in the reserves note.

Under **FRED 22**, gains and losses on disposal of fixed assets would be reported in the **'other gains and losses'** section of the statement of financial performance. However, **gains and losses** that represent **marginal adjustments to depreciation, impairments, or the reversals of impairments** would be reported in the **operating section** of the performance statement.

## 50  JUNE

> **Tutor's hint**. FRS 14 is a relatively recent accounting standard. Part (a) asks why changes were required and why diluted EPS needs to be disclosed. Plan your time carefully, giving adequate time to Part (a)(ii) before getting into the fine detail of Part (b). Part (b) was a complicated question, requiring knowledge of the impact of bonus issues, share option schemes and other capital instruments. It also required a ranking of the dilutive elements, ignoring the anti-dilutive elements. If you present clear workings and deal with the information logically, there are enough relatively basic points to take you over half marks easily.

(a)  (i)  **FRS 14 changes**

(1)  **All** ordinary shares are now included in the EPS calculation, not just shares ranking for dividend.

(2)  Guidance is given as to *when* shares are to be included.

(3)  **Bonus issues** and share splits occurring after the year end but prior to the issue of the accounts are now included.

(4)  **Diluted EPS** is now calculated using a **determination of the sequence** in which EPS is diluted by potential ordinary shares.

(5)  Guidance has been given regarding EPS calculations where **contingently issuable shares** exist.

(6)  If basic EPS is **negative** it is **disclosed**.

(7)  **Exemption** from disclosure of diluted EPS on **materiality** grounds is **no longer possible**.

(8)  The distinction between the **net and nil** basis of calculation has gone.

(9)  The so called **'imputed earnings'** method used to determine EPS where options and warrants exist has **gone**.

**Reasons for the changes**

- International discussions and developments meant that SSAP 3 was no longer appropriate.

- FRS 14 achieves comparability with IAS 33.

- Some aspects of SSAP 3 were unsatisfactory (eg the 'imputed earnings' method).

(ii) Basic EPS only takes account of shares in issue and future diluting events are excluded. Many companies use convertible debt, options and warrants these days for corporate financing and many purchases include deferred share issues so the **diluted EPS figure reflects commercial realities** and gives a more realistic measure of future likely EPS levels. Diluted EPS thus acts as a 'warning' to investors that future earnings could be affected by future diluting events.

(b) **Basic EPS**

|  | £'000 |
|---|---|
| Profit attributable to members | 12,860 |
| Preference dividend | (210) |
| Other non equity appropriation | (80) |
| Basic earnings | 12,570 |

Weighted average number of shares ('000)

| | Shares | In issue to 31 March 20X9 | Weighted |
|---|---|---|---|
| At 1 June 20X8 | 10,100 | $\frac{12}{12}$ | 10,100 |
| Issued 1 January 20X9 | 3,600 | $\frac{5}{12}$ | 1,500 |
| Options 1 March 20X9 | 1,200 | $\frac{3}{12}$ | 300 |
| Purchased 1 April 20X9 | (2,400) | $\frac{2}{12}$ | (400) |
| 31 May 20X9 | 12,500 | | 11,500 |
| Bonus issue 1 for 5 1 July 20X9 | | | 2,300 |
| | | | 13,800 |

Basic EPS = $\dfrac{£12,570,000}{13,800,000}$ = 91p

The bonus issue is included (per FRS 14) because it occurred prior to publication of the accounts.

**Diluted EPS**

A calculation is needed to show whether potential ordinary shares are dilutive or antidilutive.

| | Profit £'000 | Shares | EPS(p) |
|---|---|---|---|
| Net profit: continuing operations | 18,270 (W) | 13,800 | 132 |
| Options $1,200 \times \dfrac{5-2}{5} \times \dfrac{9}{12}$ | | 540 | |
| $2,000 \times \dfrac{5-3}{5}$ | | 800 | |
| $1,000 \times \dfrac{5-4}{5}$ | | 200 | |
| | 18,270 | 15,340 | 119 (dilutive) |
| 6% bond | | | |
| $6\% \times 6,000 \times 0.65$ | 234 | 12,000 | |
| | 18,504 | 27,340 | 67.7 (dilutive) |
| 7% convertible redeemable shares | 210 | | |
| Redemption premium | 80 | 2,000 | |
| | 18,794 | 29,340 | 64.1 (dilutive) |

All adjustments are dilutive and should be taken into account.

Calculation of diluted EPS:

|  | £'000 |
|---|---|
| Basic earnings | 12,570 |
| Interest saved on convertible debt | 234 |
| Dividends/costs of preference shares | 290 |
|  | 13,094 |
| Ordinary shares (as above) | 29,340 |

$$\text{Diluted EPS} = \frac{£13,094,000}{29,340,000} = 44.6\text{p}$$

*Working: Net profit from continuing operations*

|  | £'000 |
|---|---|
| Operating profit | 26,700 |
| Fixed assets profit | 2,500 |
| Interest | (2,100) |
| Taxation (7,500 – 100) (note (v) of question) | (7,400) |
| Minority interest (540 + 600) | (1,140) |
| Preference dividend | (210) |
| Other appropriation | (80) |
|  | 18,270 |

## 51   PREPARATION QUESTION: SSAP 25

(a)   Ignoring comparative figures, Multitrade plc's segmental report would look like this.

CLASSES OF BUSINESS

|  | Group £'000 | Division A £'000 | Division B £'000 | Division C £'000 |
|---|---|---|---|---|
| *Turnover* |  |  |  |  |
| Total sales | 1,200,023 | 846,071 | 226,949 | 127,003 |
| Inter-segment sales | 335,962 | 304,928 | 31,034 | - |
| Sales to third parties* | 864,061 | 541,143 | 195,915 | 127,003 |
|  |  |  |  |  |
| *Profit before taxation* |  |  |  |  |
| Segment profit/(loss) | 172,818 | 162,367 | 18,754 | (8,303) |
| Common costs** | 96,724 |  |  |  |
| Operating profit | 76,094 |  |  |  |
| Net interest | 10,028 |  |  |  |
| Group profit before tax | 66,066 |  |  |  |
|  |  |  |  |  |
| *Net assets* |  |  |  |  |
| Segment net assets | 427,016 | 281,123 | 65,348 | 80,545 |
| Unallocated assets | 67,211 |  |  |  |
| Total net assets | 494,227 |  |  |  |

GEOGRAPHICAL SEGMENTS

|  | Group £'000 | United Kingdom £'000 | Middle East £'000 | Pacific fringe £'000 | Europe £'000 | North America £'000 |
|---|---|---|---|---|---|---|
| *Turnover* |  |  |  |  |  |  |
| Turnover by destination*** |  |  |  |  |  |  |
| Sales to third parties* | 864,061 | 57,223 | 406,082 | 77,838 | 195,915 | 127,003 |

\*   Turnover, profit, net interest and net assets should be the same as those shown in the consolidated accounts.

    **\*\***      Common costs and unallocated assets are those items in the consolidated accounts which cannot reasonably be allocated to any one segment nor does the group wish to apportion them between segments. An example of a common cost is the cost of maintaining the holding company share register, and an example of an unallocated asset might be the head office building.

    **\*\*\***     Turnover by destination must be disclosed in accordance with the Companies Act 1985. If Multitrade's divisions were not all in the UK, then another analysis would be required by SSAP 25 on the same lines as that shown for classes of business but analysed between the geographical origins of turnover.

(b)   What do we learn from Multigrade's segmental report?

    (i)      The relative sizes of each division. Here, A is obviously the most important.

    (ii)     The profitability of each division. A has the highest net profit margin and return on capital employed. C is a loss maker.

    (iii)    A depends most heavily on inter-segment sales.

    (iv)    A high proportion of the group's sales are to areas with a high political risk and nearly 95% are export, exposing it to considerable exchange risks.

  What *don't* we learn from the report?

    (i)      Which division trades in the riskiest areas?

    (ii)     How old are each division's assets?

    (iii)    How many staff does each division employ?

    (iv)    How much of a mark-up do A and B earn on their sales to other divisions?

    (v)     Which divisions are benefiting from inter-segment purchases at potentially advantageous prices?

  As usual with ratio analysis, the information provided in segmental reports can only suggest further avenues of enquiry. However, such reports are useful in indicating which parts of a business are out of step with the rest in terms of:

    (i)      Profitability
    (ii)     Potential for future growth
    (iii)    Rate of past growth
    (iv)    Degree of business or economic risk

(c)   In May 1996, the ASB issued a discussion paper on segmental reporting. The paper seeks comments on two **international proposals**.

    (i)      E 51 *Reporting financial information by segment* (IASC)
    (ii)     *Reporting disaggregated information about a business* (US FASB)

  The **key issues** in this area are:

    (i)      The division of operations into segments
    (ii)     The information to be given for each segment
    (iii)    Whether the information given is verifiable and easy to understand

  The **IASC proposals** develop the risks and returns approach used in the current UK SSAP 25. The IASC envisages that segments should be identified by the different **risks and returns** an entity faces, either through providing different products or services or through providing products or services in different geographical locations.

  The IASC proposes that **more information** should be given for each primary segment (the dominant source of risk for the entity) than is currently required for a segment under SSAP 25. The information should be prepared on the same basis as that given in the external financial statements.

The **FASB proposals** reflect a **managerial approach** under which segments reflect the way management disaggregates the entity for making operating decisions. Amounts reported by segment would be based on the information used internally by the chief executive or equivalent management committee to manage the business.

Although the IASC and the FASB approaches differ, the effect in practice, at least in the identification of segments, may be similar in that the IASC notes that the **dominant source of risk** affects how most enterprises are organised and managed. An enterprise's organisational structure and its internal financial reporting system should thus normally be the basis for identifying its segments under the IASC proposals.

**52    AZ**

> **Tutor's hint.** This question tested your knowledge of segmental reporting by asking about the importance of segmental data and the advantages and disadvantages of the managerial approach and the risk and return approach to analysing segmental data. Part (b) asked for a discussion of the implications of certain events for the determination of segmental information to be provided. Part (a) of the question focuses on the main issues which have been flagged as key by the examiner. In the new syllabus, a requirement such as (b) might now be set as a 'report advising the directors'.
>
> **Examiner's comment.** Part (a) was well answered, but in part (b) candidates focussed too much on FRS 3 at the expense of SSAP 25.

(a)  (i)   The information content is improved by including segmental data for several reasons.

(1)  **Different risks** may attach to individual business segments.

(2)  Segments may have **different growth prospects** and trading factors caused by regional and economic characteristics.

(3)  **Investors** are becoming more **sophisticated** and expect the information.

(4)  The reasons for **changes in performance** will become apparent from segmental data.

(5)  **Demergers** are becoming an important feature of modern business and segmental analysis helps users to understand this by focussing on the newly emerged segments.

(ii)  The **'risk and returns' approach** means that the segmental analysis reflects the approach taken in the accounts for **external reporting**.

**Advantages**

(1)  The data can be reconciled to the accounts.
(2)  It is a consistent method.
(3)  The method helps to reveal the profitability, risks and returns of segments.

**Disadvantages**

(1)  Segment determination is subjective.
(2)  Management may report segments which are not consistent with those used for internal reporting for control purposes.

The **managerial approach** means that segmental data is reported on the same basis as that used for **internal reporting**.

**Advantages**

(1) It is cost effective because the marginal cost of reporting segmental data is low.

(2) The users can be sure that the segmental data reflects the operational strategy of the business.

**Disadvantages**

(1) The data maybe commercially sensitive.

(2) The segments may include operations with different risks and returns.

(3) The information is highly subjective because management determine the segments.

(b) (i) Under SSAP 25 *Segmental reporting*, the directors determine the reported segments subject to guidance in general terms. **Significant segments** (10% of external turnover, profit and assets) should be **disclosed**. For the airline, segments may be determined by the **destination of the aircraft**, the geographical location of assets, the nature of the trade. The main problem is that the revenue earning assets (aircraft) can move between segments.

(ii) **Turnover** for each segment should be **analysed** by third party turnover and inter segment sales. The basis of inter segment sales need not be disclosed and there is scope for creativity in reporting.

(iii) SSAP 25 predates FRS 3 *Reporting financial performance* and the required disclosures of exceptional and extraordinary items.

SSAP 25 requires segment analysis before tax, minority interest and extraordinary items.

It would appear that, to comply with FRS 3, **exceptional losses** should be included in a particular segment results with disclosure.

(iv) Under FRS 3, **disclosure of discontinuance** is required if material and if the **conditions** for reporting discontinuance are met. Typically, discontinued operations are aggregated and not shown as separate items.

It is likely that the holiday business would be reported as a **discrete segment**, albeit discontinued, on materiality grounds.

(v) SSAP 25 requires disclosure of associates if a material part of group results or group assets, (20% threshold) unless **commercially prejudicial**. Eurocat may express the view that commercial judgements preclude disclosure.

## 53  RP GROUP

> **Tutor's hint**. You could have gained good marks for this question if you understood the nature and disclosure of related party transactions.
>
> **Examiner's comment**. Part (a), which relied more on knowledge than application was not as well answered as part (b).

(a) (i) Related party relationships (RP) are part of **normal business activity**. RP exist for sound commercial reasons and often have a material impact on the financial position of companies. Inter company trading between members of a group is a common example.

However, the existence of RP should be **disclosed** in order that users appreciate that not all transactions have been undertaken genuinely at arm's length. **Users will expect** that, in the absence of disclosure of the details of an RP, all the transactions have been undertaken at **arm's length**.

Even if there are no transactions between RP, the results of a group can still be affected by the relationship. For example, a newly acquired subsidiary can be compelled to finish a trading relationship with another company in order to benefit other group companies.

(ii) Disclosure of RP details is **equally important** to the users of **small company** accounts as it is for users of the accounts of large companies.

If the RP transaction involves **individuals** who have an interest in a small company then the significance of the RP transaction could be disproportionately high because of the degree of **influence** exercised by the individual concerned. The cost of providing RP disclosures is difficult to evaluate but **normal cost benefit considerations may not apply** to this because of the potential benefits to users of full disclosure.

The **FRSSE** requires disclosures of material transactions with an RP including personal guarantees given by the directors.

The objective of the FRS 8 and the FRSSE was to extend the Companies Act 1985 disclosures to provide a comprehensive set of rules in the area of related party transactions.

(b) (i) FRS 8 does not require disclosure of the details of the relationship and transactions between a reporting entity and providers of finance in the normal course of business.

Thus, as RP is a bank, there are **no requirements to disclose** because of this relationship. However, RP does hold **25%** of the equity of AB and FRS 8 would **presume** that a party holding or controlling in excess of 20% of voting rights is a **related party**.

An investor with 25% equity holding and board presence would be expected to **influence policies** in such a way as to be able to inhibit the pursuit of the separate interests of the two parties. If it can be shown that no such relationship exists then there is no related party relationship. Merely having common directors does not guarantee that there is a related party situation.

Under FRS 8 a relationship of **investor/associate** is **deemed** to be a **related party** relationship. Under FRS 9, the exercise of **significant influence** is required to establish associate status. Banks tend to regard companies in which they invest as investments not associates and FRS 9 recognises this situation by stating that if the business of the investor is to provide capital plus advice/guidance then the holding should be accounted for as an investment rather than as an associate. In any event, the holding of the other 75% equity is critical to determining the ability to exercise significant influence.

The decision as whether RP is a related party is **complex** in this case. If it is decided that it is a related party, all material transactions will require disclosure including the terms of loans, fees, interest and dividends paid.

(ii) **No disclosure of intra-group transactions** and balances eliminated on consolidation is required. Transactions with related parties will be disclosed to the extent that they were undertaken when X was not part of the group. Transactions between RP and X in the period from 1 July 20X9 to 31 October

20X9 will be disclosed but transactions prior to 1 July will be eliminated on consolidation. There is no related party relationship with Z as it is an ordinary business transaction, unless there is some influence or control which has led to a subordination of interests by the parties involved.

(iii)  **Pension schemes** for employee benefits **are related parties** of the entity. Contributions to the pension scheme are exempt under FRS 8 but any other transactions must be disclosed. The transfer of the fixed assets and the administrative cost recharge must therefore be disclosed. The **scheme's investment manager** is **not usually** considered a **related party** of the reporting company unless the investment manager can influence the financial and operating policies of RP through his non executive directorship. **Directors are** deemed by FRS 8 to be **related parties**. The fee is considered immaterial, but this does not mean it should not be disclosed. Materiality is defined by reference to the other related party, ie the manager, and it is likely that £25,000 is material and will require disclosure.

## 54  MAXPOOL

> **Tutor's hint**. This question required an understanding of FRS 8 *Related party disclosures* shown by a discussion and a practical problem.
>
> *Prizewinners' points*. If you mentioned IAS 24 you will have greatly impressed the examiner. However, you would gain almost as much credit if you simply said that the ASB wished to bring UK practice into line with international practice.

(a)  (i)  Whilst the CA 1985 and Stock Exchange disclosure requirements are extensive, FRS 8 *Related party disclosures* adds to the disclosure requirements to ensure that *all* user groups are aware of the existence and effect of related party transactions.

The FRS requires extensive disclosures and it is important that auditors identify instances where material related party transactions exist. Not all related party transactions are necessarily illegal nor misleading. However, it could be argued that the financial statements do not give a 'true and fair' view unless adequate disclosure occurs.

FRS 8 extends the definition of related parties by dealing with issues such as:

(1) control
(2) common control
(3) influence
(4) common influence

The ASB also has an objective of bringing the UK more into line with international practice and IAS 24 contains greater disclosure obligations which have been incorporated into FRS 8.

(ii)  (1)  Exposure drafts issued subject to the receipt of comments from a wider audience are more likely to gain the respect of users and preparers of financial statements. Hence the resulting standards are likely to prove more readily acceptable.

(2)  Exposure drafts are issued for comment to ensure consistency with other UK standards and also with international standards.

(3)  Where anomalies and conflicts do emerge, it is important that these are publicly discussed.

(4) The former Accounting Standards Committee was often criticised for not widely consulting, so the ASB had to address the need for wider consultation.

(b) (i) *Year ended 31.12.X6*

(1) Bay plc is an investor owning more than 20% of Ching and therefore is presumed to be a related party. Accordingly, details of the transaction must be disclosed in both sets of accounts. It is important that the determination of the price by an independent party is disclosed.

(2) Maxpool and Bay both have investments in Ching - but this does not make (M) and (B) related parties. There appears to be no relationship between them and no disclosure in Maxpool's accounts is needed. An exception to this would occur if Bay plc persuaded Maxpool to sell the factory at less than market value because of control or influence.

However, Maxpool may have to disclose the transaction under Stock Exchange rules where transactions between a listed company (and subsidiaries) and its shareholders holding 10% or more of the voting rights must be disclosed.

(ii) *Year ended 31.12.X7*

(1) Maxpool is presumed to be a related party of Bay as the holding is more than 20%.

(2) Maxpool is a related party of Ching but any transactions are exempted by FRS 8 from disclosure as Maxpool now owns 90% of Ching.

(3) Bay plc is not necessarily a related party of Ching because there is no presumption that the holders of 10% of the shares have the required influence.

(4) The relationship between Bay and Ching would probably not require disclosure as a related party relationship, the purchase of the vehicles by Bay plc was at a price determined using open market principles so there is no indication that Ching has subordinated any of its interests in these assets or that Bay has exerted influence over the price charged.

(5) However, Bay is an associate of Maxpool and is therefore automatically a related party of Maxpool. Therefore Maxpool must disclose the transaction in the group accounts.

(6) In addition, Stock Exchange rules may mean further disclosure of the transaction between Bay and Ching.

## 55 PREPARATION QUESTION: FRS 12

> **Tutor's hint.** You should expect a question like this on Section B of the paper. The examiner says candidates often fail to do themselves justice in discussion questions, so make sure you explain your arguments carefully.

(a) It is **overstating the matter** to imply that the concept of prudence has been abandoned in the balance sheet. Neither is it necessarily the case that the profit and loss account is going to become much more volatile all of a sudden.

FRS 12 seeks to **outlaw so-called 'big bath' provisions**, and, of lesser importance provisions which are larger than the company actually needs in order to meet its obligations. An example of this is provisions for re-structuring. These will be made later than is presently the case with some companies, and the provisions will be for a smaller amount. This is because provisions will only be allowed for obligations at the balance sheet date.

The FRS also attempts to put an **end to 'smoothing'** of results where this represents a distortion. For example, before FRS 12 it was permissible to provide in advance for such items as future repairs. Now the **costs** will have to be **charged to the profit and loss account** in the **year in which they are incurred**, that is when the work is actually carried out. Costs relating to the year 2000 problem fall into this category.

However, it could be argued that some aspects of FRS 12 will make profits **more, not less, consistent**. 'Big bath' provisions for re-structuring gave rise to big one-off hits against earnings. By contrast FRS 12 forces such charges to be made in **smaller, more frequent chunks**, with the result that earnings appear more stable than they did previously. In this way expenditure is matched more satisfactorily against revenue.

One effect of FRS 12 on the **balance sheet** is to make it not so much less prudent as rather **different from previously**. Provisions for abandonment or decommissioning costs used to be built up over a facility's working life. Now the obligation to restore the site must be **recorded in full** (although discounted) **when the damage is done**, as this is when it is incurred. Usually the debit increases the cost of the asset, so the effect on the profit and loss account is broadly neutral over the asset's life. The effect on net assets in the balance sheet is also mainly neutral, but **gross assets and liabilities are increased** significantly.

(b) FRS 12 *Provisions, contingent liabilities and contingent assets* states that only obligations that arise from past events that are independent of an entity's future actions can be recognised as provisions. The FRS notes that provision should not be made for expenditure planned to operate in a particular way in the future, because the entity can avoid that expenditure by changing its method of operation. In addition, a restructuring provision should not include expenditure associated with the entity's ongoing activities.

The proposed one-off compensation payment that is associated with the future operations could be avoided by switching overtime production to another plant. For this reason, it should not be provided for in advance at the year end. However, if agreement for the payment had been reached with the unions by the year-end and the payment was no longer dependent on future events, i.e. the structure and recipients of the payment had been identified, the situation would be different. In this case FRS 12 would require a liability to be recognised at the year end for the payment.

## 56  VACS

> **Tutor's hint**. In Part (b)(ii) provision (2) could be discounted to the present value of the cost, where the difference is material to the accounts.

(a)                                          MEMORANDUM

To:       The Directors of Vacs Ltd
From:     G Force, Chief Accountant
Date:     14 November 20X3
Subject:  Financial statements for the year ended 30 September 20X3

Set out below are the implications for the financial statements for the year ended 30 September 20X3 of the items mentioned at our recent meeting.

(i)  **Overdraft guarantee**

The company has guaranteed to pay an overdraft if its associated company cannot repay it, and must now assess whether a provision is necessary.

The giving of the guarantee gives rise to a **legal obligation** at the balance sheet date as the **result of a past event**.

However, a **provision** for this will only be made if it is **probable** that a **transfer** of **economic benefit** will arise. Thus to comply with FRS 12 *Provisions, contingent liabilities and contingent assets* you will need to make an assessment of the likelihood of Vacs Ltd having to settle the associate's overdraft.

If this outcome is considered **more likely than not**, then a **provision** should be made for the best estimate of the amount expected to be paid.

Assuming that any payment by Vacs Ltd is **not considered likely**, then **disclosure** should be made in the notes, covering the existence of the guarantee, and an estimate of the financial effect (by disclosing the amount of the associate's overdraft).

Following FRS 12, if payment is considered **remote**, then **no mention need be made** in the accounts. However, generally accepted accounting practice following Companies Act 1985 requirements for disclosure of contingent liabilities would be to give disclosures mentioned above.

(ii)  **Claim by former director**

In the case of legal claims, it is **unclear** whether an **obligating event** has happened or not (ie some form of wrongful dismissal). This will be decided by a court case or a settlement.

Thus once again, as directors, you must **assess the likelihood** of this liability existing, and again provide for any payments that are considered more likely than not to arise.

Consideration should be given to such factors as:

(1)  The legal opinion you have received that any claim by the former director is unlikely to succeed

(2)  Potential legal costs that will be incurred if the case goes to court

(3)  Any potential out-of-court settlement that may be being considered

If payments are **not probable**, then the claim would be treated as **a contingent liability**, and disclosures covering the nature of the uncertainties and an estimate of the financial effect should be made. However, if the likelihood of making any payments is considered remote, then no such disclosure needs to be made.

We will need to review the basis of your £50,000 provision in the light of these considerations and discuss the likely outcome of events. Based on legal advice received to date, the **provision appears unnecessary** and should be removed.

(iii)  **Realisable value of stock**

The post balance sheet reduction in the net realisable value of stock is the result of the competitor's product development, a condition which did **exist at the balance sheet date**. This is an **adjusting event** per SSAP 17 *Accounting for post balance sheet events*.

The net realisable value of stock at the balance sheet date should be adjusted downwards to £373,750 (see working). The Companies Act 1985 requires stock to be stated at the lower of cost and net realisable value. The stock should thus be written down by £201,250, from its cost of £575,000 to its net realisable value of £373,750.

By virtue of its size the write down should be treated as an **exceptional item** and **disclosed** by way of note to the profit and loss account, giving a description of the item and the amount.

(iv) **Sale of building**

SSAP 17 states that sales of fixed assets constitute non-adjusting post balance sheet events and, whilst the accounts would not normally be amended to reflect the event, it should be disclosed in the notes.

However, it appears that in this case the sale price is **evidence of an impairment** of the building at the year end and, unless it can be shown that the conditions causing the impairment arose from post year end circumstances, the **accounts should be adjusted** to reflect the reduction in recoverable amount.

The impairment will be **disclosed as exceptional** in the operating profit note.

The **building**, being a former head office, should also be disclosed as a current **asset** at the year end, as its disposal appeared to be an intended event.

(v) **Nationalisation**

**Government actions**, such as nationalisation, are **normally** treated as **non-adjusting events**, requiring only disclosure in the notes to the accounts. Full provision for the loss arising from the nationalisation would only be made in this year's accounts if the going concern were in doubt.

*Working: NRV of stock*

|  | £ |
|---|---|
| Cost of stock | 575,000 |
| Normal selling price (130% × 575,000) | 747,500 |
| New selling price (50% × 747,500) | 373,750 |

(b) (i) **Recognition criteria**

FRS 12 has greatly restricted the instances in which provisions can be created and maintained in the balance sheet. This is to prevent the misuse of provisions, where in the past companies may have:

(1) Created large general 'big bath' provisions to release against unspecified future costs in times of low profits

(2) Provided against future costs which they could realistically avoid

This therefore makes sure that costs are included in the profit and loss only in the period in which they have been incurred (rather than predicted).

In layman's terms the recognition criteria are explained below.

(1) **Obligation**

The company must have **done** something in the past which means it has no realistic alternative to paying out cash.

For example, it may have announced to the world its commitment (a 'constructive obligation') or it may have a contractual obligation (it has a contract and has already recorded the benefits from that contract – so now it needs to provide for the costs).

(2)   **Probability**

There is more than a 50% chance of the obligation resulting in a cash payout ('more likely than not').

(3)   **Measurement**

The cost can be measured (or estimated) with reasonable reliability.

(ii)   **Costs of Scarey Ltd**

In view of the conditions set out above, accounting will be as follows.

(1)   **Warranty costs**

Scarey Ltd **can provide** for estimated costs of repairing goods it has sold before the year end under warranty.

By making the sale the company has created a **contractual obligation** to repair.

The only issues will be in making a **reliable estimate** of those costs (which it should be able to do based on past experience and levels of post year end repairs), and determining which costs are covered under the warranty (eg parts) and which are payable by the customer (eg labour).

(2)   **Environmental damage**

Scarey Ltd **should provide** for the costs of removing or replacing the soil in five years' time. It has a **contractual obligation** to make good, and by spilling paint has **incurred** the obligation.

It should therefore charge the profit and loss account for the year with the expected cost, and credit the balance sheet with the provision.

(3)   **Retraining**

The company **cannot provide** for the future costs of retraining.

This is because it has no 'obligation' to retrain its staff. It has a realistic alternative – it **could decide not to** retrain/not to produce tandems.

Only when the costs are actually incurred (ie when the retraining occurs) can they be charged to the profit and loss account.

(4)   **Onerous lease**

If the company cannot terminate the lease of the old factory, or offset its costs by sub-letting it to a third party, the lease is described as '**onerous**'.

Because Scarey Ltd is no longer getting any benefits from the lease (but still has to pay its rental costs), **FRS 12 allows the full remaining costs to be provided for** from the date the contract becomes onerous.

# Advanced Corporate Reporting
# BPP Mock Exam 1:
# June 2002

| Question Paper: | |
|---|---|
| Time allowed | **3 hours** |
| **This paper is divided into two sections** | |
| **Section A** | **This question is compulsory and MUST be attempted** |
| **Section B** | **THREE questions ONLY to be answered** |

**Disclaimer of liability**

Please note that we have based our predictions of the content of the June 2002 exam on our long experience of the ACCA exams. We do not claim to have any endorsement of the predictions from either the examiner or the ACCA and we do not guarantee that either the specific questions, or the general areas, that are forecast will necessarily be included in the exams, in part or in whole.

We do not accept any liability or responsibility to any person who takes, or does not take, any action based (either in whole or in part and either directly or indirectly) upon any statement or omission made in this book. We encourage students to study all topics in the ACCA syllabus and the mock exam in this book is intended as an aid to revision only.

# paper 3.6

DO NOT OPEN THIS PAPER UNTIL YOU ARE READY TO START

UNDER EXAMINATION CONDITIONS

**Section A - This question is compulsory and MUST be attempted**

1   The following draft financial statements relate to the Baron Group plc.

DRAFT GROUP PROFIT AND LOSS ACCOUNT
FOR THE YEAR ENDED 30 NOVEMBER 20X7

|  | £m | £m |
|---|---|---|
| Turnover | | |
| Continuing operations | 4,458 | |
| Discontinued operations | 1,263 | |
| | | 5,721 |
| Cost of sales | | (4,560) |
| Gross profit | | 1,161 |
| Distribution costs | 309 | |
| Administration expenses | 285 | |
| | | (594) |
| | | 567 • |
| Income from interests in joint venture | | 75 |
| Defence costs of take-over bid | | (20) |
| Operating profit | | |
| Continuing operations | 438 | |
| Discontinued operations | 184 | |
| | | 622 |
| Loss on disposal of tangible fixed assets | (7) | |
| Loss on disposal of discontinued operations (note (a)) | (25) | |
| | | (32) |
| Interest receivable | 27 | |
| Interest payable | (19) | |
| | | 8 |
| Profit on ordinary activities before taxation | | 598 |
| Tax on profit on ordinary activities (note (c)) | | (191) |
| Profit on ordinary activities after taxation | | 407 |
| Minority interests - equity | | (75) |
| Profit attributable to members of the parent company | | 332 |
| Dividends - ordinary dividends | | (130) |
| Retained profit for the year | | 202 |

GROUP STATEMENT OF TOTAL RECOGNISED GAINS AND LOSSES
FOR THE YEAR ENDED 30 NOVEMBER 20X7

|  | £m |
|---|---|
| Profit attributable to members of the parent company | 332 |
| Deficit on revaluation of land and buildings | (30) |
| Deficit on revaluation of land and buildings in joint venture | (15) |
| Gain on revaluation of loan | 28 |
| Total recognised gains and losses relating to the year | 315 |

## DRAFT GROUP BALANCE SHEET AS AT 30 NOVEMBER 20X7

|  | 20X7 £m | 20X6 £m |
|---|---|---|
| *Fixed assets* | | |
| Intangible assets | 60 | 144 |
| Tangible fixed assets (note (d)) | 1,415 | 1,800 |
| Investments (notes (b) and (e)) | 600 | - |
|  | 2,075 | 1,944 |
| *Current assets* | | |
| Stocks | 720 | 680 |
| Short term investments (note (e)) | 152 | 44 |
| Debtors (note (f)) | 680 | 540 |
| Cash at bank and in hand | 24 | 133 |
|  | 1,576 | 1,397 |
| Creditors: amounts falling due within one year (note (g)) | (1,601) | (1,223) |
| *Net current assets* | (25) | 174 |
| *Total assets less current liabilities* | 2,050 | 2,118 |
| Creditors: amounts falling due after more than one year | (186) | (214) |
| Provision for liabilities and charges - bid defence costs | (30) | (15) |
| Minority interests - equity | (330) | (570) |
|  | 1,504 | 1,319 |
| *Capital and reserves* | | |
| Called up share capital | 440 | 440 |
| Share premium account | 101 | 101 |
| Revaluation reserve | 33 | 50 |
| Profit and loss account | 930 | 728 |
| Total shareholders' funds - equity | 1,504 | 1,319 |

The following information is relevant to the Baron Group plc.

(a) The group disposed of a major subsidiary Piece plc on 1 September 20X7. Baron held an 80% interest in the subsidiary at the date of disposal. Piece plc's results are classified as discontinued in the profit and loss account.

The group required the subsidiary Piece plc to prepare an interim balance sheet at the date of the disposal and this is as follows.

|  | £m | £m |
|---|---|---|
| Tangible fixed assets (depreciation 30) | | 310 |
| Current assets | | |
| Stocks | 60 | |
| Debtors | 50 | |
| Cash at bank and in hand | 130 | |
|  | 240 | |
| Creditors: amounts falling due within one year (including corporation tax - £25m) | (130) | |
|  | | 110 |
|  | | 420 |
| Called up share capital | | 100 |
| Profit and loss account | | 320 |
|  | | 420 |

The consolidated carrying values of all the assets and liabilities at that date are as above. The depreciation charge in the profit and loss account for the period was £9 million. The carrying amount relating to goodwill in the group accounts arising on the acquisition of Piece plc was £64 million at 1 December 20X6. The loss on sale of discontinued operations in the group accounts comprises:

|  | £m |
|---|---|
| Sale proceeds | 375 |
| Net assets sold (80% × £420m) | (336) |
| Goodwill | (64) |
|  | (25) |

The consideration for the sale of Piece plc was 200 million ordinary shares of £1 in Meal plc, the acquiring company, at a value of £300 million and £75 million in cash. The group's policy is to amortise goodwill arising on acquisition but not in the year of sale of a subsidiary. The amortisation for the year was £20 million on other intangible assets.

(b) During the year, Baron plc had transferred several of its tangible assets to a newly created company, Kevla Ltd, which is owned jointly by three parties. The total investment at the date of transfer in the joint venture by Baron plc was £225 million at carrying value comprising £200 million in tangible fixed assets and £25 million in cash. The group has used equity accounting for the joint venture in Kevla Ltd. No dividends have been received from Kevla Ltd but the land and buildings transferred have been revalued at the year end.

(c) The taxation charge in the profit and loss account is made up of the following items.

|  | £m |
|---|---|
| Corporation tax | 171 |
| Tax attributable to joint venture | 20 |
|  | 191 |

(d) The movement on tangible fixed assets of the Baron Group plc during the year was as follows.

|  | £m |
|---|---|
| Cost or valuation 1 December 20X6 | 2,100 |
| Additions | 380 |
| Revaluation | (30) |
| Disposals and transfers | (680) |
| At 30 November 20X7 | 1,770 |
|  |  |
| Depreciation |  |
| 1 December 20X6 | 300 |
| Provided during year | 150 |
| Disposals and transfers | (95) |
| At 30 November 20X7 | 355 |
|  |  |
| Carrying value at 30 November 20X7 | 1,415 |
|  |  |
| Carrying value at 1 December 20X6 | 1,800 |

(e) The investments included under fixed assets comprised the joint venture in Kevla Ltd (£265 million), the shares in Meal plc (£300 million), and investments in corporate bonds (£35 million). The bonds had been purchased in November 20X7 and were deemed to be highly liquid, although Baron plc intended to hold them for the longer term as their maturity date is 1 January 20X9.

The short term investments comprised the following items.

|  | 20X7 £m | 20X6 £m |
|---|---|---|
| Government securities (Repayable 1 April 20X8) | 51 | 23 |
| Cash on seven day deposit | 101 | 21 |
|  | 152 | 44 |

(f)  A prepayment of £20 million has been included in debtors against an exceptional pension liability which will fall due in the following financial year. Interest receivable included in debtors was £5 million at 30 November 20X7 (£4 million at 30 November 20X6).

(g)  Creditors: amounts falling due with one year comprise the following items.

|  | 20X7 £m | 20X6 £m |
|---|---|---|
| Trade creditors | 1,300 | 973 |
| Corporation tax | 181 | 150 |
| Dividends | 80 | 70 |
| Accrued interest | 40 | 30 |
|  | 1,601 | 1,223 |

**Required:**

**Prepare a group cash flow statement using the 'indirect method' for the Baron Group plc for the year ended 30 November 20X7 in accordance with the requirements of FRS 1 *Cash flow statements* (revised 1996). Your answer should include the following.**

**(a)   Reconciliation of operating profit to operating cash flows**

**(b)   An analysis of cash flows for any headings netted in the cash flow statement**

(Candidates should distinguish net cash flows from continuing and discontinued operations.)                                                                                      **(25 marks)**

The notes regarding the sale of the subsidiary and a reconciliation of net cash flow to movement in net debt are not required.

## Section B - Three questions only to be answered

2    Provisions are particular kinds of liabilities. It therefore follows that provisions should be recognised when the definition of a liability has been met. The key requirement of a liability is a present obligation and thus this requirement is critical also in the context of the recognition of a provision. However, although accounting for provisions is an important topic for standard setters, it is only recently that guidance has been issued on provisioning in financial statements. In the UK, the Accounting Standards Board has recently issued FRS 12 *Provisions, contingent liabilities and contingent assets.*

### Required:

(a) (i)    **Explain why there was a need for more detailed guidance on accounting for provisions in the UK.**    (7 marks)

   (ii)    **Explain the circumstances under which a provision should be recognised in the financial statements according to FRS 12** *Provisions, contingent liabilities and contingent assets.*    (6 marks)

(b)    **Discuss whether the following provisions have been accounted for correctly under FRS 12** *Provisions, contingent liabilities and contingent assets.*

   World Wide Nuclear Fuels plc disclosed the following information in its financial statements for the year ended 30 November 20X9.

   *Provisions and long-term commitments*

   (i)    Provision for decommissioning the Group's radioactive facilities is made over their useful life and covers complete demolition of the facility within fifty years of it being taken out of service together with any associated waste disposal. The provision is based on future prices and is discounted using a current market rate of interest.

   *Provision for decommissioning costs*

|  | £m |
|---|---|
| Balance at 1.12.X8 | 675 |
| Adjustment arising from change in price levels charged to reserves | 33 |
| Charged in the year to profit and loss account | 125 |
| Adjustment due to change in knowledge (charged to reserves) | 27 |
| Balance at 30.11.X9 | 860 |

   There are still decommissioning costs of £1,231 m (undiscounted) to be provided for in respect of the group's radioactive facilities as the company's policy is to build up the required provision over the life of the facility.

   Assume that adjustments to the provision due to changes in knowledge about the accuracy of the provision do not give rise to future economic benefits.    (7 marks)

   (ii)    The company purchased an oil company during the year. As part of the sale agreement, oil has to be supplied for a five year period to the company's former holding company at an uneconomic rate. As a result a provision for future operating losses has been set up of £135m which relates solely to the uneconomic supply of oil. Additionally the oil company is exposed to environmental liabilities arising out of its past obligations, principally in respect of remedial work to soil and ground waste systems, although currently there is no legal obligation to carry out the work. Liabilities for environmental costs are provided for when the Group determines a formal plan of action on the closure of an inactive site and when expenditure on remedial work is probable and the cost can be measured with reasonable certainty. However, in this case, it has been decided to provide for £120m in respect of the environmental liability on the acquisition of the oil company. World Wide Nuclear Fuels has a reputation for ensuring that the environment is preserved and protected from the effects of its business activities.          (5 marks)

**(25 marks)**

**3**    You have been asked by the new chairman of a group of companies to prepare a report advising the chairman about some of the existing practices within the group. These practices are:

(a)  Weekly monitoring and analysis of the company's register of shareholders.

(6 marks)

(b)  The evaluation of performance within the semi-autonomous subsidiaries of the group by means of the return on investment within the subsidiary.     (10 marks)

(c)  The purchase of the company's 'Z' score, based upon multiple discriminant analysis, every three months from a leading business school.          (9 marks)

**Required:**

**In each case discuss the usefulness and problems (if any) of the practice and briefly discuss possible modifications to existing practice that might be of value.**

**(25 marks)**

**4**    Planet plc has provided the following draft consolidated balance sheet as at 30 November 20X1.

PLANET PLC
GROUP BALANCE SHEET AS AT 30 NOVEMBER 20X1

|  | £'000 |
|---|---|
| *Fixed assets* | |
| Intangible assets | 10,360 |
| Tangible assets | 76,240 |
|  | 86,600 |
| *Net current assets* | 55,800 |
| *Total assets less current liabilities* | 142,400 |
| *Creditors: amounts falling due after more than one year* | (25,400) |
| *Provisions for liabilities and charges* | (1,800) |
|  | 115,200 |
| *Minority interests* | (18,200) |
|  | 97,000 |
| *Capital and reserves* | |
| Called up share capital | 32,200 |
| Share premium account | 10,000 |

| | |
|---|---|
| Profit and loss account | 54,800 |
| Shareholders' funds | 97,000 |

The group accountant has asked your advice on several matters. These issues are set out below and have not been dealt with in the draft group financial statements.

(i)   Planet purchased a wholly owned subsidiary company, Moon, on 1 December 20W9. The purchase consideration was based on the performance of the subsidiary. The vendors commenced a legal action on 31 March 20X1 over the amount of the purchase consideration. An amount had been paid to the vendors and included in the calculation of goodwill but the vendors disputed the amount of this payment. On 30 November 20X1 the court ruled that Planet should pay an additional £16 million to the vendors. The directors do not know how to treat the additional purchase consideration and have not accounted for the item. Goodwill is written off over five years and there is no time apportionment in the year of purchase.

*Note.* Ignore the effect of the time value of money.

(ii)   Planet has corporate offices under an operating lease. A requirement of the operating lease for the buildings is that the asset is returned in good condition. The operating lease was signed in the current year and lasts for six years. Planet intends to refurbish the building in six years time at a cost of £12 million in order to meet the requirements of the lease. This amount includes the renovation of the exterior of the building and is based on current price levels. Currently there is evidence that due to exceptionally severe weather damage the company will have to spend £2.4 million in the next year on having the exterior of the building renovated. The company feels that this expenditure will reduce the refurbishment cost at the end of the lease by an equivalent amount. There is no provision for the above expenditure in the financial statements.

An 80% owned subsidiary company, Galaxy, has a leasehold property (depreciated historical cost £16 million). It has been modified to include a swimming pool for the employees. Under the terms of the lease, the property must be restored to its original state when the lease expires in ten years' time or earlier termination. The present value of the costs of reinstatement are likely to be £4 million and the directors wish to provide for £400,000 per annum for ten years. The lease was signed and operated from 1 December 20X0. The directors estimate that the lease has a recoverable value of £19 million at 30 November 20X1 and have not provided for any of the above amounts.

Additionally Planet owns buildings at a carrying value of £40 million which will require repair expenditure of approximately £12 million over the next five years. There is no provision for this amount in the financial statements. Depreciation is charged on owned buildings at 5% per annum and on leasehold buildings at 10% per annum on the straight line basis.

(iii)   On December 20X0, Planet entered into an agreement *— is a forward contract.* with a wholly owned overseas subsidiary, Dimanche, to purchase components at a value of 4.2 million krona on which Dimanche made a profit of 20% on selling price. The goods were to be delivered on 31 January 20X1 with the payment due on 31 March 20X1. Planet took out a foreign currency contract on 1 December 20X0 to buy 4.2 million krona on 31 March 20X1 at the forward rate of £1 = 1.4 krona.

At 30 November 20X1, Planet had two-thirds of the components in stock. The spot rates were as follows.

|  | *£1 equivalent* |
| --- | --- |
| 1 December 20X0 | 1.3 krona |
| 31 January 20X1 | 1.46 krona |
| 31 March 20X1 | 1.45 krona |
| 30 November 20X1 | 1.35 krona |

The initial purchase of the stock had been recorded on receipt at the forward rate and the forward rate had been used for the year end valuation of stock. The directors are unsure as to how to treat the items above both for accounting and disclosure purposes but they have heard that the simplest method is to translate the asset and liability at the forward rate and they wish to use this method.

(iv)  Galaxy has developed a database during the year to 30 November 20X1 and it is included in intangible fixed assets at a cost of £6 million. The asset comprises the internal and external costs of developing the database. The cost of the database is being amortised over 10 years and one year's amortisation has been charged. The database is used to produce a technical computing manual which is used by the whole group and sold to other parties. It has quickly become a market leader in this field. Any costs of maintaining the database and the computing manual are written off as incurred. The computing manual requires substantial revision every four years.

**Required:**

**(a) Explain how the above four issues should be dealt with in the consolidated financial statements of Planet. Show the accounting entries that need to be made.**                                                   (19 marks)

**(b) Prepare a revised group balance sheet at 30 November 20X1 taking into account the four issues discussed in part (a).**                         (6 marks)

**(25 marks)**

5     (a)  In December 2000 the ASB issued FRS 19 *Deferred tax*. This requires full provision. The partial provision method of accounting for deferred tax had lost favour, mainly because it anticipates future events, which is considered inconsistent with other accounting treatments and with many international standard setters.

FRS 19 was issued in order to facilitate the process of harmonisation of accounting for deferred tax. However, full provision for deferred tax under FRS 19 is entirely different to that of equivalent accounting standards internationally. Under these standards full provision is based on 'temporary differences' whereas FRS 19 has a system based on 'timing differences'. There is strong opposition within the ASB to accounting for deferred tax using temporary differences rather than timing differences. Another important difference is that FRS 19 allows discounting of deferred tax balances.

**Required:**

(i)   **Discuss the arguments for and against discounting long-term deferred tax balances.**   (6 marks)

(ii)  **Explain the differences between accounting for deferred tax using timing differences as opposed to temporary differences.**   (6 marks)

(b)  FP plc will be applying the provisions of FRS 19 to its financial statements for the year ending 30 November 20X1. The amounts of deferred taxation provided and unprovided in the group financial statements for the year ending 30 November 20X0 were as follows.

|  | Provided £m | Unprovided £m |
|---|---|---|
| Capital allowances in excess of depreciation | 76 | 24 |
| Other timing differences | 22 | 28 |
| Pensions and other post retirement benefits | 124 | - |
| Losses available for offset against future taxable profits | (68) | (84) |
| Corporation tax on capital gains arising on the disposal of property which has been deferred under the rollover provisions | - | 330 |
| Tax that would arise if properties were disposed of at their revalued amounts | - | 280 |
|  | 154 | 578 |

The following notes are relevant to the calculation of the deferred tax provision under FRS 19 as at 30 November 20X1.

(i)   The excess of capital allowances over depreciation is £360 million as at 30 November 20X1. It is anticipated that the timing differences will reverse according to the following schedule.

|  | 30 Nov 20X2 £m | 30 Nov 20X3 £m | 30 Nov 20X4 £m |
|---|---|---|---|
| Depreciation | 2,200 | 2,200 | 2,200 |
| Capital allowances | 2,100 | 2,080 | 2,060 |
|  | 100 | 120 | 140 |

Other timing differences amount to £180 million as at 30 November 20X1. It is anticipated that they will all reverse in the year to 30 November 20X2.

(ii)  FP acquired a 100% holding in an overseas company several years ago. The subsidiary has declared a dividend for the financial year to 30 November 20X1 of £16 million. The dividend has been accrued but no account has been taken of the tax liability on this dividend of £4 million payable on 30 November 20X2. During the year FP had supplied the subsidiary with stock amounting to £60 million at a profit of 20% on selling price. This stock had not been sold by the year end and the tax rate applied to the subsidiary's profit was 25%. No other adjustments to deferred taxation are required for the subsidiary other than those required by this note.

(iii) Corporation tax on the property disposed of becomes payable on 30 November 20X4 under the rollover relief provisions. There had been no sales or revaluations of property during the year to 30 November 20X1.

BPP PUBLISHING

(iv) Corporation tax is assumed to be 30% for the foreseeable future and the company wishes to discount any deferred tax liabilities at a rate of 4%.

(v) It is envisaged that any unrelieved tax losses will be offset in equal proportion against taxable profits for the years ending 30 November 20X2 and 20X3. The auditors have concurred with the directors of the company as regards the future recovery of the unrelieved tax losses. No further losses arose in the year to 30 November 20X1. The tax losses provided for at 30 November 20X0 were offset against profits for the year ended 30 November 20X1.

(vi) The amount of the deferred tax provision required for pensions and other post retirement benefits has risen to £180 million as at 30 November 20X1. FP has an actuarial valuation of the pension fund every three years.

**Required:**

**Calculate the provision for deferred tax required in the group balance sheet of FP plc at 30 November 20X1 using FRS 19. Comment on the effect that the application of FRS 19 will have on the financial statements of FP plc.**

(13 marks)

**(25 marks)**

# ANSWERS

**DO NOT TURN THIS PAGE UNTIL YOU
HAVE COMPLETED THE MOCK EXAM**

# WARNING! APPLYING THE BPP MARKING SCHEME

If you decide to mark your paper using the BPP marking scheme, you should bear in mind the following points.

1   The BPP solutions are not definitive: you will see that we have applied the marking scheme to our solutions to show how good answers should gain marks, but there may be more than one way to answer the question. You must try to judge fairly whether different points made in your answers are correct and relevant and therefore worth marks according to our marking scheme.

2   If you have a friend or colleague who is studying or has studied this paper, you might ask him or her to mark your paper for you, thus gaining a more objective assessment. Remember you and your friend are not trained or objective markers, so try to avoid complacency or pessimism if you appear to have done very well or very badly.

3   You should be aware that BPP's answers are longer than you would be expected to write. Sometimes, therefore, you would gain the same number of marks for making the basic point as we have shown as being available for a slightly more detailed or extensive solution.

It is most important that you analyse your solutions in detail and that you attempt to be as objective as possible.

---

**Professional Examination - Paper 3.6**                                **Marking Scheme**

**Advanced Corporate Reporting**

This marking scheme is given as a guide to markers in the context of the suggested answer. Scope is given to markers to award marks for alternative approaches to a question, including relevant comment, and where well-reasoned conclusions are provided.

---

# A PLAN OF ATTACK

If this were the real Advanced Corporate Reporting exam and you had been told to turn over and begin, what would be going through your mind?

The answer may be 'I can't do this to save my life'! You've spent most of your study time on groups and current issues (because that's what your tutor/BPP Study Text told you to do), plus a selection of other topics, and you're really not sure that you know enough. The good news is that this may get you through. The first question, in Section A, is very likely to be on groups. In Section B you have to choose three out of four questions, and at least one of those is likely to be on current issues – a new FRS, FRED or discussion paper. So there's no need to panic. First spend **five minutes or so looking at the paper**, and develop a **plan of attack**.

## Looking through the paper

The compulsory question in Section A is, as usual, on groups, in this case, a group cash flow statement. It looks horrendous, but don't worry about this for now. In **Section B** you have **four questions on a variety of topics:**

- Question 2 deals with provisions, and is part straightforward explanation, part application. It looks a good bet.

- Question 3 is a gift if you've revised this topic. Of course you may not have done – it looks a bit obscure, but the Study Guide for Paper 3.6 does give this area some emphasis.

- Question 4 looks at first like a group accounting question. But it isn't really about groups at all. It requires a discussion of four accounting issues: FRS 7 and fair values, FRS 12 and provisions, FRS 13 and derivatives (and a straightforward intercompany adjustment) and FRS 10/SSAP 13 and intangible assets. Then you have to revise a group balance sheet.

- Question 5 is your current issues question, on a very recent standard, FRS 19.

You **only have to answer three out of these four questions.** You don't have to pick your optional questions right now, but this brief overview should have convinced you that you have enough **choice** and variety to have a respectable go at Section B. So let's go back to the compulsory question in Section A.

## Compulsory question

**Question 1** requires you to **prepare a group cash flow statement**. This question looks daunting and you can expect it to be time pressured because of the sheer volume of information, covering several pages of the examination paper. However, the question is relatively straightforward, provided that you provide methodical, clearly set out workings, you remember the treatment of disposals of subsidiaries in cash flow statements and you can calculate the minority interest dividend payment.

## Optional questions

Deciding between the optional questions is obviously a personal matter – it depends how you have spent your study time. However, here are a few pointers.

In our opinion, **everyone should do Question 2, on provisions**. You should know FRS 12 by now as you have studied it for Paper 10/2.5. This question, though by no means a walkover, contains no nasty hidden traps.

**Question 4** is a good question to do, despite its rather strange requirements. This is because it is **broken down into, in effect, five chunks**. You are likely to know something about the areas covered, because you have met the standards before. Producing a revised balance sheet may be a surprise, but there is no mystery to it.

Choosing between Questions 3 and 5 may seem like choosing between 'the devil and the deep blue sea'. 'Z' scores or deferred tax – which is it to be? You will be able to make up your mind fairly quickly, though – **if you've studied corporate failure in detail, go for Question 3**, which is straightforward bookwork. If not, have a stab at **Question 5 – you should have studied deferred tax at a basic level** for Paper 10/2.5 and should be able to get at least some of the marks.

## Allocating your time

BPP's advice is always allocate your time **according to the marks for the question** in total and for the parts of the question. But **use common sense**. If you're doing Question 4 but haven't a clue what Part (a)(iii) is getting at (derivatives and hedging), you'd be better off stating that the unrealised profit must be eliminated and spending more time on the other parts of the question.

## Forget about it!

And don't worry if you found the paper difficult. More than likely other candidates will too. The paper is marked fairly leniently and always has a good pass rate. If this were the real thing, you would need to **forget** the exam the minute you left the exam hall and **think about the next one**. Or, if it's the last one, **celebrate**!

1

> **Tutor's hint**
>
> If you got the analysis into continuing and discontinuing operations completely right - well done. You could, however, easily pass the question without doing so. There are a lot of basic calculations in this question, eg movement on provisions, dividends paid and so on. Don't let the length of the question put you off.

BARON GROUP PLC
CASH FLOW STATEMENT FOR THE YEAR ENDED 30 NOVEMBER 20X7

|  | £m |
| --- | --- |
| Cash inflow from operating activities (note 1) | 875 |
| Returns on investment and servicing finance (note 2) | (214) |
| Taxation (W7) | (115) |
| Capital expenditure (note 2) | (312) |
| Acquisitions and disposals (note 2) | (80) |
| Equity dividends paid (W6) | (120) |
| Cash inflow before use of liquid resources and financing | 34 |
| Management of liquid resources (note 2) | (143) |
| Decrease in cash | (109) |

*Notes*

1   *Reconciliation of operating profit to operating cash flows*

|  | Continu-ing £m |  | Discon-tinued £m |  | Total £m |
| --- | --- | --- | --- | --- | --- |
| • Operating profit (W1) | 458 |  | 184 |  | 642 |
| Depreciation | 141 | (150 – 9) | 9 | (note (a)) | 150 |
| Goodwill amortisation | 20 | (note (a)) |  |  | 20 |
| Share of joint venture profit | (75) |  |  |  | (75) |
| Increase in stocks $s$ (incl Piece) | (40) |  | (60) |  | (100) |
| Increase in debtors $\circ$ (incl Piece) | (119) | (W2) | (50) | (Piece) | (169) |
| Increase in creditors $c$ (incl Piece) | 327 | (note (g)) | 105 | (Piece) | 432 |
| Operating activities continuing operations | 712 |  | 188 |  | 900 |
| Bid defence | (5) | (W3) |  |  | (5) |
| Pension prepayment | (20) |  |  |  | (20) |
|  | 687 |  | 188 |  | 875 |

2   *Gross cash flows*

*Returns on investment and servicing finance*

|  | £m |
| --- | --- |
| Interest received (4 + 27 – 5) | 26 |
| Interest paid (30 + 19 – 40) | (9) |
| Minority interest dividend (W4) | (231) |
|  | (214) |

| *Capital expenditure* | £m |
|---|---|
| Purchase of tangible fixed assets (note (d)) | (380) |
| Sale of tangible fixed assets (W5) | 68 |
| | 312 |

| *Acquisitions and disposals* | |
|---|---|
| Cash paid to acquire interest in joint venture (note (b)) | (25) |
| Cash disposed on sale of subsidiary (note (a)) | (130) |
| Cash element of disposal proceeds (note (a)) | 75 |
| | (80) |

| *Management of liquid resources* | |
|---|---|
| Purchase of corporate bonds (see note (e)) | (35) |
| Purchase of government securities (increase) (see note (e)) (51 – 23) | (28) |
| Cash on seven day deposit (increase) (see note (e)) (101 – 21) | (80) |
| | (143) |

*Note.* None of the above are deemed to be 'cash' under the terms of FRS 1 revised.

*Workings*

1 *Operating profit*

| | £m |
|---|---|
| Operating profit per P&L (continuing operations) | 438 |
| Add back bid defence costs | 20 |
| | 458 |
| Operating profit on discontinued operations | 184 |
| | 642 |

2 *Debtors*

| | £m |
|---|---|
| At 30.11.X7 | 680 |
| Pension prepayment (note (f) in question) | (20) |
| Interest receivable (note (f) in question) | (5) |
| | 655 |
| At 30.11.X6 | 540 |
| Interest receivable (note (f) in question) | (4) |
| | 536 |
| Increase (before allowing for disposal) | 119 |

3 *Bid defence*

| | £m |
|---|---|
| 20X6 Provision b/f | 15 |
| 20X7 P&L charge | 20 |
| | 35 |
| 20X7 Provision c/f | 30 |
| Paid | 5 |

4 *Dividend paid to minority interest*

MINORITY INTEREST MEMORANDUM WORKING ACCOUNT

| | £m | | £m |
|---|---|---|---|
| Disposal of MI in Piece | | | |
| (420 × 20%) | 84 | Balance b/f 1.12.X6 | 570 |
| Balancing figure = cash paid | 231 | P&L: minority interest share | 75 |
| Balance c/f 30.11.X7 | 330 | | |
| | 645 | | 645 |

5   *Disposal of fixed assets*

|  | £m |
|---|---|
| Net book value of all disposals (note (d)) (680 – 95) | 585 |
| Assets of Piece sold (at NBV) | (310) |
| Assets transferred to joint venture (note (b)) | (200) |
| NBV of fixed assets sold | 75 |
| Loss on disposal (per P&L account) | (7) |
| Sale proceeds | 68 |

6   *Equity dividends paid*

|  | £m |
|---|---|
| Balance b/f 1.12.X6 (note (g)) | 70 |
| P&L appropriation | 130 |
| Balance c/f 30.11.X7 (note (g)) | (80) |
| Paid | 120 |

7   *Taxation*

|  | £m |
|---|---|
| Balance b/f 1.12.X6 | 150 ✓ |
| Taxation balance disposed on sale of subsidiary | (25) |
| Taxation attributable to joint venture | (20) ✓ |
| P&L tax charge for year | 191 |
| Balance c/f 30.11.X7 | (181) ✓ |
| Tax paid | 115 |

---

### Marking scheme

|  | *Marks* |
|---|---|
| Cash flow from operating activities | 10 |
| Returns on investments and servicing of finance | 3 |
| Taxation | 2 |
| Capital expenditure | 3 |
| Acquisitions and disposals | 3 |
| Equity dividends | 2 |
| Management of liquid resources | 3 |
| Exceptional cash outflows | 2 |
| Presentation | 5 |
| **Available** | **33** |
| **Maximum** | **26** |

---

2

---

**Tutor's hint**. In part (b) make sure that your answer uses all the various details in the mini-scenarios and is specific to the question. Vague points about FRS 12 will not score well here whereas good basic knowledge applied to the question will.

---

(a)   (i)   **Need for guidance**

> (1)   Different companies accounted for provisions in different ways leading to **inconsistent reporting**.

> (2)   Provisions were used as '**income smoothing**' devices, ie setting up a provision and then either releasing it or charging expenses to it and thus bypassing the profit and loss account.

225

(3)  Provisions were not always recognised in the balance sheet. Alternatively **spurious provisions** were recognised which led to the balance sheet's worth being undermined.

(4)  SSAP 18 only dealt with contingencies. The Companies Act rules on provisions were **insufficiently precise**.

(5)  In the light of the definition of liabilities in the ASB *Statement of Principles*, FRS 12 now makes the definition of a provision consistent with that definition of a liability.

(6)  **Improved disclosure** rules have been introduced.

(7)  The **timing of recognition** and the **measurement** of provisions have been addressed by FRS 12.

(ii)  Provisions are only recognised in restricted circumstances.

(1)  There is a constructive or legal **obligation** arising from **past events**.

(2)  It is probable that the liability will be settled by a **transfer of economic benefits.**

(3)  A **reliable estimate** of the amount required to settle the obligation can be made. Alternatively, there may be a range of possible outcomes.

(4)  **No provision** can be recognised for **expected future costs** - if the company can avoid the expenditure by future action then no provision is required.

(5)  **No provision** for **future operating losses** should be recognised.

(6)  Provisions for **restructuring** should only be recognised when there is a **constructive obligation**.

(7)  If a company has an **'onerous contract'** then the present obligation should be recognised as a provision.

(8)  FRS 12 takes a **balance sheet view** of provisions by concentrating upon the recognition of liabilities rather than the recognition of the profit and loss account expense charges.

(b)  (i)  The company is building up the provision over the life of the facility on the 'units of production' method.

FRS 12 requires the **full liability** to be recognised for the obligations which exist. The provision can be capitalised as an asset if it provides access to future economic benefits, otherwise it is chargeable to the profit and loss account.

The decommissioning costs (£1,231m) are brought onto the balance sheet at present value and a corresponding asset created.

The method used to **discount the provision is inconsistent**. FRS 12 requires companies to use current prices discounted by real interest rates or future prices discounted by nominal rates. The company currently uses a mixed method. The rate used should be a risk free rate when future cash flows already reflect risk. A good rate to use would be the government bond rate.

The company makes a reserve adjustment for changes in price levels. Such adjustments should be made through the profit and loss account consisting of two parts.

(1)  An adjustment to the provision for changes in the discount rate.

(2)  An element representing the 'unwinding' over time of the discount.

The profit and loss account would be charged with the amortisation of the asset set up and also an adjustment for changes in interest rates and the unwinding of the discount.

Any subsequent changes in the provision should be charged to the profit and loss account if they do not give rise to future economic benefits. The £27m **should not therefore be charged to reserves**.

(ii) Following FRS 12, no provision for operating losses in the future could be set up. If the company has an '**onerous contract**' then a **provision can be established**. Onerous contracts are contracts where the costs of fulfilling the contract exceed contract receipts and where compensation is payable if the contract is terminated.

The provision of £135m can remain and would affect the fair value at acquisition.

Provisions for **environmental liabilities** can only be recognised if the **conditions in FRS 12** regarding recognition of provisions are met. There is no current obligation, but it is possible that a **constructive obligation could arise** subject to agreement with the auditors because of the company's reputation.

---

## Marking scheme

|  |  | Marks |
|---|---|---:|
| **(a)** (i) | Subjective | 7 |
| | *Maximum* | 7 |
| (ii) | Liability | 1 |
| | Legal/constructive obligation | 2 |
| | Reasonable estimate | 1 |
| | No alternative | 1 |
| | Recognition | 1 |
| | Do not need to know identity | 1 |
| | Onerous contracts | 1 |
| | *Available* | 8 |
| | *Maximum* | 6 |
| **(b)** (i) | Full liability | 2 |
| | Accounting | 3 |
| | Discounting | 2 |
| | Price level adjustment and interest | 2 |
| | Amendment of provision | 1 |
| | *Available* | 10 |
| | *Maximum* | 7 |
| (ii) | No provision for future losses | 1 |
| | Onerous contract | 2 |
| | Provision stays | 1 |
| | Environment costs – obligation | 2 |
| | Mere existence | 1 |
| | *Available* | 7 |
| | *Maximum* | 5 |
| | **Available** | **32** |
| | **Maximum** | **25** |

**3**

> **Tutor's hint**. The answer should be in the form of a report to the chairman of the group. In part (b) the possibility of manipulation and distortion of return on investment within subsidiaries should be taken into account, as well as the impact on the ratio of long term group strategic decisions. Explain how the 'Z' score may be used by external parties as well as its direct use to the group in failure prediction.

To:     Chairman
From:   Accountant                                    Date: 12 December 20X2

EXISTING FINANCIAL PRACTICES

*Introduction*

This report provides an appraisal of some of the existing financial practices within the group.

**Analysis of the register of shareholders**

The benefits of weekly monitoring and analysis are as follows.

(a)  Analysis of movements in shareholdings can assist in understanding recent movements in the share price.

(b)  Monitoring the register can provide early indications of stake building in advance of a possible hostile takeover bid. Such knowledge enables rapid preparation of a defence document.

(c)  Understanding the composition of the shareholders can assist in deciding the most appropriate dividend policy to adopt. It should also be taken into account when trying to determine what level of risk is appropriate in investment appraisal.

(d)  Knowledge of the structure of the shareholders allows the board to maintain informal relationships with the principal shareholders. This will be useful when the board needs their support in making major strategic moves eg the acquisition of another company.

Thus it is useful for the board to be aware of the composition of and changes in the shareholders' register. However, it is debatable whether a weekly report is the most appropriate timescale for this. If a hostile bid is anticipated, then the register should be monitored more often than once a week. However at other times, and for the purposes described in points (a), (c) and (d) it is probably not necessary to undertake the exercise at such regular intervals and this may be a waste of resources. Monthly monitoring is probably adequate.

**The use of ROI in subsidiary performance evaluation**

Return on investment (ROI) is a common method of subsidiary performance evaluation within a group of companies. The measure commonly used is:

$$\frac{\text{Profit before interest and tax}}{\text{Total capital employed}}$$

This ratio relates the total amount of profit earned to the funds used to generate it. It is commonly analysed into two sub-ratios:

$\dfrac{\text{Profit}}{\text{Sales}}$ measures return on sales, or margin;

$\dfrac{\text{Sales}}{\text{Capital employed}}$ measures asset turnover, the intensity with which assets are being used.

The main benefit of using this measure is that it permits the direct comparison of performance between semi-autonomous subsidiaries which are not directly comparable in other ways. However, it may be subject to the following drawbacks.

(a)  It is very dependent on the net book value of the assets employed. This might make managers reluctant to make long term improvements to the asset base since this could depress ROI in the short term. It also means that the ratio is sensitive to the depreciation policies used. If these are not subject to group standards, this will lead to distortions in the comparison of subsidiaries.

(b)  Allocation of central overheads can distort the ratio.

(c)  Transfer pricing policies within the group may distort the profit figure and therefore make realistic comparison of the ratio difficult.

(d)  The group may have directed a subsidiary to undertake a long term strategic move, such as moving into a new market which is not currently very profitable but which offers the prospect of good returns in the future. In this situation direct comparison of the ratios is not realistic.

(e)  In a conglomerate group, the subsidiaries may operate in different economic sectors where different levels of ROI are regarded as acceptable. The group may wish to maintain this diversification even though it means that some subsidiaries are less profitable than others.

Thus ROI is of value in performance evaluation, but subject to certain constraints. It should not be used in isolation, but in conjunction with other measures. Examples of other appropriate measures include net present value of the cash flows generated, and trends in some of the component ratios making up ROI such as movement in market share.

**Three monthly purchase of 'Z' scores**

'Z' scores were developed by Altman as a tool for predicting company failure. Five key ratios were identified which were weighted as factors in an equation to produce the 'Z' score for a given firm:

(a)  Working capital : total assets
(b)  Retained earnings : total assets
(c)  Earnings before interest and tax : total assets
(d)  Market value of equity : book value of total debt
(e)  Sales: total assets

Altman identified three categories of score:

(a)  More than 2.7: non-failure
(b)  1.8 - 2.7: uncertain
(c)  Less than 1.8: probable failure

The sample used was small and related to US firms. Subsequent researchers have developed similar models using different combinations and weightings of ratios to produce predictors of failure in different countries and market sectors.

Regular appraisal of the group's 'Z' score may therefore be useful if the group is in a critical financial condition, either approaching or within the uncertainty zone. However it can be argued that the management should know better than an external organisation what the current financial health of the group is like. Further, purchased 'Z' scores are dependent upon the information provided in reported group accounts, and the management should have access to far more detailed financial information.

Although it may appear that regular purchase of the 'Z' score is only likely to be useful when the group is in financial problems, it must be remembered that banks, investors, suppliers, customers and other providers of credit will use the tool in evaluating the status of the group. Thus it could be argued on these grounds that the group should keep abreast of its perception within the market and be able to take steps to ensure that it is not misrepresented.

An alternative but more subjective method of predicting possible corporate failure based on non-financial information such as on organisation and systems is the technique of 'A' scores developed by Argenti.

**Conclusions**

The existing practices are likely to continue to be of value, with the following caveats.

(a)   The timescale over which movements in the register of shareholders are monitored and analysed may need to be changed.

(b)   ROI should be used in conjunction with other measures of subsidiary performance, and must be evaluated in the context of wider group strategic decisions.

(c)   Regular purchase of the 'Z' score is justified in order to keep in touch with market perceptions of the group, and at times when financial conditions are critical.

---

**Marking scheme**

|  |  | Marks |
|---|---|---:|
| Analysis of register of shareholders: | Usefulness | 5 |
|  | Problems | 3 |
| Use of ROI: | Usefulness | 7 |
|  | Problems | 6 |
| 'Z' scores: | Usefulness | 6 |
|  | Problems | 5 |
|  | **Available** | **32** |
|  | **Maximum** | **25** |

---

**4**

(a)   (i)   **Additional purchase consideration**

The company should **recognise a liability of £16 million and additional goodwill of £16 million**. Although FRS 7 *Fair values in acquisition accounting* sets a time limit for recognition of fair value adjustments this applies only to the acquired assets and liabilities. There is **no time limit** for the recognition of **goodwill relating to contingent consideration** (FRS 7 paragraph 57).

The increase in goodwill is an adjustment to an accounting estimate made in a previous period. Therefore it should be amortised over four years (the remaining useful economic life of the goodwill).

The accounting entries required are:

|  |  | £'000 | £'000 |
|---|---|---:|---:|
| DEBIT | Profit and loss account (amortisation) | 4,000 |  |
| DEBIT | Intangible assets (goodwill) | 12,000 |  |
| CREDIT | Creditors: Amounts falling due within one year |  | 16,000 |

(ii) **Buildings**

In each case the main issue is whether Planet should recognise a provision for future repair and refurbishment expenditure.

*Operating lease*

FRS 12 *Provisions, contingent liabilities and contingent assets* states that a provision should only be recognised if there is a **present obligation resulting from a past event**. The terms of the lease contract mean that Planet has an obligation to incur expenditure in order to return the buildings to the lessee in good condition. The past obligating event appears to be the signing of the lease.

However, **future repairs and maintenance costs** relate to the future operation of the business. They are **not present obligations** resulting from past events. If FRS 12 is interpreted strictly, no provision should be recognised. The repair costs should either be charged as operating expenses in the period in which they occur or capitalised as assets.

Despite this, there is a strong case for recognising a provision for at least some of the expenditure. An Appendix to FRS 12 explains that where a lessee is required to incur periodic charges to **make good dilapidations** or other damage occurring during the rental period, these liabilities **may be recognised, provided that the event** giving rise to the obligation under the lease **has occurred**. Damage to the building has occurred because of the severe weather and therefore a provision should be recognised for the £2.4 million needed to rectify this damage.

Whether any further amounts should be provided depends on the event that gives rise to the present obligation. It is possible to argue that the obligating event is the occurrence of specific damage to the building, but the cost of repairing actual dilapidation to the building during the year would be **difficult to estimate accurately**. It could also be argued that the obligating event is the passage of time, because some expenditure would be necessary if the lease were terminated immediately. Therefore a further £1,600,000 should be provided (£12 million less £2.4 million divided by six). The total provision is £4 million.

The accounting entries required are:

|  | | £'000 | £'000 |
|---|---|---|---|
| DEBIT | Profit and loss account | 4,000 | |
| CREDIT | Provisions for liabilities and charges | | 4,000 |

*Leasehold property*

In this case the company has a present obligation to incur expenditure as a result of a past event (the creation of the swimming pool). Under FRS 12 a **provision should be recognised for the full restoration cost** of £4 million. It is not possible to build up the provision over ten years as the directors propose.

Because the swimming pool represents access to future economic benefits, the future cost also represents an **asset** and this **should be recognised**. The asset will be depreciated at 10% per annum.

The carrying value of the leased building is £19.6 million (£16 million + £4 million – £400,000). This is above the recoverable amount of £19 million and therefore an impairment loss of £600,000 should be recognised.

The accounting entries required are:

|  |  | £'000 | £'000 |
|---|---|---|---|
| DEBIT | Tangible fixed assets | 4,000 | |
| CREDIT | Provisions for liabilities and charges | | 4,000 |
| | | | |
| DEBIT | Profit and loss account (group retained profits) | 320 | |
| DEBIT | Minority interest | 80 | |
| CREDIT | Tangible fixed assets (depreciation) | | 400 |
| | (4,000 × 10%) | | |
| | | | |
| DEBIT | Profit and loss account (group retained profits) | 480 | |
| DEBIT | Minority interest | 120 | |
| CREDIT | Tangible fixed assets (impairment) | | 600 |

*Owned buildings*

Future repair expenditure does **not** represent a **present obligation** of the company because there has been **no past obligating event**. The repairs relate to the future operations of the company and in theory the expenditure **could be avoided** by selling the buildings. Under FRS 12 no provision can be recognised.

Any loss in service potential of the asset should be reflected in the depreciation charge. If the repairs are necessary to restore the service potential of the asset the expenditure should be capitalised.

(iii)   **Agreement with subsidiary**

This has several implications for the financial statements. Because two thirds of the stock remains unsold, the **unrealised inter-company profit** of £400,000 (2/3 × 4.2 million dinars ÷ 1.4 × 20%) **must be eliminated**.

The accounting entries required are:

|  |  | £'000 | £'000 |
|---|---|---|---|
| DEBIT | Profit and loss account (group retained profit) | 400 | |
| CREDIT | Stock | | 400 |

In addition, because Planet is a listed company it must comply with the requirements of FRS 13 *Derivatives and other financial instruments: disclosures*. The **forward contract is a derivative** financial instrument. By entering into the contract the company has fixed the price of the stock and has avoided the effect of changes in the exchange rate. **No exchange gain or loss is recognised** on the transaction. The company is required to **disclose its accounting policy** in respect of hedge accounting, which is to translate its foreign currency assets and liabilities at the forward rate at the date of delivery (as permitted by SSAP 20 *Foreign currency translation*). It is also required to disclose certain information about the contract, including details of any gains and losses carried forward in the balance sheet at the balance sheet date and the extent to which these are expected to be recognised in the profit and loss account in the next accounting period.

Because Planet entered into the contract without incurring any costs, the **book value** and the **fair value** of the forward contract were **nil** at its inception date. The cost of the stock to the company was £3 million (4.2 million ÷ 1.4) but by 31 March 20X1 (the settlement date), exchange rates had moved so that the company would only have paid £2,896,552 for the stock at the spot rate of 1.45. Therefore the company has made a **loss** of £103,448. **One third** of this (£34,482) relates to the **stock sold** and has effectively been **recognised** in the **profit and loss account for the year**. The **remainder** (£68,966) is **carried forward in the value of stock** and will be recognised in the profit and loss account in the next accounting period. There is an argument for **reducing this figure by 20%** as this is the amount of the **inter-company profit** which is eliminated on consolidation. The amount of the loss to be disclosed under FRS 13 is therefore £55,173.

(iv) **Database**

The issue here is whether the cost of developing the database can be capitalised as an intangible asset. FRS 10 *Goodwill and intangible assets* states that **internally generated** intangible assets may **only be capitalised** if they have a **readily ascertainable market value**. This means that the asset must belong to a **homogenous population** of assets that are equivalent in all material aspects and there must be an **active market**, evidenced by frequent transactions, for that population of assets. The database very clearly fails to meet these criteria.

However, the expenditure has resulted in a new product which is now generating income for the group. Under SSAP 13 *Accounting for research and development* the cost of using of scientific or technical knowledge in order to produce new or substantially improved products **may be capitalised as development expenditure** provided that the project meets certain **criteria**. There must be a clearly defined project, the expenditure must be separately identifiable, the outcome of the project must be capable of being assessed with reasonable certainty, future revenue must exceed costs and adequate resources must exist to enable the project to be completed. As the project has been completed and the manual has quickly become a market leader it appears that these conditions have been met.

Because the manual will require substantial **revision every four years** the development costs should be **amortised over this period** (rather than the ten years proposed by the directors).

The accounting entries required to record the additional depreciation are:

|  |  | £'000 | £'000 |
|---|---|---:|---:|
| DEBIT | Profit and loss account (group reserves) | 720 | |
| DEBIT | Minority interests | 180 | |
| CREDIT | Intangible fixed assets ((6,000 ÷ 4) – 600) | | 900 |

(b) **PLANET PLC**
**REVISED GROUP BALANCE SHEET AT 30 NOVEMBER 20X1**

|  | £'000 |
|---|---:|
| *Fixed assets* | |
| Intangible assets (10,360 + 12,000 – 900) | 21,460 |
| Tangible assets (76,240 + 4,000 – 400 – 600) | 79,240 |
| | 100,700 |
| *Net current assets* (55,800 – 16,000 – 400) | 39,400 |
| *Total assets less current liabilities* | 140,100 |
| *Creditors: amounts falling due after more than one year* | (25,400) |
| *Provisions for liabilities and charges* (1,800 + 4,000 + 4,000) | (9,800) |
| | 104,900 |
| *Capital and reserves* | |
| Called up share capital | 32,200 |
| Share premium | 10,000 |
| Profit and loss account (W) | 44,880 |
| | 87,080 |
| *Minority interests* (18,200 – 80 – 120 – 180) | 17,820 |
| | 104,900 |

*Working: profit and loss account*

| | £'000 |
|---|---:|
| Draft | 54,800 |
| Amortisation of additional goodwill (contingent consideration) | (4,000) |
| Provision for repairs (operating lease) | (4,000) |
| Additional depreciation (leased property) | (320) |
| Impairment loss (leased property) | (480) |
| Unrealised profit (inter-company sales) | (400) |
| Amortisation of development expenditure (database) | (720) |
| | 44,880 |

---

### Marking scheme

| | | *Marks* |
|---|---|---:|
| **(a)** | Fair value of consideration | 3 |
| | Operating lease | 4 |
| | Finance lease | 4 |
| | Owned assets | 2 |
| | Hedged transaction: stock | 3 |
| | disclosure | 4 |
| | Database | 5 |
| | *Available* | 25 |
| | *Maximum* | 19 |
| **(b)** | Goodwill | 1 |
| | Operating lease | 1 |
| | Finance lease | 3 |
| | Intercompany profit | 1 |
| | Database | 2 |
| | *Available* | 8 |
| | *Maximum* | 6 |
| | **Available** | **33** |
| | **Maximum** | **25** |

---

5

**Tutor's hint.** Review your answer carefully, noting particularly

The rule about revaluations

The treatment of unrelieved losses

The fact that deferred tax relating to a timing difference based on an already discounted figure (eg pension liabilities) does not have to be discounted.

(a)   (i)   **Arguments for and against discounting**

The purpose of discounting is to measure future cash flows at their **present value**. Therefore **deferred tax balances** should **only** be **discounted** if they represent **future cash flows** that are **not already measured at their present value**.

There is a case for discounting some types of timing differences. Where accruals are made for expenses that will only be paid some time into the future and the tax relief will only be received when the expense is paid, that tax relief represents a future cash flow. However, some expenses, such as **retirement benefits**, are

234

usually **measured on a discounted basis** and therefore they are **already stated at their present value**.

Many timing differences arise because **capital allowances** are received before an asset is depreciated. The resulting deferred tax is a liability that is postponed to future accounting periods. It can be argued that this **postponed liability** is effectively an **interest free loan** from the tax authorities. Discounting the liability reflects this benefit to the entity. There will be a future cash flow because future tax liabilities are higher than they would have been.

It can also be argued that discounting deferred tax on capital allowances is **not appropriate** because the **cash inflow** (in the form of a reduced tax charge) has **already occurred**. Therefore the deferred tax **provision** is **already** stated at its **present value**.

Possibly the most persuasive argument against discounting is that for most entities, the **cost** of calculating the deferred tax charge is likely to **outweigh the benefit** of reducing the liability. In addition, the calculation is **subjective,** as it involves estimating the reversal of timing differences and arriving at a suitable discount rate. A further argument against discounting is that it is inconsistent with international practice. (IAS 12 and the US accounting standard specifically prohibit it.) For these reasons, **FRS 19 allows discounting, but does not require it.**

(ii) **Timing differences and temporary differences**

**Timing differences** arise because some gains and losses are recognised in the financial statements in **different accounting periods** from those in which they are **assessed to tax**. This results in differences between an entity's reported profit in the financial statements and its taxable profit. Timing differences originate in one period and **may reverse** in one or more subsequent periods.

**Temporary differences** are **differences** between the amount at which an asset or liability is **recognised in the financial statements** and the amount that will be **deductible or taxable in the future**. The temporary difference approach recognises the future tax consequences of these differences by looking at the tax that would be payable if the assets and liabilities were realised for the amounts at which they are stated in the balance sheet. The rationale behind this approach is that an asset will generate pre-tax cash flows at least equal to its carrying value. Any tax payable on these cash flows is a liability of the entity and should be provided.

The two approaches consider deferred tax from **different perspectives**. The **timing differences** approach focuses on the **profit and loss account** while the **temporary differences** approach focuses on the **balance sheet**.

The **temporary differences** approach normally results in a **higher tax charge** than the timing differences approach. This is because **temporary differences** may **include permanent differences** as well as timing differences. For example, in theory deferred tax would be provided when an asset or liability is first recognised.

The **timing differences approach is relatively simple** to apply in practice as it is usually easy to identify timing differences from tax computations. It is normally more difficult to identify and measure temporary differences.

(b)  **Calculation of deferred tax liability**

|  | 20X2 £m | 20X3 £m | 20X4 £m |
|---|---|---|---|
| Accelerated capital allowances | 100 | 120 | 140 |
| Other timing differences | 180 | | |
| Tax losses (84 ÷ 0.3 × 50%) | (140) | (140) | |
| Corporation tax on capital gains (330 ÷ 0.3) | | | 1,100 |
| Inter company profit in stock (Note 2) | (12) | | |
| | 128 | (20) | 1,240 |
| | | | |
| Deferred tax liability (30%) | 38.4 | (6.0) | 372.0 |
| Dividend from subsidiary (Note 3) | 4.0 | | |
| | 42.4 | (6.0) | 372.0 |
| Discounted (4%) | 40.8 | (5.6) | 330.8 |
| | | | |
| Total discounted liability (40.8 – 5.6 + 330.8) | | 366 | |
| Plus pension provision (Note 4) | | 180 | |
| Total | | 546 | |

*Notes*

1    FRS 19 states that deferred tax should not be provided on revaluation gains or losses unless the company has a binding sale agreement and has recognised the expected gain or loss. It is assumed that this is the case here.

2    Deferred tax should be provided on the inter company profit in stock. The rate of tax is the rate applicable to the supplying company (FP).

3    FRS 19 states that deferred tax should not be provided on the unremitted earnings of subsidiaries unless there are dividends accrued as payable or there is a binding agreement to distribute past earnings. The dividend has been accrued and therefore a provision of £4m is required.

4    The pension provision does not require further discounting because it has already been discounted as a result of the actuarial valuation.

**The effect of applying FRS 19**

The change to full provision will cause the **deferred tax liability** to **increase** by £392 million. This will **reduce earnings per share, distributable profits and net assets** and will **increase gearing**. This means that the directors may have to reduce dividend payments and the company may find it more difficult to raise finance.

However, users of the financial statements should already have been aware of this potential tax liability, as **SSAP 15 required disclosure of the amount of any unprovided deferred tax**, analysed into its major components. This means that the company's **share price** is **unlikely to be greatly affected** by the change from partial provision to full provision.

## Marking scheme

|  |  | | *Marks* |
|---|---|---|---|
| **(a)** (i) | Subjective | | 6 |
| | | *Maximum* | 6 |
| (ii) | Timing differences | | 4 |
| | Temporary differences | | 4 |
| | | *Available* | 8 |
| | | *Maximum* | 6 |
| **(b)** | Calculation | | 10 |
| | Comment | | 3 |
| | | *Available* | 13 |
| | | *Maximum* | 13 |
| | | **Available** | **27** |
| | | **Maximum** | **25** |

BPP PUBLISHING

# Advanced Corporate Reporting

# BPP Mock Exam 2: Pilot Paper

| Question Paper: | |
| --- | --- |
| Time allowed | 3 hours |
| This paper is divided into two sections | |
| Section A | This question is compulsory and MUST be attempted |
| Section B | THREE questions ONLY to be answered |

# paper 3.6

DO NOT OPEN THIS PAPER UNTIL YOU ARE READY TO START
UNDER EXAMINATION CONDITIONS

**Section A - This question is compulsory and MUST be attempted**

1   Portal Group, a public limited company, has prepared the following group cash flow statement for the year ended 31 December 20X0.

PORTAL GROUP PLC
GROUP STATEMENT OF CASH FLOWS
FOR THE YEAR ENDED 31 DECEMBER 20X0 (DRAFT)

|  | £m | £m |
|---|---|---|
| *Net cash inflow from operating activities* | | 875 |
| *Returns on investments and servicing of finance* | | |
| Interest received | 26 | |
| Interest paid | (9) | |
| Minority interest   =) DIV- PAID TO MS. | (40) | |
| | | (23) |
| *Taxation* | | 31 |
| *Capital expenditure* | | |
| Purchase of tangible fixed assets | (380) | |
| Disposals and transfers of fixed assets at carrying value | 1,585 | |
| | | 1,205 |
| *Acquisitions and disposals* | | |
| Disposal of subsidiary | (25) | |
| Purchase of interest in joint venture | (225) | |
| | | (250) |
| *Net cash inflow before management of liquid resources and financing* | | 1,838 |
| *Management of liquid resources* | | |
| Increase in short term deposits | | (143) |
| *Increase in cash in the period* | | 1,695 |

The accountant has asked your advice on certain technical matters relating to the preparation of the group cash flow statement. Additionally the accountant has asked you to prepare a presentation for the directors on the usefulness and meaning of cash flow statements generally and specifically on the group cash flow statement of Portal.

The accountant has informed you that the actual change in the cash balance for the period is £165 million, which does not reconcile with the figures in the draft group cash flow statement above of £1,695 million.

The accountant feels that the reason for the difference lies in the incorrect treatment of several elements of the cash flow statement of which he had little technical knowledge. The following information relates to these elements.

(a)   Portal has disposed of a subsidiary company, Web plc, during the year. At the date of disposal (1 June 20X0) the following balance sheet was prepared for Web plc.

|  | £m | £m |
|---|---|---|
| Tangible fixed assets: valuation | | 340 |
| depreciation | | (30) |
| | | 310 |
| Stocks | 60 | |
| Debtors | 50 | |
| Cash at bank and in hand | 130 | |
| | 240 | |
| Creditors: amounts falling due within one year | | |
| (including taxation £25 million) | (130) | |
| | | 110 |
| | | 420 |
| Called up share capital | | 100 |
| Profit and loss account | | 320 |
| | | 420 |

The loss on the sale of the subsidiary in the group accounts comprised:

|  | £m |
|---|---|
| Sales proceeds: ordinary shares | 300 |
| cash | 75 |
| | 375 |
| Net assets sold (80% of 420) | (336) |
| Goodwill | (64) |
| Loss on sale | (25) |

The accountant was unsure as to how to deal with the above disposal and has simply included the above loss in the cash flow statement without further adjustments.

(b) During the year, Portal has transferred several of its tangible assets to a newly created company, Site plc, which is owned jointly with another company.

The following information relates to the accounting for the investment in Site plc.

|  | £m |
|---|---|
| Purchase cost: fixed assets transferred | 200 |
| cash | 25 |
| | 225 |
| Dividend received | (10) |
| Profit for year on joint venture after tax | 55 |
| Revaluation of fixed assets | 30 |
| Closing balance per balance sheet - Site plc | 300 |

The cash flow statement showed the cost of purchasing a stake in Site plc of £225 million.

(c) The taxation amount in the cash flow statement is the difference between the opening and closing balances on the taxation account. The charge for taxation in the profit and loss account is £191 million of which £20 million related to the taxation on the joint venture.

(d) Included in the cash flow figure for the disposal of tangible fixed assets is the sale and leaseback of certain land and buildings. The sale proceeds of the land and buildings were £1,000 million in the form of an 8% loan note repayable in 20Y2 at a premium of 5%. The total profit on the sale of fixed assets, including the land and buildings, was £120 million.

(e) The minority interest figure in the statement comprised the difference between the opening and closing balance sheet totals. The profit attributable to the minority interest for the year was £75 million.

(f) The net cash inflow from operating activities is the profit on ordinary activities before taxation adjusted for the balance sheet movement in stocks, debtors and creditors and the depreciation charge for the year. The interest receivable credited to the profit and loss account was £27 million and the interest payable was £19 million.

**Required:**

(a) **Prepare a revised group cash flow statement for Portal plc, taking into account notes (a) to (f) above.**                                   (18 marks)

(b) **Prepare a brief presentation on the usefulness and information content of group cash flow statements generally and specifically on the group cash flow statement of Portal plc.**                            (7 marks)

**(25 marks)**

## Section B – Three questions only to be answered

2    The financial director of Axe, a public limited company, has heard of the recent discussions over accounting for leases but is unsure as to the current position. Additionally the company has undergone certain transactions in the year and the director requires assistance as to how these transactions should be dealt with in the financial statements. The financial year end of the company is 31 December 20X0.

On 1 January 20X0, Axe sold its computer software and hardware to Lake, a public limited company, for £310 million. The assets were leased back for four years under an operating lease whereby Lake agreed to maintain and upgrade the computer facilities. The fair value of the assets sold was £190 million and the carrying value based on depreciated historic cost was £90 million. The lease rental payments were £45 million per annum, payable on 1 January in advance, which represented a premium of fifty per cent of the normal cost of such a lease.

Additionally, on 1 January 20X0 Axe sold plant with a carrying value of £200 million. The fair value and selling price of the plant was £330 million. The plant was immediately leased back over four years which is the remaining useful life of the asset. Axe has guaranteed a residual value of £30 million and the plant is to be sold for scrap at the end of the lease. Axe will be liable for any shortfall in the residual value. The lease cannot be cancelled and requires equal rental payments of £87 million at the commencement of each financial year. The 'normal' cost of such a lease without the residual value guarantee would have been £95 million per annum. Axe pays the costs of all maintenance and insurance of the plant.

The company has also leased motor vehicles on 1 January 20X0 for the first time. Fifty vehicles were leased at an annual rental of £5,000 each, payable on 1 January in advance. In addition an extra 20p per mile is payable if the mileage exceeds 60,000 miles over the three year rental period. The excess mileage charge reflects fair compensation for the additional wear and tear of the vehicle. Axe returns the vehicle to the lessor at the end of the lease. The lessee maintains and insures the vehicles. (A discount rate of 10% should be used in all calculations. The present value of an ordinary annuity of £1 per period for three years at 10% is £2.49.)

**Required:**

(a) Discuss the new approach to accounting for leases which is being developed by the Accounting Standards Board in its Discussion Paper *Leases: implementation of a new approach.*                              (8 marks)

(b) Advise the financial director on the way in which the above transactions would be dealt with under current accounting standards and how this would change if the recommendations in the Discussion Paper were implemented.                                                                        (17 marks)

**(25 marks)**

3   X, a public limited company, owns 100 per cent of companies Y and Z which are both public limited companies. The X group operates in the telecommunications industry and the directors are considering three different plans to restructure the group. The directors feel that the current group structure is not serving the best interests of the shareholders and wish to explore possible alternative group structures.

The balance sheets of X and its subsidiaries Y and Z at 31 May 20Y1 are as follows:

|  | X plc £m | Y plc £m | Z plc £m |
|---|---|---|---|
| Tangible fixed assets | 600 | 200 | 45 |
| Cost of investment in Y | 60 | | |
| Cost of investment in Z | 70 | | |
| Net current assets | 160 | 100 | 20 |
|  | 890 | 300 | 65 |
| Share capital - ordinary shares of £1 | 120 | 60 | 40 |
| Profit and loss account | 770 | 240 | 25 |
|  | 890 | 300 | 65 |

X acquired the investment in Z on 1 June 20X5 when the profit and loss account balance was £20 million. The fair value of the net assets of Z on 1 June 20X5 was £60 million. Company Y was incorporated by X and has always been a 100 per cent owned subsidiary. Goodwill is written off over four years. The fair value of the assets of Y at 31 May 20Y1 is £310 million and of Z is £80 million.

The directors are unsure as to the impact or implications that the following plans are likely to have on the individual accounts of the companies and the group accounts.

The three different plans to restructure the group are as follows.

*Plan 1*

Y is to purchase the whole of X's investment in Z. The directors are undecided as to whether the purchase consideration should be 50 million £1 ordinary shares of Y or a cash amount of £75 million.                                                                        (10 marks)

*Plan 2*

A new company, W, is to be formed which will issue shares to the shareholders of X in exchange for X's investment in Y and Z. W is to issue 130 million ordinary shares of £1 to the shareholders of X in exchange for their shares held in Y and Z. The group is being split into two separate companies W and X which will be quoted on the Stock Exchange.                                                                        (8 marks)

*Plan 3*

The assets and trade of Z are to be transferred to Y. Company Z would initially become a non-trading company. The assets and trade are to be transferred at their book value. The consideration for the transfer will be £60 million which will be left outstanding on the inter company account between Y and Z.                     (7 marks)

**Required:**

**Discuss the key considerations and the accounting implications of the above plans for the X group. Your answer should show the potential impact on the individual accounts of X, Y and Z and the group accounts after each plan has been implemented.**

(The mark allocation is shown in brackets next to each 'plan'.)            **(25 marks)**

4    Engina, a foreign company, has approached a partner in your firm to assist in obtaining a Stock Exchange listing for the company. Engina is registered in a country where transactions between related parties are considered to be normal but where such transactions are not disclosed. The directors of Engina are reluctant to disclose the nature of their related party transactions as they feel that although they are a normal feature of business in their part of the world, it could cause significant problems politically and culturally to disclose such transactions.

The partner in your firm has requested a list of all transactions with parties connected with the company and the directors of Engina have produced the following summary.

(a)  Engina sells £50,000 of goods per month to Mr Satay, the financial director. The financial director has set up a small retailing business for his son and the goods are purchased at cost price for him. The annual turnover of Engina is £300 million. Additionally Mr Satay has purchased his company car from the company for £45,000 (market value £80,000). The director, Mr Satay, owns directly 10% of the shares in the company and earns a salary of £500,000 a year, and has a personal fortune of many millions of pounds.

(b)  A hotel property had been sold to a brother of Mr Soy, the Managing Director of Engina, for £4 million (net of selling cost of £0.2 million). The market value of the property was £4.3 million but in the overseas country, property prices were falling rapidly. The carrying value of the hotel was £5 million and its value in use was £3.6 million. There was an over supply of hotel accommodation due to government subsidies in an attempt to encourage hotel development and the tourist industry.

(c)  Mr Satay owns several companies and the structure of the group is as follows.

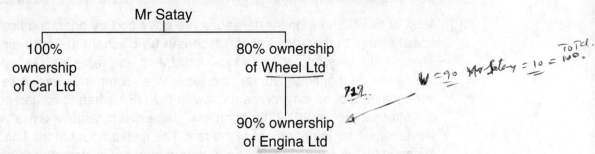

Engina earns 60% of its profit from transactions with Car and 40% of its profit from transactions with Wheel.

**Required:**

**Write a report to the directors of Engina setting out the reasons why it is important to disclose related party transactions and the nature of any disclosure required for the above transactions under the UK regulatory system before a Stock Exchange quotation can be obtained.**

**(25 marks)**

The mark allocation will be as follows:

| | Marks |
|---|---|
| Style/layout of report | 4 |
| Reasons | 8 |
| Transaction   (a) | 4 |
|                      (b) | 5 |
|                      (c) | 4 |
| | 25 |

5   The directors of Glowball, a public limited company, had discussed the study by the Institute of Environmental Management which indicated that over 35% of the world's 250 largest corporations are voluntarily releasing green reports to the public to promote corporate environmental performance and to attract customers and investors. They have heard that the main competitors are applying the *Global Reporting Initiative* (GRI) in an effort to develop a worldwide format for corporate environmental reporting. However, the directors are unsure as to what this initiative actually means. Additionally they require advice as to the nature of any legislation or standards relating to environmental reporting as they are worried that any environmental report produced by the company may not be of sufficient quality and may detract from and not enhance their image if the report does not comply with recognised standards. Glowball has a reputation for ensuring the preservation of the environment in its business activities.

Further the directors have collected information in respect of a series of events which they consider to be important and worthy of note in the environmental report but are not sure as to how they would be incorporated in the environmental report or whether they should be included in the financial statements.

The events are as follows.

(a)   Glowball is a company that pipes gas from offshore gas installations to major consumers. The company purchased its main competitor during the year and found that there were environmental liabilities arising out of the restoration of many miles of farmland that had been affected by the laying of a pipeline. There was no legal obligation to carry out the work, but the company felt that there would be a cost of around £150 million if the farmland was to be restored.

(b)   Most of the offshore gas installations are governed by operating licences which specify limits to the substances which can be discharged to the air and water. These limits vary according to local legislation and tests are carried out by the regulatory authorities. During the year the company was prosecuted for infringements of an environmental law in the USA when toxic gas escaped into the atmosphere. In 20X9 the company was prosecuted five times and in 20X8 eleven times for infringement of the law. The final amount of the fine/costs to be imposed by the courts has not been determined but is expected to be around £5 million. The escape occurred over the sea and it was considered that there was little threat to human life.

(c) The company produced statistics which measure their improvement in the handling of emissions of gases which may have an impact on the environment. The statistics deal with:

(i) Measurement of the release of gases with the potential to form acid rain. The emissions have been reduced by 84% over five years due to the closure of old plants.

(ii) Measurement of emissions of substances potentially hazardous to human health. The emissions are down by 51% on 20X5 levels.

(iii) Measurement of emissions to water which removes dissolved oxygen and substances that may have an adverse effect on aquatic life. Accurate measurement of these emissions is not possible but the company is planning to spend £70 million on research in this area.

(d) The company tries to reduce the environmental impacts associated with the siting and construction of its gas installations. This is done in a way that minimises the impact on wildlife and human beings. Additionally when the installations are at the end of their life, they are dismantled and are not sunk into the sea. The current provision for the decommissioning of these installations is £215 million and there are still decommissioning costs of £407 million to be provided as the company's policy is to build up the required provision over the life of the installation.

**Required:**

**Prepare a report suitable for presentation to the directors of Glowball in which you discuss the following elements.**

**(a) Current reporting requirements and guidelines relating to environmental reporting.** (10 marks)

**(b) The nature of any disclosure which would be required in an environmental report and/or the financial statements for the events (a) – (d) above.**

(15 marks)

**(25 marks)**

*BPP* PUBLISHING

# ANSWERS

**DO NOT TURN THIS PAGE UNTIL YOU
HAVE COMPLETED THE MOCK EXAM**

# WARNING! APPLYING THE BPP MARKING SCHEME

If you decide to mark your paper using the BPP marking scheme, you should bear in mind the following points.

1 The BPP solutions are not definitive: you will see that we have applied the marking scheme to our solutions to show how good answers should gain marks, but there may be more than one way to answer the question. You must try to judge fairly whether different points made in your answers are correct and relevant and therefore worth marks according to our marking scheme.

2 If you have a friend or colleague who is studying or has studied this paper, you might ask him or her to mark your paper for you, thus gaining a more objective assessment. Remember you and your friend are not trained or objective markers, so try to avoid complacency or pessimism if you appear to have done very well or very badly.

3 You should be aware that BPP's answers are longer than you would be expected to write. Sometimes, therefore, you would gain the same number of marks for making the basic point as we have shown as being available for a slightly more detailed or extensive solution.

It is most important that you analyse your solutions in detail and that you attempt to be as objective as possible.

---

**Professional Examination - Paper 3.6**       **Marking Scheme**

**Advanced Corporate Reporting**

This marking scheme is given as a guide to markers in the context of the suggested answer. Scope is given to markers to award marks for alternative approaches to a question, including relevant comment, and where well-reasoned conclusions are provided. This is particularly so in the case scenario questions where there may be more than one definitive solution.

# A PLAN OF ATTACK

Doing the Advanced Corporate Reporting paper would probably not be your preferred way of spending three hours. You'll have worked through an enormous syllabus and been told that knowledge on its own is not enough and you need to think deeply about the issues, whatever that means! But you've got to get through. If this were the real exam and you had been told to turn over and begin, what would be going through your mind?

The answer may be 'Panic'! You've spent most of your study time on groups and current issues (because that's what your tutor/BPP Study Text told you to do), plus a selection of other topics, and you're really not sure that you know enough. The good news is that this may get you through. The first question, in Section A is very likely to be on groups. In Section B you have to choose three out of four questions, and at least one of those is likely to be on current issues – a new FRS, FRED or discussion paper. So calm down. First spend five minutes or so looking at the paper, and develop a plan of attack.

## Looking through the paper

The compulsory question is, as is generally the case, on groups, in this case, a group cash flow statement. In Section B you have **four questions on a variety of topics**:

- Question 2 is, in effect, a 'current issues' question. It is about leasing and the approach of the new Discussion Paper on the subject.

- Question 3 is a largely numerical question on group re-organisation.

- Question 4 is a straightforward looking question on FRS 8.

- Question 5 is a wordy looking thing on environmental reporting.

You **only have to answer three out of these four questions**. You don't have to pick your optional questions right now, but this brief overview should have convinced you that you have enough choice and variety to have a respectable go at Section B. So let's go back to the compulsory question in Section A.

## Compulsory question

Question 1 requires you to **revise a group cash flow statement** prepared by an accountant who was not quite sure what he was doing. Questions of this type, where you are playing an **advisory role** are likely to come up under this new syllabus. There isn't a huge amount of high speed number crunching in Part (a), but there is a lot of thinking. You need to think carefully whether you are **adding or subtracting** in your workings. Your task is to **adjust** a cash flow statement rather than to prepare one from scratch. Part (b) of this question looks like a good source of easy marks, but you must remember to discuss the usefulness of **group** cash flow statements, not just cash flow statements in general. In part (b) you should also be sure to relate your answer to the **cash flow statement of Portal**.

## Optional questions

Deciding between the optional questions is obviously a personal matter – it depends how you have spent your study and revision time. For simplicity, let's suppose you fall into one of two categories.

- Type 1 – the **number-cruncher**. You can work through calculations at high speed.
- Type 2 – the **wordsmith**. You like analysing, writing and presenting arguments.

When choosing between Questions 3 and 5, a **number-cruncher** would be advised to **go for 3**. Assuming you have studied the topic, this is a straightforward question, but time consuming if you are slow at presenting lots of different balance sheets to illustrate a point.

By contrast a **wordsmith** should definitely **go for Question 5**. It looks intimidating because there is a lot of information, but the good news is you don't need a high level of technical knowledge, although **you do need analytical skills** and the ability to think round the subject. Whatever type of person you are, if your technical knowledge is lacking, you may find it easier to pick up marks on Question 5, because **you can always write something**.

In our opinion, **everyone should do Question 4, on related party transactions**. You should know FRS 8 by now as you have studied it for Paper 10/2.5. This question, though by no means a walkover, contains no nasty hidden traps.

Whether or not you do **Question 2** depends, of course, on how well you know the Discussion Paper on leasing. There is no scope for waffle if you don't.

### Allocating your time

The golden rule is always allocate your time **according to the marks for the question** in total and for the parts of the question. But **be sensible**. If you don't know the leasing Discussion Paper **and** you have only a hazy grasp of group re-organisations, you may be better off trying to pick up some extra marks on the questions you **can** do.

### Afterwards

Don't be tempted to do a post mortem on the paper with your colleagues. It will only worry you and them and it's unlikely you'll be able to remember exactly what you put anyway. If you really can't resist going over the topics covered in the paper, allow yourself a maximum of half an hour's 'worry time', then put it out of your head!

**1**

> **Tutor's hint**. The examiner for the new syllabus paper has stated that the emphasis is on advising management and on realistic scenarios. Part (b) could come under the heading of advice and Part (a), which involves using your knowledge to correct the accountant's work, could come under both headings. This is a slightly different slant on cash flow statements, requiring adjustments to be made to an incorrectly prepared statement. The best approach would be to use the same workings as for a normal preparation question, piece together the details from the question, then recalculate the correct cash effects. Leave sufficient time for Part (b).

(a)  PORTAL GROUP
     CASH FLOW STATEMENT FOR THE YEAR ENDED 31 DECEMBER 20X0

|  | | Working | £m | £m |
|---|---|---|---|---|
| O | *Net cash inflow from operating activities* | | | 692 |
| D | Dividend received from joint venture | | | 10 |
| | | | | 702 |
| R | *Returns on investments and servicing of finance* | | | |
| | Interest received | | 26 | |
| | Interest paid | | (9) | |
| | Dividend paid to minority interest | w-2 | (31) | |
| | | | | (14) |
| T | Taxation | w-3 | | (115) |
| | *Capital expenditure* | | | |
| | Purchase of tangible fixed assets | | (380) | |
| | Sale of tangible fixed assets | 4 | 195 | |
| | | | | (185) |
| | *Acquisitions and disposals* | | | |
| | Disposal of subsidiary | | 75 | |
| | Cash of subsidiary disposed of | | (130) | |
| | Purchase of interest in joint venture | | (25) | |
| | | | | (80) |
| | *Net cash inflow before use of liquid resources and financing* | | | 308 |
| | Increase in short term deposits | | | (143) |
| | *Net cash inflow* | | | 165 ✓ |

*Workings*

1   *Net cash inflow from operating activities*

|  | £m |
|---|---|
| Per question = op-profit | 875 |
| 1. Add back loss on disposal | 25 |
| 2. Adjustments for current assets/liabilities of subsidiary* | |
|  • Stock | (60) |
|  • Debtors | (50) |
|  • Creditors (130 – 25) | 105 |
| 3. Deduct pre-tax profit on joint venture (55 + 20) | (75) |
| 4. Interest receivable | (27) |
| 5. Interest payable | 19 |
| 6. Deduct profit on sale of fixed assets | (120) |
| | 692 |

*Note*. The movements in <u>current assets</u> used by the accountant to calculate net cash inflow from operating activities incorrectly include amounts relating to the subsidiary disposed of.

2    *Dividend paid to minority interest*

|  | £m |
|---|---|
| Difference per question (balance sheet movement) | 40 |
| Profit for year  ~~To m I~~ | 75 |
| Sale of subsidiary (20% × 420)  ~~[NA+R]~~ | (84) |
|  | 31 |

3    *Taxation*

|  | £m |
|---|---|
| Per question (balance sheet movement) | 31 |
| Tax on joint venture | 20 |
| Tax on subsidiary disposed of | 25 |
| Tax on profit | (191) |
| Cash outflow | (115) |

4    *Sale of tangible fixed assets*

|  | £m |
|---|---|
| Per question (carrying value) | 1,585 |
| Transferred to joint venture | (200) |
| Subsidiary disposed of | (310) |
| Sale and leaseback | (1,000) |
| Profit on sale  = ~~NON c·F~~ | + 120 |
| Cash inflow | 195 |

(b)    *Cash flow statements: presentation to directors of Portal plc*

**General purpose**  ~~need to speak on all the adj. on the C.F.S.~~

The purpose of cash flow statements is to **provide information which is not shown in the other financial statements**. This information is important because the success and survival of every reporting entity depends on its ability to generate or obtain cash. For example, the tax authorities require an **actual cash payment**, which will differ for a number of reasons from the tax charge shown in the profit and loss account. Some of the information, such as the purchase or sale of tangible fixed assets, is apparent or can easily be computed from the balance sheet or profit and loss account, but the **complexity** of the financial statements may make this hard to see in respect of some items.

**Group cash flow statements**

Consolidated profit and loss accounts and balance sheets can hide the amount of cash actually paid to acquire a subsidiary, or received on disposal, in situations where part of the consideration is in the form of shares. FRS 1 requires **cash flows relating to the consideration** to be reported under acquisitions and disposals in the consolidated cash flow statement. Similarly, the dividend paid to minority interest is shown, as is the dividend received from associates or joint ventures.

However, a possible limitation of consolidated cash flow statements is that they can **obscure the cash profile of companies within the group**. For example, if there were two subsidiaries, one with a high cash flow from operations and one with high returns on investments, consolidation would obscure this. This is a limitation of consolidated accounts generally.

**Accounting ratios**

Useful information derived from the cash flow statement can be used in **accounting ratios** for analysis purposes. In the case of Portal plc, it might be useful to show proportion of net cash inflow from operating activities which has been spent on purchasing fixed assets:

$$\frac{\text{Purchase of tangible fixed assets}}{\text{Net cash inflow from operating activities}} = \frac{380}{692} = 54.9\% \text{ of cash to buy FA}$$

It would be useful to know how much of this relates to maintenance of existing operating capacity and how much relates to increasing capacity with a view to enhancing future earnings. However, this information cannot be derived from the cash flow statement.

It would also be useful to know **how the cash flow after investment has been utilised.** This can be done by comparing the net cash inflow before use of liquid resources and financing with the net cash increase in the period. In the case of Portal this works out as (308 – 165)/308 = 46.4%. In other words 46.4% of this net cash inflow has been used to take out short term deposits.

Another useful ratio is **interest cover**, based not on profit before interest and tax as in conventional ratio analysis, but on operating cash flow: PBIT

$$\frac{\text{Net cash flow from operating activities}}{\text{Interest paid}} = \frac{692}{9} = 76.8 \text{ times}$$

### Further limitations

*   The cash flow statement does not provide information about future cash flows.

*   The reconciliation can be misinterpreted. Naïve investors may perceive the adding back of depreciation/amortisation as sources of funds.

*   Some regard the cash flow statement as derivative.

| | Marking scheme | | Marks |
|---|---|---|---|
| **(a)** | Net cash inflow | | 8 |
| | Taxation | | 3 |
| | Sale of tangible fixed assets | | 4 |
| | Minority interest | | 2 |
| | Joint venture | | 2 |
| | Disposal of subsidiary and cash disposed of | | 2 |
| | | *Available* | 21 |
| | | *Maximum* | 18 |
| **(b)** | Subjective | | 7 |
| | | **Available** | **28** |
| | | **Maximum** | **25** |

2

> **Tutor's hint.** When you review your answer, consider whether you addressed the requirements properly.
>
> In (a), the 'discussion' should look at the reasons for the new proposals, not just list out rules.
>
> In (b), the requirement gives a good indication as to where to find marks. There are three lease transactions to consider under two sets of rules. As long as you can find at least one point to make on each of these six 'sub-requirements' and two on a few of them, the 50% needed to pass should be straightforward, even if some of the more complicated calculations went wrong.

(a)   The current treatment of leases under SSAP 21 is open to criticism.

   (i)     The distinction between treatment as a finance lease or operating lease is based on **quantitative rather than qualitative criteria**.

   (ii)    Many operating lease transactions have been **designed to fit** the quantitative criteria when in substance they are finance leases.

   (iii)   The 90% present value criterion may be satisfied by using a **contingent rental clause**. Contingent rentals would not come into the calculation.

   (iv)    The interest rate implicit in the lease may not be available, in which case an alternative estimated rate can be used. This can lead to the **present value criterion being circumvented.**

   (v)     **Material assets and liabilities** arising from operating lease contracts are **omitted** from the balance sheet.

   (vi)    The approach of SSAP 21 is 'all or nothing', while modern transactions are more complicated than this.

   For some time, users have called for **finance leases and operating leases to be treated consistently.**

   The ASB published a Discussion Paper *Leases: implementation of a new approach* in December 1999. The Discussion Paper presents a Position Paper that has been developed by the (now defunct) G4+1 group.

   The paper recommends that **all leases should be reflected in financial statements in a consistent manner** and it explores the principles that should determine the extent of the assets and liabilities that lessees and lessors would recognise under leases.

   At the beginning of a lease the lessee would **recognise an asset and a liability equivalent to the fair value of the rights and obligations that are conveyed by the lease** (usually the present value of the minimum payments required by the lease). Then the accounting for the lease asset and liability would **follow the normal requirements for accounting for fixed assets and debt**. The lessor would report financial assets (representing amounts receivable from the lessee) and residual interests as separate assets.

   Leases that are now treated as operating leases and therefore 'off balance sheet' would give rise to assets and liabilities. However, the difference may not be significant. **Where a lease is for a small part of an asset's useful economic life, only that part would be reflected in the lessee's balance sheet.**

   The Discussion paper also examines the principles for accounting for more complex features of lease contracts. These include renewal options, contingent rentals, residual value guarantees and sale and leaseback transactions.

(b)   **Computer software and hardware**

   Under SSAP 21 *Accounting for leases and hire purchase contracts* the computer software and hardware **sold and leased back** should be treated as **a sale** and the operating lease rentals charged against profit. The lease is not shown on the balance sheet. If the transaction is at **fair value**, the profit or loss on the sale should be **recognised immediately**. If the transaction is **above fair value**, the **profit based on fair value** (£190m – £90m, ie £100m) may be **recognised immediately**. The balance of profit in **excess of fair val**ue (£310 – £190m, ie £120m) should be **deferred and amortised** over the shorter of the lease term and the period to the next lease rental review. In this case this would be amortised over four years, ie £30m per annum.

However, as the sales value is not the fair value, the operating lease rentals (£45m) are likely to have been adjusted for the excess price paid for the assets. For Axe plc, the sale value is considerably more than the fair value, and according to FRS 5 *Reporting the substance of transactions*, **the substance** of the transaction is one of **sale of asset and a loan** equalling the deferred income element. The premium of £15m would be viewed as a financing cost, with the excess over the fair value of £120m being shown as a loan, with part of the costs of the operating lease being treated as repayment of the loan plus interest.

Under the Discussion Paper, the accounting treatment would be very different. The Paper would view this as **one transaction with a dual purpose**:

(i)    The raising of finance
(ii)   The disposal of an interest in the property

The sale is for more than its fair value, but this is compensated for by an onerous lease.

The required entries are:

| | | |
|---|---|---|
| DEBIT | Cash | 310 |
| CREDIT | Lease liability *lease* | + 157 (£45m + (£45m × 2.49)) |
| | Carrying value of assets | − 72.5 $\left(\dfrac{310-157}{190}\times 90\right)$ |
| | Profit | 80.5 |

The asset would need to be reviewed for impairment. As a result of this treatment the company's gearing would increase and its profit would reduce.

**Plant**

The sale and leaseback appears to create a **finance lease** as the present value of the minimum lease payments is greater than 90% of the fair value of the plant. The lease runs for the useful life of the plant and Axe has a guaranteed residual amount of £30m. Therefore the minimum lease payments are:

| | £m |
|---|---|
| £87m + (£87m × 2.49) | 303.6 |
| £30m residual value discounted at 10% | 20.5 |
| | 324.1 |

Under FRS 5 the asset should **remain in the lessee's balance sheet at carrying value** and the sale proceeds (£330m) are shown as a creditor representing the finance lease liability. As payments are made they are treated partly as a repayment of the creditor and partly as a finance charge against income. The rental payments have been reduced because Axe has guaranteed a residual value of £30m, which is probably more than its scrap value, which is likely to be low.

Under the Discussion Paper, the treatment would not change.

**Motor vehicles**

**SSAP 21** would treat the lease of the motor vehicles as an **operating lease**. The rentals would be charged to the profit and loss account on a straight line basis over the term of the lease, regardless of the due dates for payment.

The treatment would change under the **Discussion Paper**. An **asset and liability** would be **recognised** on the balance sheet. This would be the present value of three payments, calculated as follows.

Annual payment: 50 × £5,000 = £250,000
Present value of three payments: £684,000

The 20p per mile payable if the mileage exceeds 60,000 is a contingent rental. It is fair compensation for additional wear and tear, and as such the option has little value and should be ignored. Such additional rentals would be recognised as incurred.

Again, as a result of the Discussion Paper, the gearing ratio of the company would be adversely affected, as a liability would be recognised which is not recognised under SSAP 21.

---

### Marking scheme

|  |  |  |  | *Marks* |
|---|---|---|---|---|
| **(a)** | | Subjective | | 8 |
| **(b)** | (i) | Current standards | | 4 |
| | | Discussion paper | | 5 |
| | (ii) | Current standards | | 4 |
| | | Discussion paper | | 1 |
| | (iii) | Current standards | | 1 |
| | | Discussion paper | | 4 |
| | | | *Available* | 19 |
| | | | *Maximum* | 17 |
| | | | **Available** | **27** |
| | | | **Maximum** | **25** |

---

3

There are a number of reasons why a group may re-organise.

- To reduce gearing by floating a business
- Companies may be transferred to another business during a divisionalisation process
- To create efficiencies of group structure for tax purposes

The impact of each of the proposed structures is discussed below.

### Plan 1

The implications of this plan will be different, depending on the choice of purchase consideration.

### Share for share exchange

If the purchase consideration is in the form of shares, then a share premium account will need to be set up in the books of Y. This share premium account must comprise the minimum premium value, which is the excess of the book value of the investment over the nominal value of the shares issued: £70m − £50m = £20m.

The impact on the individual company accounts and on the group accounts is as follows.

| | *Note* | *X*<br>*£m* | *Y*<br>*£m* | *Z*<br>*£m* | *Group*<br>*£m* |
|---|---|---|---|---|---|
| Tangible fixed assets | | 600 | 200 | 45 | 845 |
| Cost of investment in Y | 1 | 130 | | | |
| Cost of investment in Z | 2 | | 70 | | |
| Net current assets | | 160 | 100 | 20 | 280 |
| | | 890 | 370 | 65 | 1,125 |
| Share capital | 3 | 120 | 110 | 40 | 120 |
| Share premium | 4 | | 20 | | |
| Profit and loss account | 5 | 770 | 240 | 25 | 1,005 |
| | | 890 | 370 | 65 | 1,125 |

*Notes*

1   *Cost of investment in Y*

This is increased by the total value of the shares issued: £50m + £20m = £70m.

2   *Cost of investment in Z*

Transferred to Y. The book value of the investment is preserved.

3   *Share capital*

Y's share capital is increased by the nominal value of the shares issued, £50m.

4   *Share premium*

This is as discussed above.

5   *Profit and loss account*

Goodwill arising on the purchase of Z is £10m (£70m – (£40m + £20m)). This will have been written off to reserves. The group profit and loss account is calculated as follows.

|  | £m |
|---|---|
| X | 770 |
| Y | 240 |
| Z's PARR (25 – 20) | 5 |
| Goodwill (post-acquisition) | (10) |
|  | 1,005 |

*Cash purchase*

If the purchase consideration is in the form of cash, a gain or loss on the sale of Z will arise in the books of X. This does not count as a distribution as the cash price of £75m is not in excess of the fair value of the net assets of Z, £80m. The effect on the accounts would be as follows.

|  | Note | X £m | Y £m | Z £m | Group £m |
|---|---|---|---|---|---|
| Tangible fixed assets |  | 600 | 200 | 45 | 845 |
| Cost of investment in Y |  | 60 |  |  |  |
| Cost of investment in Z | 1 |  | 75 |  |  |
| Net current assets | 2 | 235 | 25 | 20 | 280 |
|  |  | 895 | 300 | 65 | 1,125 |
| Share capital |  | 120 | 60 | 40 | 120 |
| Profit and loss account | 3 | 775 | 240 | 25 | 1,005 |
|  |  | 895 | 300 | 65 | 1,125 |

*Notes*

1   *Cost of investment in Z*

This is the cash consideration of £75m.

2   *Net current assets*

X's cash increases by £75m and Y's cash decreases by £75m.

3   *Profit and loss account*

X's profit and loss account has been increased by £5m, being the profit on the sale of the investment in Z. This is eliminated on consolidation as it is an intra-group transaction. The consolidated profit and loss account is calculated in exactly the same way as in the share for share exchange.

**Plan 2**

This restructuring plan involves a demerger of Y and Z from the X group and the formation of a separate W group. The transaction may be viewed as a distribution by X to its shareholders in the form of shares in W.

It is likely that this group reconstruction will qualify as a merger under FRS 6 *Acquisitions and mergers*. This will get round the necessity of creating a share premium account. Assuming that the FRS 6 criteria are met, and that no other inter-company transactions involving transfers of shares and cash had taken place, the effect on the accounts will be as follows.

|  | *Note* | *X*<br>£m | *W*<br>£m |
|---|---|---|---|
| Tangible fixed assets |  | 600 | 245 |
| Net current assets |  | 160 | 120 |
|  |  | 760 | 365 |
| Share capital | 1 | 120 | 130 |
| Profit and loss account | 2 | 640 | 235 |
|  |  | 760 | 365 |

*Notes*

1   *Share capital*

    W issued 130m £1 shares.

2   *Profit and loss account*

|  |  | £m |
|---|---|---|
| *X* |  |  |
| Per question |  | 770 |
| Less distribution |  | (130) |
|  |  | 640 |

|  | £m | £m |
|---|---|---|
| *W* |  |  |
|    Y's profit and loss |  | 240 |
|    Z's profit and loss |  | 25 |
|  |  | 265 |
| Share capital balance on merger account |  |  |
|    W shares issued | 130 |  |
|    Y share capital | (60) |  |
|    Z share capital | (40) |  |
|  |  | (30) |
|  |  | 235 |

**Plan 3**

This restructuring plan is a rationalisation, aimed at simplifying the group structure. An important point to take into account is that the investment in Z in the books of X may be impaired. Z was originally purchased for £70m, with goodwill of £10m arising, but the assets have been transferred to Y at book value of £60m. Z will be a shell company with a net asset value of £60m and this will be shown as an intercompany account with Y. The cost of X's investment in Z should be reduced to £60m, with a corresponding charge to the profit and loss account. The accounts would appear as follows.

| | Note | X £m | Y £m | Z £m | Group £m |
|---|---|---|---|---|---|
| Tangible fixed assets | | 600 | 245 | | 845 |
| Cost of investment in Y | | 60 | | | |
| Cost of investment in Z | 1 | 60 | | | |
| Net current assets | 2 | 160 | 60 | 60 | 280 |
| | | 880 | 305 | 60 | 1,125 |
| Share capital | | 120 | 60 | 40 | 120 |
| Revaluation reserve | 3 | | 5 | | |
| Profit and loss account | 4 | 760 | 240 | 20 | 1,005 |
| | | 880 | 305 | 60 | 1,125 |

*Notes*

1   *Cost of investment in Z*

| | £m |
|---|---|
| Per question | 70 |
| Less impairment | (10) |
| | 60 |

2   *Net current assets*

Y's net current assets are £100m + £20m less intercompany creditor £60m.

Note that this calculation is based on the assumption that the £10m loss in X's books, the revaluation gain in Y's books and the loss on the transfer of assets to Y in Z's books are intercompany items and can be ignored. The calculation of group profit and loss account is then the same as for Plan 1.

3   *Revaluation reserve*

This is the gain on the purchase of the assets from Z: £65m – £60m.

4   *Profit and loss account*

X's individual profit and loss account is £770m less the impairment of £10m, which gives £760m.

The group profit and loss account is calculated as follows.

| | £m |
|---|---|
| X | 770 |
| Y | 240 |
| Z (post acquisition) | 5 |
| | 1,015 |
| Less goodwill | (10) |
| | 1,005 |

Z's profit and loss account is £20m, ie £25m less £5m loss on transfer of assets.

**Summary and conclusion**

There are advantages and disadvantages to each of the three plans. Before we could make a recommendation we would need more information about why the group wishes to restructure.

**Plan 1** does not change the group financial statements. From an internal point of view it results in a **closer relationship** between Y and Z. This may be advantageous if Y and Z are close geographically or in terms of similarity of business activities. Alternatively, it might be advantageous for tax reasons.

**Plan 2** does have a **dramatic effect on the group financial statements**. Total **distributable profits fall** from £1,005 to £875m (X £640m, W group £235m). However, the W group may benefit from being more closely knit, and this may enhance overall growth.

**Plan 3** is an example of **divisionalisation**: the assets and trade of Z are transferred to Y and Z becomes a shell company. This could result in cost savings overall. Furthermore, Z becomes a non-trading company and this could be used for some other purpose. It should be noted that, with Plan 3, there is no effect on the group financial statements.

---

### Marking scheme

|  |  | *Marks* |
|---|---|---:|
| **Plan 1** | Share premium | 2 |
| | Shares at discount | 1 |
| | Gain or loss | 1 |
| | Distribution | 1 |
| | Calculations:  share | 5 |
| |   cash | 3 |
| | *Available* | 13 |
| **Plan 2** | Share premium | 2 |
| | Merger accounting discussion | 2 |
| | X financial statements | 2 |
| | W group | 3 |
| | *Available* | 9 |
| **Plan 3** | Cash consideration | 1 |
| | Impairment | 2 |
| | Calculations | 3 |
| | Intercompany items | 2 |
| | *Available* | 8 |
| | **Available** | **30** |
| | **Maximum** | **25** |

---

**4**

**Tutor's hint..** A good test of your ability to apply FRS 8 to a practical scenario.

Notice the mark allocation before starting to produce your answer. Take time to think about the presentation and structure of the report and ensure you allocate your time appropriately over the headings and keep sentences and paragraphs short to make your answer easy to mark.

When you review your answer, think about whether it is written in a good professional style as well as checking the technical details.

---

*see p 200 .*

### REPORT

To:   The Directors
       Engina Co
       Zenda
       Ruritania

From:   A N Accountant

Date:    12 May 20X1

*Subject :- Related Party Transactions*   *FRS 8.*

The purpose of this report is to explain why it is necessary to disclose related party transactions. We appreciate that you may regard such disclosure as politically and culturally sensitive. However, there are **sound reasons for the required disclosures**. It should be emphasised that related party transactions are a normal part of business life, and the disclosures are required to give a fuller picture to the users of accounts, rather than because they are problematic.

Prior to the issue of FRS 8, disclosures in respect of related parties were concerned with directors and their relationship with the group. The ASB extended this definition and also the required disclosures. This reflects the objective of the ASB to provide useful data for investors, not merely for companies to report on stewardship activities.

Unless investors know that transactions with related parties have not been carried out at 'arm's length' between independent parties, they may fail to ascertain the true financial position.

Related party transactions typically take place on **terms which are significantly different** from those undertaken on normal commercial terms.

FRS 8 brings the UK more into line with **international practice** and requires all material related party transactions to be disclosed.

It should be noted that related party transactions are not necessarily fraudulent or intended to deceive. Without proper disclosures, investors may be disadvantaged – FRS 8 seeks to remedy this.

### (a) Sale of goods to the directors

Disclosure of related party transactions is only necessary when the transactions are **material.** FRS 8 applies only to material related party transactions. For the purposes of FRS 8, however, transactions are material when their disclosure might be expected to influence decisions made by users of the financial statements, irrespective of their amount. Moreover, the materiality of a related party transaction with an individual, for example a director, must be judged by reference to that individual and not just the company. In addition, disclosure of contracts of significance with directors is required by the Stock Exchange.

Mr Satay has purchased £600,000 (12 × £50,000) worth of goods from the company and a car for £45,000, which is just over half its market value. The transactions are not material to the company, and because Mr Satay has considerable personal wealth, they are not material to him either. However, **while not material**, any transactions with directors could be viewed as **sensitive**, and therefore ought to be disclosed in accordance with **best practice and good corporate governance.**

### (b) Hotel property

The hotel property sold to the Managing Director's brother is a **related party transaction**, and it appears to have been undertaken at **below market price**. FRS 8 requires disclosure of 'any other elements of the transactions necessary for an understanding of the financial statements'.

However, not only must the transaction be disclosed, but the question of **impairment** needs to be considered. The value of the hotel has become impaired due to the fall in property prices, so the carrying value needs to be adjusted in accordance with FRS 11 *Impairment of fixed assets and goodwill*. The hotel should be shown at the lower of carrying value (£5m) and the recoverable amount. The recoverable amount is the higher of net realisable value (£4.3m – £0.2m = £4.1m) and value in use (£3.6m). Therefore the hotel should be shown at £4.1m.

The sale of the property was for £100,000 below this impaired value, and it is this amount which needs to be disclosed.

*(c)* **Group structure**

Companies legislation and the Stock Exchange require **disclosure of director's interests** in a company's share capital. Thus Mr Satay would need to disclose his ownership of the share capital of Engina, being 10% direct and 90% through his ownership of Wheel.

The rules in FRS 8 are not consistent with this. The FRS **exempts from the disclosure** requirements group companies where the parent company owns **90% or more** of the subsidiary's share capital. Engina does not therefore need to disclose transactions with Wheel Ltd, provided that Wheel Ltd prepares consolidated accounts.

However, Engina's transactions with Car Ltd will need to be disclosed. FRS 8 states that companies under **common control** are related parties, and the two companies are under the common control of Mr Satay. Car is not part of the Wheel group and so will not be entitled to exemption on that basis.

| Marking scheme | |
| --- | --- |
| | *Marks* |
| Style of letter/report | 4 |
| Reasons | 8 |
| Goods to directors | 4 |
| Property | 5 |
| Group | 4 |
| **Available** | **25** |
| **Maximum** | **25** |

*(margin handwritten notes)* Director interest. / sub 90] exempt group cos. / Common control

5

> **Tutor's hint**. A good test of report writing skills. To produce a good answer here you need to be able to explain the main issues in environmental reporting and to identify these in a scenario. Don't forget to think about FRSs, especially FRS 12 when reading the scenario. Your answer should read well as a report to the directors, as well as addressing all the technical issues

## REPORT

To:     The Directors
        Glowball plc

From:   A N Accountant
Date:   12 May 20X1

*Environmental Reporting*

### Introduction

The purpose of this report is to provide information about current reporting requirements and guidelines on the subject of environmental reporting, and to give an indication of the required disclosure in relation to the specific events which you have brought to my attention. We hope that it will assist you in preparing your environmental report.

### Current reporting requirements and guidelines

Most businesses, certainly those in the UK, have generally ignored environmental issues in the past. However, the use and misuse of natural resources all lead to environmental costs generated by businesses, both large and small.

There are very few rules, legal or otherwise, to ensure that companies disclose and report environmental matters. Any **disclosures tend to be voluntary**, unless environmental matters happen to fall under standard accounting principles. Environmental matters may be reported in the accounts of companies in the following areas.

- Contingent liabilities
- Exceptional charges
- Operating and financial review comments
- Profit and capital expenditure focus

The voluntary approach contrasts with the position in the United States, where the SEC/FASB accounting standards are obligatory.

While nothing is compulsory, there are a number of **published guidelines** and **codes of practice**, including:

- The *Valdez Principles*
- The Confederation of British Industry's guideline *Introducing Environmental Reporting*
- The ACCA's *Guide to Environment and Energy Reporting*
- The Coalition of Environmentally Responsible Economies (CERES) formats for environmental reports
- The Friends of the Earth *Environmental Charter for Local Government*
- The Eco Management and Audit Scheme Code of Practice

The question arises as to verification of the environmental information presented. Companies who adopt the Eco Management and Audit Scheme must have the report validated by an external verifier. In June 1999, BP Amoco commissioned KPMG to conduct an independent audit of its greenhouse gas emissions in the first ever **environmental audit**.

**Comments on 'environmental events'**

(a) Of relevance to the farmland restoration is FRS 12 *Provisions, contingent liabilities and contingent assets*. Provisions for environmental liabilities should be recognised where there is a **legal or constructive obligation** to rectify environmental damage or perform restorative work. The mere existence of the restorative work does not give rise to an obligation and there is no legal obligation. However, it could be argued that there is a constructive obligation arising from the company's approach in previous years, which may have given rise to an **expectation** that the work would be carried out. If this is the case, a provision of £150m would be required in the financial statements. In addition, this provision and specific examples of restoration of land could be included in the environmental report.

(b) The treatment of the **fine** is straightforward: it is an obligation to transfer economic benefits. An estimate of the fine should be made and a **provision** set up in the financial statements for £5m. This should be mentioned in the environmental report. The report might also **put the fines in context** by stating how many tests have been carried out and how many times the company has passed the tests. The directors may feel that it would do the company's reputation no harm to point out the fact that the number of prosecutions has been falling from year to year.

(c) These statistics are good news and need to be covered in the environmental report. However, the emphasis should be on **accurate factual reporting** rather than boasting. It might be useful to provide target levels for comparison, or an industry average if available. The emissions statistics should be split into three categories:

*[Handwritten margin note, top right: SSAP 13 would only tell us how to treat the exp (4.6). a Rev. exp ∴ or (P+L) or capitalized (-FA) → only if conditions are met. Here, conditions are not met.]*

- Acidity to air and water
- Hazardous substances
- Harmful emissions to water

*[Handwritten above: SSAP 13]*

As regards the aquatic emissions, the £70m planned expenditure on **research** should **be mentioned in the environmental report**. It shows a commitment to benefiting the environment. However, **FRS 12 would not permit a provision** to be made for this amount, since an obligation does not exist and the **expenditure is avoidable**. Nor does it qualify as development expenditure under SSAP 13. .

(d) The environmental report should mention the steps the company is taking to minimise the harmful impact on the environment in the way it sites and constructs its gas installations. The report should also explain the policy of dismantling the installations rather than sinking them at the end of their useful life.

*[Handwritten margin note, left: "Present obligation" Or Prov. on Cost g Decom. + Then dep over the Life]*

Currently the company builds up a provision for decommissioning costs over the life of the installation. However, FRS 12 does not allow this. Instead, the **full amount must be provided** as soon as the obligation to transfer economic benefits exists. The obligation exists right at the beginning of the installation's life, and so the full £407m must be provided for. A corresponding asset is created.

---

**Marking scheme**

|  |  | *Marks* |
|---|---|---|
| **(a)** | Current reporting requirements | 10 |
| **(b)** | Restoration | 5 |
| | Infringement of law | 4 |
| | Emissions | 4 |
| | Decommissioning activities | 4 |
| | Report | 4 |
| | **Available** | **31** |
| | **Maximum** | **25** |

---

See overleaf for information on other
BPP products and how to order

# ACCA Order

To BPP Publishing Ltd, Aldine Place, London W12 8AA
Tel: 020 8740 2211. Fax: 020 8740 1184
email: publishing@bpp.com    online: www.bpp.com

Mr/Mrs/Ms (Full name)

Daytime delivery address

Postcode

Daytime Tel

Date of exam (month/year)

| | 2/01 Texts | 1/02 Kits | 9/01 Passcards | MCQ cards | Tapes | Videos |
|---|---|---|---|---|---|---|
| **PART 1** | | | | | | |
| 1.1 Preparing Financial Statements | £19.95 | £10.95 | £5.95 | £5.95 | £12.95 | £25.00 |
| 1.2 Financial Information for Management | £19.95 | £10.95 | £5.95 | £5.95 | £12.95 | £25.00 |
| 1.3 Managing People | £19.95 | £10.95 | £5.95 | | £12.95 | £25.00 |
| **PART 2** | | | | | | |
| 2.1 Information Systems | £19.95 | £10.95 | £5.95 | | £12.95 | £25.00 |
| 2.2 Corporate and Business Law (6/01) | £19.95 | £10.95 | £5.95 | | £12.95 | £25.00 |
| 2.3 Business Taxation FA 2001 (for 2002 exams) | £19.95 | (8/01) £10.95 | £5.95 (1/02) | | £12.95 | £25.00 |
| 2.4 Financial Management and Control | £19.95 | £10.95 | £5.95 | | £12.95 | £25.00 |
| 2.5 Financial Reporting (6/01) | £19.95 | £10.95 | £5.95 | | £12.95 | £25.00 |
| 2.6 Audit and Internal Review (6/01) | £19.95 | £10.95 | £5.95 | | £12.95 | £25.00 |
| **PART 3** | | | | | | |
| 3.1 Audit and Assurance Services (6/01) | £20.95 | £10.95 | £5.95 | | £12.95 | £25.00 |
| 3.2 Advanced Taxation FA 2001 (for 2002 exams) | £20.95 | (8/01) £10.95 | £5.95 (1/02) | | £12.95 | £25.00 |
| 3.3 Performance Management | £20.95 | £10.95 | £5.95 | | £12.95 | £25.00 |
| 3.4 Business Information Management | £20.95 | £10.95 | £5.95 | | £12.95 | £25.00 |
| 3.5 Strategic Business Planning and Development | £20.95 | £10.95 | £5.95 | | £12.95 | £25.00 |
| 3.6 Advanced Corporate Reporting (6/01) | £20.95 | £10.95 | £5.95 | | £12.95 | £25.00 |
| 3.7 Strategic Financial Management | £20.95 | £10.95 | £5.95 | | £12.95 | £25.00 |
| **INTERNATIONAL STREAM** | | | | | | |
| 1.1 Preparing Financial Statements | £19.95 | £10.95 | £5.95 | £5.95 | | |
| 2.5 Financial Reporting (6/01) | £19.95 | £10.95 | £5.95 | | | |
| 2.6 Audit and Internal Review (6/01) | £19.95 | £10.95 | £5.95 | | | |
| 3.1 Audit and Assurance services (6/01) | £20.95 | £10.95 | £5.95 | | | |
| 3.6 Advanced Corporate Reporting (6/01) | £20.95 | £10.95 | £5.95 | | | |
| **SUCCESS IN YOUR RESEARCH AND ANALYSIS PROJECT** | | | | | | |
| Tutorial Text (9/01) | £19.95 | | | | | |

SUBTOTAL £

## POSTAGE & PACKING

**Study Texts**

| | First | Each extra | |
|---|---|---|---|
| UK | £3.00 | £2.00 | £ |
| Europe* | £5.00 | £4.00 | £ |
| Rest of world | £20.00 | £10.00 | £ |

**Kits/Passcards/Success Tapes/MCQ cards**

| | First | Each extra | |
|---|---|---|---|
| UK | £2.00 | £1.00 | £ |
| Europe* | £2.50 | £1.00 | £ |
| Rest of world | £15.00 | £8.00 | £ |

**Breakthrough Videos**

| | First | Each extra | |
|---|---|---|---|
| UK | £2.00 | £2.00 | £ |
| Europe* | £2.00 | £2.00 | £ |
| Rest of world | £20.00 | £10.00 | £ |

**Grand Total** (Cheques to *BPP Publishing*) I enclose
a cheque for (incl. Postage) £

Or charge to Access/Visa/Switch

Card Number

Expiry date          Start Date

Issue Number (Switch Only)

Signature

We aim to deliver to all UK addresses inside 5 working days; a signature will be required. Orders to all EU addresses should be delivered within 6 working days. All other orders to overseas addresses should be delivered within 8 working days. * Europe includes the Republic of Ireland and the Channel Islands.

## REVIEW FORM & FREE PRIZE DRAW

All original review forms from the entire BPP range, completed with genuine comments, will be entered into one of two draws 31 July 2002 and 31 January 2003. The names on the first four forms picked out on each occasion will be sent a cheque for £50.

Name: _____    Address: _____

_____

_____

**How have you used this Kit?**
*(Tick one box only)*

☐ Self study (book only)

☐ On a course: college (please state)_____

_____

☐ With 'correspondence' package

☐ Other _____

**Why did you decide to purchase this Kit?** *(Tick one box only)*

☐ Have used the complementary Study Text

☐ Have used other BPP products in the past

☐ Recommendation by friend/colleague

☐ Recommendation by a lecturer at college

☐ Saw advertising in journals

☐ Saw website

☐ Other _____

**During the past six months do you recall seeing/receiving any of the following?**
*(Tick as many boxes as are relevant)*

☐ Our advertisement in *Student Accountant*

☐ Our advertisement in *Pass*

☐ Our brochure with a letter through the post

☐ Our website

**Which (if any) aspects of our advertising do you find useful?**
*(Tick as many boxes as are relevant)*

☐ Prices and publication dates of new editions

☐ Information on product content

☐ Facility to order books off-the-page

☐ None of the above

When did you sit the exam? _____

**Which of the following BPP products have you used for this paper?**

☐ Study Text    ☑ Kit    ☐ Passcards    ☐ Success Tape    ☐ Breakthrough Video

Your ratings, comments and suggestions would be appreciated on the following areas of this Kit.

| | Very useful | Useful | Not useful |
|---|---|---|---|
| 'Question search tools' | ☐ | ☐ | ☐ |
| 'The exam' | ☐ | ☐ | ☐ |
| 'Background' | ☐ | ☐ | ☐ |
| Preparation questions | ☐ | ☐ | ☐ |
| Exam standard questions | ☐ | ☐ | ☐ |
| 'Tutor's hints' section in answers | ☐ | ☐ | ☐ |
| Content and structure of answers | ☐ | ☐ | ☐ |
| Mock exams | ☐ | ☐ | ☐ |
| 'Plan of attack' | ☐ | ☐ | ☐ |
| Mock exam answers | ☐ | ☐ | ☐ |

| | Excellent | Good | Adequate | Poor |
|---|---|---|---|---|
| Overall opinion of this Kit | ☐ | ☐ | ☐ | ☐ |

Do you intend to continue using BPP products?    ☐ Yes    ☐ No

**Please note any further comments and suggestions/errors on the reverse of this page. The BPP author of this edition can be e-mailed at: katyhibbert@bpp.com**

**Please return this form to: Katy Hibbert, ACCA range manager, BPP Publishing Ltd, FREEPOST, London, W12 8BR**

**REVIEW FORM & FREE PRIZE DRAW (continued)**

Please note any further comments and suggestions/errors below.

**FREE PRIZE DRAW RULES**

1 Closing date for 31 July 2002 draw is 30 June 2002. Closing date for 31 January 2003 draw is 31 December 2002.

2 Restricted to entries with UK and Eire addresses only. BPP employees, their families and business associates are excluded.

3 No purchase necessary. Entry forms are available upon request from BPP Publishing. No more than one entry per title, per person. Draw restricted to persons aged 16 and over.

4 Winners will be notified by post and receive their cheques not later than 6 weeks after the relevant draw date.

5 The decision of the promoter in all matters is final and binding. No correspondence will be entered into.